The Caribbean

The Caribbean

The Genesis of a Fragmented Nationalism

FRANKLIN W. KNIGHT
Johns Hopkins University

THIRD EDITION

New York   Oxford

OXFORD UNIVERSITY PRESS

Oxford University Press, Inc., publishes works that further Oxford University's
objective of excellence in research, scholarship, and education.

Oxford New York
Auckland   Cape Town   Dar es Salaam   Hong Kong   Karachi
Kuala Lumpur   Madrid   Melbourne   Mexico City   Nairobi
New Delhi   Shanghai   Taipei   Toronto

With offices in
Argentina   Austria   Brazil   Chile   Czech Republic   France   Greece
Guatemala   Hungary   Italy   Japan   Poland   Portugal   Singapore
South Korea   Switzerland   Thailand   Turkey   Ukraine   Vietnam

For titles covered by Section 112 of the US Higher Education Opportunity Act,
please visit www.oup.com/us/he for the latest information about pricing
and alternate formats.

Published by Oxford University Press, Inc.
198 Madison Avenue, New York, New York 10016
http://www.oup.com

Oxford is a registered trademark of Oxford University Press

Library of Congress Cataloging-in-Publication Data
Knight, Franklin W.
The Caribbean, the genesis of a fragmented nationalism
Franklin W. Knight.
   p. cm. Includes bibliographical references
   ISBN-13: 978-0-19-538133-7 pbk
1. Caribbean Area—Economic conditions—1945–
2. Caribbean Area—Social conditions—1945–
3. Caribbean Area—Politics and government—1945–   I. Title.
   HC155.K58   1990   330.9729—dc20   89–49185

CONTENTS

MAPS AND TABLES   vii

PREFACE TO THE THIRD EDITION: THE CARIBBEAN IN
MODERN HISTORY   ix

INTRODUCTION TO THE FIRST EDITION   xv

1   The Political Geography of the Pre-Hispanic
Caribbean   1

2   Settlements and Colonies   19

3   Patterns of Colonization in the New World   46

4   Imperialism and Slavery   62

5   Social Structure of the Plantation Society   85

6   Imperial Fragmentation and Colonial Social
Reconstruction, 1793–1886   113

7   Caribbean Nation Building 1: Haiti and the
Dominican Republic   138

8   Caribbean Nation Building 2: Cuba,
1868–2010   165

9   Caribbean Nation Building 3: Puerto Rico and the
Ambivalent Identity   189

10   Caribbean Nation Building 4: The Commonwealth
Caribbean   204

11   State and Nationalism in the Contemporary
        Caribbean   228

        CHRONOLOGY   249
        TABLES   259
        INDEX   271

MAPS AND TABLES

MAPS

The Caribbean   4
Economic Resources   238

TABLES

Table 1.   Africans Supplied to Barbados, 1673–1684   259
Table 2.   Slave Importation Distribution by Percentages, 1600–1870   260
Table 3.   Sugar Production and Slave Population Figures in
           Selected Colonies, 1643–1860   261
Table 4.   Caribbean Population by Castes, Early Nineteenth Century   262
Table 5a. British Antilles Sugar Production and Exports, 1815–1894   265
Table 5b. Non-British Caribbean Sugar Production and Exports,
           1815–1894   265
Table 6.   Haitian Export Before and After the Revolution   266
Table 7.   Caribbean Political Configuration, 2007   267
Table 8.   Caribbean Populations, 2007   268
Table 9.   Organized Workers and Unemployment, 1988   269
Table 10. Caribbean Profiles, 2007   270

The Caribbean in Modern History

The ways in which the term *Caribbean* is employed remain remarkably varied and disconcerting but nevertheless understandable. The description derives from the Caribbean Sea, the body of water lying between the Gulf of Mexico on its western frontier and the Atlantic Ocean to the east. Along the Atlantic lies the string of exceptionally beautiful islands stretching from the Bahamas in the northwest to Trinidad in the southeast. The islands as well as the sea constitute the core region of the Caribbean. But the Caribbean represents more than its core islands and bordered sea. Major parts of the surrounding mainland or continental areas also border the Caribbean. The Florida peninsula thrusts out into the Caribbean Sea, as does the Yucatán peninsula of Mexico. The Caribbean Sea also washes the entire Central American coastline from Guatemala to Panama, although many Central Americans like to speak of their Atlantic Coast. Within the Caribbean region itself, history, custom, and culture have resulted in ambiguous variations in the use of the term. The Spanish, English, French, Dutch, and Danes all had Caribbean colonies, and the inescapable legacy of that imperial reality is that, in the nature of empires, all tended to speak as though their sector of the Caribbean represented the entire region. From the perspective of empire it was an identity that was rational. But from such careless use of language were great misunderstandings born.

To speak of the Spanish Antilles, the British West Indies, the French *Caraïbes*, or the Dutch or Danish Antilles clearly denotes a subcategory of the region. This is especially so nowadays in the postimperial phase of the Caribbean. To avoid terminological confusion, it is essential that the term *Caribbean* always connote a broader, more regional application than the parochial connotation of a language or cultural sphere, for the Caribbean does form a cohesive geographic and cultural area, although one that is neither uniform nor united. That this is so requires little explanation. States, even nation-states, are notoriously diverse. One has only to think of the subdivisions of Great Britain, the United States, Germany, France, or Italy. Perhaps the closest comparison of the Caribbean situation may be observed

in modern Spain. Spain, with a population of approximately 46 million inhabitants, recognizes seventeen autonomous regional divisions and two autonomous
cities within its territory encompassing 195,364 square miles (504,030 square
kilometers). Moreover, it recognizes four regional languages as co-official with
Castilian Spanish and about a dozen unofficial but recognized local languages.
In addition, the Spanish state is part of the European community, providing its
citizens with several layers of identity.

That the individual historical experience of the various Caribbean territories
was not identical is not surprising. But it is possible to assert that the region experienced a common series of transformations although at different times. In this
way, one may regard the Caribbean experiences as systadial—comparable stage—
rather than synchronic—simultaneous occurrence. This is clearly illustrated by
the general experience of the sugar revolutions. These interrelated series of revolutions intensified gradually across the Caribbean during the two centuries between
the middle of the seventeenth century and the middle of the nineteenth century.
They began in some of the English and French colonies, such as Barbados, Nevis,
St. Kitts, Antigua, Jamaica, Martinique, Guadeloupe, and Saint-Domingue and
ended transforming production and society in Cuba, Puerto Rico, Trinidad, and
the Guianas two centuries later.

The sugar revolutions are central to the distinctive concept of the Caribbean,
but they are not singular in this regard. The history of the Caribbean remains
unique in a number of ways. Since 1492 the Caribbean region has been of
extraordinary importance in the history of the modern world, especially to the
fundamental changes in Western Europe. The Caribbean in particular and the
Americas in general were areas where the Europeans created entirely new populations, new types of societies, new political administrations, and new forms of
commerce.

In 1774, the illustrious French intellectual, Guillaume Thomas François
Raynal (1711–1796), better known as the Abbe Raynal, began his controversial
multivolume history with this declaration:

> No event has been so interesting to mankind in general, and to the inhabitants of
> Europe in particular, as the discovery of the New World, and the passage to India
> by the Cape of Good Hope. It gave rise to a revolution in commerce, in the power
> of nations; as well as in the manners, industry, and government of the whole
> world. At this period, new connections were formed by the inhabitants of the
> most distant regions, for the supply of wants they had never before experienced.
> The productions of climates situated under the equator were consumed by coun-
> tries bordering the pole; the industry of the north was transplanted to the south;
> and the inhabitants of the west were clothed with the manufactures of the east; a
> general intercourse of opinions, laws, and customs, diseases and remedies, virtues
> and voices, was established among men.

The modern Caribbean constituted the crucial proscenium of European activity in the New World. It was constructed in the wake of the arrival of Christopher

Columbus (died 1506) in the Americas and served as the cradle of exploration and European expansion for several centuries.

The Caribbean asserted its fundamental importance in five interrelated ways: its strategic geography in the days of sailing ships, the demographic transformation after 1492, the constituted economies and societies, the exchange of commodities and food crops, and the extensive political ramifications of the two great Caribbean revolutions in Saint-Domingue–Haiti (1791–1804) and Cuba (1959–2010).

As Columbus demonstrated to his fellow Europeans, the Caribbean islands were strategically located for access and egress to the Americas. The fortuitous combination of strong prevailing winds and swiftly moving currents made the Caribbean the central location for all travel to and from the Americas. Major imperial decisions, such as the tactical withdrawal of the Spanish from the Lesser Antilles and the pattern of fortified port cities, were predicated on the mobility advantages of the location of Havana, San Juan de Puerto Rico, Vera Cruz, Porto Bello, or Cartagena. Wind and current made Antigua more strategically valuable than Jamaica for the English naval forces in the Caribbean. And the central location of St. Lucia made it highly prized by all the major European colonizers in the Caribbean.

The Caribbean was important not only generally, but specifically. Columbus stumbled on them and erroneously calculated that he was on the outskirts of China and Japan. He was convinced that they lie in the latitudes where gold might be found. When he found locals wearing gold and small amounts of placer gold in Hispaniola, it was sufficient to arouse the insatiable cupidity for gold on the part of the Europeans and to have the Spanish monarchy convert its interests from commercial exploration to colonization. The Caribbean islands, then, would become the launch pad for the relentless forays on the continent that would produce more precious metals and other valuable commodities than the wildest dreams of even the most avaricious Europeans. Indeed, between 1500 and 1650, most Europeans destined for anywhere in the Americas would first visit the Caribbean. A preponderance of early American Spanish American surnames could be found among the first settlers in Hispaniola, the island that would later be formally divided in 1697 at the Treaty of Ryswick between the Spanish colony of Santo Domingo and the French colonies of Saint-Domingue.

Full-time colonization, initiated with the Spanish venture under the surly looking Nicolás de Ovando y Cáceres (1460–1518) in 1502, inadvertently created a new type of individual in the Caribbean. It resulted from the mixture of European, African, and indigenous in a bewildering array of miscegenated types. During the catastrophic decline of the native population before 1650, mixed types quickly became the normal form of Creole in the Spanish Americas, accounting for well over 60 percent of the residents of designated Spanish municipalities. The impetus to boost production—first of precious metals and then of plantation export commodities—promoted the rapid expansion of the direct transatlantic slave trade. Miscegenation created the plural society in the Caribbean. But the transatlantic slave trade resulted in the plural ethnic society and, indeed, two distinct variants of the European colonial society. One was the settler society of groups traveling overseas to try to reproduce where possible microcosms of the type of society they left at home. The other was the exploitation society, which was constructed to maximize productive efficiency but eventually ended up as a rare sort of peculiar American society of indelible mutually reinforcing social cleavages. These two dominant types fell at either end of a spectrum of social forms engendered by the American experience. Other forms along the spectrum included the intrepid free lances, described by Bernal Díaz del Castillo as adventurers who "went out to the Indies to serve god and his majesty, to bring light to them that dwell in darkness and to get rich as all men desire." They also included buccaneers, Maroons, and other unconventional transfrontiersmen. All types of society in the Caribbean were deeply affected by the sugar revolutions whether or not they participated directly in the experience.

New social organization required new political ideas, and as the Spanish, followed by other Europeans, came to the Caribbean, they would introduce and modify various forms of administrative techniques that were required in the new experience of long-distance overseas territorial control. When Antonio Nebrija dedicated his new dictionary of the Castilian language to his monarchs in 1492, indicating that it was a new tool of empire, he could never have known how correct he was. A standard language was an indispensable prerequisite for administration, yet the Caribbean and American experience would profoundly enrich both the language and the grammar of Nebrija's creation.

Another area in which the Caribbean played a major role was the transfer of fauna and flora (as well as people) during the great period of exchange and transformation. This exchange has continued through time, and today nearly 60 percent of all food crops have their origin in the Americas. The exchange, as Alfred Crosby and others have demonstrated, flowed in both directions across the Atlantic. While the Spanish and their fellow Europeans brought along animals, plants, fruit, and plants with which they were familiar, they encountered a cornucopia of useful items in the Caribbean. Apart from tobacco, sweet potato, corn, and cassava, a number of fruit abounded throughout the Caribbean. These fruit included avocado, cashew, coco plum, custard apple, guava, guinep, hog plum, mamee, paw-paw, peanut, pineapple, star apple, sour-sop, and sweetsop. The Europeans also found some useful new fibers and plants, such as agave, annatto, cotton, calabash, henequen, and indigo. These new discoveries helped sustain the early settlers in the newly found places and eventually helped transform the diets, customs, and commerce of the Atlantic World.

By the eighteenth century, the Caribbean was the center of a worldwide international trading community importing and exporting people and products globally. Then noncommercial exchanges would also follow the trade routes, the great majority of which were bilateral, rather than the often-repeated but greatly misleading description of Atlantic commerce as a form of triangular trade. The Caribbean sugar and slave trades were the foundation on which modern capitalism was constructed.

The Caribbean was never marginal to the evolving history of the Atlantic world after 1492. Rather it was central to that history. As such, therefore, it should not be surprising that the Caribbean experience should extend to the intellectual and scientific realm as well. Beginning with the famous logs of Columbus and the report of Father Ramón Pané, early travelers to the Caribbean, as well as sojourners like Bartolomé de Las Casas, Hernán Cortés, and Bernal Díaz del Castillo, constructed useful narratives that greatly shaped the overseas impressions of the lands and peoples of the Caribbean. This practice continued, and it is possible to describe numerous contributions in science emanating from the Caribbean. Nor should it be surprising that two of the seven most important political revolutions took place in the Caribbean.

The Haitian Revolution, which emerged during the French Revolution in 1789 and came into its own in 1804, not only engineered a new state—the second such in the Americas—but also attempted new, advanced forms of inclusive political participation and universal human rights. Those ideas were well ahead of their time. Without Haiti, the United States might never have become a continental power. Without Haiti, Napoleonic France might have achieved imperial greatness. The Cuban Revolution of Fidel Castro in 1959 also represented a major accomplishment that was recognized worldwide. Both the Haitian and Cuban revolutions fundamentally altered the social basis of social and political power, rather than the administrative forms. Moreover, they exalted individual human dignity.

Since the Caribbean played such an important role not only in the physical expansion of the Europeans in the New World, but in the realignment of political power in Europe over several centuries, it follows that the histories of the Americas and of Europe cannot be written without prominent attention to the region. This is already happening. A region that pioneered democracy, recognized equality before the law, and made slaves the masters of free men deserves serious attention. This book represents an attempt to look at the general patterns of challenges and changes in the Caribbean. It does not replace other such efforts. It merely complements the richly expanding literature of a region that is interesting in its own right. The history of the Caribbean is not a narrative of successive victims, disasters, and dismal decline. It is a history full of unexpected creativity, of determined resilience, of boldly confronting challenges, and of important successes. It is a new type of history because the Caribbean was a new type of place. In changing the Caribbean environment, the European intruders never calculated how much their experience in that tropical region would change their entire worlds.

NEW TO THIS EDITION OF *THE CARIBBEAN*:

This new edition

- provides a fresh contextualization of Caribbean history;
- revises, corrects, and updates the text, bringing the history to 2010;

- revises and expands the information on the indigenous societies and the contact period;
- provides a short bibliography of suggested readings for each chapter;
- expands the discussion on the Haitian and Cuban revolutions and their universal impact; and
- revises and updates the chronology and informational tables on the Caribbean.

I wish to thank the reviewers whose insights and criticism contributed to the revision of this current edition: Milagros Denis, Rutgers University; John Garrigus, University of Texas, Arlington; Anne Eller, New York University; Heidi Giusto, Duke University; Solsiree Del Moral, Penn State; Roderick A. McDonald, Rider University; and Lomarsh Roopnarine, University of the Virgin Islands, St. Croix.

INTRODUCTION TO THE FIRST EDITION

Ever since the entry of man into the Caribbean region, there have been two contradictory patterns at work. One trend has been toward homogeneity, the other toward diversity. Such are the common trends of all societies and cultures at all times. Groups are either coming together or falling apart, playing out at various speeds the age-old struggle between centrifugalism and centripetalism, the priorities of the individual against the requirements of the group. At the collective or group level, the victory of one force, however temporary, creates one type of society, state, or nation. But no victory results in a permanent situation. Today's dominant nation forms tomorrow's client substate.

The victory of centripetalism establishes large nation-states or confederations, albeit sometimes artificially contrived and precariously maintained. Within the Western Hemisphere, Canada, the United States of America, Mexico, Venezuela, Brazil, and Argentina are the results of the dominance of a politically strong center to restrain the irredentist forces of the periphery. But all these nation-states were themselves parts of larger political groupings, called empires. On the other hand, the independent states of the Caribbean, Central America, and the Andean region demonstrate the failure of the cohesive forces of centripetalism. The eventual results of group conflict—whether in the form of maxi-nation-state or mini-nation-state—are more often the consequences of chance than of historical laws. Circumstances are forever changing, and to individuals and groups alike, what appears logical and desirable one moment soon ceases to be so the next.

Yet both the nation and the nation-state are merely convenient forms of identification along a spectrum, ranging from the narrow, local self-consciousness—termed in this book, *patriachiquismo*—to the vast empire. No one has so far been able to ascertain the precise time at which a local self-consciousness transforms itself into a national sentiment. Nor can one incontrovertibly assert why some forms of diversity seem at one time to be a political asset and at others, a political liability. The Caribbean is caught up in the movement of political consciousness, but it is not at all certain that all the units are moving simultaneously in one direction or the other.

In treating the Caribbean region, I have made certain assumptions, which, I hope, will not be outrageously unfamiliar to anyone who has read about or traveled to or lived in the area. The major assumption is that while the separate units pass through the same general experience, they do so at different times—hence comparisons of the Caribbean should be systadial rather than synchronic. Another assumption is that the sum of the common experiences and understandings of the Caribbean outweigh the territorial differences or peculiarities. To speak therefore of Haitian, Jamaican, Cuban, or Caribbean characteristics should not be to speak of them as mutually exclusive; the first are merely variations or components of the last. Yet another assumption is that the forces that have resulted in the Balkanization of the region have varied more in degree than in kind. This assertion, however, does not imply any underestimation of the accumulative impact of historical traditions, linguistic forms, administrative differences, and general ignorance. To deny these differences would be to deny the political realities of the Caribbean. The separate political identities of the Caribbean are as patently strong as they are inescapable. They can no more easily be banished by the written word and wishful thought of a historian than the denial of any politician can banish his action.

Political boundaries do not necessarily make, or conform to, cultural boundaries. The concept of the Caribbean that is endorsed in this book emphasizes cultural commonalities rather than political chronology, without neglecting the importance of the latter. In my view, the region comprises one cultural area in which common factors have forged a more-or-less common way of looking at life, the world, and their place in the scheme of things. All the societies of the Caribbean share an identifiable *Weltanschauung*, despite the superficial divisions that are apparent. The differences in beliefs, values, and attitudes of the Trinidadian and the Guyanese are perhaps no greater than those between the English and the Welsh or the Castilian and the Andalucian. Moreover, the Caribbean peoples, with their distinctive artificial societies, common history, and common problems, seem to have more in common than the Texan and the New Yorker or the Mayan Indian and the cosmopolite of Mexico City.

This history traces the genesis of the Caribbean from a decidedly international Caribbean and New World perspective. Many other histories are written from the viewpoint of European and imperial affairs, rendering the transformation of the region as a coincidental by-product of other presumably larger and more important events. Such histories do not deny that the Caribbean had its day in the sun. But to change the metaphor, the history of the Caribbean was written merely as an act within a play. Here the act *is* the play, the main event. It is, of course, valid to view Caribbean history from the political and economic perspective of Africa, Europe, or mainland America—especially for Africans, Europeans, and mainland Americans. But the validity of that view cannot, and should not, invalidate the local perspective. This is the only conscious "slant" that this history provides: to look from the inside out (for someone on the inside) is not only legitimate, it is the only view.

One further admission is necessary. The criteria for dividing this history rest more on socioeconomic considerations than on political ones. The book begins by reviewing the processes of social formation in the Caribbean, and it culminates with the political factors (or realities) that impinge on the social and economic structures. It is a history, therefore, without designated heroes and significant dates—though some concessions have been made with a political chronology. This is a deliberate act. The heroes are what the Cuban poet Nicolas Guillén would call *Juan Nadies,* or common folk, too numerous to mention; the significant dates are not specific years, but various periods slipping almost imperceptibly by. Such has been the history of the Caribbean and the nature of change in that part of the world. The history of the Caribbean is the examination of fragments that, like looking at a broken vase, still provide clues to the form, beauty, and value of the past.

The research and writing of this book leave me greatly indebted to a number of institutions and individuals. The Research Institute for the Study of Man made available its magnificent collection on the contemporary Caribbean, and its director, Dr. Vera Rubin, combined a generosity of spirit, intellect, and charm that I found pleasantly contagious. The Latin American, Portuguese, and Spanish Division of the Library of Congress provided excellent facilities for more than two years, while Mrs. Georgette Dorn and Mr. Everett Larsen pampered me. The Johns Hopkins University Seminars provided a preliminary audience for some of the early chapters, and the keen verbal exchange forced me to clarify some of the earlier thinking. Walter and Margaret Bauer, Fernando and Françoise de Mateo, and Anne Perotin-Dumon all extended material kindnesses at a crucial moment. In addition, I derived much help from the following colleagues and friends: Margaret Crahan, Philip Curtin, Jack Greene, Barry Higman, Asunción Lavrin, and Johanna Mendelson. Edward Cox corrected my thinking on the Eastern Caribbean and kindly allowed me access to his research and provided a quotation that he had transcribed from the British Public Record Office. Ingeborg Bauer Knight and Sheldon Meyer have been models of patience, tolerance, and understanding while making suggestions that I have tried to meet. I do remain, however, entirely responsible for all errors and shortcomings of this work.

The Caribbean

CHAPTER 1

The Political Geography of the Pre-Hispanic Caribbean

They very willingly traded everything they had. But they
seemed to me a people very short of everything.
—CHRISTOPHER COLUMBUS,
Friday, October 12, 1492

Throughout the journals of Christopher Columbus (1451–1506), references to the physical geography of the Caribbean islands appear very often. Although he did not know it at the time, the physical geography has been, from pre-Hispanic times to the present, one of the dominant and inescapable influences on the pattern of life and society in the region. Islands, especially small islands, produce powerful influences on people. The topography and ecology of the Caribbean islands have been major influences in the types of societies that have developed there since the time of the earliest inhabitants.

Conventionally, the designation of the Caribbean has been limited to the thousands of islands of various sizes that stretch like an inclined backbone from the southern tip of the Florida peninsula to the slanting northern coastline of South America. Included in this regional depiction are the enclaves that today comprise the mainland states of Belize in Central America and Guyana, Suriname, and French Guiana in South America. Given the geographic location of these enclaves, they, too, could be regarded as islands, separated from the rest of the continent by a sort of no-man's-land of jungles. The true Caribbean islands form an irregular outer gate to both the Caribbean Sea and the Gulf of Mexico. Altogether they span an area from longitude 59 degrees west to longitude 85 degrees west and range within roughly latitude 10 degrees north and 25 degrees north—almost totally within the tropics if one excludes the northern Bahamian Islands. The distances between the islands are not very great. Nor, with the possible exceptions of Cuba (more than 44,000 square miles or 120,000 square kilometers) and Hispaniola (more than 27,000 square miles or 76,000 square kilometers), are the islands very large.

Geologically, most of the islands are limestone with granite and coral. Some islands, as well as parts of many others, have steep, rough, and disconcertingly inhospitable terrains. This type of topography is commonly found in Dominica, Grenada, Montserrat, Guadeloupe (especially Basse-Terre), northern Hispaniola, eastern Jamaica, and southeastern Cuba. Barbados and Antigua are flat, with the highest mountains barely exceeding one thousand feet. Central and western Cuba present broad vistas of gently undulating hills breaking the monotony of the extensive palm-studded plains. Some islands are precariously minuscule, such as those in the Grenadines, Anguilla, the Bahamas, and the Caymans. The larger northern islands—Cuba, Jamaica, Haiti, and the Dominican Republic (which together occupy the island of Hispaniola), and Puerto Rico—form the Greater Antilles. The double chain of islands found between Puerto Rico and Trinidad form the Lesser Antilles. During the days of sailing ships, the more northerly of these islands were called the Leeward Islands, while the more easterly ones—that is, those more toward the wind—were called the Windward Islands. Sometimes this geographic distinction formed the basis for an administrative division, and while the designations have remained to the present day, the jurisdictional separation of windward and leeward has always conformed more to convenience than to geography.

The Caribbean islands all lie within a potentially salubrious environment, highly conducive to the growth of populations and the development of complex societies. As such, the islands had been continuously inhabited for a long time before the arrival of Christopher Columbus and his "doom-burdened caravels." While no firm date can be established for the first arrival of man on the islands, it is certain that the first permanent settlers came from the tropical forest peoples of Central and South America. These peoples had been living for centuries on the islands when Columbus arrived, claiming that they were Indians (in his mistaken notion that he was on the outskirts of India or Japan) and giving rise to the description of the hemisphere that Peter Martyr would irrevocably impose some years later, "The New World."

Agricultural activity is not difficult in the Caribbean. In general, the soils of the larger islands contain coral limestone pockets of varying fertility, and the coastal plains have sandy loams. These soils are easily cultivated once the dense tropical forest covers have been removed, and in some cases, the area has been in continuous cultivation for centuries. Rainfall is constant: adequate to abundant during the rainy season from May to November, with quantities varying from about thirty inches on the leeward plains to approximately two hundred inches in the thick forests of the windward mountains. Light showers infrequently moisten the dry, often hot "winter" months running from December through March. Temperatures, which at sea level fluctuate between seventy degrees and ninety degrees Fahrenheit throughout the year, combine with the rainfall to provide a long growing season and a pleasant harvest time. And although, like much of the rest of the world, ecological changes have begun to affect rainfall and climate, the Caribbean still remains an area where the living can be easy for the acclimated, and the natural topographical beauty can be most alluring.

Nevertheless, the alluring natural beauty tends to obscure the accompanying physical hazards of life in the Caribbean: the frequent destructive hurricanes, the prevalence of endemic and epidemic diseases, the violence of earthquakes and volcanoes, the constricting limitations of physical size, the savage fury of the floods that accompany the hurricanes, and the dense clouds of insects—especially mosquitoes—that plagued the crews of Columbus and today still pester tourists and locals alike. So, although the living can be easy in the Caribbean, it often is not; and at the same time that some see the region as a tantalizing magnet, others find themselves expelled by its natural and artificial hazards.

The difficulties and frustrations of perpetuating a cohesive and sophisticated society in the Caribbean preceded the arrival of the Spanish explorers and conquerors of the late fifteenth century. The history recovered by persevering archeological research supports some useful generalizations about the pre-Hispanic populations and the types of societies that they had fashioned and were continuing to fashion when they were overtaken by the series of events beginning in 1492 when Columbus sailed into the region and forever altered their history. For the world of the Caribbean, the arrival of Columbus constituted a major turning point.

Although we have a good idea of the lifestyles of the various people who lived on the islands when Columbus arrived, we have no reliable estimate of their number. Despite the imaginative calculations of the size of the indigenous population in 1492, it is no easier to figure out how many people were living on these islands than to figure out how many Africans were brought to the New World during the four-century-long course of the transatlantic slave trade. Christopher Columbus, who gave as good a description of the early inhabitants as any other writer, was understandably vague or misleading about the size of the groups he met. But it must be understood that he was often trying to justify his expensive voyages by insinuating that the possibilities for important trade relations existed. He was not interested in counting people, and, in any case, estimating crowds is not easily done. Bartolomé de las Casas, who later gained considerable notoriety as the originator of the anti-Spanish "Black Legend," produced some incredible figures for the local population at the time of the Spanish arrival, but those estimates ought not to be taken too seriously. Las Casas had an axe to grind and wanted to show that Spanish colonization was an unmitigated disaster for the local people. In order to emphasize the scale of the destruction brought about in a short time, he exaggerated the estimate of the indigenous inhabitants. The majority of the early firsthand reporters and the popularizers who based their accounts on these first reports merely repeated the estimates that they found. No censuses could have been made, and the relative inaccessibility of the interior to the intrusive early colonists precluded any demographic description before the catastrophic epidemiological consequences of the encounter of Europeans and Americans had taken place.

The indigenous populations of all the islands of the Caribbean probably did not exceed three-quarters of a million, the great majority of whom lived on the island of Hispaniola. Such an estimate is debatable of course. But it seems highly unlikely that a larger population could have been supported by the community organizations that the first Europeans described. Columbus himself did not witness any large concentrations of people, and modern science has failed to unearth evidence of extensive occupation or cultivation. Moreover, the process of immigration

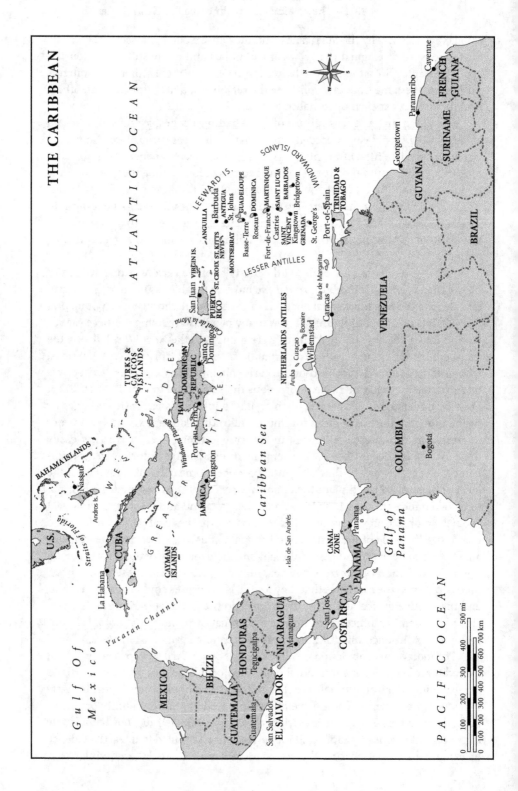

THE CARIBBEAN

ATLANTIC OCEAN

LEEWARD IS.

WINDWARD ISLANDS

ANGUILLA
Barbuda
ANTIGUA
St. Johns
GUADELOUPE
Basse-Terre
Roseau DOMINICA
Fort-de-France MARTINIQUE
Castries
SAINT LUCIA
SAINT VINCENT
Kingstown BARBADOS
GRENADA Bridgetown
St. George's

MONTSERRAT
ST. KITTS
NEVIS
VIRGIN IS.
St. Croix
PUERTO RICO
San Juan
Canal de la Mona

LESSER ANTILLES

Port-of-Spain
TRINIDAD & TOBAGO

Isla de Margarita

Caracas
VENEZUELA

NETHERLANDS ANTILLES
Aruba Curaçao Bonaire
Willemstad

TURKS & CAICOS ISLANDS

Santo Domingo
DOMINICAN REPUBLIC
HAITI
Port-au-Prince
Windward Passage

BAHAMA ISLANDS
Nassau
Andros I.

CUBA
La Habana
Straits of Florida

U.S.

Yucatan Channel

CAYMAN ISLANDS

JAMAICA
Kingston

GREATER ANTILLES

WEST INDIES

Caribbean Sea

Isla de San Andrés

PANAMA
Panama
CANAL ZONE

Gulf of Panama

PACIFIC OCEAN

COSTA RICA
San José

NICARAGUA
Managua

HONDURAS
Tegucigalpa

EL SALVADOR
San Salvador

GUATEMALA
Guatemala

BELIZE

MEXICO

Gulf of Mexico

COLOMBIA
Bogotá

GUYANA
Georgetown

SURINAME
Paramaribo

FRENCH GUIANA
Cayenne

BRAZIL

0   100   200   300   400   500 mi
0 100 200 300 400 500 600 700 km

from the South American mainland, while steady over a long period, had failed to produce any population explosion on the islands. Cuba, the most westerly of the larger islands, had about fifty thousand persons living there. Hispaniola, by virtue of its size and central location (therefore, probably of longer settlement and social development), might have been the most densely settled with a population in 1492 of perhaps half a million individuals. Jamaica had several thousands, probably not exceeding twenty thousand inhabitants. Very few islands had the population concentrations found on the mainland in places like the Central Valley of Mexico or Yucatán or the higher Andean valleys. Some of the smaller Caribbean islands like Barbados and Antigua did not appear to have been permanently inhabited at all.

Three different types of people made up this relatively sparse population at the end of the fifteenth century: the Ciboney or Guanahuatebey; the Taino Arawak; and the Carib, from whom the region and the sea derive their name. These pre-Hispanic peoples originated with the Arawak-speaking populations of Central and northern South America, and the Taino are sometimes referred to by language rather than by culture. Ciboneys, Tainos, and Caribs formed the earliest societies of the Caribbean, and in some cases, these people were the ancestors of the present population. In any case, their impact on the culture of the region and the world remain in a number of ways, from the use of hammocks and tobacco to the various words and utensils commonly found throughout the region. The indigenous peoples were not without problems, nor did they inhabit a world unfamiliar with change. Indeed, some of the social and political problems of the middle of the fifteenth century were not strikingly different from similar ones at the end of the twentieth century.

In 1492, the indigenous inhabitants were trying to come to grips with their environment in many creative ways. In some respects they were succeeding; in other respects they were failing. But these early inhabitants form the baseline of our understanding about the region and its societal genesis, as scholars like Ricardo Alegría have pointed out, and we cannot neglect their contribution to our present reality. The fact that we still know very little about the indigenous inhabitants and that we find it hard to unearth more information does not obscure their vital history.

There is no such thing as a people without history. All peoples have their history. And while all history may not necessarily be recorded in books, every history is recorded somehow, somewhere. Some peoples leave their history in their pottery, their paintings, and their works of art. Others leave their history in their buildings, their statues, their sculptures, and their tools. Their history is a particular combination of their beliefs, their myths, their customs, their philosophies— their articulations of reality and the transcendental. We who share part of their legacy may not understand it all, but we ought to respect it and strive diligently and unceasingly to understand it, for in so doing, we know not only a little more about their world, but a lot more about our own world.

And so from archeological evidence—often from negative criteria or from what researchers have failed to find rather than what they have found—we can partially reconstruct the societies and cultures of that past whose world was completely transformed by the accidental discovery by Christopher Columbus and the other peripatetic Europeans who followed him into what was, for them, the New World.

The Ciboney, the most westerly of the Caribbean residents, were probably the oldest cultural group in the region. Ciboney sites have been found scattered throughout Cuba and the southwestern peninsula of Hispaniola. Columbus encountered some of these people when his expedition arrived somewhere near the present-day Holguín in Cuba. Unfortunately, the failure to communicate linguistically—Columbus had brought along interpreters skilled in Hebrew, Latin, and Aramaic (the group of Semitic languages spoken in Mesopotamia)—as well as the evident poverty (in Christopher Columbus's own terms) meant that not much time was spent with, or much information gleaned from, these simple people. Like all the peoples of the out-islands, they were comparatively unsophisticated in military technology and unencumbered by much clothing. Although Columbus reported that the Ciboney were sometimes enslaved by the Taino, their fellow inhabitants on the islands, the true relationship between the two groups cannot be properly ascertained. Such slavery, if it were slavery, could not have been anywhere as arduous as the slavery that awaited all the inhabitants after the Spanish began to settle on the islands. Nor could it have been of the type that was established by the Spanish and the other Europeans with the use of Africans throughout the New World.

Ciboney middens already examined reveal no pottery, no domestic utensils or weapons, and no evidence of organized ritualistic religion or of complex social organizations. Largely on the basis of the lack of common artifacts used for the social and cultural reconstruction of indigenous communities, one hypothesis presents itself: that the Ciboney were hunters and gatherers with a political organization that probably did not develop beyond that of the nomadic band.

The Ciboney clearly present a major historical enigma. M. R. Harrington, in his study, *Cuba Before Columbus,* done in 1921, posited the view that the Ciboney migrated to the islands from the south by way of the Lesser Antilles chain. The argument is plausible since both wind and current would have facilitated such a maritime migration, and the distances covered were not, after all, great. One problem, however, remains. Ciboney sites comparable to those in Cuba and Hispaniola were never discovered on any of the smaller eastern islands. This absence of archeological evidence initially led Irving Rouse and Cornelius Osgood to reject the theory of Ciboney origins from South and Central America. They suggested that a point of origin in Florida could have been equally plausible.

Further research, however, modified this view. The failure to discover comparable artifacts anywhere in Florida and Rouse's later extensive excavations in Haiti and Venezuela guided Rouse toward a modified version of the old Harrington thesis. Rouse later supported a view that the Ciboney may have come from the South American mainland, but neither as a homogeneous migrant group nor necessarily at the same time. This position took into account the geographic history of the area. It is obvious that autonomous human evolution in the Caribbean is all but precluded owing to the geological youth of the islands. The inhabitants had to migrate from someplace. This being so, the archeological data from Haiti and Venezuela substantiate such a migration.

Irving Rouse, probably the most authoritative archeologist of the Caribbean area, used five steps to verify his theory of migrant peoples: (1) He identified the migrating unit as intrusive to the region; (2) he traced the unit back to its original site or homeland; (3) he determined that the archeological findings of the unit were contemporaneous; (4) he established the existence of conditions favorable for migration; and (5) he demonstrated that some other hypothesis, such as independent invention or diffusion of traits, did not better fit the facts of the situation.

Using Rouse's formula, it is easy to establish that the Ciboney must have been migrants by virtue of the improbability of autonomous local evolution, which we have already suggested. The second stage, however, requires an assumption that the term *Ciboney* covers all the earlier arrivals of preagricultural peoples to the Caribbean. Such an acceptance enables us to establish some connection and contemporaneity of the artifacts discovered both in Venezuela and in Hispaniola. Migration between the Venezuelan mainland and the Caribbean islands would have been facilitated by favorable winds and currents, except during the months of November to March. During that season—winter in the Northern Hemisphere— the prevalence of the northeast trade winds would tend to inhibit, though not totally deter, maritime travel between the southern mainland and the larger Antillean islands.

Of course, one accepts these hypotheses provisionally. The possibility—and high probability—remains that at irregular intervals the indigenous inhabitants of the Central American mainland could have inadvertently made the passage between Yucatán and the islands, where, if their numbers were insufficient and their culture not reinforced, they could have been absorbed into the local societies, thereby losing the historical record of their arrival. To date, there has been no positive evidence of any cultural impact from the societies north of the isthmus. No firm suggestion, therefore, can be made at this date of contact between North and Central America and the Antilles during the early stages of the migration of man onto the islands.

Ciboney society was the simplest of the three groups of pre-Hispanic inhabitants. They were mere troglodytic bands with an unsophisticated artistic ability, despite the shell and stove designs that have been found. They also had no knowledge of ritualistic religion or of the cassava (manioc) culture that existed throughout the other islands and on the South American continent. Nor did they possess the complex military technology to enable them to resist successfully the intrusions of the later tropical forest groups. Instead, their military strategy involved simple wooden clubs and stones thrown by hand at their opponents. Not geared for warfare, they succumbed to their attackers, and if Columbus is to be believed, some Ciboney were being held in a form of slavery by the agricultural Taino.

If the Ciboney remain largely obscured in the archeological and historical record, their rivals, the Taino and the Caribs—by virtue of their superior numbers and their bold resistance to the Spanish intrusion—left a much better account of themselves. Thanks to the meticulous records kept by Christopher Columbus and quoted extensively by Bartolomé de las Casas, we have a considerable descriptive account of Arawakan society. With communities dotting the islands from the Bahamas to the Venezuelan coastline, they were by far the most numerous people in the region. Columbus picked up an interpreter on one of the first islands on which he landed—historians are divided on whether that was San Salvador (supported by Samuel Eliot Morison) or Samana Cay (selected by a team from the *National Geographic* in 1986) or further to the northwest on Egg Island (as Arne Molander strongly believes)—and that interpreter was useful all the way to Hispaniola, a reflection of the linguistic uniformity that existed. Tainos, therefore, occupied all the larger islands of the Antilles (Cuba and Hispaniola, which they shared with the Ciboney, as well as Jamaica and Puerto Rico), the Lesser Antilles (which today constitute the British and American Virgin Islands), and the rest of the chain of Leeward and Windward islands. Columbus wrote glowingly of the Taino on his first voyage:

> They very willingly traded everything they had. But they seemed to me a people very short of everything.
>   All the men I saw were young. I did not see one over the age of thirty. They were all very well built with fine bodies and handsome faces. Their hair is coarse, almost like that of a horse's tail, and short; they wear it down over their eyebrows except for a few strands at the back, which they wear long and never cut. They are the color of the Canary Islanders, neither black nor white, and are heavily painted. Some of them paint themselves black, others white, or any color they can find. Some paint their faces, some their whole bodies, some only their eyes, some only their nose. They do not carry arms, nor know them. For when I showed them swords, they took them by the edge and cut themselves out of ignorance. They have no iron. Their spears are made of cane. Some, instead of an iron tip have a fish's tooth and others have points of different kinds. They are fairly tall on the whole, with fine limbs and good proportions. I saw some who had the scar from wounds on their bodies and I asked them by signs how they got these and they indicated to me that people came from other islands nearby who tried to capture them and they defended themselves. I supposed, and still suppose, that they come from the mainland to capture them for slaves. They should be good servants, and very intelligent, for I have observed that they soon repeat anything that is said to them, and I believe that they would easily be made Christians, for they appeared to me to have no religion. God willing, when I make my departure I will bring half a dozen back to their Majesties so that they can learn to speak. I saw no animals of any kind on this island except parrots.

The log books of Columbus, despite some occasional glaring inaccuracies and ethnocentricity, provide the basis for a closer look at the structure of the Taino Arawak communities that existed in the region at the end of the fifteenth century. Taino culture has also been reconstructed and evaluated by ethnographic and archeological methods, since both the language and the surviving artifacts provide a solid basis for research. Not surprisingly, therefore, the general knowledge and understanding of Taino culture is far better than for the other two groups in the Caribbean at that time.

Anthropologists describe the Taino society as composed of theocratic chiefdoms similar to those found over a wide area from eastern Bolivia northward through the interior of Brazil and through Colombia and Venezuela. The Taino Arawak formed one of a variegated group of such peoples, similar in culture though linguistically diverse, which inhabited the region. Unlike their ancestors on the mainland—groups such as the Chibcha, Warao, Yanomamö, Caracas, Palenque, Caquetío, or the Jirajara of the Colombia-Venezuela tropical forest belt—the island Taino were generally a nonmilitaristic people with a hierarchically structured society of manioc-producing agriculturalists.

When Columbus wrote that the people of the Bahamas had "no religion" (*que me pareció que ninguna secta tenían*), he merely meant that the Taino were not Christians. They did have a highly organized religion based on a hierarchy of gods and men. Their religious spirits were called *zemis* and were represented by icons of wood, stone, bones, or even human remains. Each individual had a pantheon of *zemis*, with the quantity reflecting the social position of the individual possessor. *Zemi* icons resembled grotesque anthropomorphic figures, often with exaggerated sex organs, presumably fashioned according to the supernatural dictates of the owner.

Village chiefs, who varied in power and influence depending on the size of their village community, had the greatest number of *zemis*, and it seems that those *zemis* were publicly venerated. The public ball courts found in Cuba, Puerto Rico, and Hispaniola suggest a ceremonial function. But nowhere in the Caribbean did the priest-temple-idol cult develop the aggressive militarism and the proselytizing fervor that characterized the societies of the mainland empires of the Aztec, Maya, or Inca. Indeed, the island Taino seem to have been one of the least aggressive peoples of the Americas. The exact relationship between the chiefs, whom Columbus frequently referred to as "kings" (as the Europeans were wont to call all political leaders whom they encountered on their initial voyages into the wider world), and the religious life of the community has never been clearly established. It seems, however, that the chiefs did have great power within their communities. Yet the simplicity of their social relations and the openness that they showed to the Spanish brought them not reciprocal kindness but rather deception—and eventually death and annihilation. Columbus was greatly impressed by Taino magnanimity when he described how the Tainos of Hispaniola helped him and his men after the shipwreck of December 24, 1492:

> On hearing the news the king wept, showing great sorrow at our disaster. Then he sent all the inhabitants of the village out to the ship in many large canoes. Thus we began to unload her and in a very short time we had cleared the decks. Such was the help that this king gave us. After this, he himself, with his brothers and relations, did everything they could both in the ship and on shore to arrange for

our comfort. And from time to time, he sent various of his relatives to implore me not to grieve, for he would give me everything he had.

I assure your Highness that nowhere in Castille would one receive such kindness or anything like it. He had all our possessions brought together near his palace and kept there until some houses had been emptied to receive them. He appointed armed men to guard them, and made them watch over them right through the night. And he and everyone else in the land wept for our misfortune as if greatly concerned by it. They were so affectionate and have so little greed and are in all ways so amenable that I assure your Highness that there is in my opinion no better people and no better land in all the world. They love their neighbors as themselves and their way of speaking is the sweetest in the world, always gentle and smiling. Both men and women go naked as their mothers bore them; but your Highness must believe me when I say that their behavior to one another is very good and their king keeps marvelous state, yet with a certain kind of modesty that is a pleasure to behold, as is everything else here.

Taino settlements, as we have indicated, ranged from single units of many families to towns of one thousand houses and probably three to four thousand persons. The village houses were arranged around the ball courts (where there were ball courts) and the straw-roofed huts of the chiefs, called *bohíos*—a term Cubans still use for the straw houses of the rural peasants. Settlements seem to have been located in areas favorable for agriculture—on the leeward side of mountains and somewhat inland. The villagers produced two crops per year of potatoes (botanical name, *solanum tuberosum*), sweet cassava (*manioca*), peanuts (*arachis hypogaea*), peppers (probably *capsicum*), beans (*phaseolus*), and arrowroot (*maranta arundinacea*). Unlike on the mainland, maize, while cultivated, was unimportant as a staple food. The dietary supplements included coneys, agouti, lizards, spiders, and a variety of insects and reptiles. Chiefs reserved the right to eat certain kinds of agouti and iguanas. The Taino had no domesticated animals except a type of mute dog (which was sometimes eaten).

In addition to agriculture, which was the main economic activity, the Taino also fished with nets, hooks, spears, and storage pens. If fishing was secondary to crop cultivation, this could not have resulted from any dearth of fish in the surrounding seas, as anthropologists Julian Steward and Louis Faron suggest, for Caribbean waters are quite shallow in some places—well-known fishing banks still survive around the Bahamas, Cuba, Jamaica, and Hispaniola—and fish are plentiful throughout the region. What appears more probable is the deliberate subordination of fishing to the successful pursuit of agriculture. Moreover, until the crisis of the postconquest period, the local societies were adequately supplied by agriculture and probably considered fishing a form of supplementary undertaking, providing variety and nutritional balance to the daily meals. Nevertheless, the Tainos' supposed indifference to fish is a tradition that seems to have been carried down to the present population of the Caribbean, where the eating of fish is still not a major dietary habit.

The political unit varied considerably in the Caribbean. A chiefdom, over which ruled a *cacique*, consisted of villages or a single village of several families.

In 1500, Hispaniola had six chiefdoms for its estimated population of 500,000 inhabitants, while Puerto Rico had eighteen for its estimated population of 45,000. Apparently the chiefs had considerable authority and prestige but no real political power—and political competition seems to have been quite unimportant among these peaceful people. Chiefs officiated over village rites and ceremonies. They led the singing, dancing, and festivities in return for the privileges of special houses, superordinate *zemis*, elaborate titles of address, distinctively large canoes, especially prepared food, and colorful dress and body ornamentation. But as a political or economic elite, the *caciques* were chronically weak. They could requisition men and food for military enterprises—usually along the hostile Carib frontier to the east. They settled village disputes and organized communal work. But they had no special training, no special skills that could establish them as a cohesive, self-perpetuating elite with a distinctive esprit de corps. Above all, the chiefs received no tribute that could be accumulated and converted into wealth. The entire political structure was inadequate to mobilize resistance to the constant marauding pressure of the Carib invasions originating from the eastern chain of islands. Altogether, the social structure contained some fundamental weaknesses that had to be modified if the Taino type of society were to survive—and these weaknesses preceded the advent of the Spanish and other Europeans to their world.

Matrilineal inheritance characterized Taino society. Bride price, bride service, and polygamy were social customs. Postmarital residence was patrilocal. In the absence of an heir of the female line of a chief, succession could be by one's son or by female relatives. Likewise, heirs of chiefs who showed no promise for leadership were rejected in preference for a locally elected member of the common people. It was a society, therefore, that had internal flexibility and mobility.

Taino pottery, especially from the larger communities on Cuba and Hispaniola, showed some progressive stylization and sophistication. In general, Antillean pottery also bore strong resemblances to that found in northeast Venezuela. The men of Gonâve Island, off the western coast of Hispaniola, had some regional reputation for their woodwork, while the men on the mainland demonstrated some minor metalurgical skills. But from the European point of view, as reflected in the journals of Christopher Columbus, the Tainos were "a people short of everything."

"A people short of everything" was patently a European description reflecting differences of culture, attitude, and material wealth. Antillean society appears to have been self-sufficient in its simple needs. Luxuries were few, the parasitical elite class was small, and the food base was perfectly adequate to support the existing population. Carl Sauer, the geographer, concluded that "in productivity the West Indian native economy cannot be rated as inferior." It is not surprising, therefore, that trade between the islands or with the mainland was not only limited, but also restricted to the barter of pottery for ornamental gold. In any case, the economic and commercial trading aspects of Antillean society have not received much attention in the literature about these communities. Assumptions of inter-island or islands-mainland trade derive mainly from the almost uniform response of the Tainos to the persistent Spanish queries about the source of the gold that they wore on their bodies. On each island, the natives kept pointing tantalizingly to the east—which, if Columbus were right that he had been off the China coast, would have indicated yet another island rather than the mainland. But despite this, it is not at all certain that the gold was obtained through regular trade as we understand the term. And the later Spanish colonists who followed Columbus did eventually find gold along some riverbanks in the interior of Hispaniola.

The rapid disappearance of the Taino population during the first century of Spanish colonization in the Caribbean does not indicate that they failed to have any impact on the future social evolution of the region. Indeed, just like on the mainland, successful European settlement depended on the support of the local native population. In the first place, it is a fair assumption that a goodly number of the early Spanish settlers mated with the Taino women and procreated. Rumor has it that the destruction of the first Spanish colony on the northern coast of Hispaniola resulted from the quarrel over women between the Europeans and the locals. As late as 1570, Indians outnumbered Spanish in the colonial enclaves established by the arriving settlers, and already a significant demographic impact had resulted from the contact of the two groups. The miscegenated offspring of that union were in all likelihood culturally absorbed into the mainstream of the Spanish colonial society in the same way that they had been on the mainland. But it should be pointed out that as late as the final decades of the sixteenth century, the Spanish recognized Indians and granted them privileges that were commonly bestowed on fellow Spaniards. For example, the Town Council of Havana in March 1569 accepted a petition from an Indian named Alonso who referred to himself as "an Indian, a citizen of this town [*Indio, vecino desta villa*]." And as though to emphasize the frontier nature of Spanish colonial society in those days, the Town Council, acting in the name of the monarch, gave several grants of land—called *mercedes de tierra*—to several nonwhites of African ancestry. When the society matured a century later, Indians and persons of African descent were no longer recognized as legitimate "citizens" of the town.

In the second place, the Indians taught the Spanish about herbs, food crops, and housing. In addition to the food crops and animals that the Spanish brought with them from Iberia, within a short time they were also cultivating tobacco, potatoes, peanuts, manioc, maize, pumpkins, beans, and other native American crops. Finally, the Taino made an indelible impression on Spanish speech, with the addition of a number of nouns that remain a part of the language of Castile: words such as *bohío* (a rural hut), *guagua* (a truck or bus), *cacique* (a chief), *caney* (a type of palm-thatched house), *conuco* (a provision ground), *guajiro* (rural peasant), and *calpulli* (a district or zone within the town).

The Caribs were the third immigrant group in the Caribbean islands. While much has been written of these fierce, proud, and dignified people, they are probably no better known than the Taino—and only slightly better known than the simple Ciboney (Guanahuatebey). Although the Caribs survived the Tainos (or rather, because the Caribs survived better than the Tainos), they occasioned a wider, more unsympathetic press. Indeed, as Richard B. Moore and William Sturtevant have shown, much of the writing on the Caribs is replete with gross inaccuracies or patent contradictions. Much of this can be blamed on the early reports of Christopher Columbus.

Hopelessly confused in his geographic location, firmly convinced that he was somewhere near the outskirts of China, and quite unfamiliar with the local languages, Columbus gave the names "Carib," "Caribbean" Sea and islands, and "cannibals" to the area and its peoples. The names, like most nicknames, stuck. Even before he met them, Columbus had been predisposed against the Caribs by charges made by the Taino leader on Hispaniola. Hernando Columbus, son of the famous discoverer, described how the Tainos maligned their neighboring rivals, the Caribs, residing in the eastern islands while Columbus was temporarily shipwrecked off the coast of Hispaniola on or about December 26, 1492:

> He then prepared to go ashore, inviting the Admiral to a feast of sweet potatoes and yucca, which are the principal foods, and giving him some masks with eyes and large ears of gold and other beautiful objects which they wore around their necks. He then complained about the Caribs, who captured his people and took them away to be eaten, but he was greatly cheered when the Admiral comforted him by showing him our weapons and promising to defend him with them.

From that day on, every reference to the Caribs made by Columbus accused them of eating humans. And so the connection between cannibal and Carib became established.

The Caribs were the latest of the three migrant groups to enter the island chain. Their society was, from all accounts, highly mobile. By 1500, they had expelled or incorporated all the Taino communities of the eastern Caribbean islands and dominated the region. Perhaps because of their recent occupation, their social organization was less complex than that of the Taino. When they settled down, they selected sites that facilitated both agriculture and fishing. Their dual interest in fishing and sedentary agriculture falls within the classification of "Tropical Forest peoples" made by anthropologists Julian Steward and Louis Faron. Nevertheless, military strategy may have been one of the determinants of settlement sites. Irving Rouse described these sites as placed on elevated land to the windward slopes of the mountains, near running water. While much has been made of these locations, the Caribs might just have learned from experience that such positions offered some limited protection from the frequent hurricanes and floods, or the locations could have been accidental placements.

Carib houses tended to be small wooden-framed structures with oval or rectangular thatched roofs, surrounding a central plaza or communal fireplace. Unlike the Tainos, the Carib villages had no ceremonial ball courts. Instead, the fireplace served the functions of ceremonial center and social gathering place. Household furniture, such as it was, closely resembled that of the Tainos: small wooden tables, *metates*, griddles, stools (the ceremonial ones called *dujos* were carved from one piece of wood), hammocks, gourds, and pottery. The diet, too, remained similar to that of the Tainos: fish, lizards, crabs, agouti, corn, sweet potatoes, yams, beans, and peppers. Men and women engaged in canoe making, beer brewing, basket making, and weaving.

Given the information that we have for the Caribs and the Tainos, it appears that both societies were closely affiliated culturally. Indeed, Carib island society recruited its female members from the neighboring Taino—a practice that might have fueled the rumors of cannibalism. Taino women probably had a tremendous influence on the structure of Carib society, since the socialization of the mixed offspring within the family would have reflected strong Taino customs and some degree of bilingual and bicultural skills on the part of the women. Moreover, the predominance of Taino women probably explains the presence of Taino artifacts in Carib middens excavated by some archeologists.

Further details on Carib organization, however, are difficult to ascertain. The records and reports of early observers make no mention of inheritance practices, kinship relations, social ranking, or economic organization beyond a few elementary points: land was communally held, canoes and ornaments were personal property, and tobacco served as currency—just as it did in the early English colonies in North America.

The social and political organization of Carib society reflected both their military inclination and their immigrant status. Villages were small and consisted of members of an extended family. The leader of the village, often the head of the family, supervised the food-gathering activities, principally fishing and cultivation. He also settled internal disputes and served in a military group of the most experienced and accomplished warriors in raids against surrounding groups. But raiding, while carefully planned, was an ad hoc activity designed primarily to furnish women for the local young men.

Warfare was the most serious group activity of Carib males, and before the arrival of the Spanish, they had a reputation as the premier fighting force among the island peoples. Their arsenal contained bows, poisoned arrows, javelins, and clubs. Huge war canoes, made from the trunks of single trees and each capable of carrying more than a hundred men, made their escapades a threat to the more peaceful Taino. While women and children were taken away to be wives and slaves, men were killed and sometimes probably ritualistically cooked and eaten. It was perhaps this ritualistic consumption of males that led to the charges of cannibalism. It is not at all certain, however, that Caribs considered human flesh a staple food item.

Carib religion lacked the elaborate ritual of the Taino or of any of the major mainland civilizations. The Carib had no *zemis*. Each Carib had a personal diety that had many representative forms and to which he or she occasionally offered some manioc (cassava). Good and evil spirits battled constantly, not only within his body but also everywhere in nature, and the society supported *shamans* who attempted to resolve the conflicts of the spirits on behalf of one or another of the contending parties.

The differences between Caribs and Tainos—as among all three groups of island inhabitants at the time of the arrival of the Spanish—were differences of degree rather than of kind. There was a certain fluidity as the three groups merged in one locale. The Ciboney-Guanahuatebey had almost been absorbed by the Tainos. The Tainos had been partially expelled and partially incorporated by the Caribs. But the Caribs must have been undergoing some severe transformation of their own as their migration became increasingly successful and their society was increasingly influenced by the continual absorption of captured Taino women. Above all, the relative lateness of the Caribs' arrival in the islands did not give them sufficient time to crystallize their social forms and customs. And by the time that we have detailed ethnographic accounts of these people by the French in the seventeenth and eighteenth centuries, they had already radically acculturated to the new reality of the European influences.

What seems clear, however, is that all the indigenous Caribbean peoples were already undergoing critical internal change when the Spanish arrived to establish permanent colonies at the end of the fifteenth century. Taino society, despite its aesthetic achievements and complex social structure, could not defend itself adequately against the invading Caribs. Yet the Tainos—despite their peaceful reputation—did not simply surrender quietly to the Carib invaders. On the eastern frontiers that were more prone to attacks from the Caribs, some Taino communities were beginning to make adjustments to combat the new peril. They were abandoning their traditional pacific inclinations and, rather than responding to the Carib aggressions with the conventional tactic of evasion, were making weapons similar to those of their attackers and were resisting strenuously. Whether this particular type of response would have become more generalized throughout the Taino communities or whether a more broadly based defense would have thwarted eventual Carib domination of the Caribbean is impossible to ascertain. But it is interesting to speculate what such Carib domination would have produced. Even the Tainos did not surrender gently to the Spanish intrusion, and the history of the early conquest details the numerous campaigns of pacification waged by the Spanish. In eastern Cuba, a local leader, Hatuey, tried to bring together a confederation of fighting forces to resist the Spanish takeover. Had the Caribs been more numerous and their culture not radically transformed, they would have provided a more broadly based military elite—as they showed in the Eastern Caribbean—that would have made the early Spanish colonization more difficult and probably more costly in human terms. But delay would not have been the equivalent of defeat, and the Spanish conquest could not have been indefinitely averted.

Caribbean subordination to the Spanish was inevitable, given the differences in technology. While stubborn resistance might have slowed the progress of Spanish colonization, the Spanish dominated the region not only because they were militarily superior to the indigenous peoples, but because they inadvertently introduced infectious diseases that decimated the local populations. These diseases were, perhaps, the most potent weapons in the Spanish arsenal, and the ability of the Caribs to survive Spanish colonization is closely related to the relative inaccessibility of those people on the fringes of the area to which the Spanish directed their attention. Once gold and silver were discovered on the mainland, the interest in the Caribbean had to be modified. Geographically strategic islands were held and fortified, but the rest of the region was relegated to a lower priority. This strategic withdrawal permitted the Caribs to survive as viable communities—and later allowed competing non-Iberian Europeans to penetrate Spain's New World successfully, although not with impunity.

It is difficult to contemplate the nature of the society that would have emerged had the Spanish delayed their entry into the Caribbean. Carib society was also undergoing changes in significant ways, as I noted before. J. A. Bullbrook deduced from his archeological work on Trinidad that the Caribs there had apparently forsaken their "cannibalism" and had become sedentary farmers, fishermen, and gatherers. Bullbrook's suggestion derives from the failure to find human bones or spears in the excavated middens on that island. Yet if the Caribs never ate members of their own community—or more likely, if the eating of humans were ritualistic rather than dietary—then the absence of these bones could be quite easily explained. Trinidad lies too far to the south and to the east of the moving frontier along which the more germane practices of militant Carib society would have been manifested and their communities reinforced by plunder and pillage. Instead, it seems that they reverted to the habits and customs of the peoples of the Tropical Forest from where they originated, supporting themselves by fishing and agriculture and modifying their customs to conform with the recruited female component of the society.

Carib survival in the Eastern Caribbean, I have also implied, stemmed from fortuitous circumstances, not from the effective challenge that they represented to the Spanish invaders. The Caribs, after all, were no more hostile than the Aztecs and the Incas of the Mexican and Peruvian highlands, and those warrior kingdoms eventually succumbed to the men on horseback with their cannons and shields and unrelenting zeal and self-confidence. The Spanish came with a long tradition of fighting, and at the beginning of the fifteenth century, they probably represented the best warriors anywhere in Europe. The Caribs of the Eastern Caribbean survived for a number of reasons. They inhabited the smaller peripheral islands, and the limited human resources of the Spanish precluded total colonization of all the islands and the mainland simultaneously. The domain of the Caribs lay off to windward, outside the main direction of sailing ships—and outside the main interest of the Spanish after the discovery of gold and silver on the mainland converted Mexico and Peru into veritable Meccas for the Spanish. So, the smaller Caribbean islands lost whatever importance they might have offered at the outset as potential settlement bases for the European intrusion into the Americas.

By the time that the English and French arrived permanently, more than a century after the Spanish had established their American empire, the Caribs had undergone vast internal changes, making it difficult to differentiate between the truly indigenous and the creative adaptations from the Europeans. The process of borrowing that had started with the Taino simply continued with the Europeans, the new neighbors of the Caribs. The most marked innovations occurred in the technology of naval transportation. Canoe sizes increased, for the Caribs no longer restricted sizes to the trunks of single trees. Sails were incorporated, fashioned from plaited palm leaves or cotton cloths—a clear imitation of the Europeans. But the military and technological superiority of the Spanish restricted the transfer of these innovations to the eastern islands. The Caribs were circumscribed. Carib society eventually became more sedentary than its natural disposition warranted, and the Caribs began farming the crops imported by the Spanish—sugarcane, oranges, lemons, bananas—and herding cattle, goats, and hogs introduced by the Europeans. Nevertheless, the Caribs remained militaristic enough to be a great nuisance to the colonizing efforts of the English and the French on the outer islands during the seventeenth and eighteenth centuries. And descendants of these Caribs still live on Dominica.

The pre-Hispanic peoples as a group were the first victims of the peculiar characteristics of the Caribbean, of the perpetual crisis and transition of Caribbean society. The physical geography of the islands conditioned and circumscribed their societies and their cultures as it would those succeeding them. Responding to external forces, these island peoples have been especially vulnerable to influences from the outside, and their societies have been more a reflection of eclectic adaptation than original creation. Originally peopled from the nearby mainland, the region moved from the periphery of American sociopolitical development in the fifteenth century to the center of European political, economic, and social attention in the eighteenth century—and the receiving zone for the largest proportion of involuntarily emigrated Africans. The pendulum of interest and influence would return to the American mainland again, but the pattern of crisis and transition remained an integral aspect of Caribbean social, political, and economic life. That pattern of change after 1500 represented a substantially different form than before. That is why for the original inhabitants of the New World, the arrival of the three caravals from Spain in 1492 meant inexorable doom. Demographically, the Indians might have survived, but for their societies and their cultures, the end began then. The arrival of Christopher Columbus began the integration of the Atlantic world.

SUGGESTED READINGS

Alegría, Ricardo. *Las primeras representaciones gráficas del Indio Americano, 1493–1523.* San Juan: Instituto de Cultura Puertorriqueña, 1978.

Alegría, Ricardo. *Apuntes para el estudio de los caciques de Puerto Rico.* San Juan: Centro de Estudios Avanzados de Puerto Rico y El Caribe, 1979.

Bercht, Fatima, Brodsky, Estrellita, Farmer, John Alan, and Taylor, Dicey, eds. *Taíno: Pre-Columbian Art and Culture from the Caribbean.* New York: Monacelli Press, 1997.

Denevan, William M., ed. *The Native Population of the Americas in 1492.* Madison: University of Wisconsin Press, 1976.

Jennings, Francis. *The Invasion of America: Indians, Colonialism, and the Cant of Conquest.* Chapel Hill: University of North Carolina Press, 1975.

Pané, Ramón. *An Account of the Antiquities of the Indians.* A new edition, with an introductory study, notes, and appendixes by José Juan Arrom. Translated by Susan C. Griswold. Durham, N.C.: Duke University Press, 1999.

Rouse, Irving. *The Taínos: Rise and Decline of the People Who Greeted Columbus.* New Haven, Conn.: Yale University Press, 1992.

Sued-Badillo, Jalil. *Los caribes: realidad o fábula.* San Juan: Instituto de Cultura Puertorriqueña, 1978.

Sued-Badillo, Jalil, ed. *General History of the Caribbean. Volume 1. Autochnonous Societies.* Paris and London: UNESCO Publishing and Macmillan, 2003.

Wilson, Samuel, ed. *The Indigenous People of the Caribbean.* Gainesville: University of Florida Press, 1997.

Wolf, Eric. *Sons of the Shaking Earth: The People of Mexico and Guatemala—Their Land, History, and Culture.* Chicago: University of Chicago Press, 1959.

CHAPTER 2

Settlements and Colonies

The Indians [shall] live in community with the Christians of
the island and go among them, by which means they will help
each other to cultivate, settle, and reap the fruits of the island,
and extract the gold which may be there, and bring profit to
my Kingdom and my subjects.
—QUEEN ISABELLA TO NICOLÁS DE OVANDO,
December 20, 1503

The first abrupt intrusion into the complacent indigenous tranquillity of the
Caribbean world came from the restless, bellicose Spanish in the late fifteenth
century. Driven by the internal effervescence and the centrifugal forces that were
then engrossing Western Europe, the Spanish set out to establish a trading-post
empire patterned closely after the Portuguese model. The Portuguese, especially
under the leadership of Prince Henry the Navigator (1394–1460), had successfully
established a system of trading factories and forts along the West African coast
and were slowly exploring the eastern Atlantic on a route that would eventually
lead them into the Indian Ocean and to the fabled wealth of the spice trade. If the
Portuguese were after "Christians and Spices"—as Vasco da Gama confessed when
he arrived off the coast of India—then the Spanish, as may be implied from the letter of the Castilian queen to Nicolás de Ovando, her governor in Hispaniola in 1503,
were after Christians and gold. Indeed, that is exactly what Bernal Díaz del Castillo,
the articulate soldier of fortune and follower of Hernán Cortés thought when they
and the other conquistadors finally stumbled on much gold in Mexico in 1519.

While Christopher Columbus might not have been the first European to arrive
in the New World, his voyages of discovery had a greater impact than all the previous ones. The first voyage of Columbus in 1492 fortuitously discovered a whole
new world and set in motion a chain of events whose profound consequences gave
new directions to the histories of Europe, Africa, the Americas, and Asia. It was the
voyages of Columbus and those who followed him that brought the Americas into
the consciousness of the Europeans. And the discovery of the New World began the
permanent links that eventually made possible the Atlantic world community.

But initially the dispersed lands and peoples discovered by Columbus
throughout the Caribbean had neither the commodities nor the inclination to
trade in ways to which the Europeans were accustomed. The little gold that the

local island people wore ornamentally merely tantalized the early Spaniards, and Columbus himself died before knowledge of the availability of the substantial gold and silver deposits of Mexico and Peru reached Spain. For Queen Isabella and King Ferdinand—the Spanish Catholic monarchs in whose names the imperial discovery was made—the idea of a rewarding trade-post empire quickly faded. If wealth were to be derived from the overseas empire, it would have to be forcefully squeezed from the native inhabitants or produced by the directed industry of Spanish colonists under Spanish supervision. The first Spanish plans, prognosticated on the error that the Caribbean was an Asian sea, lasted seven years. In those seven years, Columbus made three voyages under the original feudal authority that had been granted to him prior to his first expedition in 1492. He discovered the paths to the mainland—although he was unaware of the full extent of his geographic discovery—started a settlement of Spanish colonists on Hispaniola, and created a viable beachhead for later Spanish-American activity. An inept administrator and an incurable romantic, Columbus produced neither riches for his monarchs in faraway Spain nor peace among his followers in the New World. Queen Isabella, despite earlier promises, replaced him with the firm Francisco de Bobadilla in May 1499, and in 1502 she sent out Nicolás de Ovando with a motley group of about twenty-five hundred settlers to reinforce the Spanish hold on Hispaniola and to spread the Christian influence throughout the Indies.

The arrival of Ovando marked the first turning point in the history of the Spanish Caribbean. Semiprivate entrepreneurship, which brought great reward to the Portuguese along the African coast and inspired the first expeditions of Columbus, ceased. The Spanish monarchs introduced a selected, coordinated, and highly centralized policy of immigration to and colonization of the Americas. The theory and the high hopes of a series of successful trading posts throughout the western Atlantic yielded to the reality of Spaniards settled in defensible enclaves, re-creating as far as possible the familiar social and political patterns of Iberia. The *reconquista*, the romantic nationalist reconquest of Iberia from the Muslim occupants, moved to America.

After 1502, Spanish governors went out to the Caribbean—and later viceroys went to the mainland. These governors received their orders from Spain, and while they retained of necessity the flexibility of nonobedience common to all distant peripheral bureaucrats, they nevertheless were servants of the Spanish Crown. The Americas west of the line of demarcation mutually agreed upon by the Treaty of Tordesillas in 1494 became the imperial realm of Castile. American bureaucrats, therefore, were responsible first to the Casa de Contratación (or House of Trade) and then, after ideas of a viable trading empire faded, to the Council of the Indies. The original instructions given to Ovando and repeated frequently afterward included prohibitions against the admission into the colonies of Moors, Jews, converts to Roman Catholicism from either group, and later Protestants from anywhere in northwestern Europe, as well as Gypsies of any variety. The new Spanish colonies were designed to be orthodox and unified in religion and Castilian and Spanish in both culture and nationality.

Castilian exclusiveness, however, was a fiasco from the very beginning. Neither the Spanish Crown nor its colonial governors could prevent converted Catholics from going out to the Indies. Following the unification of the Crowns of Spain and Portgual in 1580, an increasing number of Jews and Portuguese moved across to Spanish America and the Caribbean from several nearby locations of the Portuguese empire. Indeed, 19 Portuguese appeared among the 260 *vecinos*, or male heads of households, eligible for military duty and public service in the *padrón*, or civil register, of the city of Havana in 1582. Four of the 19 ranked among the most esteemed in social status; while Manuel Diaz, one of the 4, served as the city's *contador*, or tax collector.

Royal government did not prevent the wandering of free-lance Spanish explorers in the Americas. Indeed, the contest between the free lances and the Crown continued until after the civil wars in Peru in the 1550s. But the action of Queen Isabella in sending out Nicolás de Ovando in 1502 clearly indicated an end to the linear expansion of feudal powers from Spain to the Americas. No other individual ever got the power originally conceded to Christopher Columbus—although the grant to Hernán Cortés in New Spain came close. All subsequent explorers and conquerors felt the proximity of the Spanish colonial administration. That did not change until the eighteenth century.

Hispaniola, the first designated site of settlement, was not merely a Spanish colony. It was the private domain of the Castilian monarchs. Spanish settlers there, as in the rest of the Americas later, became vassals of Castile. Hispaniola—and later Cuba and Puerto Rico—became recruitment bases for the expeditions that expanded Spanish influence on the mainland, or *tierra firme*. This constant drain depleted the populations of the islands much as it had parts of the metropolis. Cuba, by one account, lost approximately 60 percent of its Spanish population between 1502 and 1600 to the mainland. Yet, despite the dwindling populations, the islands proved extremely conducive to the propagation of Spanish crops and animals. Within a short time after their effective occupation by Spanish settlers, the islands provided an abundance of familiar Castilian animals and local and imported fruit—horses, mules, cattle, pigs, sheep, goats, figs, maize, melons, oranges, yucca (the local manioc), peppers, pomegranates, and sugarcane—in excess of that available in the mother country. Nevertheless, the early period was difficult for Indian hosts as well as Spanish arrivals.

Until 1509, Santo Domingo—or as the Spanish preferred to call it, Española or Hispaniola—remained the focus of Spanish interest and their only true settlement in the Americas. The native pre-Hispanic populations were pacified in a long campaign during the summer and autumn of 1503 in which Ovando, Diego Velázquez, Juan de Esquivel, and Ponce de León exercised the unrestrained barbarity that the last three were to extend later to Cuba, Jamaica, Puerto Rico, and Florida. Local Indian leaders were executed, and the surviving subjugated adult males were distributed in *encomienda*, or service grants, among the conquering Spanish warriors.

The pacification of Hispaniola undoubtedly diminished the prospect of further Indian uprisings, but it also undermined the potential agricultural productive capacity of the local inhabitants and considerably reduced the available population that was liable for continued distribution in *encomienda* grants. With or without the service of subjugated Indians, the Spanish were determined to settle, as they had previously done in the reconquered Moorish lands in the south of the Iberian peninsula. They therefore established fifteen towns that were strategically located alongside, or near, both the preexisting Indian pueblos, or towns, and near the newly discovered gold mines. Of the fifteen towns, ten—Santo Domingo, Azua, San Juan de la Maguana, Buenaventura, Salvaleón de Higuey, Santa Cruz, Bonao, Concepción de la Vega, Santiago, and Puerto de Plata—were founded in the eastern part of the island (in what is now the national state of the Dominican Republic). The other five were west of the Neiba River, carved out of the former Indian territories of Bainoa and Gaucayarima (in land that today forms part of the national state of Haiti): Puerto Real, on the site of Cap-Haïtien; Lares de Guahaba, north of Gonaïves; Verapaz, just north of Port-au-Prince; Salvatierra de la Sabana, near Les Cayes; and Villaneuva de Yaquimo, near Jacmel. These fifteen towns all got their coat of arms in 1508. The establishment of the towns legitimated the Spanish presence on the island of Hispaniola.

Many names later to become famous in the annals of sixteenth-century Spanish expansion were associated with some of these early towns established under the authority of Ovando. Alonso de Ojeda, who came out on the second voyage of Christopher Columbus, explored the Guianese and Venezuelan coasts, discovered the pearl fisheries of Margarita, and retired to Villaneuva to engage in the dyewood trade. Vasco Nuñez de Balboa, the first known European to view the Pacific from the Isthmus of Darien, was a farmer in Salvatierra, and so was Diego Velázquez, who later conquered Cuba. Ponce de León settled first in Santa Cruz along with the curious, restless, *encomendero* Bartolomé de las Casas. The former wandered around the Caribbean looking for a fountain of eternal youth, discovered Puerto Rico, and lost his life in Florida. The latter, also a regional wanderer, eventually returned to Spain to be the notorious "Protector of the Indians" and gadfly in the Court of Charles V. (In a series of debates against the jurist, Juan Ginés de Sepúlveda, Las Casas argued in Valladolid in 1550–1551 that the Spanish had no territorial right to the Americas. He also inadvertently initiated the "Black Legend" against Spain by claiming that the Spanish colonists had wantonly destroyed millions of native Indians in the Caribbean.) Hernán Cortés, the conqueror of Mexico, and Francisco Pizarro, the conqueror of Peru, both lived in Azua, while Juan de Esquivel, the explorer of Jamaica, came from Salvaleón de Higuey.

The influx of Spanish settlers was rapid and heavy. By 1508, according to Troy Floyd, Hispaniola had a population of approximately twelve thousand Spaniards, and its economic base had been stretched to the limit. The administration of Ovando, then drawing to a close, had been generally peaceful and attractively prosperous once the initial pacification of the Indians was completed. The preceding six years represented the acme of early Caribbean prosperity prior to the introduction of the large-scale sugar industry in the seventeenth century. Already the pattern of Spanish-American colonization, with its strong reliance on mining and grazing, was becoming apparent. The economy of the island was also largely self-sufficient in basic foodstuffs.

Mining centered around the towns of Santiago, Concepción de la Vega, Bonao, and Buenaventura. The laborers as well as the foodstuffs, hides, and other mining accessories came from the surrounding towns of Puerto de Plata, Santa Cruz and Salvaleón de Higuey on the north coast, Azua and Santo Domingo on the south coast, and San Juan de la Maguana in the extremely fertile valley of the Yaque del Sur River. The eastern port towns also supplied the mines by transshipping through the nearby ports of Santo Domingo—already in 1509 a rather bustling city—Puerto de Plata, and Santa Cruz. The animals introduced by the Spanish multiplied so rapidly and roamed so freely that they soon became pests, greatly outnumbering the human population and often destroying the cultivated *conucos*, or cultivated parcels, of the Indians and Spanish. Wild pigs took over the forests, and wild cattle and horses dominated the plains in such profusion that pioneers found abundant meat in the interior, as did later runaway slaves. Even the Indians became carnivorous. Indeed, the ready availability of these animals gave rise to the transient, transfrontier society of buccaneers during the late sixteenth and early seventeenth centuries. The most abundant food crop was the manioc (cassava or yucca), a high-yielding, subsurface-feeding, pre-Hispanic tuber popular in the diet of the circum-Caribbean peoples. Wheat, one of the few imports that failed to prosper in the tropics, was scarce, so cassava bread rapidly became the standard dietary fare for both settled colonists and transient sailors.

The pattern of the society existing in 1509 in Hispaniola presaged, in many ways, the future for Spanish colonization throughout the New World. At the top in social esteem and in local political power wielded through the town councils were the arrogant Spanish settlers who saw themselves as the natural heirs of the entire hemisphere. They were a quite variegated group, dominated by Andalucians. Peter Boyd-Bowman calculated that 60 percent of the colonists officially leaving for the Spanish Indies originated in Seville, with a substantial portion of the remainder coming from the infertile, semi-desert, and relatively unproductive Extremadura region. But most provinces of Spain had representatives among the early emigrants, although very few left from Galicia, Navarra, Aragón, Cataluña, Valencia, Baleares, Murcia, the Canary Islands, or the new zones created from the recently reconquered kingdom of Granada. Later these locales would be more heavily represented in Spanish emigration to the New World. Interestingly enough, despite the royal prohibitions against non-Castilians emigrating, more than 140 foreigners, including 44 Portuguese and 61 Italians, obtained legal permits to sail to the New World in the first decades after the conquest. Contrary to popular belief, only a few of the early emigrants were criminals. A substantial number were decent, honest, hardworking individuals who went out to seek a fortune or to find a better life. Many of these colonists distinguished themselves as leaders in the early history of the Caribbean, although most, in common with others of their class, were illiterate. But at that time, literacy was not a prerequisite for political office, upward social mobility, or the pursuit of wealth. The Spanish men who ventured to the Indies in the early sixteenth century represented a cross section of the Spanish society at that time, and they held a wide range of the common medieval motivations for territorial expansion and military strife.

Until 1519, the Spanish Caribbean tried desperately to assume the sociopolitical profile of a newly reconquered Andalucian territory. Spanish settlement took place in carefully constructed towns with local administration placed in the hands of municipal councils in which the local equivalents of a prosperous class were represented. These were the *vecinos* of substance and influence, whose rising prosperity had been tied to the number of local Indians they held in *encomienda*, a service arrangement with links to the Iberian frontier of medieval times. As established, Spanish-American towns had the same functions and status as their metropolitan equivalents and became the lowest level of local political organization. The pattern of colonial expansion in Hispaniola represented a direct continuation of the Spanish process in the Canary Islands.

The Spanish Church became prominent during the period of Ovando's governorship in Hispaniola, then more frequently referred to as Santo Domingo after its principal port and city. At least seventy-eight priests—mainly Franciscans, joined by the Dominicans after 1510—sailed to the Indies during the first two decades after the arrival of Columbus. Spreading the Christian gospel and converting the natives were, after all, integral parts of the westward expansion and a part of what the Spanish seriously considered to be their divine mission. Like the rest of the immigrants to Hispaniola, the priests also represented virtually all regions of the metropolitan Spanish state. Of the first seventy-eight priests in the *católogo de pasajeros*, the official list of emigrants at the time analyzed by Peter Boyd-Bowman, the regional representation appeared as follows: twenty-two from Andalucia, seventeen from Old Castile, eight from New Castile, twelve from Extremadura, nine from León, and one each from Catalonia and the Basque regions. The remaining eight were non-Spaniards.

The early migration formed a microcosm of Spanish society transplanted to the Antilles. With the first wave of settlers led by Ovando in 1502, entire families moved, with wives, children, servants, and slaves—the distinction between these last two categories appropriately blurred at the time—following the men to maintain or re-create the structure and functional organization of the social expansion taking place since the middle of the fourteenth century along the moving southern Iberian frontier.

Nevertheless, the linear continuity of the *reconquista* could not be sustained in the Antilles. The local conditions of the Caribbean created a major difference. The wide cultural gap between the invading Spanish and the host Tainos never paralleled the narrow gap between the Spanish and the Moors in Iberia. In many respects, the Moors represented an advanced culture with more sophisticated forms of technology. A symbiotic relationship was feasible in Iberia. In the Antilles, however, the vast technological gap between the two groups precluded the type of symbiosis that infused the frontier society in Iberia with such creative dynamism over such a long time. Spanish dominance derived from Spanish military might, and the invaders quickly and relatively easily reorganized the Indian communities, divided the families into *encomienda* grants of perpetual servitude, and exacted tribute in gold, labor, and food supplies. This socially disruptive reorganization accompanied by the tributary exactions and disturbed epidemiological environment facilitated the steady extermination of the local populations within the zones of Spanish control—and a frightful decline even outside those areas.

For the Spanish settlers, the ruthless efficiency of Ovando laid the basis for the economic success of the fledgling colony. For the Indians on Hispaniola, the European settlements were an unmitigated disaster. The increasing number of Spanish arrivals strained to the breaking point the productive capacity of the indigenous *conucos*. The greater demand for food could not be satisfied under the circumstances, even with the expanding supply of cattle and horses. The discovery of gold in the San Cristóbal-Buenaventura area of the Cordillera Central, the central mountain range, and in the Cibao in the north of Hispaniola further aggravated the situation by increasing the demand for Indians to work in the mines and placers. An ever-increasing number of Indians were withdrawn from food-crop cultivation—an activity that the Spanish seemed to spurn—thereby artificially creating the near-famine conditions of the second decade of the sixteenth century. But the general circumstances were complex. The vigorous growth of herds of semiferal animals frequently destroyed fields of food crops, while the stipulation that required Indians to work for periods of eight consecutive months in the mines and placers did not leave sufficient time for the proper pursuit of agricultural practices designed to augment the available supply of food.

The Spanish could not expect large numbers of workers for the mines and simultaneously a consistently high yield of manioc and other cultivated tubers, while the local population decreased rapidly. Of course, it is possible that the Indians might have willfully neglected their *conucos* in revengeful anticipation that by doing so they could starve the Spanish into withdrawing from the island. But after the discovery of gold (which occurred as early as 1499), the Spanish were determined to stay forever. Instead, if the Indians pursued a policy of reduced food cultivation, they unwittingly contributed to their own extermination, for it was the Indians, rather than the Spanish, who proved more vulnerable to the ravages of disease, debilitation, and scarcity in the first two decades after the Conquest.

Yet, as Nicolás de Ovando prepared to surrender his mandate in 1509, he might have had good reason to be proud of his accomplishments on Hispaniola. His had been a term of unprecedented and perhaps unequaled success. He had replaced the administrative chaos under Columbus with some order. He had completed the subjugation of the entire island; had established fifteen permanent, strategically located towns; had boosted the production of gold, dyewood, and local provisions; and converted the failing, sporadic attempts of Columbus into permanent settlements. With Ovando's effort, Spain truly arrived in the Americas.

Nevertheless, the colony had reached a critical turning point. As early as 1509, the once-populous regions were already becoming sparsely populated. The large numbers of Indians that Diego Columbus—son of the discoverer and successor to Ovando—presumably counted (and that Bartolomé de las Casas insisted with characteristic hyperbole to be "more than 3,000,000 Indians on the whole island") had largely disappeared. The *encomienda* yields started to decline, as did gold output in the mines. Food, apart from meat (as indicated earlier), became scarce, although probably not as scarce as labor. Both to local Spanish settlers and to the Spanish king, Ferdinand—appointed regent of Castile and the Indies by Isabella on her deathbed in 1504—the situation was alarming and demanded drastic action.

The immediate solutions lay in finding a new source of Indian laborers to work on Hispaniola, in diminishing the size of the local Spanish population, or in getting the Spanish to work harder to maintain themselves. The first two solutions were adopted. "Just wars" declared against the populations of neighboring islands provided a new source of slave labor. The Spanish moved out to settle on neighboring islands, thereby relieving the population pressure on Hispaniola. With regard to the third solution, there is no evidence that it received either serious consideration or sustained application. The Spanish were lords of the newfound lands.

Though the enslavement of the Caribbean Indians had always occurred, it had never been pursued actively as a policy of state. Isabella had reluctantly approved of it with reservation, carefully insisting that only the most warlike and recalcitrant Indians should be enslaved. To Isabella, the Indians were vassals, with the resultant concerns of noblesse oblige. To Ferdinand, the Indians were the indispensable link with public and private wealth, the only means of productive efficiency in the Indies. If the decline of the local populations jeopardized the continued economic viability of the overseas kingdoms, then there could be no other alternative but to introduce new Indians. These new Indians would come only as unwilling slaves. So Ovando had already resorted to slavery to establish the basis of wealth on Hispaniola.

Of course, Ovando, in proposing the general enslavement of the Indians, used two arguments of considerable weight with his king. He reasoned that the other islands were "useless," since they had no known deposits of gold, and he asserted that the enslavement of those Indians facilitated their conversion to Roman Catholicism, a duty that the monarch understood as an essential ingredient of his *patronato real,* the papal sanction for Castilian land grabbing in the Americas. The dichotomous goals of gold and God were reconciled in slavery, and the decimation of the local population that had taken place first on Hispaniola soon spread throughout the region from the Bahamas to Trinidad.

The socioecenomic salvation of the Spanish colony on Hispaniola could not be accomplished by the introduction of servile indigenous Indians alone. The resident Spanish population had to be reduced. And so began the restlessness that has remained a feature of colonial society in the Caribbean until the present, as the Spanish settlers moved on to neighboring islands seeking gold or, failing that, a sufficient number of Indians who could be enslaved. Yet by spreading out, the *vecinos* of the towns of Hispaniola were merely giving new impetus to the process of exploration that had continuously gone on since Christopher Columbus accidentally sailed into the Caribbean Sea. By 1509, the Spanish-American center

of gravity was leaving Hispaniola. The island remained the most heavily populated in the Caribbean, but within ten years, the mainland became the focus of
attention.

Before that happened, however, the action throughout the islands was fast
and furious. In rapid succession, the Spanish spread far afield. Juan Ponce de León
went to Puerto Rico in 1508 and quickly organized the local Indians into gold
miners, distributing them in *encomiendas* to the *vecinos* of the two towns that he
founded: San Juan de Puerto Rico on the northeast coast and San Germán on the
west coast near the Mona Passage. Puerto Rico produced enough gold to make
Ponce de León one of the richest men in the Americas within a year. But the demographic price was high, for the Indians died even more rapidly than on Hispaniola.
Ponce de León, rich and insatiably restless, moved on to Florida where the local
Indians did unto him as he had previously done to so many on Hispaniola and
Puerto Rico. They pierced his chest with an arrow in 1521, forcing him to retreat
to Cuba where he died from his wound.

In 1509, Nicolás de Ovando and Diego Columbus organized slave-raiding
expeditions to the Lucayan Islands, which the English later called the Bahamas.
The local population was easily "pacified" and quickly decimated. That same year,
Juan de Esquivel began the reduction of Jamaica, the third largest island in the
Caribbean chain. Like the Lucayas, Jamaica produced no gold, but possessed a
rewarding supply of Indians, who were transported to Hispaniola and sold as
slaves or indented into serfdom. A small number of Spanish settlers moved to
Jamaica and started a grazing economy on the coastal plains that ultimately produced the substantial wild herds that the English attackers so casually destroyed
after they captured the island in 1655.

By 1511, Spanish expansion had reached Cuba and Florida. In Cuba, Diego
Velázquez renewed his military confrontation with the Indian warrior, Hatuey,
who had fled earlier from western Hispaniola. Having defeated Hatuey, Velázquez,
surrounded by some familiar faces like Pánfilo de Narváez, Hernán Cortés, and
Bartolomé de Las Casas, proceeded to establish seven towns and to divide the local
population in *encomiendas*. The seven towns were Asunción (later called Baracoa),
Santiago de Cuba, Bayamo, Puerto Príncipe (later called Camagüey), Trinidad,
Sancti-Spíritus, and Havana, then on the southern coast of the island. Within three
years, the conquest and "occupation" of Cuba was complete. The minority Spanish
superimposed themselves on the local society and slowly began the process of
conversion and social transformation. The future of the colony seemed secure,
and the island replaced Hispaniola as the premier overseas possession of Castile.
Velázquez wrote to his king in 1514: "The hogs that we carried with us have multiplied to thirty thousand...and this island is so bountiful that it could provide
sufficient food for *Tierra Firme*."

Diego Velázquez served as governor of Cuba until his death in 1524. It was
a period of enormous prosperity for the governor and for those colonists who
found the large deposits of gold that had eluded Columbus. Indeed, the royal fifth
amounted to 21,000 pesos in 1517, indicating a production for that year in excess

of 100,000 pesos. At his death, Velázquez was probably the wealthiest Spaniard in the Americas.

The prosperity of Cuba did not endure. By 1518, the colony was already rife with dissension, and the successful campaign of Cortés in Mexico the following year soon reduced the island to the status of a supply base for the successive waves of war bands moving to seek their glory on the mainland. Throughout the sixteenth century, the colony virtually stagnated—challenged by pirates, buffeted by hurricanes, plagued by diseases, and steadily depopulated by the magnetic pull of the riches of Mexico and Peru. Cuba played second fiddle to the gold- and silver-producing mainland colonies for the succeeding centuries, and only its strategic location saved it from total eclipse. Havana, moved to the fine protected harbor on the north coast, became the vital collecting point for the transatlantic convoys moving between Spanish America and the home ports of Cádiz and Seville. The port prospered, but the colony as a whole did not regain its importance until the later half of the eighteenth century.

For more than a century, Spain enjoyed the undisputed dominion of the Americas west of the line demarcated by the Treaty of Tordesillas. Spanish explorers, settlers, and priests wandered hither and yon. They settled where they could, moved where they liked, and fought when the occasion arose—either against the Indians or among themselves. Some went out for gold, some for glory, some to serve God and the king. Many died; a few like Velázquez and Ponce de León got quite rich, and an undetermined number returned to Spain.

It is extremely difficult to compare the quality of life in the Indies with that in the metropolis at that time. In general, the overall quality of life in both overseas colonies and the metropolis was dismal for the vast majority of the population. Cities in the Indies were merely glorified villages of crude huts and ubiquitous squalor—except where indigenous laborers could be coerced into building impressive churches and magnificent palaces. But in general, forts took precedence over palaces. Life was uncertain. Death was frequent, and nature was deceptively violent for both visitor and native. But conditions appeared more difficult than they probably were to those Spanish who yearned for facsimile representations of what they thought they left behind in Iberia. If the Spanish spurned agriculture, it stemmed from the inordinate importance they assigned to precious metals, especially gold and silver. They prodigally destroyed Indians, cattle, and forests, not only on the islands but on the mainland as well. It was a careless attitude toward the environment that was already evident in Iberia at the time.

The physical hazards of life were somewhat assuaged by the fecundity of the land and the almost limitless political freedom that distance imposed on the Americans. It took a long time for the Crown to establish control over its newly gained territories. The Spanish prospered in America, especially from the demographic point of view. The relatively small number of emigrants increased impressively. By 1570, the Spanish Antilles had twenty-four predominantly Spanish towns, with a white population of approximately 7,500; an Indian population of about 22,150; and a new heterogeneous group of Africans, mestizos, and mulattoes numbering around 56,000. Overall, Spanish settlements in formerly Indian territories had a population composition of roughly 9 percent Spanish, 26 percent Indian, and 65 percent African or mixed. If the Spanish desired viable colonies of vassals loyal to the Castilian Crown, they would have to create the population themselves. The twin features of Spanish emigration to Mexico and Peru, combined with a slow reduction of the indigenous Caribbean populations, left the islands relatively underpopulated.

Yet, neither the extent of the Spanish conquest nor the growth of the Spanish population should be exaggerated. Spanish towns, though they claimed contiguous boundaries, were merely enclaves in the various territories, like islands in a sea of either Indian-occupied or uninhabited land. Moreover, towns designated as "Spanish" indicated a cultural rather than an ethnic or phenotypical collection of people. Neither numbers of people nor descriptions were reliably or consistently given. The example of Cuba during the sixteenth century clearly illustrates this point.

According to the *empadronamiento*, or male registration, of 1570, Cuba had between 235 and 542 *vecinos*. The lower figure represents the number of Spanish males in the towns, and the higher figure, the total of Spanish and Indian males. This Hispanized population was slightly larger than that for Puerto Rico, then estimated at 200 Spanish adult males, but smaller than that for Hispaniola, estimated at 1,000 Spanish adult males. These figures show that three generations after the Spanish colonists arrived, the islands were still relatively sparsely populated. Using the 1570 figures, Cuba had a population density of only one *vecino* per 480 square kilometers, compared with one for every 80 in Hispaniola and one for every 45 in Puerto Rico. Assuming the *vecino* to represent the male head of the household (although this was not always the case) and the household size to be five, the three islands had population densities of about 11 persons per 100 square kilometers in Puerto Rico, 6 per 100 square kilometers in Hispaniola, and just 1 per 100 square kilometers in Cuba. The official chronicler of the Indies, Juan López de Velasco, declared that Cuba had lost 60 percent of its 1520 population by 1570, although he provided no basis for his assumption.

In all probability, Juan López de Velasco got his information from the clergy. An official report of a visit made by the clergyman Juan del Castillo in 1570 contained detailed descriptions of the ten Spanish towns and their populations then in existence throughout the island. These towns were Baracoa, Santiago de Cuba, Los Caneyes, Bayamo, Puerto Príncipe (Camagüey), Trinidad, Sabana de Vasco Porcallo (probably now Sancti-Spíritus), Sancti-Spíritus (now Santa Clara), Havana, and Guanabacoa. According to Juan del Castillo, Baracoa had eight Spanish *vecinos*, whom he described as "very poor," and seventeen married Indians. Santiago de Cuba had thirty-two Spanish *vecinos*. Los Caneyes had twenty Indians. Bayamo, then described as "the best town on the island, very healthy, with many houses and much cultivated land," had more than seventy Spanish and eighty married Indians. Puerto Príncipe had twenty-five poor Spanish and forty married Indians. Trinidad had fifty married Indians. Sabana de Vasco Porcallo was described as having "twenty *vecinos*, half Spanish and half of married Indians." Sancti-Spíritus, whose church was described as the "richest on the island," had twenty Spanish and twenty married Indians. Havana, with "more than sixty *vecinos*," was already beginning to dominate the modest commerce of the island. Guanabacoa, a short distance east across the harbor from Havana, had more than sixty married Indians.

The large number of married—and therefore converted—Indians within the jurisdiction of the Spanish indicates that not only were the natives far from being annihilated, but that Spanish control of the island was restricted to small scattered settlements of largely non-Spanish populations. If we assume that all the designated men were *vecinos*, then it is notable that 56.9 percent (307) of all the heads of households (542) were Indians. Three towns were entirely inhabited by Indians: Los Caneyes, Trinidad, and Guanabacoa. In three more towns—Baracoa, Bayamo, and Puerto Príncipe—Indians composed the numerical majority. In two other towns—Sabana de Vasco Porcallo and Sancti-Spíritus—Indians controlled half the population, while in two towns—Santiago and Havana—all the citizens were Spanish. Altogether, in eight of the ten towns, the Spanish were either absent, in the minority, or comprised no more than one-half the residents. The two entirely Spanish towns together accounted for 41 percent of the Spanish *vecinos* and 17.2 percent of all *vecinos*.

In light of these figures, it is hard to accept the claim that the Indian population disappeared rapidly throughout the Antilles. Nor can the notion of an expanding Spanish colonial society equivalent to that of southern Spain be maintained when less than 50 percent of the population living within the ordered confines of the colonial state were of Spanish descent. If Indians prevailed in such large numbers within the officially controlled towns, then their numbers outside must have been greater and their demise nowhere as immediate as generally assumed. Yet it is clear that within these towns the prevailing norms were Spanish; that is, the Indians included in the register were, to all intents and purposes, no longer culturally Indian. The Spanish colonial society, then, already represented an ethnic plurality.

This ethnically plural society can be further observed when one looks at the social stratification of the island's free population as described by Juan López de Velasco. Velasco's six social categories, ranked in descending order, were *vecinos*; sons and dependents of *vecinos*, and bachelor youths; *vecinos* who lived by their labor and their children; transients, such as military and commercial representatives temporarily stationed in the towns; free blacks (presumably including free mulattoes also); and Indians. Of course, to complete the picture of society in the colony, the Indian and black slaves must be added.

This picture of the social stratification is interesting for a number of reasons. It shows a society still relatively fluid, where class distinctions—especially between the *vecinos*—appear strong and where, within the categories of the free, the African element ranked above the numerically greater Indian element. Also interesting is the omission of slaves, since slaves obviously were part of the society. This omission suggests that slavery, despite the attention given to it in the highest councils of the empire, was still a fledgling institution in the emerging social and economic life of the colony. Finally, rather curiously, there is no mention of mestizos, the racial mixture of Spanish and Indians, although it is most unlikely that such were not present in the society.

Within a decade of this report, the Spanish began the reorganization of their Caribbean empire. Unable to defend the entire hemisphere—especially after 1580 when the Portuguese empire came under Castilian jurisdiction—Spain initiated a policy of strategic withdrawal from the peripheral areas, concentrating on the precious-metal-producing mainland; fortified ports, such as Havana and Santiago in Cuba, San Juan in Puerto Rico, Vera Cruz in Mexico, and Cartagena in Colombia, and regularly (or irregularly) convoyed fleets across the Atlantic. The smaller Caribbean islands were virtually abandoned for the larger ones, and Cuba assumed increasing importance owing to its geographically strategic importance for sailing ships plying the route between the Americas and Europe. The fortifications constructed at Havana and other port cities became necessary defensive measures against the encroachments of the rival Europeans and their semiofficial bands of privateers. With the growing naval importance of Havana came a growing demand for labor to build the fortifications and residences and to provide the food for the garrisons continually stationed there. Havana slowly grew from a village to a town and from a town to a city, becoming by 1790 the third largest city in the Americas, with a total population of more than 40,000 inhabitants. This expansion put a strain on the local resources and led to the incorporation of the city and the island more fully into the Atlantic network of trade and travel.

With the increase in the local population came an increase in the stratification of the labor force. The society, formerly comprised of a few wealthy individuals and a larger number of common folk, began to accentuate social condition and social distance between castes and classes.

Indeed, as early as 1582, a register of able-bodied males in Havana indicated how much the society had changed in the twelve years since the previous accounting had been made. Called the "Register of *vecinos*, bachelors, transients, Indians and free blacks of Havana and Baracoa," it listed by name (with additional subjective evaluations of some groups) all the men who were eligible for military service in the western sector of the island. The profile of the society is truly fascinating. The 299 names on the list broke down into 168 Spanish or Spanish-Creoles, accounting for 56.2 percent of the entire group. Hispanized Indians comprised the next largest group, with 84 individuals, or 28.1 percent of the total. Then came mulattoes and mestizos, with 22 persons, or 7.4 percent, while lowest in classification were the free blacks, with 25 individuals, or 8.3 percent of the total. Altogether, the combined non-European sector accounted for 131 individuals, or 43.8 percent of the group.

A large number of the males who were listed had no occupation—and that included a fairly large number of the most important of the *vecinos* whom the military commander of the fort at Havana described as "outstanding *vecinos* with whom one can shake hands and in whom one can place one's trust." A number of mestizos and mulattoes, although, surprisingly, no Indians, were listed among the artisanal occupations, both as master craftsmen and as apprentices, or as pursuing no trade. Juan Gallego and Francisco de Santa María, both mestizos, were two of the nine master carpenters in Havana when carpentry was a very important craft on account of the shipbuilding activity. Francisco de Góngora, Pedro López, and Francisco de Yibenes were mestizo carpenter apprentices. Juan de Liçao (a name that looks suspiciously Portuguese) was listed as an apprentice tailor; Juan Mendez was listed as a mestizo apprentice shoemaker.

While this list includes only males from Havana and its environs, it does provide a picture of the social cross section of the island at that time. Foreigners appear on the list: a number of Portuguese, some Frenchmen, and one individual from Flanders. The presence of the Portuguese is less surprising than their social prominence. Perhaps the most surprising aspect of the list is that while more than thirty occupations are included, there is not a single mention of any occupation clearly or exclusively related to the production of sugar. In 1582, the age of sugar had not yet arrived in Havana. The frontier nature of the Spanish society, however, was on its way out.

The consolidation of the spheres of Spanish influence after 1580 left room in the smaller Antillean islands for encroachment by other Europeans seeking to establish American colonies. Despite the papal ruling of 1493, which divided the world into spheres of Spanish or Portuguese influence, the legitimacy of such claims appeared extremely hollow. The pope, in effect, gave the Spanish the right to proselytize in all the area west of an imaginary line drawn 100 leagues west of the Cape Verde Islands. Portugal, by shifting the line a further 270 leagues, retained the significant eastern hump of South America, which allowed her access to vast amounts of Brazilian dyewood and protected her sailing route to India. Spain reduced the competition for what it thought was the shortest sailing route to the Asian spice islands. Given the geographic information of the day, it was a reasonable compromise. But the misgivings of the legality of the papal grants seemed to have permeated the two Iberian courts to such an extent that they redrew the partition in an additional secular agreement signed at Tordesillas, a small northwestern Spanish town, in June 1494. The other European monarchs intensely disliked the arrogance implied in such a bilaterally agreed division but could do very little about it. Political influence in the papal courts as well as superior nautical technology were on the side of the Iberians.

For more than a hundred years after the Iberians initiated their settlement in the Americas, no seriously organized European threat to their monopoly developed. Individual privateers, such as the Elizabethan Englishmen Francis Drake, Walter Raleigh, and John Hawkins—sometimes with official benevolence—attempted to establish rival semiprivate colonies in the Americas during the sixteenth century. The French tried to do the same thing with an equal lack of success. Domestic political unrest and deficient nautical resources precluded a major state operation during the troubled times of either Elizabeth I, queen of England between 1558 and 1603, or Catherine de' Medici, the regent of France between 1547 and 1589. Moreover, with the election of Charles V of Spain as Holy Roman Emperor in 1519, the loyalty of the Low Countries to Spain until 1568, and the naval victory over the Turks at Lepanto in 1570, Spain became the dominant political and naval power within the European system of states. But while the Spanish could successfully discourage the permanent settlement of others in the overseas areas that they claimed, the continuous harrassment of their shipping and the relentless plundering of Spanish-American port cities forced drastic reforms that eventually made non-Spanish permanent settlement in the Americas feasible by the end of the sixteenth century.

The architect of the planned defense of Spanish America in the later half of the sixteenth century was Pedro Menéndez de Avilés (1519–1574), founder of St. Augustine, Florida, in 1565 and the most powerful and successful Spanish bureaucrat between 1550 and 1574. Menéndez attracted the attention of the Spanish court as the commander of the fleet returning from the Indies in 1555–1556. Obviously a leader of great ability, loyalty, and energy, he successively became captain-general of the Armada de la Carrera de Indias (the fleet convoying the Spanish-American merchant ships) in 1561, adviser to the Crown (1564–1566), *adelantado* (military governor) to Florida in 1565, and governor of Cuba in 1567. His major impact on the Spanish government of the Americas, and especially of the Caribbean, was twofold. First, he recognized the limited capacity of the Spanish to settle and protect all the Americas. He therefore reinforced the enclaves by the construction of fortifications and the stationing of garrisons at strategically selected sites as I noted before: Vera Cruz, Cartagena, Santo Domingo, San Juan de Puerto Rico, Santiago de Cuba, and Havana. A fortification was also built in Florida. The selection of these sites implied that the rest of the region would be given only minimal protection and that the islands themselves were of secondary importance to the bullion-producing zones on the mainland. Second, Menéndez regularized the system of protected convoys as the main basis of maritime communication between Spain and its overseas dominions. To supplement the convoys, he created a small flotilla of swift, armed vessels permanently based in the Caribbean and charged with the responsibility of attacking pirates and discouraging all sorts of non-Spanish interlopers in the region, especially would-be settlers. The system worked effectively as long as Spain was stronger militarily than its enemies. This was the case until the death of Philip II in 1598. Internal problems distracted and divided the enemies of Spain throughout the sixteenth century.

By the early seventeenth century, the European enemies of Spain were no longer divided and disunited, and in rapid succession they penetrated the perimeters of the Spanish-American world. Within the first two decades, the French had explored a great deal of eastern Canada and had set up a fur-trading empire along the Saint Lawrence River basin. Samuel de Champlain (1567–1635) roamed over areas of eastern Quebec, Ontario, and New York State, while Etienne Brulé (d. 1633) explored Lake Erie and floated down the Susquehanna River to the Chesapeake Bay. The *coureurs de bois* (trappers) eventually took French influence far afield in the great American midwestern plains and down the Mississippi

River to the Gulf of Mexico. At the same time, English explorers, encouraged by merchants and entrepreneurial courtiers, rapidly spread English influence along the Atlantic coastline from Massachusetts to Virginia. By 1620, the northwest Europeans had reconnoitered a vast expanse of the Americas outside the principal spheres of Spanish influence, and apart from the sometimes hostile Indians, they liked what they found. Although they could not successfully challenge Spain in Middle and South America, they discovered that Spain could not repel their efforts in North America. And in the outlying easterly islands of the Caribbean, the possibilities seemed especially attractive.

Yet North America had a rather hostile climatic environment, the more so in winter, that made it discouraging to all but the boldest of pioneers. It had the prospect of a refuge, but not of the type of commercially viable colony that Europeans strongly felt contributed to the grandeur of sixteenth-century Spain. Apart from tobacco, furs, and fish, the northern zones produced few commodities that paid the cost of their freight across the Atlantic. The European market showed an appetite for spices and other tropically derived products. Viable commerce with Europe, therefore, depended upon the establishment of tropical colonies. Toward that end, the probing expeditions of the northern Europeans beyond the northern perimeters of the Spanish settlements were accompanied by sallies into the vital umbilical zone of the Spanish Caribbean. The English government of Oliver Cromwell (1599–1658) drew encouragment for its Caribbean ventures from a slanted book, *The English American, or a New Survey of the West India's* [sic], written by a renegade English Catholic priest, Thomas Gage (1600–1656), who had spent twenty-four years wandering about Spanish America and the Caribbean as a member of the Dominican Order. Gage, following an opportune religious conversion, was appointed the chaplain to General Robert Venables of the "Western Design," which captured Jamaica in 1655.

Before the "Western Design" and the clumsy attempt to wrest parts of the Spanish empire away by force, quiet efforts were made at settlements on the periphery. The English, French, and Dutch tried to establish colonies in the Guianas between 1595 and 1620. The Dutch finally prevailed along the Essequibo River and in 1624 along the Berbice River. The loss of life in these early settlements in the tropics, just as along the North American littoral, was discouragingly high, but the conviction that great wealth could eventually be obtained prevailed and was sufficiently strong to fuel the desires of merchants and politicians. Finally in 1624, the English gave up in Guiana and, under the direction of Thomas Warner (d. 1649), a survivor from the Guiana campaigns, turned their attention to the Lesser Antilles. St. Christopher (later St. Kitts) in the Leewards had the dubious distinction of being not only the first English colony, but the first French colony in the Caribbean.

The early non-Spanish settlements had to contend with hostile Indian neighbors, summer hurricanes, fevers, and periodic attacks from the Spanish. Somehow they managed to survive and, with reinforcements from Europe, to expand and prosper. The 1620s were the crucial years. But the Spanish, engaged fully in the

Thirty Years' War (1618–1648) in Europe and trying to administer not only their own vast American holdings, but the more scattered Portuguese empire, found themselves increasingly less able to prevent these peripheral settlements. Moreover, the truce with the Dutch signed in 1609 expired in 1621, and the Dutch mobilized their considerable naval resources to continue the struggle against Spain on a global basis. The Dutch West India Company, chartered in 1621, aggressively took the struggle to the Spanish Indies, destroying the Spanish Atlantic fleets and violating Spanish imperial laws by illegally supplying the colonial trade centers with Dutch products. In 1624, the Dutch captured Bahía and controlled the northeast coast of Brazil for sixteen years. In 1628, Piet Heyn (1577–1629), an employee of the company, took his convoy to Cuba and captured the entire Spanish silver fleet outside Havana harbor as it was departing for Spain. This roving stratagem of unrelenting war and plunder severely disrupted Spanish military and commercial activity in the Caribbean and permanently crippled the imperial defense built by Menéndez de Avilés. Dutch naval control of the tropical Atlantic indirectly facilitated the successful penetration of the Spanish-American empire by the other northwest Europeans.

Between 1630 and 1640, the Dutch seized the miniscule islands of Curaçao, St. Eustatius, St. Martin, and Saba in order to expand the commercial activity already centered on Araya and Cumaná on the coast of Venezuela. Meanwhile, the depletion of the Spanish fleet made the Spanish colonists even more eager than before to engage in illegal trade with any foreigner who appeared in their ports. By 1640, the Dutch were clearly the most successful traders in the Caribbean, with settlements in the northeast of Brazil (from which they were expelled in 1654), Guiana, and New York (then Nieuw Amsterdam), and lucrative trading posts on six strategically located Caribbean islands. The importance of the Dutch role in vanquishing Spanish invincibility can hardly be overestimated. "It was Dutch action in the Caribbean," wrote John Parry and Philip Sherlock, "which enabled [French- and English-American] settlements to take root and grow. Dutch victories strained the overtaxed resources of Spain almost to the breaking point, and provided a naval screen behind which the English, the French, the Scots and the Danes, without much danger of Spanish interference, could build up their colonies in a long string down the Atlantic coast from Newfoundland to Barbados."

With Spanish military operations virtually crippled in the Caribbean, the English and the French quickly extended their holdings. The English, along with the Dutch, settled on St. Croix, one of the Virgin Islands in 1625. The English occupied Barbados in 1627. They took possession of Nevis in 1628, Antigua and Montserrat in 1632, and St. Lucia in 1638. An attempt to settle Tobago in 1625 failed, and the Caribs destroyed the settlement on St. Lucia in 1641. The English settlements were sponsored by rival chartered companies using influential court politicians like James Hay (d. 1636), the first earl of Carlisle, and Philip Herbert (1584–1650), the fourth earl of Pembroke, to secure conflicting patents for ill-defined areas of the Caribbean. These conflicts over jurisdiction led to early disorder in the English colonies, a situation that the English Civil War (1642–1652) greatly exacerbated.

At the same time, the French were also advancing their settlements under the auspices of the Compagnie des Iles d'Amérique (Company of the American Islands), chartered by Cardinal Richelieu (Armand-Jean du Plessis, 1585–1642) in 1635 and ordered to take over the struggling colony of Pierre D'Esnambuc (the partner of Thomas Warner) on St. Christopher and to expand French settlements to any other island not previously occupied by Europeans. In return for some very liberal privileges, the company had the arduous task of settling at least four thousand Roman Catholics in the French Antilles within twenty years. The company settled Martinique and Guadeloupe and thus gave France a permanent interest in the Caribbean and a base for expansion to St. Bartholomé, St. Martin, Grenada, St. Lucia, and the western part of Hispaniola, which was ceded by the Spanish at the Treaty of Ryswick in 1697.

The English and the French, unlike the Dutch, were serious about transplanting Europeans who would grow tropical staples—tobacco, cotton, sugarcane, and anything else they could produce easily for export—and develop a reciprocal commercial relationship with the metropolis. In this way, the colonies could become viable, semi-autonomous communities and attractive recipients for what was then commonly considered an increasingly superfluous European population. In the early stages of each colony, tobacco became the principal cash crop, and a type of free trade with the Dutch salvaged many a faltering enterprise. The Dutch, until the second Anglo-Dutch war of 1665–1667, were, after all, the main promoters of commerce in the Caribbean, far excelling all other powers in knowledge of agricultural techniques, transportation facilities, financial terms, marketing arrangements, and general economic sophistication. Unlike the Spanish settlers of the early sixteenth century, the later-arriving northwest Europeans had no large host populations to supply food, instruct them in techniques of tropical survival, and become servants and slaves. During the initial phases of their colonization in the seventeenth century, the English, French, Danish, and Swedish settlers in the Eastern Caribbean found themselves either on isolated or uninhabited islands like Barbados or among hostile warrior groups like the Caribs on Martinique, Guadeloupe, Tobago, and St. Lucia. Survival depended on self-help and on trial and error. And for all groups of newcomers, the initial toll in human lives was high. The early colonists in the smaller islands cleared the forests and cultivated their crops by themselves or with the contractual help of indented servants in the English islands or *engagés* in the French. Colonial life in the tropics was extremely difficult and often short. But the mere existence of a multinational form of colonial activity in the Caribbean had tremendous consequences for the region as well as for the European powers involved.

During the two centuries after 1625, three important transformations occurred pertaining to the relations of the region to the wider world: the Spanish-American hegemony was successfully broken, the sugar revolutions began in the Caribbean, and the Europeans began to articulate new theories about empire that affected their international relations.

By the end of the seventeenth century, Spain had clearly lost its hegemony in the Caribbean. That was the first great change, slowly evolving since the late sixteenth century when the aggressive assaults of interlopers forced an imperial policy of strategic retrenchment and armed fleets. As early as 1604, Spain recognized the right of England to trade in the Caribbean. By 1648, at the Treaty of Münster, Spain tacitly recognized both her loss in the Thirty Years' War in Europe and the eclipse of her global power. She granted the Dutch those colonies that they had occupied overseas, freedom to trade in the Caribbean, and freedom to practice their own religion. Philip IV, having recently lost the Portuguese segment of the combined Iberian empire, could no longer make political demands on his European competitors. Nor could the internal affairs of the rival European states be separated any longer from their overseas involvement—and much of that involvement was in the Caribbean. Peace in Europe and peace "beyond the line" of amity became integrally related.

The manifest naval and military weakness of Spain emboldened the English to change their colonial policy after the late 1640s. Before that, the English had followed a timid policy of trading along the African coast and of establishing colonies of Europeans outside the range of effective Spanish reprisals. By the 1650s, however, the English, acting on Thomas Gage's unreliable advice, planned a massive assault on the Spanish Caribbean with the intention of wresting the major islands from Spanish control as a prelude to carving up the mainland and simultaneously boosting the fortunes of the Cromwellian Commonwealth at home. That was the ill-fated "Western Design" of 1655 under the command of Admiral William Penn (1621–1670) and General Robert Venables. Based on its original lofty aims—to conquer Hispaniola or Cuba as a base for commerce and to displace the Dutch (with whom the English were then at war) in the Caribbean—the plan was a monumental fiasco. The English, still woefully ignorant of conditions in the New World, found that the strength of the Spanish-American fortifications and Dutch dominance at sea far exceeded their estimations. Apart from some ships bearing bullion, the English fleet managed to capture only the relatively undefended and sparsely populated island of Jamaica. Unimpressed by their endeavor, Cromwell threw Penn and Venables into the Tower of London. Their stay, however, was short. Penn's son, William, founded the colony of Pennsylvania on the North American mainland after the Restoration of the English monarchy in 1660. Venables died in obscurity. Yet the failure of the "Western Design" was not without valuable lessons. If the Spanish-American empire could not be forcefully seized, Spain was powerless to prevent incursions, and at the Treaty of Madrid in 1670, she surrendered Jamaica and accepted the de facto legitimacy of the other English colonies. When Spain also accepted the French settlements in the Lesser Antilles and on western Hispaniola at the Treaty of Ryswick in 1697, "Adam's will" was redrawn: the American world no longer belonged to the Iberian monarchs. And by the end of the century, the English and the French had effectively duplicated the Dutch commercial system with their own overseas imperial possessions. The age of mercantilism had arrived.

The second consequence of the successful challenge to Spain was a series of social and economic revolutions on the islands of the Lesser Antilles as well as on Jamaica and Saint-Domingue, as the French called their colony on the western part of the island of Hispaniola. (The Spanish began to refer to the island as Hispaniola in the seventeenth century, rather than Española, as it was previously designated, and to call their eastern section Santo Domingo, in keeping with the practice of calling islands and colonies after the chief port city.) The nature of these revolutions will be examined and discussed in Chapter 4, but the essential characteristic was the conversion of colonies of settlement based on predominantly European populations engaged in mixed small farming and seminomadic cattle ranching into full-fledged, dependent plantation colonies integrally related into an Atlantic network of trade and administration involving Africa, Europe, the Americas, and eventually India and Asia as well. As these colonies were transformed from obscure havens for restless refugees from a divided Europe to economic areas designed for the production of tropical staples, they also changed profoundly in political importance. No longer was the Caribbean a region of marginal importance to the Spanish empire. Instead, until eclipsed by India in the nineteenth century, the Caribbean islands became the most valued possessions in the overseas imperial world, "lying in the very belly of all commerce," as Carew Reynell (1636–1690) so aptly described Jamaica in the seventeenth century.

The settlement experiment in the non-Hispanic Caribbean failed for two related reasons: the lure of free land and the growing demand for labor. The Caribbean could not compete with the mainland as a lure for free citizens seeking land and a new style of life, and so the free mixed economy could not be sustained in the smaller islands. For more than forty years, the northwest Europeans had attempted to establish random settlement colonies throughout the Americas. Everywhere they had paid a frightfully high price in human terms. Everywhere they faced enormous, often crippling difficulties: hostile Indians, antagonistic Spanish, unfamiliar climates, new fatal epidemics, failing harvests, and illusory riches. The frontier conditions of tropical and temperate America took their toll equally across national and ethnic lines. Yet it was the temperate climate that Europeans found more conducive to re-creating the type of society they either had or wished for. Nevertheless, climate was not the major stumbling block to the successful perpetuation of the settler colonies in the Caribbean—and indeed, the Spanish continued with their true settlements until the late eighteenth century.

By the middle of the 1640s, the English and French settlement colonies in the Eastern Caribbean faced the same type of crisis that the Portuguese and the Spanish had encountered in Brazil and in the Caribbean a century before. An acute labor shortage jeopardized the success of a viable agricultural economy. Barter arrangements with the Indians collapsed, as did outright Indian slavery. Caribbean-grown tobacco competed neither in quality nor in quantity with the mainland product. And the exodus of the released indentureds and *engagés* to the mainland or to join the marauding bands of transfrontier buccaneers exacerbated the labor shortage. Moreover, farming proved less attractive and profitable than plunder throughout the Caribbean. In July 1642, Captain William Jackson, a buc-caneer, easily recruited 500 men from Barbados and 250 more from St. Christopher to join his free-lancing band of more than a thousand pirates on a three-year expe-dition of plunder around the Caribbean. Thousands of landless farmers flocked to join the Penn and Venables expedition against the Spanish in 1655. And more than 1,200 Barbadians moved to New England and the Middle Atlantic colonies in the 1640s and 1650s. Moreover, the unsettled state of English domestic politics of the middle seventeenth century precluded the sustained political and commercial attention necessary to succor the fledgling colonies. French domestic politics in the seventeenth century was marginally more stable than English domestic poli-tics, but French Atlantic colonization, with the possible exception of the divided colony of St. Christopher, presented equal discord. In addition to the scarcity of labor, the French colonists had the burdens of poor local administration and the rapaciousness of local merchants—grievances that would accumulate and eventu-ally explode during the Revolution of 1789.

The third consequence of the new situation resulted directly from the other two. The acquisition of possessions in the Caribbean forced the northwest European states to articulate elaborate theories about the relationship of colonies to the mother country and to try to implement these ideas in order to control the wealth and power that such colonies afforded to a metropolis. The theory and practice of imperialism closely resembled the dilemma that the Spanish had confronted—if not adequately resolved—a hundred years before in the immediate aftermath of the conquest of their American empire.

The organizational structure that Europeans fashioned for their empires responded to their perceived needs as well as the actual circumstances of the sev-enteenth century, but it prevailed, with only minor modifications, until the nine-teenth century. The structures did not vary greatly among imperial divisions, having been conscious imitations of the most successful aspects of the expansive empiricism of the age. The basis of these schemes rested on the delegation of pub-lic functions to private corporations or associations of merchants, such as the Dutch West India Company, Richelieu's Compagnie des Iles d'Amérique, or any of the numerous charters given to Roger North, William Courteen, or the earl of Carlisle. All charters and companies involved in American exploration, trade, and colonization at that time blended political activities of the medieval guilds and corporations in Europe with the cooperative stockholding concerns of the Italian and Dutch cities. They therefore possessed three characteristics: financial support through joint-stocks, with shareholders receiving a share of the profits; political supervision in their sphere of operations; and some form of economic monopoly from their chartering government.

These characteristics could be seen quite clearly in the charters granted to the French Compagnie des Iles d'Amérique. With Cardinal Richelieu as its major sponsor and stockholder, the company got a charter in 1635 to develop parts of the Americas "not previously held by any Christian prince." In 1642, Richelieu won an extension of the charter, giving the company control over all islands they could capture or settle between the equator and latitude 30 degrees north, exclusive trade with these territories, privilege to import the produce of the islands into France duty-free, and complete jurisdiction to appoint all governors and the governor-general. Not only were these extensive privileges awarded, but the Crown promised letters of ennoblement to any settler who transported fifty men to any previously uninhabited island and lived there for two years. The extent of the powers awarded to individuals and companies in the late sixteenth and early seventeenth centuries reflected the relatively weak position of the new monarchies of the various competing Europeans. Joint-stock companies with informal government control facilitated the execution of imperial policies that would be too unpopular either at home or with neighboring states. Methods changed drastically when the monarchs felt themselves stronger both within their realms and vis-à-vis their monarchical rivals.

The overlapping political and economic aims of the various states were handled by a series of institutions that did not reveal fundamental differences across imperial boundaries. This common feature of imperial organization facilitated the transfer of colonies across imperial boundaries. Some imperial systems were more successful than others, and some exhibited greater efficiency over a longer period of time. But the goals of controlling trade and fractious colonists required only a few organizational measures. Both the scheme of organization and the measures required for control can be illustrated by reference to the various imperial organizations.

At the end of the seventeenth century, it was clear that the Consejo de Indias (or Council of the Indies) handled the imperial political coordination for the vast Spanish overseas empire. Established in 1524, this imperial watchdog controlled all matters related to the empire—from the appointment of viceroys to the evaluation of incoming colonial reports—and advised the monarch on all matters relevant to the administration of the Indies. For the Portuguese empire the Conselho Ultramarino performed similar administrative functions, as did the English Parliament (usually through the Board of Trade), the French Ministry of the Navy (after the bankruptcy of the French West India Company in 1649), and the Dutch Heren XIX, the board of directors of the Dutch West India Company responsible to the four provincial governors.

Local political control was somewhat diffused. In the Spanish colonies, it resided with the captains-general, the *audiencias* (the regional Supreme Court or Tribunal), and the *cabildos* (or town councils). The English distributed local control among governors, representative assemblies of property-holding colonists modeled after the English Parliament, and patentees, who could in some cases appoint some governors. The French reorganization of the colonial structure under Jean-Baptiste Colbert (1619–1683) in 1664 gave local control to governors appointed by the newly chartered French West India Company (in effect, the front for the French government) and aided by appointed councils. Planters' interests gained representation by the appointment of planters to the local councils. The Dutch, who had less ambitious aims for settler colonies, merely appointed local governors to supervise the commercial and other affiliated interests in their essentially trading colonies.

Economic direction and control fell within three portfolios: overall economic planning for the entire empire, coordinating economic schemes with the prevailing interest groups of the metropolis; local control of trade; and management of production. The Casa de Contratación and the Consulado (or Merchant Guild) of Seville had the highest responsibility for overseas Spanish trade, although by the seventeenth century most trade to and within the Indies had passed out of effective Spanish control. The English Parliament exercised a similar control for the English empire, with the Board of Trade responsible for advising on policy matters. The French Ministry of Finance made policy, with advisory input from the commercial companies funneled through the various chambers of commerce. And although the Dutch West India Company was not solely a commercial enterprise, it had control of overall economic planning.

In the Spanish imperial system, the domestic and overseas *consulados* controlled trade at the local level and managed production, sometimes in collusion with the local town councils. Local merchants and private shippers, however, handled this operation in the three principal rival non-Hispanic systems in the Caribbean, although nominally the Dutch West India Company supervised Dutch-American affairs. Similarly, the supervision of staple production was entirely in the hands of local planters. In theory, any English subject could organize his own trading enterprise within the empire as long as he did not violate the Navigation Acts designed to ensure metropolitan domination of trade by restricting the transportation of designated colonial products to English ships with an English captain and no less than 75 percent English crew.

The formal vertical imperial structures, however, could not prevent horizontal commercial association across imperial divides. In practice, the administrative systems failed to function efficiently from their inception. A number of factors contributed to this. States made exceptions to the general rule when such exceptions were in their general interests, such as the licensed trade, or *asiento*, granted by the Spanish in violation of the orthodox mercantilistic principles. Public officials frequently bought their offices and quickly found that the perquisites of office increased more rapidly by legal noncompliance than by adherence. Moreover, laws propounded on general principles often required local, commonsense applications—a built-in mechanism for possible graft and corruption. Communication between the home office and the colonial periphery was slow and subject to conflicting political vagaries. In the final analysis, the administrative bureaucracies could be no more responsible, sensitive, and effective than the metropolitan governments, which in that age proved demonstrably short of those qualities.

The formal relationship between the European metropolises and their American colonies became increasingly more complicated as the natures, circumstances, and values of the colonists were subtly transformed through time. Creolization in the American and Caribbean context altered the attitudes and values of Europeans in various ways. The novel experiences of the successive waves of immigrants fashioned the changes between European society and colonial American society. But perhaps the single greatest element in the structuring of this separation was the involvement in slavery, the slave trade, and the colonial conversion in the Caribbean from true settlements into zones of specialized economic exploitation.

Slavery was not unfamiliar to the European social experience when Christopher Columbus, Juan de la Cosa, Amerigo Vespucci, Juan and Sebastian Cabot, Pedro Álvares Cabral, and the many other brave explorers of the fifteenth and sixteenth centuries broadened the Atlantic horizons of their fellowmen. Slavery in the Mediterranean basin had been commonplace in the fifteenth century and continued to be practiced until the nineteenth century. While the Americas were being incorporated into the Spanish domain, Spanish and Portuguese merchants bought and sold Africans in a number of Iberian port cities, especially Huelva, Cádiz, Seville, Málaga, Valencia, and Barcelona. The Iberian market for slaves, however, was relatively small, absorbing annually perhaps no more than two hundred individuals—not all of whom were Africans. Communities of ex-slaves and their descendants formed in these southern Iberian cities. These communities included a varied number of groups of diverse origins: Moors, Jews, Syrians, Lebanese, Egyptians, Russians, and native Canary Islanders.

In the Mediterranean world where slavery flourished most, slaves were an important commercial commodity, ranking just below gold, horses, and salt. But slavery was not so important a part of general commerce or society that national governments became unduly interested. Nevertheless, Christopher Columbus was sufficiently impressed by the potential economic value of slaves to take some indigenous American Indians back as samples to his monarch in Spain after his second voyage to the New World, hoping that they would be vendible products. Isabella I, queen of Castile, refused to sanction this early expansion of slavery and, preferring vassals to slaves, forbade the large-scale and unrestricted importation and sale of her newly acquired American subjects. The moral qualms of the Spanish queen were insufficient, however, to save the Antillean population from epidemiological decimation. Isabella died in 1504, and by 1510, the inadequacy and reluctance of Indian workers created a severe labor problem in the gold mines, the pearl fisheries, and the farms of the islands.

Africans had accompanied the Spanish explorers and colonists to the Caribbean from the beginning of the age of exploration. An indefinite number arrived with the expedition of Nicolás de Ovando in 1502. By 1516, Spanish-speaking Africans—most likely born in Spain—had already outnumbered the true Spanish colonists. As Spanish colonialism expanded, so did the need to find individuals who would perform the demanding physical tasks required to clear the forests, plant the crops, attend the animals, build the cities, work the mines, and dive for the pearls. Spanish colonists themselves were not sufficiently skilled, sufficiently available, or sufficiently willing. The local Tainos, coerced to perform, died in astonishingly large numbers (though not necessarily from overwork), while the Caribs demonstrated such a vigorous opposition to enslavement that the majority were left alone. The Spanish Crown abandoned the cautious scruples that had inhibited the selling of non-Christians in their American possessions, and in 1518, Charles V sanctioned the monopolistic commerce of non-Spanish-speaking Africans shipped directly to the Antilles. With this permission, the transatlantic slave trade began in earnest. During the following century, the number of Africans increased steadily. As each colony became subdued, the local Indian population dwindled. As the Indian population diminished, the African component increased. African slavery preceded the establishment of the plantation economy, the development of the *ingenio*, or sugar mill, and the virtual monocultural dominance of sugar in the export economy. After 1530, the number of Spanish-speaking Africans declined drastically in the Caribbean as metropolitan policy prevented their legal export from Spain and as earlier arrivals followed the general exodus of colonists to the mainland.

The supply of slaves became a major concern. The economic viability of the entire imperial operation came more and more to depend on manual labor—and manual labor became more and more synonymous with African slaves. Spain, by the treaties of Alcaçovas (1479) and Tordesillas (1494), had surrendered to Portugal access to the African coastal trade—the best source of slaves—for an undisturbed hegemony of whatever it encountered within the western Atlantic. With Africa (and in the first century of the trade, the Guinea Coast) providing the majority of the marketable slaves, the Spanish-American colonists had little recourse but to depend on others for their legally obtained slaves. The attitude of the Spanish Crown was that slaves could be supplied in a controlled, monopolistic fashion, supervised just like any other commercial activity by the Casa de Contratación. And it obviously was too lucrative a form of commerce to be left entirely to commoners.

Lorenzo de Garrevod, the Duke of Bresa and an intimate friend of the young Spanish King Charles V, was the first licensed American slave trader. Awarded the monopoly to supply 4,000 Africans within four years, exempt from customs duties, Garrevod quickly realized the difficulties and disadvantages of initiating direct trade between Africa and the Americas. Apart from lacking the capital for ships and goods for exchange, Garrevod and the Spanish had no contacts and no protection along the African coast. Frustrated, Garrevod sold his contract to a consortium of Genoese merchants for 25,000 ducats. The merchants, in turn, resold the permission, probably illegally, to individuals who were in a better position to effect the purchase and transportation of Guinea slaves to the Americas—Portuguese sea captains, sailors, and factors—making a profit on their investment of some 275,000 ducats. This experience demonstrated that the slave trade had become such a lucrative business that even speculating middlemen could make handsome profits. By 1528, Charles realized that there could be a profit for the Crown, too. He sold the monopoly, then regarded as an *asiento*, to two front men for a powerful German banking firm, Heinrich Ehinger and Hieronymous Seiler. With the monopoly, the Spanish Crown tried to fix both the flow of Africans—about 1,000 per year—and the selling price at the point of delivery—about 40 ducats per *pieza*, or unit of labor roughly equivalent to a physically healthy adult male slave. Unfortunately, the American colonists found, not for the last time in their history, that both the legal number and the legal price could be breached with impugnity.

In 1537, Charles granted an *asiento* to Domingo Martínez and Cristóbal Francisquimé of Seville in which they pledged to supply 1,500 Africans to the Indies in return for a onetime payment of 9,750 ducats to the Crown and the usual exemptions from the levy of customs duties. The Sevillians resold their monopoly at the usual profit. By the middle of the century, the Crown assumed the direct award of contracts, or *licencias,* to individuals as well as to groups of merchants and shippers, gently escalating the price of the permits as the demand increased and the fiscal situation of the Crown became steadily less secure. The issuance of individual permits afforded a magnificent opportunity for illicit trade with the Spanish Indies. Foreign interlopers, like the Englishman John Hawkins, found that just about anyone who could get slaves off the African coast could easily dispose of them in the Americas without fulfilling the requirements of the king of Spain and the Casa de Contratación. To stem the increase of illicit trade, Charles's successor, Philip II (1527–1598), reverted to the monopoly system in 1586, vesting the delivery of slaves in a number of Portuguese firms until 1640. Although the Crown gained a large and steady income, the American colonists remained unhappy both with the number and price of the slaves delivered. Moreover, the American demand created a boom for interlopers.

In 1640, when Portgual regained its independence from Spain, it lost its preferred position as chief supplier of slaves to the Americas. During the period after 1518, approximately 75,000 Africans had been shipped to the Spanish Americas, accounting for about 60 percent of the total transatlantic slave trade before 1600.

By the early years of the seventeenth century, conditions in Europe, in Africa, and in the Americas had changed considerably with respect to national politics and international slave trading. Spain no longer held the dominant political and military position in Europe; England and the Netherlands were no longer Roman Catholic in religion—which made commercial intercourse with those countries tantamount to endorsing heresy—and France and Spain were at war. Spain, therefore, was less able than ever before to regulate the trade to her American possessions. In Africa, slave trading had emerged as a sophisticated system of commerce, highly organized, and with accepted rules of conduct on the part of all the participants, be they Africans or Europeans. The area of the trade had expanded along the coast as well as far into the interior of West Africa, making the recruitment and exchange of slaves a complex, multifaceted operation along an interlocking system of client relationships. Almost every European state, except the Spanish, had factors, forts, and contacts along the African coast, with the Dutch ascendant until the end of the seventeenth century. In the Caribbean, as I noted, the Spanish hegemony had been effectively broken as the French, English, and Dutch established footholds in the eastern Caribbean islands and along the maritime coastlands of the North Atlantic. More colonists meant more work; more work fostered an even greater demand for Africans. After 1640, the Spanish colonists became only one sector of the American slave market and, until the nineteenth century, received an ever-declining proportion of the Africans sold in the New World. Moreover, by 1640, the sugar and plantation frontier had traveled from the Mediterranean, down the islands of the western Atlantic, and through Brazil and had arrived in the Caribbean, creating an "economy world" that Philip Curtin once called the South Atlantic System. The Atlantic world of plantation agriculture, big business, international commerce, shipping, and slavery was created. For the next two centuries, it would expand in all directions. The modest requirements of the early Spanish colonists in the sixteenth century had become an insatiable demand by the beginning of the eighteenth century. The Caribbean settler colonies were on their way to becoming exploitation slave societies.

SUGGESTED READINGS

Crosby, Alfred W., Jr. *The Columbian Exchange: Biological and Cultural Consequences of 1492.* Westport, Conn.: Greenwood, 1972.

Elliott, John. *The Old World and the New, 1492–1650.* New York: Cambridge University Press, 1970.

Elliott, John. *Empires of the Atlantic World: Britain and Spain in America, 1492–1830.* New Haven, Conn.: Yale University Press, 2006.

Emmer, Pieter, and Carrera Damas, German, eds. *General History of the Caribbean. Volume II. New Societies: The Caribbean in the Long Sixteenth Century.* Paris and London: UNESCO and Macmillan, 1999.

Fuson, John. *The Log of Christopher Columbus.* Translated by Robert H. Fuson. Camden, Maine: International Marine Publishing Company, 1987.

Gibson, Charles. *Spain in America.* New York: Harper and Row, 1966.

Greene, Jack P. *Pursuits of Happiness: The Social Development of Early Modern British Colonies.* Chapel Hill: University of North Carolina Press, 1988.

Kamen, Henry. *Empire: How Spain Became a World Power, 1492–1763.* New York: HarperCollins, 2003.

Marrero, Levi. *Cuba: Economia y sociedad,* 14 vols. Madrid and San Juan: Playor, 1972–1988.

Meinig, D. W. *The Shaping of America: A Geographical Perspective on 500 Years of History, 1: Atlantic America, 1492–1800.* New Haven, Conn.: Yale University Press, 1986.

Schwartz, Stuart B., ed. *Tropical Babylons. Sugar and the Making of the Atlantic World, 1450–1680.* Chapel Hill: University of North Carolina Press, 2004.

CHAPTER 3

Patterns of Colonization in the New World

We have not only eaten all the cattle within twelve miles of the place, but now almost all the horses, asses, mules' flesh near us so that I shall hold little Eastcheap in more esteem than the whole Indies if this trade last, and I can give or learn no reason that it should not here continue; so beside this we expect no pay here, nor hardly at home now, but perhaps some ragged land at the best, and that but by the by spoken of, for us general officers not a word mentioned.

—ANONYMOUS SOLDIER,
Jamaica, November 1655

At first glance, it is difficult to reconcile the wide variety of cultures and societ-ies that developed throughout the Americas between 1492 and 1800. These colonial societies and cultures, as already indicated, arose at different times, in different geographic areas, and under the auspices of different European national patronage. Beginning with the initial exploratory expeditions of Christopher Columbus and Pedro Álvares Cabral (c. 1467–c. 1520), the Americas went from being an Iberian monopoly to a territory theoretically mapped out by and for all the emerging nation-states of sixteenth- and seventeenth-century Europe.

At one time or another, the English, French, Dutch, Danes, and Swedes attempted to establish colonies in the Americas. Some were more successful than others. But all the colonies began haltingly as small, precarious enclaves of occu-pation in a vast expanse of an unfamiliar continent. These enclaves survived by forging ingenious relationships with one another—legally when they could, and illegally if necessary—by extensive intercourse with the local indigenous popula-tions and by strong reciprocal relations with the parent societies in Europe. As these colonies developed and succeeded politically and economically, they came to represent and reflect the accumulated experiences of their associations through time. Slowly they became new societies in a new land with new identities.

Until the end of the eighteenth century, however, the predominantly European society was merely one form of society and culture in a wide spectrum of social forms that were present in the Americas. Throughout Spanish America, Brazil, and the Caribbean, significant and vital indigenous communities continued to exist alongside the Europeans, sometimes symbiotically, sometimes antagonistically. These indigenous communities ranged in size and social sophistication from the Tupí and Puelches in the Brazilian lowlands to the Mayo, Yaqui, and Maya in the Mexican coastal valleys and the Isthmus of Tehuantepec. Also present at one time or another were the semi-European cultures that developed during the period—buccaneers in the Caribbean, Gauchos on the pampas or plains of the Río de la Plata in southeastern South America, Llaneros in the interior plains of Colombia and Venezuela, and fugitive Maroons just about everywhere that slavery was once employed as a form of labor organization.

The genesis and interrelationship of these societies have been conventionally viewed through ethnocentric European lenses, with the consequent distortion and obscurantism of not only the general pattern of evolution but of the common prevailing impact of geopolitical and geophysical factors. When viewed from the perspective of Europe, the Caribbean appears as a sidelight of European history—its events and peoples confined to the subplots of presumably larger and more important affairs.

Caribbean history and society, of course, had a logic of their own, although frequently and sometimes profoundly affected by individuals and events in the various metropolises. In this history of the Caribbean, the societies and cultures dominated by the Europeans constitute the focus of attention, but in ways that limit their variety and that diminish the value of particular national origins. Indeed, Caribbean history viewed from the Caribbean offers a quite different perspective than Caribbean history viewed from outside the region. Viewed from an internal Caribbean perspective, it is possible to place all the European colonies in the region on a spectrum bounded by two distinct and enduring types of communities in the region between 1492 and 1800: the communities or colonies of settlers and the communities or colonies of economic exploiters. Although these forms represented, consciously or unconsciously, the ideal goals of the would-be colonists—and hence would fall on the opposite ends of the spectrum—they could not be perfectly realized. They remained the unattainable ideals. The result, therefore, was a fluidity along the spectrum in which colonies moved from one form to another, usually from colonies of settlement to colonies operating almost exclusively for the maximum production of profit for their politically dominant group.

To the Europeans of the fifteenth and sixteenth centuries, America was the great unknown. Physically isolated from the contiguous Afro-Eurasian landmass, it entered the consciousness of the Europeans in the sixteenth century as the essence of that virginity and limitless opportunity that so obsessed the curious, expansive, irrepressible intruders of that period. Yet from the very beginning, Europeans demonstrated a haunting ambivalence about the meaning of America. The American impact on Europe, then, though unmistakeably broad and continuous, has been, according to an adjective used by John Elliott in *The Old World and the New,* "uncertain."

America was undoubtedly a novel and challenging ecological environment for the European newcomers. Its flora and fauna were different. Its indigenous social and economic structures were unfamiliar. Its populations lacked the common epidemiological immunities of the peoples on the eastern side of the Atlantic. And its very existence, topography, and geopolitical realities challenged, where they did not refute, the most basic conventional wisdom of the Europeans—concepts and theories about time, geography, society, theology, philosophy, and aesthetics. Naturally each traveler and each publicist saw America as he or she wanted, within the framework of a personal intellectually comfortable, inherited, cultural view of the world.

Christopher Columbus, whose journal frequently compared what he newly saw with what his Iberian readers would know and who died thinking that he was certainly on the outskirts of China, wondered why the Antilleans were such "an extremely poor people." He saw, of course, nothing faintly resembling the opulent courts of the fabulous Kublai Khan described by the Venetian, Marco Polo (c. 1254–c. 1324), in legendary narratives that fired the imagination of the European elites for centuries. But he did mention that he was entertained in a "palace" on Hispaniola. The original concept of a Spanish trading-post empire, patterned after the Portuguese experience along the West African coast, died prematurely with the initial settlement on Hispaniola and the pragmatic de facto revocation of the grandiloquent titles that the astute Isabella of Castile had granted to Columbus.

Bernal Díaz del Castillo (c. 1492–c. 1581), that charming chronicler of the most astounding military success of Spanish arms, saw America as the new venue for an updated crusade, merging the religious assumptions of his late medieval age with the pragmatic aims of his modernizing monarch. To him, the American adventure was "to serve God and his Majesty,... and to get rich, as all men desire to do." He died an optimistic pauper in the mosquito-infested wilderness of Guatemala, dazzled by his deeds but completely oblivious of their consequences.

Emperor Charles V (1500–1558), understandably impressed by the papal pronouncement *Sublimus Deus* of 1537 that Indians were rational beings, sought, through the instrumentality of the New Laws promulgated in 1542, to subordinate the ubiquitous brigandage of the indefatigable conquistadors to the organizing structure of the emerging Spanish corporate state. This political retrieval on the part of Charles V saved Spanish America for the Castilian Crown and coincided with the aims of João III (king, 1521–1557) of Portugal to convert Brazil into a true colony, rather than a geographic reference point for Portuguese sailors on their way to India.

By the middle of the sixteenth century, both the Spanish and Portuguese had decided to establish types of colonies in the Americas that failed to conform to their original notions of an overseas empire but colonies that were not entirely removed from the general European tradition of settlements beyond their native frontiers. The Caribbean settlements constituted, then, a linear expansion of the European frontier.

In every respect, the earliest Caribbean settlements were microcosms of their European metropolitan societies. The expedition of Nicolás de Ovando to settle

Española, as the Spanish at that time called the island of Hispaniola, in 1502 represented a direct continuation of the pattern of *reconquista*, or reconquest, with its curious combination of military posturing and material greed for land, wealth, and servants. In the wake of the explorers, opportunists, and free lances came a complete cross section of Spanish society, ably described by James Lockhart in *Spanish Peru* and *The Men of Cajamarca*, Peter Boyd-Bowman in his *Indice Geobiográfico*, and other scholars like Ida Altman—hidalgos, clerks, artisans, priests, merchants, and members of the lower orders of society. While the social values of the emigrants remained thoroughly Spanish, a substantial proportion of these ordinary men and women manifested little or no desire to return to Spain. Of course, the fact that a great number came from the depressed towns of Extremadura and western Andalucia made a one-way ticket even to the American unknown a rather attractive prospect. Similarly, the early English settlers in Thomas Carlisle's Barbados, John Smith's Virginia, and John Winthrop's Massachusetts represented a continuation of the English "plantations" in Ulster, Wales, and Scotland—the expansion and domination of an English social structure within an English polity.

Initially the institutions and ideas of the colony paralleled those of the metropolis. The American frontier offered space and opportunities to escape the confines of Europe and to create a quality of life and a social environment superior to that left behind. This pattern of expansion incorporating goals of economic amelioration and political and social relaxation—if not elevation—was, after all, closely associated with the eastern expansion and consequent modification of Western European feudal society during the Middle Ages.

At the core of the Spanish expansion was religion. The ethnocentric Roman Catholicism of an absolutist monarchy in Iberia prospered in Hispaniola, in New Spain, and in Peru, collaborating with the imperial bureaucracy to maintain the hegemony of the Crown. The *fazenda* (large landed estates) and the *Senado da Camara* (municipal council) held together early Brazilian colonial life, retaining as much as possible the traditions of Portugal. And Englishmen in Barbados and the other eastern Caribbean islands reflected all the political and religious vicissitudes of the motherland in the early and middle seventeenth century.

Women were important in the new colonies. A viable community necessitated a substantial proportion of women, both for procreation and for the vital function of socializing the newborns to the norms and expectations of the majority. Female mortality among the arriving settlers, however, was extremely high. As soon as the Spanish state inaugurated its policy of subordinating the free lances, it began to assure a continuous and sufficient supply of suitable females. Perhaps more than any other European group, the Spanish invested their womenfolk with all the qualities of social honor and familial responsibility and stability. The Crown not only actively discouraged sexual intercourse with the indigenous population, but fostered the migration of family units. According to Peter Boyd-Bowman, of the known 5,481 Spanish who immigrated to the Americas between 1493 and 1519, some 308, or roughly 6 percent, were women. Although this appears to be a small number, it was a fairly representative female population for that early stage of colonization. Richard Dunn in *Sugar and Slaves* found approximately the same percentage of women among the English passengers bound for Barbados in 1635—at a time when Barbados was still trying actively to promote the settler society. After 1570, in accordance with the declaration of the Council of Trent that marriage was a sacrament, the Spanish Crown forbade married men to travel overseas for periods in excess of six months unless accompanied by their families. The subsequent emigration of predominantly single males from Iberia greatly stimulated the rise of a miscegenated population throughout the Americas. The Crown did not formally approve—nor did the laws recognize—the practice of Spanish males in the overseas colonies who mated spontaneously to suit their fancy. Yet until the late seventeenth century, the Church permitted marriage regardless of social status or race or ethnic origin as preferential to wanton cohabitation.

Yet if the settler mentality responded to the possibilities of America, it was a response tempered by three related considerations operating at three different levels. In the sixteenth century, before the successful penetration into the region of the northwest Europeans and the shattering of the tenacious illusion of an Iberian monopoly of the Americas, these views could be roughly divided into (1) an official secular view, (2) an official religious view, and (3) the individual view, tempered but not confined by the former two views.

The official secular view or state policy toward the Americas was integrally connected to the early modern ideas of national power and the position of the monarchy in the European sphere of political power. The absolutist monarchy of Spain (more properly, of Castile) considered and successfully imposed the concept of the Americas as the personal domain of the king. All Americans, Spanish as well as non-Spanish, were thereby vassals of the Castilian king. The imperial bureaucracy attempted to reinforce this claim and to destroy any other manifestations of feudalistic autonomy anywhere in the Americas. The original Columbus grant was considered to be a threat to this royal patrimony. The Portuguese monarchy eventually had the only resources that could make Brazil an economically viable and politically secure part of their American empire. The French in the seventeenth century were in a similar position to the Portuguese. By contrast, early English and Dutch colonization drew their greatest stimuli from individual entrepreneurs. In the fluid political atmosphere of the sixteenth and seventeenth centuries, each colony needed, sought, and received the patronage of a state, however peripheral such a state was to the main political power configurations of Europe. Eventually it mattered little what the official attitudes to the Americas were. Europeans of every sort went forth subscribing fully or partially to the goals expressed by Bernal Díaz del Castillo: reconciling service to God and the king with the personal pursuit of riches.

In accordance with the age, state policy paralleled—when it was not identical with—an official religious policy. The pioneering Iberians had established with papal consent the division of the Americas within their sphere into two competing zones of Christians and infidels. This is exactly what had occurred along the

Eurasian frontier as William McNeill described in the *Rise of the West*. Western Christendom, fraught with multiple political jealousies, broke apart during the wars of the Reformation (1517–1648). The Treaty of Cateau-Cambrésis (1559) accepted the principle that the political head of state determined the general religious denomination of the people. That did not happen, since later notable conversions were of monarchs falling in line with the religion of the most powerful sector of their subjects. Conformity, however, proved tantalizingly unattainable, and further undermining of the metropolises (through such events as the religious wars in England and France during the sixteenth century) created a fresh impetus to settler communities overseas in the Americas—all with the conscious conviction that their microcosms conveyed the best ideals of the old societies.

Latin America and the Caribbean were spared the more extreme forms of that religious parochialism that drove John Winthrop (1588–1649) and his pilgrims to the rather inhospitable coast of North America. But the domestic English rivalry between Anglicans, Presbyterians, and Arminians affected social relations in Barbados and Jamaica, and Jews found relative security only in the early Dutch settlements—thanks in large measure to Spanish-Dutch political antagonisms.

Individuals shared to a greater or lesser degree the official positions of church and state. Nevertheless, to admit that church and state influenced the actions and the attitudes of individuals ought by no means to be construed as a necessarily harmonious relationship between these three groups. Indeed, it was with considerable difficulty that the Spanish Crown imposed its authority over the conquering free lances and their descendants in the sixteenth century. All the established societies were equally hard-pressed to dominate the essentially transfrontier groups such as the filibusters or buccaneers during the seventeenth century. Nonconforming groups of Indians and Africans defied civil authorities until the nineteenth century. In addition, many individuals who did not join groups defied the authorities, though not always successfully. Nor did all dissenters move beyond the effective reach of established society as the buccaneers and the Maroons did. Bartolomé de las Casas (1484–1566) and Thomas Gage (1600–1656) chose to remain individual dissenters, the former protesting from within the framework of Spanish society, while the latter in one fell swoop changed both his religious and his political affiliations. Las Casas and Gage were merely the extremes of individual dissent in an essentially dissenting age.

The distinction between settler colonies and exploitation colonies was not lost on contemporaries. It could be found in the observations probably best sketched by the jaundiced eye and poisoned pen of that ethnocentric Englishman, James Anthony Froude (1818–1894), regius professor of modern history at Oxford University. Writing in an entirely different context, Froude described two sets of colonies in the nineteenth century, one "as offering homes where English people can increase and multiply; English of the old type with simple habits, who do not need imported luxuries," and the other set serving Europeans to "go there and to make their fortunes which they can carry home with them." Despite Froude's unsophisticated economic view, his two categories roughly coincided with the two basic goals of European colonization in the New World. In a real sense, these two categories represent two opposite points along the kaleidoscope of ideal European colonial activity in the Americas.

To a certain extent, every settler society had its exploitation component, and every exploitation society had its settler dimension. It is important to understand not only the dynamic interchange between these two extremes (which sometimes resulted in reversals of the pattern), but the corpus of ideologies that permeated each colony, giving each a sense of community, security, and identity. Europeans went to the Americas—as they did elsewhere in the wider world—to make a profit if they could and to settle if they had to. These were never seen as conflicting goals, and whenever a colony changed its condition, there was always a satisfying rationale presented either by the colonists themselves or by their superiors in the political metropolis.

Throughout the history of the Caribbean islands can be found individuals whose careers or families did not conform to the pattern of colony in which they resided. Some of these families continued for generations, even centuries— families such as the British Codringtons, Draxes, Pickerings, and Hothersalls in Barbados; the Warners and Jeaffresons in St. Kitts; the Warners and Kaynells in Antigua; the Stapletons and Pinneys in Nevis; and the Prices, Dawkinses, Tharps, and Beckfords in Jamaica. At randomly selected periods, any of these families, viewed superficially, might appear socially and politically indistinguishable from any of the prominent settler families of New England, Virginia, New Spain, or Peru. Nevertheless, a crucial difference can be found in the attitudes that these West Indians held toward their territories or the milieu that they helped to create and that their plantations perpetuated. The British families just mentioned, for example, never ceased to be or to behave like transient English families. They never ceased to identify closely with English society and the politics of the metropolis. They prospered in the Caribbean, and that prosperity facilitated their reentry into English society. But at no time did they adapt to the Caribbean, and it never really became their home.

Between the sixteenth and the eighteenth centuries, the bewildering novelty and variety of the Americas severely challenged the colonists. The earliest settlements paid a discouragingly high price in human terms. After a century or so, the dreams of El Dorado had become nightmares to so many that spontaneous migrations overseas began to decline sharply. It became evident that the wealth of the Americas would yield only to arduous toil and constant perseverance in the mines and jungles and swampy, mosquito-infested tropical coastlands. The visions of cities of good people everywhere yielded to the geographic imperatives of the region. Settlement colonies of Europeans could prosper only under climatic conditions roughly similar to those in Europe—in the salubrious highlands of Mexico and Peru and, much later, on the peripheral lowlands of Brazil and Argentina. Tropical lowlands did not seem to provide good settlement sites. Eventually the Europeans developed the widespread myth that their upper classes could not survive well in the tropics—except as visitors and managers.

The necessities of empire and commerce required the marketing of luxury commodities of high value and small bulk that were most economically produced on the relatively insalubrious tropical low-lands. The Europeans repeated in the Americas what trial and error had already produced in Africa—a situation in which others did the toil while they reaped the profits. That was how the exploitation colony originated.

But this type of colony also responded to the developing political situation in Europe. Mercantilism provided the catalyst for the exploitation colony, merging politics and economics to serve the individual interests of the expanding states. National wealth was equated with national power, and wealth was measured by commercial activity. The role of the Dutch West India Company in the Americas was not merely to show a profit to its corporate stockholders, but to wage relentless attacks on the political might of Spain. This rationale gave impetus to the slogan "no peace beyond the line."

The typical exploitation colony was one in which a minority of Europeans usually, but not always, dominated and managed a majority of non-Europeans in a socioeconomic complex designed to produce some export commodity primarily for the European market. Unlike the settler colony, economic motivation became almost the sine qua non for European interest. The greater the prospect of economic gain, the greater the importance of the colony. Unlike the case of the settler societies, occupation, social cleavage, and social status tended to be mutually reinforcing and directly correlated with the respective level of participation in the export-commodity production. Almost everywhere these commodities were the tropical staples of tobacco, cotton, cocoa, sugar, and coffee.

Sometimes the exploitation colony was a component of a larger settler colony. The mining communities of Brazil, Upper Peru, and New Spain were exploitation enclaves par excellence, but their symbiotic relationship to the surrounding settler communities diluted their influence and mitigated their autonomy and their social impact. The mines never succeeded in moving beyond the periphery of settler social and economic relations.

This was not so with the plantations that flourished in the environment of the exploitation colony, especially where they were isolated. For this reason, the Caribbean islands, the northeast of Brazil (for all practical purposes, an island prior to the nineteenth century), northern New Granada, and the eastern Gulf Coast of New Spain formed a natural breeding ground for this strange type of social organization.

The exploitation colony came into its own in the seventeenth and eighteenth centuries, but the attempts go back to the earliest days of the Spanish presence—to the experiments of Pedro Arias Dávila's (also known as Pedrarias D'Ávila [d. 1531]) Darien community and the post-Ovando Hispaniola or the Cortes Marquesado estates in New Spain. The *encomienda* system by which the Spanish monarchs subjected Indians to the early settlers was perfectly compatible with, and conducive to, its genesis. What foiled these early attempts was the demographic disaster in the tropical American world and the exigencies of empire that precluded common Spanish contact with both the African and American fringes of the Atlanic simultaneously, thereby limiting the scale of the early Spanish slave trade. To the very end of its empire, Spain pragmatically used Indians, Africans, and the lower classes from the metropolis in the economic development of its overseas colonies but could never quite establish the equilibrium between demand and supply.

The exploitation colonies were typified by the Portuguese in the northeast of Brazil and by the Dutch when they captured the Brazilian northeast between 1624 and 1640, as well as in the Dutch Caribbean trading entrepôts of Curaçao, Aruba, St. Eustatius, St. Croix, and Surinam (later Suriname) where they had sugarcane plantations. The English converted Barbados from a settler to an exploitation colony around 1650 and established similar colonies in St. Kitts, Antigua, Nevis, Anguilla, Jamaica, and later Guiana. The French created a very successful example in Saint-Domingue, Guadeloupe, and Martinique and, to a lesser extent, St. Lucia and St. Vincent. In the later half of the eighteenth century, they lost Saint-Domingue to their slaves. St. Lucia and St. Vincent fell to the English. The Spanish belatedly converted Cuba, Puerto Rico, and Santo Domingo (eastern Hispaniola after 1697) from settlement to exploitation colonies in the early 1800s and almost succeeded in doing the same to the settlements on the northern coastlands of Colombia and Venezuela.

The imperial divisions, however, were of minor significance—a fact illustrated by the facility with which territories moved into and out of rival imperial administrative controls. The characteristics of the exploitation colony followed a logic and a tradition that were created in the twelfth-century Levantine Mediterranean basin and moved inexorably westward with the changing fortunes of the European Atlantic expansion: a small, intrusive, managerial class; a numerically preponderant, ethnically differentiated laboring class; and an economic activity that supported the community. Sugar and slavery constituted a common feature. Discernible differences occasionally appeared as the colonies responded to the vicissitudes of European political alliances, Western economics, and their own internal dynamics. Exploitation colonies developed into societies with self-conscious identities no less strong than those of the settler communities, albeit considerably more vulnerable to the prevailing winds of economic, political, and ideological change.

Nevertheless, it was precisely the distinct ethos of the exploitation society that made it somewhat anomalous in the eighteenth-century world. At a time when more intellectuals were considering social structures as rationally integrated, the exploitation society appeared to lack a rational basis for its existence. But the ethos that permeated the exploitation society, the ethos of instability and irrationality, derived from the character of both the colonists and the circumstances of the locale—character and characteristics that unsettled such local leaders as the planter Edward Long (1734–1813); Lady Maria Nugent (1771–1834), wife of the lieutenant-governor of Jamaica; and Medéric-Louis-Elie Moreau de Saint-Méry (1750–1819) of Martinique; such informed tourists as Alexander Humboldt (1769–1859) and James Anthony Froude; and such enlightened philosophers as

Guillaume-Thomas-François de Raynal (1713–1796), better known as the Abbé Raynal, and Cornelius de Pauw (1739–1799).

European settlers tried to re-create and create, to preserve and perpetuate. European exploiters merely held together as long as they could—and when the profits declined, they moved on. This difference manifested itself in the physical setting of the colony as well as in the conduct of the colonists. Transients often noted this difference.

> Kingston is the best of our West Indian towns [wrote Froude in 1888] and Kingston has not one fine building in it. Havana is a city of palaces, a city of streets and plazas, of colonades and towers, and churches and monasteries. We English have built in those islands as if we were but passing visitors, wanting only tenements to be occupied for a time. The Spaniards built as they built in Castile; built with the same material, the white limestone which they found in the New World as in the Old. The palaces of the nobles in Havana, the residence of the governor, the convents, the cathedral, are a reproduction of Burgos or Valladolid, as if by some Aladdin's lamp a Castilian city had been taken up and set down again unaltered on the shore of the Caribbean Sea. And they carried with them their laws, their habits, their institution and their creed, their religious orders, their bishops and their Inquisition.

Froude was, of course, viewing a Havana luxuriating in the fortunes of the sugar-plantation society of the nineteenth century. He did not know, and probably did not care to find out, that this splendid vista was of recent creation. Indeed, until the late eighteenth century, Havana was a rather dilapidated *gran aldea* (large village). More important, perhaps, is the similarity between the early Spanish settlers in Cuba and the early English settlers in Barbados or St. Christopher. The early English, like the early Spanish, built and behaved in the Caribbean much as they did back home in Europe.

"The early West India colonists," wrote the historian Richard Dunn, "tried their best to transfer English modes of diet, dress and housing to the tropics. Scorning to imitate the Spaniards, the Indians or the Negroes who were all experienced at living in hot countries, they clung determinedly to their own North European styles and standards."

The attempt to perpetuate the ideal settler colony in the English Caribbean failed dismally. By 1650, Barbados and the Leewards abandoned their settler destinies to pursue the lucrative path of the tropical plantation society. Many would-be settlers packed up and moved on to the mainland, to New England, and to the Middle Atlantic colonies. Those English who remained on the islands—or who came out later—no longer attempted to reproduce English societies of predominantly non-English peoples. As the islands became plantations based on imported African slave labor, the minority English tenaciously retained their Englishness, grotesquely flaunting their origins. But they could not re-create their English society. The divergence with the mainland accelerated as the settler experiments continued, with geographic modifications on the mainland especially noticeable in the contrasting patterns of New England and Virginia and the Carolinas. The plantation society produced a plantation culture, essentially ad hoc, dependent and eclectic, while the settler society produced its own settler culture with a pronounced regional influence that gradually developed into a sort of nationalism.

The settler origins left indelible traces in the physical landscape and "character" of Barbados. But Barbados could not be described as an English settler colony after the 1660s. Anthony Trollope (1815–1882), the noted English Victorian novelist famous for his description of provincial life and manners in the fictional county of "Barsetshire," visited the West Indies and the Spanish Main in 1859. Less inclined to praise than Froude was later, he found "nothing attractive about the town of Havana; nothing whatever to my mind if we except the harbour. The streets are narrow, dirty, and foul." Kingston, Jamaica, had a "ragged, disreputable, and bankrupt appearance." Barbados reminded him of "an ordinary but ugly agricultural county...[and] Bridgetown, the metropolis of the island is much like a second or third rate English town."

As long as the base population of the colonial venture remained predominantly European, settler societies faced no greater problem than adjusting constantly to the cultural variations produced by time and geography. Until the late seventeenth century, the Englishman born in the Americas was no less "English" in outlook and attitudes than the Englishman born in England. Both shared a set of assumptions and values that, while not homogeneous, had not appeared to either native Englishmen or American-born Englishmen to be fundamentally different. The same held true for the French, Portuguese, Dutch, and Spanish. The settler colonies were overseas components of the mother country—a concept that returned in political theory in the late nineteenth and twentieth centuries in the Caribbean.

The "upper-class" English colonist, if he could afford it, still went to England to complete his education. The Spanish-American Creole, while educated locally, assumed that the local universities in Mexico, Guatemala, Cuba, or Peru were inferior to those in, say, Salamanca or Alcalá de Henares. One's education was not considered complete until one had "finished" in the metropolis. This relationship made for relatively easy social communication between metropolis and colony. For example, Médèric Louis Élie Moreau de Saint-Méry (1750–1819) born in Martinique, practiced law in Saint-Domingue, founded the Museum of Paris in 1787, and was the ruler of the City of Paris for three days after the fall of the Bastille in 1789. His career was exceptional and indicated that until well into the eighteenth century, neither European power positions nor American colonial self-consciousness were insuperable social barriers. The eighteenth century saw both the resolution of political hegemony in Europe on the one hand and the maturation of the colonial American communities into a variety of Creolized societies with aspirations that conflicted with their metropolises on the other.

By the beginning of the eighteenth century, the pattern of settlement colonies and of exploitation colonies was becoming demonstrably clear. With it, too, came the divergence between Europeans and Americans. That divergence increased throughout the century. By the beginning of the nineteenth century, the Atlantic world had become engrossed in a revolution that strained the intellectual legacy of Europe and shattered the imperial tradition throughout the Americas. A Jamaican planter and member of the British Parliament, Bryan Edwards (1743–1800), described that contagious restlessness as "a spirit of subversion…which set at nought the wisdom of our ancestors, and the lessons of experience."

Yet Edwards's "spirit of subversion" did not bear the same apprehensions for both types of societies that were developing in the Americas, especially in the Caribbean. In general, settler societies interpreted this "spirit" in the best liberal intellectual tradition of the Enlightenment as both a good and a glorious thing. British North Americans, behind the banner of "No Taxation Without Representation," forsook the English empire to chart their own political destiny. Political independence, however, failed to destroy the strong cultural links with England and the rest of Europe, and the end of the American Revolution in 1783 brought only minor changes in the social structure and the social base of political power in the new, confederated states. In Latin America, under the slogan of *"Viva El Rey! Muera el mal gobierno!"* ("Long Live the King! Down with bad government!"), the Spanish-Americans dismantled the mainland empire: in the case of most of South America, to implement a more liberal constitution than that offered by the Junta of Cádiz in 1812; in the case of Mexico, to thwart the introduction of metropolitan liberalism in the 1820s—while the Brazilians established an equal Portuguese family division between Lisbon and Rio de Janeiro. Everywhere the local oligarchies, like the propertied classes in the United States of America, usurped political power and began to articulate their own ideas about the state, ideas that descended with only minor modifications from the corpus of European nationalistic and intellectual traditions.

The outstanding exception, of course, was the prosperous French colony of Saint-Domingue that flourished until 1789 on the western part of the island of Hispaniola. There, events deviated both from the centrifugal currents of the settler mainland colonies and the centripetal forces of the neighboring, mainly exploitation, islands. In Saint-Domingue, the French colonists endeavored to have their cake and eat it—pretending to be simultaneously Frenchmen and French-Caribbean colonists in an age when a choice was becoming necessary. It proved a tragic miscalculation. For them, 1789 was the wrong time and Saint-Domingue the worst place to emulate the ambiguous metropolitan generalizations of "liberty, equality and fraternity." Saint-Domingue was, after all, not Mexico or Peru or Brazil or the United States: it was not a settler society with a common understanding or common appeal that transcended class, race, and color and gave practical significance to a majority. Saint-Domingue was an exploitation colony—the exploitation colony par excellence during the eighteenth century—where the ideological miscalculation that a minority view was the general will led not only to the fratricidal civil wars of the metropolis, but to a general slave revolt and a race war unprecedented in the history of the Americas. Once war broke out, power gravitated to the numerical majority of slaves who quickly overcame the whites and their allies with the fortuitous assistance of that exotic tropical disease, yellow fever. As a result,

the only true revolution in the Americas before the twentieth century occurred
in Saint-Domingue when in 1804 Henri Christophe (1769–1820), Jean-Jacques
Dessalines (1758–1806), Alexander Petión (1770–1818), and countless unknown
others completely destroyed the old social order and reconstituted an entirely new
polity.

Whether the Haitian revolution was creative—that is, originally conceived
by François-Dominique Toussaint Louverture (d. 1803)—or reactive—that is,
responding negatively to the French attempts to reimpose slavery—the hegemony
of the slaves represented a logical extension of the leveling-down process in a pluralistic society where the intellectual paradigms of the social structure contradicted
the reality of day-to-day living. In the unconscious assumptions of the superordinate groups of literate whites and free persons of color in Saint-Domingue in 1789,
liberty and equality meant relaxation of metropolitan controls and the removal of
the political and legal disabilities of the wealthy *gens de couleur* (people of color).
To the slaves of Saint-Domingue—unschooled as they were in eighteenth-century
rational thought—liberty and equality meant complete freedom from bondage
and nothing less. In the social context of exploitation, the two connotations of
liberty were irreconcilable.

In the Caribbean, the ambiguities of this situation dissipated the strongly
nationalistic manifestations that prevailed in the settler societies elsewhere by
the end of the eighteenth century. The type of patriotism—or more accurately,
patriachiquismo (sense of local identity)—that infused the writings of John Adams
(1735–1826) of New England or Francisco Javier Clavijero (1731–1786) of New
Spain was a luxury that Caribbean whites could not afford. Nor was this the consequence of diet and disease and climate as De Pauw, Adams, and the French natural-
ist Georges Buffon (1707–1788) believed. Rather, it was the instinctive ambivalence
of a group whose hearts and minds remained adamantly European while their
bodies responded to the overpowering impact of African ethnic and cultural influences on their brittle plantation world. The Creole habits, customs, and outlook
so strongly deprecated by Long, Moreau de Saint-Méry, and Lady Maria Nugent
were contrapuntal to the Eurocentrism of the late eighteenth and early nineteenth
centuries. The exploitation society was the true melting pot of races, cultures, and
beliefs. Europeans and Africans shared a peculiar world that profoundly affected
both groups simultaneously, and the plight of the European born in such a world
or acclimatized to such conditions was a constant factor. The African component
of exploitation colonial culture constituted an important and interesting variant
on the development of the American Creole culture. These African-derived variants, wherever they were found and however they were composed, were neither
inferior nor superior derivatives of Europe or Africa. They were, and should be
regarded as, simply different. The extent to which Africans or Europeans affected
the operational values and behavior of any society in the Caribbean depended on
the proportional size of the respective component, on the cohesiveness and self-
confidence of the managerial group, and on the mode of arrival of each of the segments of the population. Afro-American behavior differed in societies in which

Afro-Americans constituted the majority of the population from their conduct when they were a minority or a mere exotic element of the community.

The apparently antagonistic ideals of settler and exploitation colonies had far-reaching consequences for the development of Creole society in Latin America and the Caribbean, consequences whose impact is often overlooked by the conventional historiographical model of treating the regions in isolated imperial compartments, chronologically divided through time. In reality, there was continual intercommunication between the various colonies in the Americas, with a commercial symbiosis between settlers and exploiters as Peggy Liss demonstrated in her book, *Atlantic Empires.*

The division of the Caribbean into settler and exploitation colonies is an oversimplification that facilitates the analysis of the region by incorporating the dynamics of social change. Both settler and exploitation societies were constantly changing, responding to their altered circumstances. These societies, therefore, should not be viewed either as frozen entities suspended in time and space or merely reactive structures intrinsically incapable of articulating their own world-view. Any systadial—rather than synchronic—description of the region reveals the continuous attempts by all segments of the colonial societies to come to grips with their particular circumstances in ways that gave meaning to their lives and coherence to their communities. The basic divisions in American colonial societies were not the simple dichotomy between masters and slaves, black and white, Iberians and Indians, Europeans and Africans, or Protestants and Catholics. The basic divisions occurred between types of societies that allowed all groups to react interdependently, each in its own way creating an environment consonant with a vision of man, nature, and society. Even in the slave societies, master and slaves acted fully aware of the reactions of their opposites.

In the settler societies, the transfer of the conventional institutions of the metropolis provided the model for conformity and socialization. Newcomers could accept such norms and usually did. Dualities of status and power could exist, although not without some internal strains. The settlers formed an enclave that was determined to succeed and consciously set about discovering ways to facilitate their domination of nature. Settlers adapted freely and pragmatically, however much they deplored such actions. The very success in taming the wilderness lent zeal to what Francisco López Camara described as *la conciencia de sí* (self-consciousness), a spirit gallantly portrayed by the character Hawkeye in James Fenimore Cooper's novel, *The Last of the Mohicans.* The perspective could, of course, be relative. If from the metropolitan perspective settler societies in the eighteenth and early nineteenth centuries appeared to display centrifugal tendencies, from the colonial viewpoint those same traits were centripetal, forging a cohesive, new, independent polity.

By contrast, exploitation societies lacked a common, unifying, institutional basis beyond the plantations and other economic enterprises. They were innovative only for self-preservation. Not only were such societies divided, they also tended to be divisive, with mutually reinforcing cleavages within the overlapping castes.

The elites lacked cohesion and self-confidence. However long the elite remained physically in situ, they were psychologically transients, with myopic confusion of social order and productive efficiency. The most enduring and sometimes the most interesting features of such societies were created by the lower orders, who were often told what they could not do but were rarely told what they ought to do.

Nevertheless, the cultural weaknesses and deficiencies of the plantation elite provided an almost unique opportunity for the coerced and subordinate African element to help fashion their society. Africans had more opportunities where they formed the dominant sector in the local communities, and so their overall impact varied across the region. The Afro-American or Afro-Caribbean tradition, then, is not a single, common one. It responded to several factors: patterns of demography, diet, colonization, Creolization, and Americanization. In short, it developed in the same way that all traditions do.

The realization of the way the societies evolved is a basic requirement for understanding the colonial experience in Latin America and the Caribbean. Despite the linguistic differences, the region forms one variegated cultural area, no more internally diverse than India, West Africa, the British Isles, Europe, Iberia, or the United States. The distinction between settler and exploitation societies should not lead to any assumption that one form was inherently superior or inferior to, or better or worse than, the other form. Such an assumption surrenders the positive characteristics of their mutual interdependence to the dictates of nationalism and chauvinism. Of course, settler and exploiter divisions refer only to the colonies within the European sphere of influence and do not exhaust the wide range of responses to the circumstances of the American frontier. Nor should the assertion that the Caribbean comprises a related cultural area indicate the absence of deep differences between the peoples and the territories. It does indicate a pervasive commonality throughout the region, a commonality imposed by the long experience with the twin yokes of European imperialism and African slavery.

SUGGESTED READINGS

Abbott, Elizabeth. *Sugar: A Bittersweet History.* London: Duckworth, 2009.

Abulafia, David. *The Discovery of Mankind: Atlantic Encounters in the Age of Columbus.* New Haven, Conn.: Yale University Press, 2008.

Altman, Ida. *Emigrants and Society: Extremadura and Spanish America in the Sixteenth Century.* Los Angeles: University of California Press, 1989.

Altman, Ida, and Horn, James, eds. *"To Make America": European Emigration in the Early Modern Period.* Los Angeles: University of California Press, 1991.

Benzo de Ferrer, Vilma. *Pasajeros a la Española, 1492–1530.* Santo Domingo, Dominican Republic: La Autora, 2000.

Curtin, Philip D. *The Rise and Fall of the Plantation Complex: Essays in Atlantic History.* New York: Cambridge University Press, 1990.

Floyd, Troy S. *The Columbus Dynasty in the Caribbean, 1492–1526.* Albuquerque: University of New Mexico Press, 1973.

Otte, Enrique. *Las perlas del Caribe: Nueva Cádiz de Cubagua*. Caracas: Fundación John Bolton, 1977.

Parry, John. *Europe and a Wider World, 1415–1715*. London: Hutchinson University Library, 1949.

Parry, John. *The Spanish Seaborne Empire*. New York: International, 1966.

Parry, J. H. *The Age of Reconnaissance: Discovery, Exploration and Settlement, 1440–1650*. New York: World Publishing, 1963.

Parry, J. H. Sherlock, Philip, and Maingot, Anthony. *A Short History of the West Indies*, 4th ed. New York: St. Martin's Press, 1987.

Pike, Ruth. *Enterprise and Adventure: The Genoese in Seville and the Opening of the New World*. Ithaca, N.Y.: Cornell University Press, 1966.

Williams, Eric. *From Columbus to Castro: History of the Caribbean, 1492–1969*. New York: Harper and Row, 1970.

CHAPTER 4

Imperialism and Slavery

It were somewhat difficult, to give you an exact account, of the number of persons upon the Island; there being such a store of shipping that brings passengers daily to the place, but it has been conjectur'd, by those that are long acquainted, and best seen in the knowledge of the Island, that there are not less than 50 thousand souls, besides Negroes; and some of them who began upon small fortunes, are now risen to very great and vast estates.

The island is divided into three sorts of men, viz: Masters, Servants and Slaves. The slaves and their posterity, being subject to their masters forever, are kept and preserv'd with greater care than the servants, who are theirs but for five years, according to the law of the Island. So that for the time, the servants have the worser lives, for they are put to very hard labour, ill lodging, and their dyet very sleight.

—RICHARD LIGON,
True and Exact History . . . of Barbadoes, 1653

The seventeenth century witnessed some fundamental changes in the political, economic, and social structures of the Caribbean. This was the century that marked the beginning of the transition from settler communities to exploitation colonies within the non-Hispanic sphere. The Hispanic Caribbean followed these changes during the eighteenth century. The most startling political change was the Balkanization of the region as the Dutch, French, and the English successfully defied the might of Spain and established permanent strongholds along the strategic outer periphery, as well Jamaica, of what had for more than a century been reluctantly conceded as the private domain of the monarchs of Castile. The success of the northwest European states coincided with—and in some cases resulted from—basic changes in the Spanish-American empire.

Three basic changes took place during the seventeenth century within the structure of the Spanish-American empire. In the first place, the center of gravity of the empire shifted from Peru to New Spain (Mexico) following the expansion of precious-metal exports. This meant that Mexican Gulf ports like Tampico and Vera Cruz took precedence over South American ports, such as Porto Bello, Cartagena, and La Guaira. In the second place, the orderly system of regular convoys that connected the metropolis to the colonies broke down. Sailings were infrequent, and commerce and communication suffered severe disruptions, inviting contraband activities. In the third place, the establishment of rival colonies accentuated the disruption of trade and promoted more illegal activities across the newly drawn imperial frontiers. The English capture of Jamaica in 1655 and the expansion of Dutch commercial activities from St. Eustatius, Saba, St. Martin, and Curaçao facilitated the economic penetration of the Spanish Americas by outsiders.

After 1700, a number of Caribbean possessions changed hands frequently among European powers. But the region remained cosmopolitan, with the tendency toward a greater rather than a lesser number of European divisions. Economically, the early outposts of the newly arriving imperialists began to assume increasing international importance owing to their conversion into major producers of tropical staples or into free markets for commercial exchanges. The older Spanish colonies, Cuba, Hispaniola, and Puerto Rico, were slow to respond to the changes and lagged behind the others in converting themselves into free markets and plantation colonies. The conversion, of course, carried a social price. Socially, the Caribbean acquired a racial-class delineation far more complex than the simple divisions of Richard Ligon's "three sorts of men" in Barbados in 1653. Indeed, politics, economics, and society became even more intimately connected with the development and inexorable expansion of the Caribbean sugar industry. But the development of the Caribbean sugar industry took place after 1650 and is connected with imperial rivalry on the mainland, especially between Dutch and Portuguese in the northeast of Brazil.

As late as 1700—and much later on the larger islands and mainland possessions—the European colonies in the Caribbean constituted expanding enclaves with moving frontiers. Until the Peace of Utrecht in 1713, there were two general types of society existing in alternating harmony and discord. The first type comprised the boisterous, violent society of struggling settlers, prospering planters, exasperated officials, machinating merchants, suffering slaves, and ambivalent free persons of color. Together these constituted the organized and formal colony. They were the true colonists who accepted, albeit often under duress, the rules, regulations, and interventions of the metropolises and subscribed to various degrees to the political integrity of the different imperial systems. The second social type generated by the considerable sociopolitical flux of the times consisted of a variegated group of individuals, commonly considered transfrontiersmen— people who chose to operate outside the conventional confines of the colonies. Such transfrontier groups ranged from the highly organized communities of Maroons, or escaped slaves, to the defiant, stateless, peripatetic collectivity of buccaneers or freebooters. These two groups—Maroons and buccaneers—were not primarily a threat to settled, organized society in the Caribbean but represented a temporary alternative to the formal colonial social structure.

The Maroons formed the most successful alternative to organized European colonial society. Born of the innate resistance to slavery, they were essentially communities of Africans and their descendants who escaped individually and collectively from the plantations and households of their masters to seek their freedom, thereby continuing a tradition begun by the indigenous Indians. The word *maroon* was first used to describe the range cattle that had gone wild during the first attempts at Spanish colonization on the island of Hispaniola. It was also applied to Indians who had escaped from the established Spanish compounds. By the middle of the sixteenth century, it was already being applied to African slaves. In any case, *marronnage*—the flight from servitude—became an intrinsic dimension of American slavery, enduring as long as the institution itself.

American plantation society spawned a variety of forms of resistance to enslavement. Acts of resistance could be categorized into two forms. The first was the temporary desertion of individual slaves. This form of escape, frequently called *petit marronnage*, reflected the strong individual inclination on the part of the slave to resist forced or unpleasant labor; to procrastinate; to defy a master or a rule; or to visit friends, family, or acquaintances in the neighborhood without the requisite permission. *Petit marronnage* was eventually accepted with due reluctance as one of the inescapable concomitants of the system and was punished with less severity than other infringements of local regulations or other patterns of behavior that jeopardized the social order. At its most serious, *petit marronnage* remained a personal conflict between the master and the slave.

This was not true of the second form of resistance, *gran marronnage*, which constituted a fully organized attempt to establish autonomous communities, socially and politically independent of the European colonial enclave. This pattern of conduct was potentially subversive to the entire socioeconomic complex of colonial life. Such independent communities—variously called *palenques* in the Spanish colonies, *quilombos* or *mocambos* in the Portuguese, and Maroon towns in the English colonies—encompassed various numbers of individuals. Some communities lasted only for very short periods of time. Others endured for centuries. In their construction and their survival may be deduced the eloquent articulation of the Africans and Afro-Americans on the real conditions of slavery and their opinions of it. Organized bands of Maroons prevailed for centuries in Jamaica, outlasting the determined communities of Bahía and Palmares in Brazil, Esmeraldas in Ecuador, or Le Maniel in French Saint-Domingue.

Detested and vehemently opposed by the European slave-owning colonists, these misnamed towns taxed the ingenuity and resourcefulness of all the participants, both for their sustenance and for their survival. Considering the extreme disadvantages under which the Maroons labored, it is most surprising that so many communities survived for such long periods of time, often in close proximity to operating plantations. The principal ingredients of success seemed to be the nature of their social organization and the physical location of the communities.

Maroon villages were composed predominantly of young able-bodied adults, although as Barry Higman pointed out in his study of the slave populations of the British Caribbean, *marronnage* involved slaves of all ages and both sexes. Until the eighteenth century, Africans tended to predominate among the Maroon communities, but gradually the composition reflected the changing demographic structure, with an increasing number of Creoles. Indeed, with the cessation of official English participation in the transatlantic slave trade after 1807, both the slave and Maroon communities acquired an increased proportion of Creoles.

During the eighteenth century, Maroons acquired a fearsome reputation. Bryan Edwards wrote a curiously admiring description of the Maroons of Jamaica in the later part of the eighteenth century that reveals as much about the writer and his society as his subject:

> Savage as they were in manners and disposition, their mode of living and daily pursuits undoubtedly strengthened their frame, and served to exalt them to great bodily perfection. Such fine persons are seldom beheld among any other class of African or native blacks. Their demeanor is lofty, their walk firm, and their persons erect. Every motion displays a combination of strength and agility. The muscles (neither hidden nor depressed by clothing) are very prominent, and strongly marked. Their sight withal is wonderfully acute, and their hearing remarkably quick. These characteristics, however, are common, I believe, to all savage nations, in warm and temperate climates; and like other savages, the Maroons have only those senses perfect which are kept in constant exercise. Their smell is obtuse, and their taste so depraved, that I have seen them drink new rum fresh from the still, in preference to wine which I offered them; and I remember, at a great festival in one of their towns, which I attended, that their highest luxury, in point of food, was some rotten beef, which had been originally salted in Ireland, and which was probably presented to them, by some person who knew their taste, *because it was putrid.*

Like banditry, successful Maroon communities depended on good fortune and the quality of their leadership. Leadership seemed to have been determined partly by military and partly by political ability, qualities that were not exclusively male. One of the most successful of the Jamaican Maroon leaders was a formidable lady called Nanny, of the Windward Maroons near Port Antonio. The most successful leaders, such as Nanny and Cudjoe in Jamaica; Macandal or Santiago in Saint-Domingue; or Ventura Sanchez, otherwise known as Coba, in Cuba, combined religious roles with their political positions, thereby reinforcing their authority over their followers. Good leaders also showed an unusually keen understanding of settled colonial society that facilitated their ability to deal with the white political leaders. Prior to the eighteenth century, most leaders tended to be rigidly authoritarian and needlessly cruel. New recruits to Maroon communities were scrupulously tested, and deserters, wanderers, and suspected spies were brutally killed. Maroons, however, had no monopoly on brutality. In 1819, Brigadier Eusebio Escudero, the military governor of Santiago de Cuba, captured Ventura Sanchez through deception. Rather than be jailed, or re-enslaved, Sanchez committed suicide. Escudero then had his head displayed in an iron cage outside the city of Baracoa for a long time, presumably as a macabre form of intimidation. Maroon communities were vulnerable to internal feuds or disenchanted defection from the ranks.

Security was a constant preoccupation of Maroon villages. The physical setting of the village became a prime ingredient in its survival and eventual evolution. All successful villages in the Caribbean depended, at least initially, on their relative inaccessibility. They were strategically located in the densely forested interior of the Sierra Maestra, in the sparsely settled areas of Pinar del Río and Las Villas, or in the rugged northern coastlands of Oriente in Cuba; on the conical limestone ridges of the Cockpit Country in western Jamaica; on the precipitous slopes of the Blue Mountains in eastern Jamaica; in the formidable *massifs* of northern and southern Haiti; in the rugged *cordilleras* of Santo Domingo; on the isolated slopes of the Windward and Leeward islands; and in the jungle interiors of the Guianas and Suriname. Where geography was not conducive to hiding, such as in cities— and urban Maroons were a serious problem in the nineteenth century—or on small islands or in less rugged terrain, such as found in Barbados, Antigua, Martinique, or Guadeloupe, *petit marronnage* rather than *gran marronnage* seemed to be the order of the day.

Early Maroon communities seemed to have suffered from a shortage of women, not a surprising occurrence, given the preponderance of males in the rural slave cohorts from which they mainly drew their recruits. The scarcity of women and the observed polygamy and polygyny of some of the leaders forced some unusual practices during the formative years of the community. One such practice was raiding for the express purpose of capturing women, usually Indian women, as occurred in the Guianas and other areas on the mainland. Another was enforced sharing of females, as was reported for some Jamaica Maroons. As the communities endured and stabilized, however, sexual imbalance adjusted itself, especially as Maroons were able to produce and nurture to adulthood their own offspring. By the nineteenth century, the Maroons appeared to have achieved a more normal sexual balance. Barry Higman noted that in 1817 all the slaves reported "at large" in Kingstown, St. Vincent, were females, and in Bridgetown, Barbados, twice as many females as males were in Maroon communities. Between 1827 and 1831, about 49 percent of the Maroons on the small island of Anguilla were female. The presence of women was crucial for the survival of any Maroon community.

Given the inhospitable environment in which most Maroons chose to set up their communities, only the fittest and luckiest survived. Starvation, malnutrition, dysentery, smallpox, and accidental poisoning from unfamiliar herbs and leaves took a high toll on the villagers. The threat of discovery and attack by the organized colonial society remained constant. Throughout the Caribbean, large-scale military expeditions to seek and destroy Maroon villages that had become too prominent were sporadic, though important, activities. Colonists in Cuba and Jamaica employed specially trained dogs to hunt and recapture Maroons, and on the mainland, the Indians were rewarded for returning Maroons, dead or alive, to the colonial authorities. Notwithstanding the hazards, Maroon communities recruited and trained enough manpower to defy local authorities, wage successful wars, and secure their own peace treaties, as the Jamaica Maroons did in 1739 and 1795. Or they secured a modus vivendi with the local communities and de facto recognition from the political rulers as they did in eastern Cuba and Le Maniel in southern Saint-Domingue.

Successful *marronnage* required the concealed cooperation of slaves, free persons of color, and free whites within the settled societies. This communication with the established societies enabled the Maroons to get firearms, tools, utensils, and, in some cases, food, and this assistance was often crucial in the early stages of subduing the forest and building the community. Later the Maroons could obtain intelligence of impending raids or, in times of cooperation, could conduct free commerce with the neighboring towns, plantations, or islands. Not only urban Maroons, but a large number of rural Maroons, gradually developed a semisymbiotic relationship with the societies from which they had withdrawn their support and unilaterally revoked their servile status.

With unfortunate irony, it was this very semisymbiosis that proved most lethal to the integrity, cultural distinctiveness, and vitality of Maroon existence. Once the Maroons succeeded in gaining legal or quasi-legal recognition, their structure, internal organization, methods of recruitment, and political attitudes underwent significant changes. In the treaties that they signed, they accepted severely limited territorial concessions, restricting their mobility. The legal status that they got in return was at the cost of some internal power and control. For example, by treaty obligations, runaway slaves could no longer be ascripted to the group but had to be handed over to the planter societies, often for a fee. This practice not only restricted the physical size of the community, but insidiously undermined the political appeal of the Maroons as a viable alternative to the organized slave society. The Maroons of Jamaica signed treaties with the English government in the eighteenth century allowing them to trade in slaves or to own slaves and obliging them to return runaway slaves to their owners—a deed that incurred a lot of ill will among the slaves. If the Maroons viewed the treaties as a form of collective security, the treaties nevertheless represented a strengthening of the very sociopolitical structure that they had formerly despised. Formal treaties with the Maroons (and other free communities surrounding slave plantations) strengthened the system of slave control by removing, reducing, or otherwise restricting one option of personal escape from slavery to freedom. Maroon communities, by agreeing to the external legal controls over basic aspects of their lives, even regarding the succession of leaders, may have done themselves more harm than good in the long run. Increased interrelations with the slave society exacted its penalty. In the familiar tradition of all groups crossing a common frontier, the various Maroon societies gradually became indistinct from their neighboring slave communities. They lacked adequate facilities and autonomous infrastructures for long-term economic and social success, a condition that was common to most transfrontier groups. Eventually, the Maroons, like the French Huguenots, ultimately were unable to overcome the severe limitations and internal contradictions of a state within a state.

Like the Maroons, the buccaneers were also the products of a certain stage of social evolution in the history of the Caribbean. The buccaneers, however, represented a shorter historical phase, whose period of glory lasted from about the middle of the seventeenth century until the beginning of the eighteenth. This period coincided with the period of greatest political and social transition in the Caribbean, following the demise of Spanish military supremacy in the region and the general recognition of "no peace beyond the line." The boundaries of empires, as well as the notions of international law, were extremely vague, facilitating fluctuating alliances or associations of European communities within the region and encouraging acts of dubious legality.

Buccaneers were essentially stateless persons who lived comfortably by commerce with the settled communities of European colonists, just as the Maroons did. According to legend, they had begun their existence by exploiting the large number of cattle, horses, hogs, and dogs that had proliferated on the tropical savannas in the wake of the early Spanish settlement. The word *buccaneer* derives from the original Indian custom of slowly drying and curing strips of meat, called "boucan," over an open fire. This delicious, relatively non-perishable product found a ready market among the increasing number of ships trafficking in Caribbean waters. Small colonies of these hunters and meat-smokers flourished during the middle decades of the sixteenth century on the northern plains of Cuba, in the western parts of Puerto Rico and Hispaniola, and on a number of the smaller neighboring islands. The economy of these groups depended on selling hides and boucan to the ships passing through the Mona Passage and the Windward Passage. Over a period of time, the hunters gradually diversified their economic base by adding piracy to their occupation and extending their operations from the mainland to the rugged but easily defensible island of Tortuga—relatively safe from the periodic Spanish search-and-destroy missions but still very close to the wild herds of northwestern Hispaniola. Eventually the buccaneers forged a community geographically and legally separated from formal colonial political control, in which the urge for adventure and plunder overrode the need to settle down. In the Anglophone Caribbean, the term *buccaneer* adhered to the amorphous group of adventurers long after they had forsaken the art of hunting and boucaning. The French preferred the term *corsairs* or *flibustiers*, while the Dutch called the group *zee-roovers*. The more notorious and successful of the buccaneers, such as Henry Morgan (1635–1688), considered themselves to be "Bretheren of the Coasts," with allegiance to no state and obligation to no laws but their own.

Buccaneers, however, more closely resembled social bandits than the Maroons. By the middle of the seventeenth century, the buccaneers had achieved international fame and had attracted a motley band, probably numbering a few thousand throughout the Caribbean. Their recruits came from shipwrecks, deserters from the regular crews of vessels sailing in the region, opportunistic fortune seekers, and men and women repelled by the regimentation and coercion of the sugar-plantation society then rapidly spreading from island to island. But the real international importance of the buccaneers undoubtedly increased because they had the capacity to perform freelance attacks on the Spanish possessions in and around the Caribbean at a time when neither the English nor the French—then riddled with civil conflicts or domestic political weakness—could undertake such action officially. With the covert support of the rival states, the buccaneers continued the attacks on Spain and, by keeping Spain off-balance in the Caribbean, contributed to the permanent success of the non-Spanish attempts at colonization in the tropical Americas. On the other hand, Spain, by trying to destroy the communities of buccaneers—especially by hitting at their subsidiary economic activity— boucaning—justified their raison d'être, piracy. Yet buccaneers insisted that they were not mere pirates and sought official support for their actions. The myth of Spanish wealth and the reality of Spanish treasure fleets assembling off Havana at frequent intervals for the annual spring sailings to the metropolis merely sharpened the cupidity of an already rapacious group.

Père Jean-Baptiste Labat (1663–1738), the radical, indefatigable Dominican priest who served in the French West Indies from 1694 to 1705 and whose memoirs were published posthumously in 1743, left a rare firsthand account of the organization and political importance of the buccaneers, albeit in their waning days. Labat's account compares favorably with that of Alexander Exquemelin, or Esquemeline (d. ca. 1680), and appears to have captured the attitudes and actions of the buccaneers during their predominantly sea-roving phase:

St. Pierre [Martinique], 6th March 1694. We were busy all this morning confessing a crew of *flibustiers* who had arrived at Les Mouillages with two prizes that they had captured from the English. The Mass of the Virgin was celebrated with all solemnity, and I blessed three large loaves which were presented by the captain and his officers, who arrived at the church accompanied by the drums and trumpets of their corvette. At the beginning of Mass the corvette fired a salute with all her cannons. At the Elevation of the Holy Sacrament, she fired another salvo, at the Benediction a third, and finally a fourth, when we sang the *Te Deum* after Mass. All the *flibustiers* contributed 30 sols to the sacristy, and did so with much piety and modesty. This may surprise people in Europe where *flibustiers* are not credited with possessing much piety, but as a matter of fact they generally give a portion of their good fortunes to the churches. If church ornament or church linen happen to be in the prizes they capture, the *flibustiers* always present them to their parish church.

The conditions of Roving are set forth in what is called *Chasse Partie [hunting regulations]*. If the vessel belongs to the *flibustiers* themselves, their booty is shared equally. The captain and the quartermaster (who is always second in command on these ships), the surgeon and the pilot receive no more than anyone else except a gift which is given to them by the rest of the crew. As a rule the captain is given a present which is equivalent to three and sometimes four extra shares. The quartermaster is presented with an additional two shares. The pilot and the surgeon each receive an extra share and a half. Boys are given a half share, and the man who first sights the prize wins an extra share.

Other items in the agreement are: That if a man be wounded he has to receive one *écu* a day as long as he remains in the surgeon's hands up to sixty days, and this has to be paid or allowed for before any man receives his share. A man receives 600 *écus* for the loss of each limb, 300 *écus* for the loss of a thumb or the first finger of the right hand, or an eye, and 100 *écus* for each of the other fingers.

If a man has a wooden leg or a hook for his arm and these happen to be destroyed, he receives the same amount as if they were his original limbs.

In the case the ship is chartered by *flibustiers*, the owners have to provision and arm the ship, and receive one-third of the prizes.

In war-time the *flibustiers* are given commissions by the governor of the different islands, who receive a tenth share in the prizes. In peace-time they were given permits to fish. But either with or without commission, the *flibustiers* pillaged the Spaniards, who hanged them as pirates whenever they caught them.

The description by Labat underlined the principal characteristics of the buccaneers that set them apart from the Maroons as transfrontiersmen. In terms of cultural distinction, the Maroons were patently further removed from settler society than the buccaneers. For the buccaneers won the admiration of their metropolitan public, even though an account such as that of Exquemelin emphasized the savagery, selfishness, excessive avarice, and utter lawlessness of the infamous international horde. Exquemelin's history of the buccaneers, first published in Dutch around 1674 as *De Americaensche zee-roovers*, was quickly translated into English, French, and German and apparently had a wide readership throughout Europe.

Although the buccaneers were essentially stateless individuals, they retained strong links with the general culture and society with which they were familiar. That is quite clear from the account just cited from Labat. The buccaneers did not try, as did the American Maroons, to create a separate culture and society. Buccaneers had their culture and knew their social origins quite well. What they sought—at least for a time—was freedom from the restraints and obligations of that culture and that society. Most of those who survived the occupational hazards of their profession returned to those societies. In any case, the leaders of the buccaneering bands always had some national identity: Alexander Exquemelin (1645–1707) was Dutch; Bartholomé Portuguez—the most famous nonswimmer in the history of the buccaneers—was Portuguese; Rock, the Dutchman, had lived once in Brazil; Francis L'Olonnois (1630–1699), also called The Cruel, was a Frenchman; Henry Morgan (1635–1688) was born in Wales, lived in Barbados, and was knighted and served as lieutenant-governor of Jamaica between 1674 and 1682; Raveneau de Lassan (1663–1690)—in all probability a nom de guerre—claimed to be a French buccaneer. To be sure, most buccaneers were not from what were then commonly called the "cultivated classes" of Europe. A large number, among them Morgan, Exquemelin, and L'Olonnois, had served as indentured servants or *engagés* in the emergent sugar plantations of the Caribbean. With the demand for labor outstripping supply, the later accusations that some of these unfortunate indentureds might have been aggressively kidnapped could have been true. But their condition of servitude, as Richard Ligon noted, engendered an enormous antipathy toward the state that supported it, not unlike that of the African slaves who replaced them in the fields.

The harsh conditions of indenture produced physically tough and spiritually callous individuals, capable of surviving the exacting and hazardous conditions of international piracy. But this occupation did not dissolve their links with settled societies, which often found the buccaneers as convenient a bulwark of defense as the Jamaican planters of the eighteenth century found Cudjoe's (d. 1760s) Maroons. In Jamaica, would-be buccaneers could buy a commission from the government for about twenty pounds sterling that allowed them to plunder towns in the Spanish Indies. One such commission, issued to Morgan in 1670, stipulated that he was solely responsible for the full cost of mounting the expedition and that the prizes from the adventure would be distributed according to the buccaneers' customary rules. The ill-gotten plunder of the buccaneers, lavishly dispensed in the local towns, boosted the local economies and compensated adequately for the otherwise detestable social manners of these men.

The economic importance of the buccaneers contributed in no small way to their general acceptance among the non-Spanish Caribbean authorities. Clarence Haring in his history of the buccaneers described the English capture of Jamaica and the entire Cromwellian "Grand Design" of 1655 as "a reversion to the Elizabethan gold-hunt...the first of the great buccaneering expeditions." John Milton (1608–1674), Oliver Cromwell's (1599–1658) Latin secretary, gave the official justification for privateering commissions as a response to (1) the cruelties of the Spanish toward the English-American colonists, (2) the Spanish cruelty toward the Indians, and (3) the Spanish refusal to sanction open English trade with their empire.

Sir Charles Lyttleton, the lieutenant-governor of Jamaica in the early 1660s, proposed six practical reasons for official support of the buccaneers, and these seem to have impressed the English metropolitan government for a time. Privateering, he argued, provided a number of able-bodied men and available ships that served to protect the island in the absence of an appointed naval squadron. Privateers had extremely valuable information on local navigation, and their practical experience would be invaluable in wartime. The international connections of the buccaneers supplied uniquely rich intelligence on the size, preparation, and potential wealth of Spanish towns and Spanish naval activities. The prizes and currency brought to Port Royal attracted merchants, contributed to the economy, and helped to reduce prices—especially for African slaves. English colonial authorities lacked the requisite naval force to destroy the bands of buccaneers, and English seamen had such admiration for the brotherhood that it was doubtful they would zealously engage in such activities. Finally Lyttleton argued that any attempt to destroy the buccaneers might simply serve to attract their aggressive retaliation on English plantations and English commerce. Opponents of the granting of commissions thought that buccaneering was dishonorable and unprofitable—or at least less potentially profitable than regular commerce.

Lyttleton knew his buccaneers well and had perhaps personally profited from his short association with them. In any case, he was familiar with their modus operandi. For buccaneers did not usually attack the colony from which the leader of the band originated or the citizens related in nationality or culture to the majority of the members. In practice, therefore, French privateers led by a Dutchman, would normally attack only Spanish or English towns and ships, and English buccaneers preferred the spoils of countries with which their nation-state was at war. Everyone, however, saw the Spanish as fair game, and Spanish shipping and Spanish colonies suffered most during the period of greatest buccaneer activity. By the beginning of the second half of the seventeenth century, although the lingua franca of the buccaneers remained French, the leadership became English, and after 1655, the main base of operation shifted from Tortuga to Port Royal, Jamaica, at the tip of the Palisadoes Peninsula, and across the harbor from Kingston.

Buccaneer wealth provided a healthy stimulus to the early local economy of some islands. Captain Henry Morgan, admiral-in-chief of the confederacy of the Jamaican buccaneers, used his returns from privateering to build a splendid city home in Port Royal, purchase several sugar plantations in the interior of the island, and achieve the socially prominent position of lieutenant-governor of the second most important English Caribbean possession at that time. Many wealthy traders in Guadeloupe depended on privateering as a regular means of commerce. Apart from the inordinate amounts of bullion and currency that the buccaneers brought and distributed to their home towns, they dealt in confiscated sugar, cocoa, indigo, logwood, slaves, jewels, silks, spices, wine, and cattle. Buccaneering during the seventeenth century was not only a potent political weapon, but a crude form of imperial revenue-sharing.

Persistent war and conflicts over trade in the Caribbean increased the strategic importance of the buccaneers for a time. Until the late 1670s, buccaneers sought formal commissions to engage in privateering raids throughout the region. Ostensibly, such commissions made them the legal representatives of the English or French Crown, and their exploits were a part of the expansion of empire. But the complicated international situation after the Restoration in England (1660)— with Charles II (1630–1685; king, 1660–1685) moving toward friendship with Spain and enmity with France—forced the award of aggressive commissions away from the center of empire to the local governors, whose authority could then be conveniently superseded should changing diplomatic relations so warrant. The legitimate cover of a commission enabled the buccaneers to equip their ships with powder, shot, cannons, and supplies, as well as to recruit men openly. But from the buccaneer point of view, political support was merely a cover—the interests of empire being of minor importance. In this way, Jérémie Deschamps, Seigneur du Rausset, obtained by duplicity simultaneous commissions from both the English and the French and successfully played one power against the other for a short period of time, while the status of his "colony" of Tortuga remained ambiguous. Deschamps finally ended up in the Bastille in Paris, where he was persuaded to cede his interest in Tortuga to Jean-Baptiste Colbert's (1619–1683) French West India Company for 15,000 livres and his freedom. On the other hand, Henry Morgan was apparently quite upset by the implication in Alexander Exquemelin's history of the buccaneers that he had sailed without a commission and sought to have the English edition of the book suppressed. In 1684, Morgan also brought a charge of libel against the publishers, for the lack of a royal commission would have erased the legal distinction between piracy, which was illegal, and privateering, which was not. Morgan got a small award of slightly more than 200 pounds sterling—much less than the 10,000 pounds that he sought. At stake was Morgan's new status as a gentleman, knight, influential planter, and recently respectable lieutenant-governor of Jamaica. By 1684, the golden age of buccaneering was fading fast.

The conditions that had proved most propitious to buccaneering activity ceased after 1670—although it was some time before the signals reached the Caribbean. The political influence of a semilegal, uncontrolled band to further the cause of colonization yielded to the diplomatic adroitness, increased military strength, and self-consciousness of Louis XIV in France (1638–1715) and Charles II in England. Moreover, Spain was no longer the power it used to be. The possessions of the French West India Company became true colonies after 1674, and after the Restoration, Charles II moved to exercise greater control over the English West Indian islands. Greater supervision of the colonies severely undermined the previous reciprocal relationship between settler societies and the transfrontier communities. Lyttleton's analysis was no longer valid. The withdrawal of formal commissions during the 1680s and 1690s meant that the same activities formerly hailed in England and France were then condemned as piracy, subject to punishment by hanging. The legal end came with the Treaty of Ryswick in 1697, when the French joined the Dutch (the Treaty of The Hague in 1673) and the English (the Treaty of Windsor in 1680) in agreeing to withdraw official support from the buccaneers. These treaties with Spain, signed outside Iberia, underlined her military decline already obvious during the Thirty Years' War. Individual, uncontrolled marauding became politically counterproductive to the genesis of exploitation societies based on slave-operated plantations and organized international commerce. In 1692, Port Royal, the most notorious stronghold of buccaneers, slipped ominously into the sea after a severe earthquake, taking along the house and tomb of Henry Morgan. The activity that had elevated Morgan and Jean-Baptiste du Casse (1646–1715) from transfrontier sea rovers to imperial governors no longer prevailed. It was the end of the age of the buccaneers.

The existence of communities of buccaneers represented a stage in the transition from pioneering colonialism to organized imperialism. The changes in the Caribbean reflected changes in Europe. England, France, and Holland had become strong enough to dictate aspects of their relations with Spain. But the Spanish had not yet become so weak that their empire could be wrested from them indiscriminately. Trade, not the export of people founding microcosmic European societies, became the major preoccupation, and the exigencies of trade demanded not only a new relationship between each metropolis and colony, but a new climate of international order. This new climate required the control, coordination, and responsibility that were the anathema of buccaneering. Thus, while the buccaneering bands displayed their skills, a series of events and circumstances ushered in a new order. Non-Hispanic European states began to expand their political influence by conquest rather than by settlement, exemplified by the capture of Jamaica in 1655 and the French advance on western Hispaniola (conceded by the Treaty of Ryswick in 1697). The French reorganized their empire under Colbert and finally brought it under the direct control of the Crown in 1674. Spanish-American silver production declined significantly, domestic Spanish industries virtually disappeared, and Spanish merchant shipping drastically diminished in Caribbean ports. By 1686, more than 90 percent of the capital and goods handled on the legal Seville-to-the-Indies trade was controlled by French, Genoese, Dutch, English, and German businessmen (often working through Spanish intermediaries), while an estimated two-thirds of all Spanish-American trade was contraband. At this time, too, the Caribbean region had already been experiencing the revolutionary reorganization of its society, its agriculture, and its commerce. With an understandable delay in the Spanish possessions, the exploiters dominated or expelled the subsistence settlers. The age of sugar and slavery had arrived.

The massive introduction of African slaves and the employment of slavery as the main form of labor organization reflected a major sociopolitical change in the status and role of the Caribbean colonies. The resort to plantation agriculture indicated the failure to re-create viable colonies of Europeans in the tropical islands and circum-Caribbean lowlands. From about the 1640s, the semifeudal European settler frontier slowly gave way to the rigidly organized, commercially integrated exploitation society of masters and slaves. The slave society, transmitted from Barbados westward across the Caribbean, brought greater and quicker profits to the private and public proponents of empire than did the former struggling enclaves of predominantly European cash-crop farming communities.

The eventual adoption of slavery as the principal labor system arose from the severe economic crisis of the middle of the seventeenth century in the Caribbean. It arose especially from the overwhelming need to establish a more competitively marketable commodity than tobacco as the basis of a colonial economy. After a short period of trial and error, sugarcane emerged as the most valuable potential agricultural crop. Sugar had become increasingly popular on the European market, and the technique of its production had been known in Mediterranean Europe since the time of the Crusades. Sugar and slavery were constant companions of the European westward expansion. Sugarcane had been successfully cultivated in Iberia, the Canaries, the African Atlantic islands, Brazil, and the Spanish Americas. Moreover, sugar provided the efficacious balance between bulk and value so crucial in the days of small sailing ships and distant sea voyages. Sugar production and export, however, demanded a considerable capital outlay and a larger, more reliable, and more consistent supply of labor than was available through contracted servants or irregularly supplied African slaves. The slave society required a new imperial order and new commercial regulations.

The relationship between a colonial export economy and its metropolis demanded a more structured political organization in the interest of efficient trade. The English circumscribed the political independence of the Barbados Assembly in the late seventeenth century, and the French Crown took over direct control of its overseas colonies. A long series of mercantilistic trade and navigation laws were passed during the succeeding century regulating commerce between the various European metropolises and their Caribbean colonies. The essence of these navigation acts was to make sure that goods between the metropolis and the colonies were carried in their own ships. In this way, the English dramatically increased the tonnage of English carrying trade in the seventeenth and eighteenth centuries, to the great all-around gain of the mother country. Metropolitan merchants advancing capital and goods largely on credit desired a stable political relationship conducive to long-term planning, as well as to the security of their investment. Each European state saw enormous potential gain in the employment of its citizens, the development of its industry, and the expansion of its merchant marine through the twin pursuits of trade within the empire and trade with other Europeans as well as Africans. Trade was the fulcrum of political power.

From the colonial perspective, however, the priorities were different. Like those in the metropolises, colonies viewed the relationship between commerce and wealth as direct. But unlike the metropolitan groups, they felt that the fewer the restrictions on trade, the more lucrative would be the relationship, especially to the individual traders. Colonial planters enjoyed the partial guarantee of the home market for their tropical commodities, but they wanted a steady supply of slaves from Africa and provisions, as well as planting equipment from Europe and North America. As they became more successful at their pursuits, they realized that mercantilism did not provide the greatest quantity of commodities at the lowest possible prices. On the other hand, free trade implied a state of commercial insecurity (especially with regard to the unsettled competitive politics of Europe) and the removal of the protection and support derived from being part of an empire. These divergent views, ideals, and practices could never be fully reconciled within the context of empire, and they precipitated within the managerial strata of Caribbean plantation societies a resentment that grew more bitter with time. Perhaps no aspect of the commercial relationship bred more mutual irritation than the supply and price of African slaves, the most important single ingredient in the economic success of the plantation society.

As early as the 1630s, the bases of a sugar system were introduced into the English Caribbean in an attempt to duplicate the Portuguese and Dutch economic success along the northeastern coast of Brazil. The Spanish sugar industry had been going on in Hispaniola, Mexico, and Cuba on a small scale since the early sixteenth century. In 1639, the French Compagnie des Iles d'Amérique, acting in response to a number of individual entrepreneurs at home and overseas, signed a contract with a Dutch immigrant from Brazil to build a pioneer sugar estate of approximately three hundred acres on the island of Martinique. It was an ambitious undertaking, but, like other such early experiments, it failed from a combination of uncertain finances and an immature infrastructure unable to coordinate the many integrated features of labor supply, agricultural management, and product marketing. Success necessitated in that period international, especially Dutch, support. The Dutch, therefore, acted as the organizational middlemen of the Caribbean sugar industry, deploying their capital, expertise, transportation and marketing facilities, and slaves throughout the English and French Caribbean. In 1647, the first successful cargoes of sugar left Barbados and Guadeloupe in Dutch ships for

Europe. By 1650, the Dutch, confident of available supplies, established a number of refineries on their small islands, a development that pleased the sugar producers as much as it irked their metropolitan rulers. For the following thirty years, the English and French fought a series of anti-Dutch naval wars in an effort to destroy Dutch influence and improve the efficacy of their own mercantile system.

If the English and the French sugar industries depended on the benevolence of the Dutch, the same was not true of the early Spanish sugar industry. On his second voyage, Christopher Columbus introduced sugarcane to Hispaniola, and by the middle of the sixteenth century, a number of relatively large estates had begun an erratic but lucrative export of sugar to Spain. Sugar production from water-powered mills became an attractive economic alternative to the *encomienda*, since both the supply of Indians and the quantity of gold had diminished greatly. Many partnerships involved the highest officials of the fledgling colony, such as the treasurer Esteban Pasamonte, the *fiscal* (district attorney) Pedro Vásquez de Mella, the *contador* (accountant) Alonso de Ávila, and the *oidores* (judges) Cristóbal Lebron and Alonso Zuazo, who imported Africans and participated in the early sugar industry. Diego Columbus had a large estate on the outskirts of the city of Santo Domingo with about forty African slaves producing sugar as early as 1522. Meanwhile Hernando Gorjón of Azua made enough money from the early sugar trade to Spain to endow the *colegio* (high school) in Santo Domingo, which eventually became the first American university.

Like its seventeenth-century Caribbean successor, the early Spanish sugar industry spread throughout the region, island-hopping in tandem with the expansion of settlements and the availability of African slaves. By 1526, Hispaniola had nineteen sugar mills and was importing about four hundred African slaves per year. Sugar mills were also established around San Germán in Puerto Rico and Santiago de la Vega in Jamaica. The gross production of these mills remains uncertain, but their exports totaling several thousand tons went to Spain, Mexico, and Cuba. Most probably as the result of the shortage of available capital, the Cuban sugar industry did not begin until the last decade of the sixteenth century. The first hydraulic mills established in the city of Havana had an export capacity of about three thousand *arrobas* (37.5 short tons) in 1600, sending their product to Spain, Campeche, and Cartagena. Spaniards who had produced sugar on estates in southern Iberia, especially around Huelva and Málaga, transferred the technique to the Americas. But most colonists utilized sugarcane as a means of making syrup, expressing the juice by a simple manual wooden press or an equally simple, relatively inefficient, rotary animal-powered press called a *trapiche* and boiling it to the desired state of crystallization. An *ingenio*, or sugar mill, required both capital and a large supply of sugarcane, both of which were beyond the individual productive capacity of most of the early colonists. Above all, as the numerous, frequently repeated petitions to the Spanish Crown indicated, a sugar industry needed a continuous supply of African slave labor.

Although the Spanish Crown supported the new industry, even to the extent of lending the early Cuban sugar producers 40,000 ducats (about 90,000 dollars) in 1595, production faltered. The high volume of Brazilian sugar exports to the European market served to depress further the Spanish-American export trade. But Spanish-American sugar production for domestic consumption remained high and economically attractive in Peru, Mexico, and the larger islands. Unfortunately, the technology of Spanish sugar production remained stagnant, and not until the late eighteenth century did the Spanish return to large-scale sugar production for export.

The supply of slaves, on which any large-scale sugar industry depended, did not increase rapidly. African coastal stations had to be found, trade relations with Africans established, and the exchange of European merchandise for Africans and other Africa-derived commercial products coordinated. Though important, the African slave trade was only one component of a complex, competitive trading system. So competitive was the international slave trade that, like in the earlier experience of colonization, private entrepreneurs sought and obtained the full support and military resources of their states to assist them in carving out and defending their niche in the system. Thus the English and Dutch fought over access rights to the African ports until the Dutch formally recognized the trading rights of the Company of Royal Adventurers of England at the Treaty of Breda in 1667.

The Company of Royal Adventurers, succeeded in 1672 by the Royal Africa Company, was the typical private front for a state enterprise. Chartered by Charles II in 1663 and having members of the royal family among its subscribers, it replaced the commerce in dyewoods, gold, and ivory with the slave trade. Enthusiastically promising to deliver three thousand Africans to the English sugar colonies annually at a cost of seventeen pounds sterling per head, the company failed miserably in achieving its goal. By March 1664, the company had landed thirty-three cargoes totaling 2,364 slaves at Barbados; the average selling price exceeded twenty pounds per slave per cargo. Despite a cost price of three pounds per African at the point of purchase, the company proved neither competitive nor profitable and went bankrupt in 1671.

The Royal Africa Company was only marginally more successful. The transatlantic slave trade stubbornly refused to be monopolized by either a single chartered company or a single trading nation. The records of the Royal Africa Company between 1673 and 1684 illustrate the problems inherent in the slave-delivering component of the South Atlantic System. In the twelve years between 1673 and 1684, the company landed eighty-four cargoes totaling 16,274 slaves for an average cargo size of 194 slaves and an average annual importation rate of 1,356 slaves. The average selling price of the slaves at Barbados over the twelve years, payable in muscovado sugar, varied between twelve pounds and twenty pounds per slave per cargo, with the highest prices got for twenty-nine slaves sold "to a Spaniard at 25 pounds per head" in 1681. This was a profitable-enough price to attract private, noncompany traders who did not have to bear the enormous overhead expenses of the company. Given the annual demand in Barbados based on the previous agreement of 1663 to deliver three thousand slaves per year, the performance of the Royal Africa Company fell far short of its promise. Indeed, it came close to the required minimum only in 1683 when it brought in eighteen cargoes with 2,963 slaves. In only two years, 1681 and 1683, did the company manage to land more than ten cargoes at Barbados, leaving considerable room for private, noncompany deliveries. Eventually, with its carrying capacity further depleted by war, the company resorted to subcontracting its quota of slaves in return for a flat fee. Nothing, however, could save the company, and finally in 1698, it lost its legal monopoly of the English transatlantic slave trade.

Despite the constant depredations of war, the importation of slaves expanded rapidly in the Caribbean after 1650. The arriving Africans not only completely offset the demographic decline of the postconquest and early settlement periods, but contributed to greater social and demographic variation. Sugar and slavery provided the catalysts for these changes, and the volume of both increased steadily until during the eighteenth century the Caribbean distinguished itself as the premier location for the importation of slaves and the production of sugar. Every colony sought to produce plantation staples of any kind, and every successful plantation depended on a constantly replenished supply of African slaves.

The Caribbean received nearly one-half of all Africans brought to the Americas in the 350-year span of the organized transatlantic slave trade. During the seventeenth century, the Caribbean accepted more than 50 percent of all arriving Africans in the New World. By 1700, the English Antillean sugar colonies had imported some 263,000 slaves. The French Caribbean had imported 156,000. The Dutch Antilles had absorbed 40,000, while the Spanish Caribbean producers had bought a fair proportion of the 292,000 slaves supplied to the Spanish-American empire during the 1600s. By comparison, Brazil had imported about 560,000 slaves, accounting for nearly 42 percent of the total Atlantic slave trade.

The growth of the slave trade and slavery paralleled the expansion of sugar production. Within forty years after the introduction of sugarcane, Barbados was producing 8,000 metric tons of sugar from about 350 estates operating in 1680. The French Antilles had about 300 estates in 1670, producing nearly 12,000 metric tons of sugar, more than one-third the total production of Brazil in that year. Guadeloupe alone in 1674 was producing 2,106 metric tons of sugar, employing the labor of about 43,000 slaves.

The eighteenth century was the heyday of the slave plantation society in the Caribbean. Sugar and slavery penetrated all parts of the Antilles. Altogether, the planters of the Caribbean bought nearly 4 million African slaves, equivalent to about 60 percent of all the slaves sold throughout the Americas between 1701 and 1810. The English Antilles imported more than 1.4 million slaves, or about 23 percent of the total transatlantic trade. The French Antilles followed closely with more than 1.3 million, or slightly above 22 percent of the trade. The Spanish Caribbean, having seriously entered the sugar business in the later half of the eighteenth century, accounted for about 580,000 slaves, or slightly less than 10 percent of the market. The Dutch, transshipping a fair proportion of those arriving in their entrepôts, accounted for some 460,000, or about 7.6 percent, while the Danish Antilles imported some 25,000. By comparison, during the same period of time,

Brazil imported slightly less than 2 million slaves, or 31 percent of the market, while British North America (after 1776 the United States of America) accepted about 350,000, approximately 6 percent.

During the nineteenth century, the system began to disintegrate, attacked both from within and from without. By 1808, the English had abolished their slave trade and had begun a serious campaign to destroy the trade everywhere. The importation of slaves to their Caribbean possessions declined sharply. The slave revolt that terminated French political hegemony on Saint-Domingue also terminated the market for slaves. Only the Spanish Antilles and Brazil continued to expand their markets. Even so, the decline of the slave trade was absolute as well as relative until it finally ended about 1870. Between 1811 and 1870, less than 2 million slaves were sold in the Americas, a sharp drop from the nearly 5 million sold in the previous century. But even before the English action to terminate the trade in 1808, the system had already entered its crisis. The figures of slaves sold in the Americas reflected the economic condition of the region, especially among the staple-producing tropical areas like the Caribbean. While the system was being constructed during the sixteenth century, slave imports averaged about 2,000 per year. Between 1601 and 1700, the annual average increased to more than 13,000 slaves per year. During the period of highest expansion between 1701 and 1810, the average importation rates climbed to more than 55,000 slaves per year—although by the 1790s the rate had already fallen to just about 40,000. And between 1811 and 1870, the rate stood at about 32,000 per year. As Philip Curtin pointed out in his book, *The Atlantic Slave Trade,* approximately 80 percent of all the Africans brought to the Americas arrived between 1701 and 1870.

Altogether, the Caribbean region formed the host society for about 5 million Africans—if we accept the total African arrivals in the Americas to be around 10 million. Given the transportation facilities of the time, this constituted one of the greatest migrations of modern times, although the migrants went unwillingly and with no prospect of ever returning to their homelands. Africans arrived at the rate of more than 14,000 per year between 1601 and 1810, with their distribution varying according to the agricultural development and hence the labor needs of any particular zone. Economic prosperity, measured in terms of the quantity of land under cultivation and the volume of tropical staple exports, constituted the most powerful magnet for the African slave traders. But a prosperity based on agricultural exports tended to be transient. As soil fertility and land availability diminished in each territory, the prospect of easy wealth from agriculture and the demand for slaves consequently fell.

This correlation between new land under cultivation and the high volume of slave imports demonstrated a sequential occurrence throughout the Caribbean involving both intra-imperial and inter-imperial trends. Seen in the conventional terms of the sugar revolutions, it is quite clear that the English Caribbean islands tended to experience the first wave of intensification, followed closely by the French, with the Spanish colonies belatedly participating. Barbados was the first English and Caribbean colony to experience the interrelated series of revolutions.

By 1680, Barbados was perhaps the most valuable tropical colony in the world, and it received the largest supply of Africans. By 1750, Jamaica had superseded Barbados, only to lose its eminence to French Saint-Domingue by 1780. Cuba eclipsed all colonies to become the largest single producer of cane sugar and the "jewel of the Spanish Crown" after 1830. As predominantly monocultural plantation exporters, the Caribbean colonies assumed a commercial importance that transcended the mere buying of slaves and foodstuffs and the selling of sugar, tobacco, indigo, and cotton. The region demanded a variety of imports that not only undermined the structure of mercantilistic imperialism, but catapulted the region into the position of being a key element of international trading during the period. The resultant multifaceted trading system, of which the Caribbean was a part, had connections with North America, South America, Europe, and Africa. From those distant regions came fish, firearms, horses, flour, meat, barrel staves, nails, lumber, tools, slaves, machinery, cloth, furniture, utensils, paper, and a range of luxury products to supply the economic, dietary, and production needs of the tropical plantation societies.

The so-called sugar colonies were never exclusively producers of sugar. Yet sugar and sugar by-products remained the mainstay of their economies and the unvarying measure of their success or failure. As such, the volume of sugar production tended to increase in direct proportion to the increase in the slave population until the beginning of a technological revolution in Cuba during the 1840s. A few examples illustrate the correlation between sugar and slavery. In 1712, Barbados produced 6,343 tons of sugar and had a slave population of 42,000. By 1800, production had stabilized at about 19,000 tons, and the slave population stood at 82,000. By 1730, Jamaica was producing about 15,000 tons of sugar and had a population of 74,500 slaves. In 1808, the slave population was 324,000 and the sugar output was 77,800 tons. In Saint-Domingue, the slave population grew from 206,000 in 1764 to 480,000 in 1791, while sugar production during the same period increased from approximately 60,000 tons to nearly 80,000 tons. For Cuba, the slave population increased from 44,300 in 1774 to 286,000 in 1827, while the production of sugar climbed from 10,000 tons to 70,000 tons. The gross totals tend to disguise the variations in sugar production as well as the fluctuations in the importation of slaves. They do indicate, however, the rapidity with which the colonies moved into high-scale sugar production with a series of social repercussions that are discussed in Chapter 5.

By the eighteenth century, "sugar was king" throughout the Caribbean. Ralph Davis graphically noted this dominance in *The Rise of the Atlantic Economies*:

> Sugar production, once it had been introduced, showed a tendency to engulf whole islands in single-crop cultivation, and it created its own form of society whose stamp still lies upon the Caribbean. There were exceptions: the small islands of Grenada and Dominica had single-crop coffee economies for some decades of the eighteenth century, and colonies with great land areas, St. Domingue and especially Brazil, could produce immense sugar crops while still retaining some variety in cultivation. But the value of the Caribbean colonies to

Europe came to be in their sugar production. So overwhelmingly did it dominate island economy and society, so vital was it even to Brazil, that the main feature of the life of Europe's tropical colonies are best set out in terms of the movement towards sugar, and the adaptation of society to the needs of its production. After 1660 England's sugar imports always exceeded its combined imports of all colonial produce; in 1774 sugar made up just half of all French imports from her West Indian colonies; over the colonial period as a whole more than half Brazil's exports of goods were sugar. Sugar made up almost a fifth of the whole English import bill of 1774, far surpassing the share of any other commodity.

Sugar and its associated by-products, rum and molasses, accounted for 81 percent of the exports of the British Caribbean in 1770. The second-place export commodity was coffee, accounting for 11 percent. At the same time, the French Antilles showed a slightly higher variation, with sugar-related exports amounting to 49 percent of exports; coffee, 24 percent; indigo, 14 percent; and cotton, 8 percent. In 1855, Cuba had an overwhelming 84 percent of its export trade in sugar, with second-place tobacco accounting for less than 8 percent. The situation varied from island to island, but except for the designedly free-port trading islands of the Dutch, such as St. Martin, St. Eustatius, and Curaçao, the situation remained the same. Sugar exports dominated most Caribbean economies.

The export-import economy was only one facet of the Caribbean economic structure, albeit an important one. The mature plantation complex not only created two societies by the late eighteenth century—one Euro-American, the other Afro-American—it also created two economies—one external, the other internal. And like the social division, the two economies coexisted in a symbiotic relationship. For if the export of plantation products and the import of consumer articles were major economic activities, they were integrally related to the system's internal marketing of local provisions, as well as the distribution and merchandising done locally by a significant sector of the population.

The import-export trade was more complex than the selling and shipping abroad of the local harvest. Each colony traded not only with its metropolis, but legally and illegally with foreigners. J. Stewart aptly captured the multilateral dimensions of colonial trade in Jamaica in the 1820s when he wrote: "The commerce of Jamaica may be classified under the following heads: The trade with the mother country—which is far more considerable than all the other branches together; the trade with British North America; and the trade with the island of Cuba and the Spanish islands, the Spanish Main or Tierra Firma [sic], and territories on the American continent formerly belonging to Spain." And indeed, Jamaica was an important trade mart. During the entire eighteenth century and as late as 1839, fully 50 percent of the trade of Cartagena was conducted with Jamaica. The necessities of trade transcended the neatness of imperial boundaries. In the 1850s, Cuba traded with its metropolis, Spain, the United States, England, Germany, France, Mexico, Venezuela, and Jamaica. Figures for Puerto Rico in 1843 amply demonstrate how complex external trading had become by that time. The island exported its products in British ships to the West Indian islands, England, and

Canada; in Danish, American, Hanseatic, and Dutch ships to England; and in Spanish ships to Spain and Canada. The exported items included sugar, tobacco, dry and salted hides, horses, mules, cattle, coconuts, coffee, beans, tortoise shells, and timber. Imported items included olive oil, brandy, beer, gin, wine, salted beef and pork, hams, figs, fish, raisins, rice, cocoa, flour, lard, butter, cheese, potatoes, garlic, onions, barrel staves, lumber, iron hoops, plates and bars, nails, glass, agricultural tools, soap, utensils, medicines, tobacco, candles, perfumes, and domestic supplies.

The absence of a coordinated banking system and adequate common currencies restricted much of the trade to the form of a complicated system of barter, in which locally produced goods were accepted and then reexported along with a variety of coins. This lack of any systematic banking system plus the perennial shortage of coins for small-scale transactions were continual complaints of colonists in the tropics until the middle of the nineteenth century.

Strategically located free ports supplemented the direct importation and export of commodities. Janet Schaw, the elusive "Lady of Quality" from Edinburgh, Scotland (and third cousin of Sir Walter Scott 1771–1832), who visited St. Eustatius on January 19, 1775, wrote a very graphic description of one of the most bustling Caribbean free ports at that time:

> We landed on St. Eustatia, a free port, which belongs to the Dutch; a place of vast traffic from every quarter of the globe. The ships of various nations which rode before it were very fine, but the Island itself the only ugly one I have seen. Nor do I think I would stay on it for any bribe. . . . The whole riches of the Island consist in its merchandize, and they are obliged to the neighbouring Islands for subsistence; while they in return furnish them with contraband commodities of all kinds. . . . But never did I meet with such variety; here was a merchant vending his goods in Dutch, another in French, a third in Spanish, etc. etc. They all wear the habit of their country and the diversity is really amusing. . . . From one end of the town of Eustatia to the other is a continued mart, where goods of the most different uses and qualities are displayed before the shop-doors. Here hang rich embroideries, painted silks, flowered Muslins, with all the Manufactures of the Indies. Just by hang Sailor's Jackets, Trousers, shoes, hats, etc. Next stall contains most exquisite silver plate, the most beautiful indeed I ever saw, and close by these, iron pots, kettles and shovels. Perhaps the next presents you with French and English Millinary wares. But it were endless to enumerate the variety of merchandize in such a place, for in every store you find everything, be their qualities ever so opposite. I bought a quality of excellent French gloves for fourteen pence a pair, also English thread-stockings cheaper than I could buy them at home.

Miss Schaw was lucky, for the next year the outbreak of the American Revolution brought unrelieved depression to the free ports of the Caribbean. St. Eustatius would never again be as exotic as she saw it.

The other side of the economic coin was the internal, or interisland, marketing system. This internal economy had two dimensions. The first was the coastal and interisland retail trade that took the goods of the large commission merchants in the principal ports and distributed them via small coastal vessels of less than seventy tons to smaller merchants who served the planting as well as free village communities. Here, as in the export trade, barter and credit were the major operating media, although all items bore a discounted cash price. "A wharfinger's receipt for a puncheon of rum, endorsed by a payer," wrote Stewart, "passes in payment as readily as a bill or draft would do; so that these articles become a sort of circulating medium, and it is not unusual for a puncheon of rum, or other commodity, to pass through twenty or more different hands, without ever being moved from the wharf-store where it was deposited by its original owner, into whose possession it may again ultimately return."

The other dimension of the internal marketing system consisted of the local markets with their hawkers who supplied the plantations and the free citizens with ground provisions, livestock, smallstock, poultry, and eggs. Unlike the other facets of trade, however, these peddlers dealt mainly in cash, further accentuating the scarcity of specie in the colonies. The internal marketing system was dominated by free persons of color. Slaves participated too, but during the eighteenth century, a series of laws gradually proscribed their economic activities. The Jamaica Assembly in 1711 prohibited slaves from owning livestock or from selling meat, fish, sugarcane, or any manufactured item without the written permission of their masters. The authorities in St. Lucia passed laws in 1734 and 1735 that prevented slaves from dealing in coffee or cotton, the principal export crops. The French Antilles also passed laws in 1744 and 1765 that removed the opportunities for slaves either to trade in cattle or to engage in the occupation of butcher, while huckstering by slaves was prohibited on plantations or in towns. In 1767, St. Vincent forbade slaves to plant or sell any crop exported from the island. In the 1840s, the Cubans restricted the occupations and movement of the free, nonwhite members of the society, thereby precluding their huckstering and other means of working.

The planter class that formulated the laws restricting the economic activities of the nonwhites were motivated by self-interest. They disliked unnecessary local competition, and economic subordination facilitated the social control of the majority of the population. Nevertheless, the laws could not be effectively enforced, and the gradual collapse of the economic and political worlds of the slaveholders opened more and more opportunities for the nonwhites. By the middle of the nineteenth century, nonwhites were, individually and collectively, buying up bankrupt and abandoned estates throughout the Caribbean, and peasant economies were competing strongly with the plantation economies for land and labor.

SUGGESTED READINGS

Cañizares-Esguerra, Jorge, and Seeman, Erik R., eds. *The Atlantic in Global History, 1500–2000.* Upper Saddle River, N.J.: Prentice Hall, 2007.

Canny, Nicholas, and Pagden, Anthony, eds. *Colonial Identity in the Atlantic World, 1500–1800.* Princeton, N.J.: Princeton University Press, 1987.

Coclanis, Peter A., ed. *The Atlantic Economy During the Seventeenth and Eighteenth Centuries: Organization, Operation, Practice, and Personnel.* Columbia: University of South Carolina Press, 2005.

Curtin, Philip D. *The Atlantic Slave Trade: A Census.* Madison: University of Wisconsin Press, 1969.

Eltis, David. *The Rise of African Slavery in the Americas.* Cambridge, England: Cambridge University Press, 2000.

Ely, Roland T. *Cuando reinaba su majestad el azúcar: estudio histórico-sociológico de una tragedia Latino-Americana,* 2nd ed. Havana: Imagen Contemporánea, 2001.

Garrigus, John D., and Morris, Christopher., eds. *Assumed Identities: The Meanings of Race in the Atlantic World.* Arlington, Tex.: A&M Press, 2010.

Goveia, Elsa V. *Slave Society in the British Leeward Islands at the End of the Eighteenth Century.* New Haven, Conn.: Yale University Press, 1965.

Hamilton, Douglas J. *Scotland, the Caribbean and the Atlantic World, 1750–1820.* Manchester, England: Manchester University Press, 2005.

Higman, B. W. *Slave Population and Economy in Jamaica, 1807–1834.* Cambridge, England: Cambridge University Press, 1976.

Higman, B. W. *The Slave Populations of the British Caribbean, 1807–1834.* Baltimore, Md.: Johns Hopkins University Press, 1984.

Higman, B. W. "The Sugar Revolution." *Economic History Review,* 53 (May 2000): 213–236.

Klein, Herbert S. *The Atlantic Slave Trade.* New York: Cambridge University Press, 1999.

Klein, Herbert S., and Vinson, Ben III. *African Slavery in Latin America and the Caribbean.* 2nd ed. New York: Oxford University Press, 2007.

Moreno Fraginals, Manuel. *El ingenio: el complejo económico-social cubano del azúcar, 1760–1860.* 3 vols. Havana: Ciencias Sociales, 1976.

Thomas, Hugh. *The Slave Trade: The Story of the Atlantic Slave Trade: 1440–1870.* New York: Simon & Schuster, 1997.

Whyte, Iain. *Scotland and the Abolition of Black Slavery, 1756–1838.* Edinburgh: Edinburgh University Press, 2006.

CHAPTER 5

Social Structure of the Plantation Society

Virginia and Barbados were first peopled by a sort of loose,
vagrant People, vicious and destitute of means to live at home
(being either unfit for labour, or such as could find none to
employ themselves about, or had so misbehaved themselves by
Whoring, Thieving, or other Debauchery, that none would set
them to work) which Merchants and Masters of Ships by Their
Agents (or Spirits as they were called) gathered up about the
streets of London, and other places, cloathed and transported
to be employed upon Plantations....

—JOSIAH CHILD,
New Discourse on Trade, 1688

Throughout the Caribbean the slave-labor plantation complex inexorably
succeeded the faltering attempts to create a viable settler society patterned
after European antecedents. Designed to produce tropical staples for the temperate, mainly European markets, these slave-based plantation complexes eventually
evolved from artificial communities to composite societies. But they were societies
with some unusual characteristics. Nowhere throughout the plantation Caribbean
did enslaved social units procreate and maintain their demographic viability as
other social units did in Africa, Europe, and the indigenous American communities. As a rule, the Caribbean plantation society demonstrated some erratic,
eclectic, and artlessly contrived traits: predominantly male, predominantly adult,
predominantly nonfree, and relentlessly coerced. Nevertheless, it would be a gross
exaggeration to assert that these societies were not dynamic, resilient, creative, and
strong. By the late eighteenth century, when the Caribbean slave society attained
its highest stage of development, it had assumed a distinctive form. Masters and
slaves, merchants and shippers, rulers and ruled, free and nonfree, white and nonwhite all constituted a closely integrated, mutually interdependent grouping of
distinct castes and classes. In the Caribbean case, however, castes were neither as
rigid nor as impermeable as the classic Indian caste system.

Within the plantation complex, no one group—neither the masters nor their
slaves—fashioned this strange world all by themselves. Rather, it was a world that

developed slowly as a result of the equal participation of both the masters and the slaves. To speak of a "world the slaveholders made" provides a catchy, eloquent phrase but does less than full justice to the confusing reality. Masters and slaves did not, and could not, form two totally independent communities. Together, both masters and slaves formed a curious world apart from the normal original American, African, or European experience. Time and the exigencies of the plantation export economy hallowed their Creolized traditions, calcified their peculiar relationships, and tended to freeze such views as the inhabitants of the region had of themselves and their role in the universe of production and commerce. Thus arose the misleading and static view that many nineteenth-century writers portrayed of the vast, variegated region stretching from the North Atlantic seaboard to the Northeast of Brazil, which they deemed "Afro-America." The Caribbean plantation complex formed the center of this spectrum of societies and cultures—and it was a very important economic center until the whole system began to fall apart during the nineteenth century.

Before this prolonged process of disintegration, however, some notorious internal ambiguities and contradictions manifested themselves within these slave societies. And nowhere were these ambiguities and contradictions more pronounced than in the overlapping structures of castes and classes. The caste system represented the most notable aspect of the plantation society. The typical slave society had three legally defined castes that were stubbornly supported partly by force, partly by custom, and partly by impromptu legal ingenuity. In ascending order of social status (and often population size), these three castes were the slaves, the free persons of color, and the white persons. Each component required a separate set of criteria to define and distinguish it, which further contributed to the contradictions and ambiguities. Occupation and stipulated legal disabilities patently separated the subordinate slave component from the two free sectors of the society. Slaves were slaves only because they were bought as such and condemned legally to that status. Originally the relationship with African descent was merely coincidental. In the earliest period of constructing the complex, servants and slaves were often interchangeable labels applied indiscriminately to servile Europeans or Africans, but by the end of the seventeenth century, the term *slave* connoted African origin and menial occupation. A narrowing of the definition had already begun to take place. At the same time, within the realm of the free, ethnicity, phenotype, and attributed status largely determined the caste boundaries between the white sector and the other nonwhite sector, subdivided into free blacks and free mulattoes. As far as the distinction could be made, free mulattoes represented the result of inescapable miscegenation within the complex.

This general description of the castes sometimes broke down in specific circumstances. Small islands, such as Bermuda, the Caymans, St. Barthélemy, Carriacou, and the Grenadines; commercial entrepôts, such as Curaçao; or economically undeveloped territories, such as Puerto Rico, tended to approximate less the classic structure of the plantation society than the larger, more productive places. The prevailing ambiguities and inherent contradictions of the plantation structure continually operated to undermine rigidity and permitted vagueness, uncertainty, overlap, and social "passing" on a limited scale—most notably along the peripheral penumbra of the two free castes, as well as between free colored and slaves. Slaves could become members of the free colored community, and occasionally free coloreds could become members of the white community.

Each caste was further internally subdivided into classes or ranks. Each social class varied in size, function, and consequently in the intensity of its acceptance of, or hostility to, the overall system. And like the definition of castes, class and status designations were also complex. Within the white caste, economic and occupational indices figured prominently in designating individual social position and status. Normally prestige correlated with the ownership of slaves and plantations. Within the intermediate stratum of the free persons of color, race and color—or more precisely complexion and shades of color—determined status and rank. In most cases, free mulattoes were considered (and considered themselves) to be superior in status to free blacks. Race and color distinguished the free groups, and freedom, however tenuously held, separated them from the status of slaves. Among the slaves, occupation was probably the most important criterion for social ranking. Skilled and domestic slaves generally enjoyed higher social status than did non-skilled field slaves. Each caste therefore had its elaborate pecking order, a factor that might have contributed to internal social mobility either laterally across the vertical divisions of caste or upward through the horizontal divisions of classes or ranks. This internal social mobility contributed to the cohesion and longevity of the slave society, but it also generated enormous discontent within the various segments and eventually contributed to its demise.

The conventional demographic profile of the slave society was that of a narrow-peaked triangle, horizontally divided into three segments. The broad base of this triangle represented the vast majority of slaves. In the fifteenth and early sixteenth centuries, these slaves were entirely African- or Iberian-born, but as the demand grew and the system expanded, an increasing proportion was born in the Americas. Nevertheless, throughout the history of slavery, the society depended more on imports than procreation to maintain its population. Africans constituted the first major immigrant stream to enter the Americas after the fifteenth century, albeit in bondage. African-born slaves were called *bozales*, while those born in the Americas were called Creoles or Afro-Americans.

Miscegenation between the imported African slaves and all the other ethnic groups also produced a new mixed-blood substratum of individuals designated mestizo or mulatto who fell into the categories of slave and free. Eventually the mixed population formed the middle band of the triangle, an important, intermediate segment uncomfortably juxtaposed between the upper and the lower orders of society, between the fully free and the thoroughly enslaved, between white and nonwhite. Generally this group was labeled the free people of color, uncharitably referred to by an English colonial governor as "the unappropriated people." The free people of color shared qualities of both the free and the nonfree. Ethnically divided into black and mulatto like the slave sector, they suffered a circumscribed freedom that probably accentuated their ambiguity and contributed to their psychological disorientation. Throughout the eighteenth century and after, the free persons of color fought doggedly to preserve their individual liberty and legal status.

The small apex of the triangle represented the white population. Small in number, diverse in background, and varied in original culture, this group possessed the economic and political power within the society and exercised an inordinate influence on local culture. The Caribbean, after all, served the purposes of Europe and the Europeans.

The pyramidal illustration of Caribbean slave societies, however, reflects only the most fully developed systems found primarily in the English and French Caribbean during the eighteenth and early nineteenth centuries. There, the white population represented between 3 percent and 11 percent of the total colonial population, respectively. The proportion of slaves and free varied considerably from place to place, reflecting the degree of agricultural development or the nature of the local economy. In some places, the whites consistently formed a large group. In the early nineteenth century, the white population comprised 23 percent of the inhabitants of the Bahamas, 48 percent in Bermuda, 44 percent in Cuba, and 51 percent in Puerto Rico. That the presence of plantations played a major role in determining the population composition may be seen in the case of the Dutch Caribbean in the nineteenth century. On the trading islands of St. Eustatius, St. Martin, and Curaçao, the whites accounted for slightly more than 17 percent of the population. By sharp contrast, in the plantation colony of Surinam (now Suriname), the whites, although equal to the number in Curaçao, represented slightly more than 4 percent of the population.

By custom and often by law, any person of European birth or ancestry, regardless of economic circumstance, intellectual ability, or educational achievement, enjoyed a social status superior to that of every nonwhite person. As the slave-based plantation economic system matured throughout the eighteenth century, a concomitant social complex based on the mutually reinforcing cleavages of race, color, and occupation not only manifested itself throughout the Caribbean, but became indelible and pervasive. On the plantations as well as in the cities away from the plantations, the color of one's skin immediately and effectively fixed both social position and occupation, with blackness indicating low status and arduous menial labor and whiteness indicating superiority and leisure. Such was the condition of the Caribbean colonies until the later decades of the nineteenth century, when association with the plantation and its occupational structure no longer provided a reliable index of either caste or class. When that occurred, however, the plantation complex was already in an advanced stage of disintegration.

Fully developed plantation societies all exhibited common characteristics. Both the concentration on export agriculture and population composition indicated the degree of participation in and the stage of maturity of the particular colony within the context of the South Atlantic System. In general, the most vigorous and most mature structures revealed a preponderance of Africans and Afro-Americans. In plantation zones, slaves outnumbered the free by ratios varying

between two to one and thirty to one. At the beginning of the nineteenth century, the entire population of the Caribbean islands and their neighboring enclaves
of Berbice, Demerara, Essequibo, Surinam, Guiana, and British Honduras (now
Belize) amounted to about 2 million inhabitants, with about two-thirds of that
number being slaves.

The size and composition of local populations fluctuated according to the
nature and state of the economy. In times of prosperity, the total number of people
increased. Economic depressions or shrinking fortunes diminished the community, especially among the white, plantation-owning sector. For example, in 1781
the small Dutch island colony of St. Eustatius (commonly called Statia) was both a
flourishing free port and a prominent sugar exporter. Of a total of approximately
twenty thousand inhabitants, nearly fifteen thousand were slaves working on a
number of sugar plantations. The English captured and sacked the island, and its
fortunes rapidly declined. By 1840, the population of St. Eustatius had dwindled to
less than four hundred white persons and two thousand slaves. The Spanish island
of Cuba presented an opposite change. In 1774, Cuba had a population of 171,620
of which only 44,333 (25.8 percent) were slaves. By 1827, with the sugar revolution fairly advanced, the total population of the island increased dramatically to
704,487, of whom 286,942 (40.7 percent) were slaves. The common feature of the
sugar revolutions in the Caribbean was the rapid increase of a servile black population at the expense of the free-white settler population. The plantation complex
changed the focus of agricultural enterprises and the composition of the local population. This created economic, demographic, and social changes of considerable
importance.

The Caribbean slave societies were very complex social organizations.
Although the slaves formed the lowest castelike stratum of the entire population,
they were just as elaborately subdivided for purposes of occupation, management, and rank as the free castes. The most basic division was along lines of color,
between the African and Afro-Caribbean slaves (usually referred to as the "black"
slaves) on the one hand and the miscegenated or "colored" slaves (most frequently
called mulattoes or *pardos* in the Spanish islands) on the other. Slaves of mixed
race, however, do not seem to have been a significant factor in the overall slave
population before the nineteenth century. The overall decline of the slave trade—
facilitated by the abolition of the English transatlantic slave trade in 1808—and
normal increases in the birthrate produced an increasing proportion of mulattoes,
mestizos, and other persons of mixed blood throughout the region.

In 1800, the mixed slave population on Worthy Park Estate in central Jamaica
accounted for only about 5 percent of the estate's slave labor force. This percentage does not seem to vary significantly from the general pattern for agricultural
populations recently involved in intensive plantation production. Indeed, Barry
Higman, reviewing the situation for the British Caribbean in the early nineteenth
century, suggested that "around 1817 slaves of color made up roughly 12 percent
of the total slave population in the first-phase sugar colonies [Antigua, Barbados,
Jamaica, Nevis, Montserrat, and St. Kitts], 10 percent in the marginal colonies

[Anguilla, the Bahamas, Barbuda, British Honduras, and the Cayman Islands], 8 percent in the second-phase sugar colonies [Dominica, Grenada, St. Vincent, and Tobago], and 4 percent in the third-phase sugar colonies [Berbice, Demarara, Essequibo, St. Lucia, and Trinidad]." In Cuba, as late as 1846, the mulatto slaves accounted for 12,791 of a total slave force of 323,759—slightly less than 4 percent. Higman found that the slave registers reveal that the overall mulatto slave population might have been between 10 and 12 percent of the total Jamaican slave population in 1820. Such an increased percentage would not necessarily be at variance with the Worthy Park Estate findings of Michael Craton and James Walvin, since the proportion of mulattoes would have increased after the termination of the English slave trade. Moreover, since colored slaves were more frequently found among domestic and urban slaveholdings than rural ones, the increase could also be explained by an increased urban concentration as the Jamaican sugar economy declined during the nineteenth century.

Urban centers seemed to have produced a greater concentration of persons of mixed blood—slave as well as free—than did the plantations. Many travel accounts made this observation. Janet Schaw, the Scottish "lady of quality" who traveled through the West Indies and South Carolina on the eve of the American Revolution, described "crouds [sic] of Mullatoes [sic]...in the streets, houses and indeed everywhere" in the town of St. Johns, Antigua. Most Caribbean towns would have given a similar impression, especially to the eye that could not discriminate between the free and the slave. In Havana, according to the census of 1828, the colored slaves numbered 1,010, or 12.6 percent of a total slave population of 8,005. By contrast, the free coloreds numbered 8,215 of a total free nonwhite population of 23,562, a proportion slightly less than 35 percent. On the island of Puerto Rico, the free-colored population in 1860 represented 41.3 percent (241,037 persons) of a total 583,181 inhabitants, and combined with the colored slaves, probably represented the largest component of the population.

Slaves of mixed ancestry were not generally regarded as good field workers. As a result, there was a concentration of these slaves in urban areas and in the domestic, skilled, and artisanal trades. These occupations provided both the exposure and the income that facilitated the movement from slavery to freedom, thereby reinforcing the notion that lightness of skin color lubricated upward social mobility. Consequently, slaves of mixed heritage felt that they were generally superior in rank to African and Afro-American slaves, and this sentiment permeated every society in which the norms for grace and beauty were those established by the superordinate white sector.

Other subtle distinctions followed. Slaves born in the Caribbean felt socially superior to their relatives and colleagues who were not. Obviously these Creole slaves had some advantages over their African counterparts. They were physically acclimatized as well as mentally socialized to the conduct and routine of the plantation and local culture, and in some cases they spoke and understood the local languages. Yet familiarity brought few material benefits to Creole slaves. Moreover, the curious Creole Afro-Caribbean sentiment of enhanced status may have been based solely on the reflected impressions and unquestioned acceptance of the pre-vailing white biases. The white colonists, after all, continuously condemned the Africans as "savages," claimed that exposure to the rigors of the tropical plantation "civilized" them, and in some cases were willing to pay more for locally born black slaves than for recently imported African ones.

If color provided one criterion for rank among slaves, occupation provided another. Edward Brathwaite, in his study of Jamaica, divided the slaves into five occupational groups on the basis of the convenient distribution of functions on the plantation and in the economy: field slaves, usually called praedial slaves; mechanic and domestic slaves; slaves working as hired hands; and skilled, pro-fessional, or semiprofessional and managerial slaves. Some of these categories depended to a great extent on the type of society, the size of the category engaged in the activity, and the number of slaves held by the slave owner. Nevertheless, cer-tain common patterns emerged. Field slaves, as indicated earlier, were generally considered lowest in rank. They were the most numerous group. Edward Long estimated that about 160,000 of the approximately 220,000 slaves in Jamaica in 1787 were field slaves, more than 72 percent. Rural slaves accounted for the vast majority of slaves throughout the Caribbean, although it should be noted that the difference between rural and urban in the nineteenth century could not be sharply defined. In 1855, at the height of the Cuban sugar revolution, about 81 percent of the slaves were registered as rural slaves, indicating an extremely high proportion of field slaves.

But even these field slaves had their own internal social ranking as well as their own preference for certain tasks, and these rankings and preferences did not necessarily correspond with those of their masters. Nevertheless, the records of the masters predominate in the historical archives. Slave masters ranked slaves accord-ing to their utility in the production process or their personal needs. Ranking, however, was an arbitrary procedure, more common on established, large, special-ized estates than on small, multicrop estates. On Irwin Estate in St. James Parish in Jamaica, the slaves were listed in the following order: first gang, second gang, third gang, tradesmen, pen-keepers, domestics, watchmen, grass cutters, invalids, young children. The cattle were also listed in an order that suggested value: work-ing stock, bulls, young working stock, mules, cows, calves, fattening cattle. The listing of slaves was similar on Peruvian Vale Estate in St. Vincent, with the order being first gang, second gang, third gang, tradesmen, jobbers, domestics, watch-men, stockkeepers, cattle and mule boys, "at works," superannuated, children, and sick. The Peruvian Vale Estate task-allocation pattern clearly indicated that some flexibility occurred in assigning tasks, depending on the season and the needs of the plantation routine. When Rose Price took personal control of Worthy Park Estate, Jamaica, in the early 1790s, he divided his 483 slaves into seventeen differ-ent categories based on his assessment of their relation to production. This was a refinement of the seven or so categories into which the slaves were divided before his arrival. Slaves and cattle were the perennial concerns of the Caribbean planta-tion owner: their value, their health, their number, and their disposition.

Field slaves were the backbone of the plantation and the economy. The division into gangs represented the various degrees of physical strength and permitted the deployment of workers as units, whether the demands were heavy and rigorous, as they were during the crop season when the mill operated, or light and sporadic, as during the planting season and *tiempo muerto.* Gangs maximized productive efficiency and facilitated group management. The first gang on any estate was comprised of the most able-bodied males and females, with subsequent gangs organized according to a descending order of physical strength and ability. Some planters simplified the groupings, as did J. Stewart, who based his descriptions on his experiences in Jamaica:

> The plantation slaves are divided into three classes or *gangs*, as they are called, according to age and condition. The first gang consists of the ablest of both sexes, from sixteen to about fifty years of age, and are employed in the most laborious of the work; the second gang contains the elderly and weakly men and women, and boys and girls of from twelve to sixteen who have lighter work assigned to them; and the third, or what is called *small gang*, consists of the children of about six to twelve, attended by a female driver, and are employed in weeding the young plant-canes, and other easy work adopted to their strength. In most of the jobbing-gangs the different classes, with the exception of children, are improperly blended together. When the slaves are rendered unfit, by age or infirmity, for field labor, they are employed in occupations that require little bodily exertion; the men are placed as watchmen over the canes and provisions, and the women to take care of the children, or in other light employments.

Since a great deal of the labor on any estate—from the basic planting to the harvesting and ultimate preparation of the crop for export—remained repetitive, newly imported Africans could fit into the routine of the plantation without considerable difficulty or dislocation. After a period of seasoning and acclimatization that could last for up to three years, new slaves were placed alongside the older ones to learn the routine of the plantation. Most purchased Africans began and ended their enslavement working with the field gangs.

One frequently overlooked aspect of plantation slavery was the high degree of participation by women in all aspects of field and factory labor. Plantations in general demanded prime workers and placed their emphasis on able-bodied males in the fourteen-to-forty age category. For a number of reasons, women made up a large proportion of the workers on the older plantations. Their presence derived from the needs of social control as well as from the natural consequences of differential mortality rates and reproduction or the exigencies of an irregular market-supply mechanism. Sexual imbalance was not a pronounced feature of large estates. In Cuba during the middle years of the nineteenth century, male slaves in rural areas outnumbered the females by a ratio of slightly less than two to one. In 1857, the official returns for slaves gave a rural slave force of 193,187 males and 114,188 females. Urban slaves showed a slight majority of females, with 34,762 females and 30,848 males. Barbados, one of the first islands to complete its sugar revolution, consistently had more female than male slaves throughout the nineteenth century. In 1832, the island possessed 43,738 female slaves and 37,762 male slaves, or about 86 male slaves for every 100 female slaves. Until 1817, males outnumbered females in Jamaica. After that date, however, the female population gradually outnumbered the male population. In 1829, Jamaica had 164,167 females and 158,254 males in a total slave workforce of 322,421. The predominance of male slaves, then, was a feature of the moving plantation frontier found in rural Trinidad, Demerara, Essequibo, central Cuba, and the Ponce area of Puerto Rico during the nineteenth century. As the system matured, the imbalance tended to redress itself. As soon as the initial task of clearing the virgin forests of the tropical lands was completed, women served just as efficiently as men in the daily routine of cultivation, harvest, and manufacture.

In every colony, women worked alongside men in the majority of the occupations. In his study of the slave population of the British Caribbean, Barry Higman reported that "females were totally excluded from skilled trades other than sewing, and rarely worked in transportation and fishing, or served as 'watchmen'" and that "males were excluded only from washing and sewing." For many large established sugar estates, women may even have had a proportionately greater share of the arduous fieldwork than did men. On the Jamaican Worthy Park Estate, this was certainly the case at the end of the eighteenth century, and there is no reason to believe that the situation did not persist afterward. In 1789, Worthy Park Estate had a labor force of 339 slaves, 162 female and 177 male. Slightly more than 43 percent of its females (70 slaves) worked in the field gang, while just over 16 percent of the males (29 slaves) did. During the efficient reorganization by Rose Price between 1791 and 1793, the situation remained the same. In 1793, the labor force increased to 528 slaves, 244 women and 284 men. But again almost 44 percent of the women (107 slaves) worked in the fields, while only slightly more than 32 percent of the men (92 slaves) did so. A similar situation prevailed on La Ninfa Estate in Cuba in the 1820s. This large progressive estate, owned jointly by Francisco Arango y Parreño and the intendant, Pablo José Valiente, had 350 slaves. According to Manuel Moreno Fraginals, during the harvest of 1827 "cane was cut and loaded exclusively by women—who cut an average of 300 arrobas (3.5 tons) a day."

One curious, though probably typical, observation on the female labor force emerged from Higman's study of the Jamaican slave population just prior to emancipation in 1834. Higman found that women worked in the fields much longer, on average, than did men, probably corresponding to their longer life expectancy. He noted that "males were put to a fairly wide range of occupations, whereas females were confined almost entirely to field or domestic tasks." He also found relatively few female slaves of color among the field slaves. Indeed, the recruitment of black women for domestic work declined as soon as female slaves of color could be found. This pattern prevailed throughout the Caribbean and most likely reflected concepts about race, color, and physical ability held by the slave owners.

The slave system was a constantly changing one, but it responded to the demographic patterns. The relatively low percentages of field-labor participation by the two sexes on Worthy Park Estate indicate a regional trend throughout the nineteenth century. The system of slavery did not produce a very efficient process of labor employment. On the typical sugar estate—the largest employers of slaves—only about 50 percent of the workhands were capable, healthy, able-bodied participants in the field-production process. On La Ninfa in Cuba, an 1829 daily register of slaves showed that of 340 slaves, 26.5 percent (90 slaves) were infants, invalids, or deserters, and only 54.4 percent (185 slaves) were employed in the fields. Barbados appeared to be unique in the region for its large gangs of young children working in the fields under the supervision of a female driver. More men than women worked in the factory, however, while an unduly large number of slaves seemed to be in domestic service, especially while the owners were in residence.

Again, the Worthy Park experience was indicative. The great house, while normally vacant, employed two full-time domestics to maintain it. With the owners in residence, however, the number increased to a high figure of seventeen slaves. Robert Ellis, the overseer, began with one slave and within six years had a domestic staff of thirty-six slaves to serve only six white persons in 1795. Domestic slaves tended to form a larger category in the Spanish and French colonial societies than in the English, perhaps owing to the relatively larger residential white populations in the former societies. Nevertheless, domestic slaves were not merely servants of the white population, and their lives were not invariably superior to those of their rural counterparts. In reality, the distinction between domestic and field could be muted among slaves of small holdings, especially holdings in rural areas. On sugar estates in the English Caribbean, about 10 percent of the female slaves were domestics, but about 20 percent of the female slaves among the small holdings of coffee, cotton, cocoa, and ground-provision plantations or grazing pens were domestics.

As the historian Edward Brathwaite pointed out, domestic slaves sometimes considered themselves to be of a higher rank than field slaves. Some masters reinforced this impression by distinguishing the dress and nurturing the civility of the group and treating—in the most benevolent cases—their domestic slaves as part of a large extended family. Banishment to field labor was utilized as a form of punishment for disobedient or disgraced domestic slaves. One imperial master decreed that his mulatto stable boy be "stripped of his livery, degraded to a field negro" as punishment for some unspecified misdeed. In the Cuban antislavery novel, *Francisco*, written by Anselmo Suárez y Romero, the author has the protagonist whipped and condemned to join the field slaves by a cruel, jealous master. Despite this impression of a great gulf between field and domestic slaves, most domestic slaves served as either cooks or washerwomen, two tasks that could be both arduous and difficult—especially for fastidious owners.

Domestic slaves, like the general category of urban, skilled, or semi-independent slaves, did have certain advantages that were denied to most field slaves. They probably had more leisure time, were under less coercive control, and had more opportunities for self-purchase or *coartación* than their rural companions. Nevertheless, domestic and urban slaves displayed a dislike equal to that of field slaves of the entire system of slavery and demonstrated an equal proneness to flee the system.

Specialist slaves were found in both domestic and field categories and participated in a variety of occupations. They could be skilled, such as mechanics, carpenters, coopers, masons, sugar boilers, rum distillers, potters, weavers, seamstresses, tailors, shoemakers, assorted hired hands, superannuated watchmen, and caretakers of children, the last affectionately called *criolleras* in Cuba. Not all these skills were practiced full time throughout the year, and not all were necessary on all plantations. Small cocoa, coffee, and spice plantations, for example, often did without the services of skilled slaves of any sort.

Highest in privilege and importance on the estate were the slave drivers and chief sugar makers, whom the Jamaican planter, Matthew Lewis, felicitously called "principal persons." Drivers were a feature of large slaveholdings, normally containing more than fifty slaves, and led the various gangs. Some gangs had two drivers, often referred to as the "head driver" and the "under driver." The order, loyalty, and productivity of slave forces rested almost entirely in the hands of the slave drivers. In most cases, they constituted the crucial managerial force of the entire operation. The drivers not only controlled the daily routine of the plantation, but performed the essential liaison functions between the Europeans and the Africans. Moreover, drivers could administer corporal punishment, with or without the instruction of the white overseer. As long as these low-level supervisory personnel remained satisfied and loyal, coordinated resistance to the system of slavery could not meet with significant success. In recognition of this fact, slave owners tended to bestow special privileges on these male and female slave drivers. Often they gave the slave drivers their own residences separate from the community of slaves, greater rations, and more leeway in the ordinary rules and regulations of the plantations. The treatment of the drivers provided a clear illustration of the positive incentives that the system used to maintain social control.

On sugar estates, the skill and experience of the master sugar boiler was equally valuable for the economic success of the enterprise. His keen sense of the proper elaboration of sugar could make the difference between the financial success of the estate and disaster. In terms of purchase price, however, drivers and sugar boilers cost less than those specialists who made possible the reliable, trouble-free operation of the entire machinery of sugar production: carpenters, millwrights, coppersmiths, coopers, sawyers, and masons. Together these groups appeared to constitute a hierarchy among the slaves with a great deal of personal freedom of movement on the estates. Occasionally they were hired out to supplement the income of their owners or to acquire the capital to purchase their own freedom or that of their relatives.

Outside the plantations, a vast number of slaves plied trades, filled occupations, and participated in the two overlapping, symbiotic economies—the export and the domestic economies. Some slaves engaged in huckstering (called "higglering" in the British Caribbean), operating as middlemen between the growers of ground provisions in the rural areas and the consumers in the towns and on the estates. Predominantly female, huckster slaves operated as itinerant or fixed vendors, often competing with the free and white merchants and causing no small degree of inconvenience to the authorities. Slaves also operated small coastal boats and were fishermen, musicians, craftsmen, guides, or rat catchers. In short, any jobs that provided an income and were not, or could not be, adequately filled by the free population fell to the slaves.

Some of these occupations gave the slaves tremendous control over their time and their activity, eventually blurring the legal and customary distinctions between slavery and freedom. For this reason, runaways found it quite easy to engage in these occupations as one means of survival until more organized connections could be established. These occupations, connecting as they did the internal marketing economy and the export economy, proved a viable way of circulating the wealth of the society throughout the three castes. At any given time, a considerable proportion of the liquid capital in any colony would be in the hands of the slaves, and at the end of slavery, slaves were able to purchase a number of bankrupt estates and establish themselves as peasant farmers.

Runaways and individual slaves working independently or semi-independently merged imperceptibly into the lower ranks of the heterogenous intermediate group identified as free persons of color. This category represented a mélange of somatic-norm images as so many travelers to the Caribbean remarked from time to time. It ran the spectrum from indistinguishably white to unmistakably black. John Stewart, in his anonymously published *Account of Jamaica and Its Inhabitants*, put it this way:

> Between the whites and the blacks in the West Indies, a numerous race has sprung up, which goes by the general name of people of colour: these are subdivided into Mulattos, the offspring of a white and a black; Sambos, the offspring of a black and a Mulatto; Quadroons, the offspring of a Mulatto and a white; and Mestees or Mestisos, the offspring of a Quadroon and a white. Below this last denomination, the distinction of colour is hardly perceptible; and those who are thus removed from the original negro [sic] stock, are considered by the law as whites, and competent, of course, to enjoy all the privileges of a white. Between these particular *castes,* an endless variety of nondescript shades exist, descending from the deep jet to the faintest tinge of the olive; by gradations which it were impossible to mark and to designate.

Stewart's graphic description neither reflected the full legal distinctions of biological and complexional mutations nor accurately portrayed the composition of the free colored in Caribbean society. The Spanish managed to get twenty-five possible hybrid variations in their range of color, although only a small number of descriptions were precise enough to be practically useful. Few outside the esoteric realm of primitive biological specialists bothered to trace bloodlines so carefully. The random selections of genetic transmissions frustrated the general desire to have phenotype conform regularly to genealogical heritage. Combinations of white and nonwhite did not fall neatly into designated categories of shades of color, and a range of characteristics could be found within the same family. For all practical purposes, therefore, most designations were the simple, visually correct but biologically false, categories of mulattoes and Sambos (persons of mixed African and indigenous American ancestry).

But the free colored group was not confined merely to persons of mixed African, European, and American heritage. By the nineteenth century, a large number of blacks had become bona fide members of this group. The free colored group was not uniformly one of freedom in the sense that all members were once slaves. Some were the descendants of successive generations of free individuals of unaltered African ancestry. To describe them as freedmen, with the connotation of a group recently manumitted, is as misleading as describing contemporary Americans as Europeans or Latin Americans as Spanish and Portuguese.

The origins of the free coloreds in the Caribbean rested predominantly in the miscegenated results of the unions of European masters and their non-European slaves. Gradually the group developed its own internal marital affiliations, procreative impulses, and hereditary continuities. With the passage of time, opportunities for self-purchase and other forms of unrestricted freedom allowed fluctuating numbers of African slaves to move into the legal category of free persons, though carefully distinguished from free white persons. Some of these Africans formed biological unions with persons of mixed ancestry or non-Africans, further contributing to the biological mélange. Others preferred their own kind, thereby continuing to reinforce a distinct, and often legally designated, subcategory of free blacks.

As a proportion of the entire population, the free nonwhite sector varied considerably from colony to colony and even across time within the same colony. The free coloreds made up a high 43.5 percent of the total population of the Dutch colony of Curaçao in 1833. In plantation Surinam (now Suriname)—likewise a Dutch colony—the free population constituted less than 9 percent of the total colonial society. In Puerto Rico, the free coloreds remained 41.3 percent of the island's total population in 1860, about the same proportion as it was in 1830. In Cuba, the percentage of free colored remained likewise virtually constant, changing from 15.1 percent of the total population in 1827 to 16.2 percent in 1860. In the English and French colonies, the proportion varied between the low of 1 percent in Berbice (later part of British Guiana) and a high of 12.6 percent in the Bahamas in 1810. In Barbados, the free coloreds represented 6.5 percent of the island's total population in 1834. In Jamaica, it was 10.2 percent in 1800. In French Saint-Domingue, the free coloreds were 5.3 percent of the total for the colony in 1791, while Martinique had a proportion of 5.4 percent in 1789.

The data presented in table 4 provide only a frozen "snapshot" view of the demographic profile of the Caribbean. But "frozen" representations, however graphic they may be, cannot reveal the inherent dynamism of the social groups. The history of the free colored population is one of continual response to an ever-varying number of influences through time. One of the most prominent influences on the behavior of the free nonwhite population as a category was the changing economic fortunes of the plantation-based export economy. Fluctuating economic conditions, of course, had an equal impact on all sectors of the colonial society.

A few examples illustrate the vagaries of economy and population. During the eighteenth century, the plantation economy expanded in Surinam until 1788, when the colony had 591 plantations and 50,000 slaves of a total population of 55,000 inhabitants. By 1813, the number of plantations had declined to 369, and in 1863, when slavery was abolished, the number was 210. At the same time, the collapse of the Amsterdam exchange in 1773 began an irreversible process of the withdrawal of capital from agriculture. In 1863, the total population of the colony was less than in 1830. Other subtle changes also took place. Plantations fell into absentee ownership, with more than 80 percent (297) of all plantations in 1813 in this category. The number of free coloreds, especially in the female mulatto group, increased dramatically. Dutch plantation owners and their families left the colony in large numbers, allowing Jews to become the predominant element among the superordinate white sector. At the same time, bachelor whites sent out from Holland to administer foreclosed estates further accentuated the male-dominant sexual imbalance among the whites. Between 1768 and 1834, the free colored population spurted from about 3,500 to 35,000, a tenfold increase that boosted their proportion from 16 percent of the total free group to about 70 percent. During the period, the white population fell by almost 50 percent, and the number of slaves—by an entirely unrelated coincidence—nearly doubled. In Martinique, where the plantation economy declined precipitately during the Napoleonic wars of the early nineteenth century, the free colored sector increased from 7.1 percent of the total population in 1802 to 24.9 percent in 1835. In Cuba, on the other hand, the plantation economy expanded rapidly between 1774 and 1827, and the free nonwhite sector declined from 20.3 percent to 15.1 percent of the population.

The free nonwhite sector, wherever they were found and regardless of the circumstances under which they flourished, manifested a number of common traits. It tended to be predominantly female, largely urban, and almost self-consciously differentiated from the slave sector. In Trinidad in 1811, 56.7 percent of the free nonwhite population was female, with adult females outnumbering adult males by 2,830 to 1,790. Barbados presented a slightly anomalous picture, with females predominating in all three castes. In 1817, for example, females made up more than 54 percent of the slave and white sectors and more than 51 percent of the free nonwhites. Free nonwhite females outnumbered free nonwhite males in Cuba, too, where in 1841 the 78,843 free nonwhite women outnumbered the free nonwhite men by 3,140 and proportionately exceeded the latter by 51 percent to 49 percent. In the new colonies of Demerara and Essequibo, free nonwhite adult females outnumbered free nonwhite adult males 1,096 to 487; while in small Tobago, the adult free nonwhite women numbered 153, and the free adult nonwhite men numbered 92. The numerical superiority of women among free nonwhite populations did not prevail among children. In most cases, boys outnumbered girls in all segments of the Caribbean societies, slave or free.

With some notable exceptions, the residential pattern of the free nonwhites throughout the Caribbean tended to be urban. In the eighteenth century, free nonwhites predominated in the southern departments of French Saint-Domingue. In the nineteenth century, a substantial number of this population continued to exist in the rural areas of Cuba, Puerto Rico, Spanish Santo Domingo, and Trinidad. Even in Cuba, a far heavier concentration of free colored persons lived in the cities of Havana, Santiago de Cuba, Manzanillo, and Trinidad than in the plantation zones of Cárdenas, Colon, and Matanzas. In Barbados the situation was the same. After 1809, about 61 percent of all the free Barbadian nonwhites lived in the parish of St. Michael, and there is a strong indication that the majority of this group resided in or near the capital of the island, Bridgetown. In 1829, in any case, 3,140 of the 5,146 free nonwhites in Barbados lived in St. Michael Parish. A greater number of nonwhites lived in Belize City than anywhere else in British Honduras, and more lived in Kingston than in the rest of the island of Jamaica. Trinidad was the only exception in the British Caribbean, having a larger free colored population in the rural areas than in the towns.

The urban residence pattern fulfilled certain physical as well as psychological conditions for the free colored population. Although some free coloreds figured among the wealthy plantation owners and slave owners—most prominently in Jamaica, Puerto Rico, Spanish Santo Domingo, Saint-Domingue, Martinique, Trinidad, and Surinam—most working free coloreds derived their livelihood from trades and services. The cities provided a far more conducive ambience for the pursuit of these occupations than the rural plantation zones, where they would face some degree of competition from the slave workforce. Moreover, like the slaves, the miscegenated free were generally recognized to be less than ideal manual workers on the plantations. Once the magnetic pattern of urban residence and association was established, it could not be easily reversed. Towns offered the critical mass necessary to project opportunities for economic gain and social recognition. The rural exodus of the free coloreds might also have had powerful subconscious motivations. The social mores of the Caribbean plantation society consistently denigrated those who did manual and menial labor. For this reason, plantation field slaves represented the lowest social category. And in an atmosphere in which the correlation between a black skin and the status of slavery was almost taken for granted, free nonwhites in rural areas faced the unavoidable and continuous problem of proving their freedom. Increasing the social distance between slavery and freedom for the Afro-Caribbean population might have meant increasing the physical distance as well.

Yet the flight to the cities, although providing many opportunities for upward social mobility, created and intensified economic and political competition, especially at the two ends of the spectrum. At the lower end of the economic scale, the free Afro-Caribbean population faced competition from jobbing slaves, often working zealously to purchase their freedom while being indirectly subsidized by their owners. At the upper end of the scale, the free nonwhites competed with the artisan, commercial, and semiskilled service sector of the lower orders of the white group.

The whites often used their political power, or their access to political power, to define and broaden the economic and occupational gap between themselves and the free colored sector. Laws distinguishing comportment, dress, and residence or denying the practice of certain occupations or limiting the material inheritance of the free colored population were commonplace throughout the Caribbean during the early years of the nineteenth century. The constriction of the range of occupations, the personal liberties, and the political rights of the free nonwhite sector tended to run concurrently with the expansion of a plantation economy of a colony. Throughout the eighteenth century, therefore, the French Antilleans sought to restrict intermarriage across ethnic boundaries and to curtail nonwhite participation in shipping, commerce, and the military. The Jamaica Assembly passed an act in 1762 restricting the inheritance of any free person of color to no more than two thousand pounds sterling. In 1783, the Assembly of the Virgin Islands passed a law that restricted the amount of land that free coloreds could buy to a maximum of eight acres, prohibited them from inheriting lots of more than fifteen slaves, and imposed public whipping as the punishment for striking whites. Similar types of restrictions were introduced in Cuba during the nineteenth century—at the time when the British Caribbean was moving in the direction of removing distinctions within the free population.

One area of colonial life in which the free coloreds found ready opportunities for service was in the military. Slaves had always been impressed for emergency military service and were often rewarded with freedom for their military valor in all European colonies in the New World. Gradually free colored males were organized into separate militia units designed to serve alongside the whites in local defense. In Cuba the free coloreds were formally constituted into a separate unit in the military reforms at the end of the sixteenth century, thereby becoming the first colored soldiers recognized by any European state anywhere in the Caribbean. Between 1600 and the late 1800s, the number of free colored militia companies increased from one to sixteen in Cuba, and nearly one-third of all the local militia came from the free colored sector. In the French Antilles, integrated units of whites and free coloreds existed before the end of the seventeenth century. In 1697, a separate free black militia company was recognized in Saint-Domingue, and by 1730, the free nonwhites formed their own companies under white officers. In Jamaica, where the free coloreds were required by law to serve in the segregated island militia, they constituted more than 54 percent of the troops in 1828. The free colored militia not only sought to defend the island against foreign attack, but fought against the Maroons in 1739 and again in 1795 and stood ready to contain slave revolts. Barbados, which had a relatively larger resident white population than Jamaica and had less to fear from slave revolts or foreign attacks, showed a greater reluctance to admit free nonwhite companies into the volunteer militia. Nevertheless by 1833, fully 25 percent of the militia were drawn from the free colored population—a sharp contrast with the less than 5 percent serving at the time of the American Revolution.

The free colored population throughout the Caribbean, then, was a considerably heterogeneous group, struggling to assert itself and to establish its identity under a variety of ever-changing conditions. In Santo Domingo, the Bahamas, Bermuda, and a number of the smaller islands in the Eastern Caribbean, the local economies remained virtually constant, and the social structures reflected this stability in their pattern of slow evolution. Elsewhere the situation was far more volatile, far more dynamic. In 1789, Saint-Domingue erupted at the height of its prosperity, and the society experienced the first thorough revolution in the Western Hemisphere. There, change went far beyond a political rearrangement. The slaves destroyed not only their bondage, but the symbols of their servitude—the white masters, the large plantation complex, the whole pattern of latifundium, and the export-oriented economy. In the early nineteenth century, the export economies of a number of the British Caribbean colonies were on the verge of collapse. The politically dominant white minorities waged a determined but futile campaign to forestall the emancipation of their slaves and the gradual political participation of the nonwhite majorities. By 1834, both goals were lost as the British government accepted the abolition of slavery throughout the British empire and began to take measures to secure the civil rights of the free nonwhites. In 1844, the Cuban whites, basing their action on a presumed islandwide conspiracy, staged a sort of preemptive massacre that virtually decimated the intellectual and economic leadership of the Afro-Cuban population. That action, called the Conspiracy of the Ladder, signified the highest point of local racial tension during the century.

Despite the monumental handicaps, free colored individuals achieved outstanding successes in many spheres of activity. Where the opportunities presented themselves, members of the free colored community participated ably and enthusiastically. In Trinidad and Puerto Rico, free coloreds made up nearly one-third of all landowners in the early nineteenth century. Throughout the region, the free coloreds were noted for their participation in the printing trades, in literature, in music, in dance, and in other aspects of local culture, sometimes performing better than the whites. Considerations of class, color, and the inescapable ambiguity of being neither fully free nor plainly servile for so long might have definitely inhibited the cohesion of the nonwhites. Until the nineteenth century, the local white groups tried to marginalize, demoralize, and eliminate this important component of the society. It could not be done. Like the slaves, this sector survived and eventually came into its own.

Like the free persons of color, the white sector was also quite a heterogeneous group. Their division along socioeconomic class lines was almost as pronounced as the color divisions within the free colored caste: *peninsulares* and *criollos* in the Spanish colonies, *grands blancs* and *petits blancs* in the French colonies, and "principal whites" and "poor whites" in the English colonies. As indicated before, some of these social attributes derived from the relationship to the plantation structure in the exploitation colonies. In the settler colonies, place of birth assumed some importance, with greater status attributed to whites born in the metropolis.

This distinction did not diminish even when the colony was transformed into a plantation colony. By the end of the eighteenth century, colonial-born whites were already becoming so self-conscious that their attitude became a source of some political friction in Cuba and Saint-Domingue.

But the white community was further divided in other ways. Every colony had a mixture of national origins and religious denominations within the white ranks. Sometimes this situation restricted cooperative action on the part of the whites and may have retarded the growth of a local nationalism. Nowhere was this illustrated better than on the island of Trinidad, captured and retained by the English from the Spanish in 1797. Trinidad had never been an important Spanish colony, lying as it did just off the Venezuelan coast and outside the axis of the Spanish-American empire. During the later half of the eighteenth century, the Spanish had attempted to encourage Catholic settlers to boost the population and had enthusiastically welcomed refugees from war-torn French Saint-Domingue. At the time of its capture, the island already had a mixed population of whites, and the diversity increased. In 1811, the white population of Trinidad numbered 4,353 persons, representing ten different national or regional origins. Indigenous Indians numbered 1,736, constituting the largest white group at about 40 percent of the population. English whites totaled 1,280, or 29.4 percent. The French settlers numbered 681, or nearly 15 percent. The Spanish component was 559, or almost 12.8 percent. In addition, there were 25 Germans, 20 Americans, 20 Corsicans, 18 Italians, 10 Maltese, and 4 Portuguese. National origin and religious affiliation, however, were lesser considerations than was merely being white in a colony where color was more important than condition. The English placed the colony under a government that continued to respect Spanish law and custom—but not those laws and customs that supported the civil rights of the nonwhite sector.

Every slave society struggled to preserve its carefully delineated hierarchical order and only reluctantly accepted the unavoidable breaches of social boundaries. This was as true within the white sector as between the races. The genial Lady Maria Nugent, an American Creole born in Perth Amboy, New Jersey, of mixed Scottish, Irish, and Dutch ancestry, a loyalist refugee from the American Revolution as well as the wife of the governor of Jamaica, left a classic description of the colonial society in which she lived for five years. Lady Nugent found Jamaican upper-class conduct a source of exasperation and bemusement and well below her metropolitan expectations:

> In this country it appears as if every thing were bought and sold. Clergymen make no secret of making a traffic of their livings; but General N. [her husband, General George Nugent, governor of Jamaica, 1801–1806] has set his face against such proceedings, and has refused many applications for this purpose. He is determined to do all he can towards the reformation of the church, and thus rendering it respectable. It is indeed melancholy, to see the general disregard of both religion and morality, throughout the whole island. Every one seems solicitous to make money, and no one appears to regard the mode of acquiring it. It is extraordinary to witness the immediate effect that the climate and habit of living in this country

have upon the minds and manners of Europeans, particularly of the lower orders. In the upper ranks, they become indolent and inactive, regardless of everything but eating, drinking, and indulging themselves, and are almost entirely under the domination of their mullatto favorites. In the lower orders, they are the same, with the addition of conceit and tyranny; considering the negroes as creatures formed merely to administer to their ease, and to be subject to their caprice; and I have found much difficulty to persuade those great people and superior beings, our white domestics, that the blacks are human beings and have souls. I allude more particularly to our German and other men-servants.

It was curious to observe, when we were entering any town, the number of trunks, band-boxes, & c. that were hurrying to the different houses, and the same at our departure, all going back to the country again, and all on negroes' heads; for whenever the ladies go to town, or are to appear in society, their black maids and other attendants start off with their finery in cases or their boxes, on their heads. Trunks of any size are carried in the same manner. In short, everything is put upon the head, from the largest to the smallest thing; even a smelling-bottle, I believe, would be carried in the same way. I have often, on our tour, seen twelve or fourteen negroes in one line of march, each bearing some article for the toilette on his head.

The creole language is not confined to the negroes. Many of the ladies who have not been educated in England, speak a sort of broken English, with an indolent drawling out of their words, that is very tiresome if not disgusting. I stood next to a lady one night, near a window, and, by way of saying something, remarked that the air was much cooler than usual; to which she answered, "Yes, ma-am, *him rail-ly too fra-ish.*"

Despite its stuffiness, Lady Nugent's remarkably perceptive observations on Jamaican colonial society could be made, *mutatis mutandis,* of just about any other Caribbean colonial society. The "corruption" of clergy and public officials, the laxity of European moral standards, the stereotypical social behavior of mulatto females, the gluttony (always under the guise of generosity), the prodigal use of labor, and the profligate obsession with materialism could be observed equally in Cuba, Martinique, Barbados, or Surinam (now Suriname)—in any of the wealthier European colonies in the Caribbean. These were common behavioral traits of the upper classes of whites and nonwhites in the plantation society. They probably were one indication of the effects that the mercantile mentality and occupational servility of slavery had on the Europeans overseas. It was not merely the climate of the tropics, but the process of Creolization within the peculiar socioeconomic structure of their own creation that surreptitiously undermined their original "Europeanness." By the eighteenth century, this process had led to a marked difference between metropolitan whites and Creole whites.

The two basic social classes within the category of Euro-Caribbean whites formed four distinct social ranks. At the very summit—and closest to what might otherwise be called an elite—were the noble and seminoble families and the wealthy owners of large, successful plantations. In the Spanish and French colonies, some of these noble families had titles that ranked among the most distinguished in their respective metropolises. Cuba, for example, had twenty-nine titled families in 1810, including thirteen marquesses and sixteen counts. Most of these families arrived in the island as true settlers in the sixteenth or early seventeenth centuries, although their titles dated only from the eighteenth century. This was true of the Pedroso, González de la Torre, Roxas, Santa Cruz, Cárdenas, Cepero, and Sotolongo families of Havana; the Porcallo de Figueroa, Varona, and Guerra families of Bayamo; the De la Torre family of Puerto Príncipe; and the Estrada family of Santiago de Cuba. Lower members of the nobility also sojourned for various periods in the British islands, brought out by the call of duty, the lure of pleasure, or the desire for profit. William Scarlet, a wealthy landowner in St. James Parish, Jamaica, was knighted on becoming chief justice of the island in the 1720s. He was the brother of Lord Abinger (James Scarlett, 1769–1844, of Duckett's Spring, St. James), attorney general and chief baron of the Exchequer in England. Simon Taylor, the wealthy landowner, left his extensive properties in Jamaica to his nephew, Sir Simon Taylor. Indeed, founding families of the British West Indian plantation societies formed, by the late eighteenth century, a core of old planters, whose advice was often influential in the realm of imperial as well as local politics.

Along with the titled nobility and the old plantocracy came a mixed group of wealthy—sometimes distinctly nouveaux riches—planters, bureaucrats, senior officers in the military and naval services, and wealthy merchants, often the proud owners of lavish country estates. The difference between these two strata of the white upper class was not great. Indeed, kin affiliations occurred frequently between the two groups. The most distinguished and dominant Cuban families provided offspring who gave valuable service in the Spanish military, bureaucracy, and clergy throughout the empire. H. P. Jacobs reported in his study, *Sixty Years of Change*, that members of the old plantocracy in the British Caribbean often sent their sons to fight and die in the military service of the British empire in faraway places, such as Spain, Egypt, and India, convinced that they were fighting for their monarch and their country. By the nineteenth century, however, a division had developed within the ruling elite. As Jacobs noted: "The old plantocracy had frequently a deep love for Jamaica and a feeling of responsibility; but they were not completely identified with it. The new plantocracy looked for advancement through Jamaica and through Jamaica alone." Both groups, old and new, formed a powerful alliance, stubbornly defending the economic and political interests of the white planting sector against the legitimate aspirations of the nonwhites.

Below the upper group of old and new planters and their bureaucratic peers came the middling merchants and the important professionals, such as doctors and clergymen. These groups together formed a third rank within the white sector. The expansion of commerce and the complex semibartering nature of the export economy provided opportunities for the expansion of the commercial and professional classes. The plantation society was, above all, a major consumer society importing necessities and luxuries from a variety of sources. Bills of lading for the Port of Havana in 1852 demonstrate the universality of its commercial contacts and the diversity of the imported products. A partial selection of the list included among the imports fine cloths, furniture, and mirrors from England, Holland, France, and North America; flour, wine, spices, olive oil, and shoes from Spain; codfish and salted meat from Newfoundland, New York, Philadelphia, Baltimore, and Vera Cruz; silverware from Manchester and Birmingham; bricks, clay pots, and stones from Toledo in Spain; tiles and ceramic ware from Puebla, Mexico, and Talavera de la Reina in Spain; and timber from neighboring Jamaica. With certain variations in the sources, the selection could have been representative of the commerce for Curaçao, Port-of-Spain, Bridgetown, Point-à-Pitre, or Kingston. The merchant groups were a diverse, sometimes socially well-connected class. Some were the scions of great families. This was particularly noticeable in Cuba in the early nineteenth century. Others, especially in the French colonies, were connected to prominent merchant houses in Nantes, Bordeaux, and La Rochelle. Still others were simple adventurers of uncertain origin. Basques and Catalans virtually controlled the trade of the Hispanic Caribbean during the nineteenth century. Jews, Syrians, and Lebanese were prominent in the Dutch and British colonies. Eventually the most successful merchants who stayed on in the colonies found acceptance into the social circles of the plantation elite. Jews in some British Caribbean colonies, while conceded freedom of worship and movement, suffered from some political disabilities. They could neither vote nor serve in the military services until the general enfranchisement of all free nowhites, beginning with the Jamaica law of 1830.

Merchants were a large and active part of municipal life throughout the Caribbean. The most successful merchants established impressive urban and rural dwellings and acquired country estates. As a group, they were never generally regarded as the social equivalent of the specialist planting classes, and it is ironic that in the French and British colonies the merchants were sometimes considered absentee owners and blamed for many of the economic ills of the colony. The nineteenth-century modus operandi of the commercial craft necessitated travel, not just abroad to suppliers and customers, but throughout the interior of the colony. It is perhaps unlikely that a greater proportion of merchants than planters retired abroad. Moreover, the tone of all the large Caribbean cities—Havana, San Juan, Kingston, Bridgetown, Fort-de-France, or Willemstad—was set by the merchant groups that pioneered (albeit with great self-interest) some of the fledgling police and fire protection services that have survived as major municipal occupations. After 1805, merchants made up more than half the Kingston Vestry Jurors' Lists.

The fourth rank was the largest white grouping. They were labeled with a variety of terms, some of which, regardless of the language, carried a pronounced pejorative connotation: *petits blancs*, poor whites, "lesser orders," *campesino, quajiro, mambí, jíbaro*, "walking buckra," or "red legs." At one time or another, the category included small independent farmers, petty shopkeepers, lawyers, taverners and hosteters, day laborers, itinerant preachers, teachers, policemen, firemen, bookkeepers, bill collectors, commission agents, gunsmiths, blacksmiths, coppersmiths, goldsmiths, druggists, midwives, nurses, undertakers, hairdressers, seamstresses, porters, cooks, gardeners, bakers, barbers, tailors, coachmakers, coopers, watchmakers and repairers, shoemakers, sailmakers, wharfingers, shipwrights, carpenters, cabinetmakers, bricklayers, masons, printers, and stationers. Since these whites gained their employment mainly in the service occupations, they competed with jobbing slaves and the free nonwhite population, a coincidence that did not enhance their social status. This motley group also included a small number of unskilled, unemployed, and socially unsuccessful persons who formed a part of the poor white community in every colony. But in general, members of the poorer white classes were employed, industrious, and filled with the hope of enormous pecuniary gain and eventual upward social mobility that helped form the magnetic attraction for their sojourn in the tropics. Moreover, regardless of their economic circumstances, the accidental factor of race and color invested all whites with a superior status in the colonies.

The white segment was not more homogeneous than any other, but it tended to display a far greater cohesiveness and unity than any other group, especially after the revolution in Saint-Domingue. Whites emphasized their racial and color differences, and they dominated all the major institutions of the society. Whites virtually controlled the export economy, monopolized the political structure before the late nineteenth century, and set what they arrogantly presumed to be the cultural norms for the entire society. Nevertheless, the scathing criticisms of visitors and some long-term residents indicated that in most cases, the local white Creole culture was merely a parody of that in the metropolis. The white subgroup suffered from the class prejudices of the elite, as Edward Long described graphically in his remarkable *History of Jamaica* published in 1774:

> The lower order of white people (as they are called here), are, for the most part, composed of artificers, indented servants, and refugees...carpenters, who never handled a tool; bricklayers, who scarcely know a brick from a stone; and bookkeepers, who can neither write nor read. Many of these menial servants, who are retained for saving a deficiency, are the very dregs of the three kingdoms. They have commonly more vices, and much fewer good qualities, than the slaves over whom they are set in authority; the better sort of whom heartily despise them, perceiving little or no difference from themselves, except in skin, and blacker depravity. By their base familiarity with the worst-disposed among the slaves, they do a very great injury to the plantations; causing disturbances, by seducing the Negroes [sic] wives, and bringing *odium* upon the white people in general, by their drunkenness and profligate actions. In fact, the better sort of Creole Blacks disdain to associate with them, holding them in too much contempt, or abhorrence.

Long's antagonistic attitude was probably not widely held by the majority of upper-class whites who passed their lives in the colonies among a far greater number of enslaved Africans and their descendants. For them, race and color, rather than class and nationality, became a consoling, fraternal bond. Such were the peculiarities of the plantation slave society that the conventional class divisions and social distinctions of the metropolis largely broke down in the overseas colonies. Even as Long wrote in the later eighteenth century, he was aware that some fundamental changes had already taken place—the autocracy of the plantation owner had yielded to a community of common law, and the colonial society had become, in many ways, a pale reflection of the mother country.

The essentially frontier conditions of the tropical American colonies facilitated a fantastic upward mobility among the whites that often made a mockery of metropolitan class consciousness. But there was more at work than the frontier. Bryan Edwards, the experienced Jamaican planter and member of the British Parliament, wrote apprehensively of white colonial social relations in the 1790s as the French Revolution engulfed the Continent and the distant colony of Saint-Domingue:

> It appears to me [he wrote in 1793] that the leading feature [among the whites] is an independent spirit, and a display of conscious equality throughout all ranks and conditions. The poorest white person seems to consider himself nearly on a level with the richest, and, emboldened by this idea approached his employer with extended hand, and a freedom, which in the countries of Europe, is seldom displayed by men in the lower orders of life toward their superiors. It is not difficult to trace the origin of this principle. It arises, without doubt, from the preeminence and distinction which are necessarily attached even to the complexion of a White Man, in a country where the complexion, generally speaking, distinguishes freedom from slavery.

The simple facts of Caribbean life everywhere permitted sufficient examples of the dramatic rise from dismal poverty and humble status to Croesus-like wealth and the most highly esteemed social rank. It was not impossible for a poor white to become the governor of a colony. Henry Morgan, a poor Welsh indentured servant-turned-buccaneer, ended his fascinating life as a highly respected planter and the lieutenant-governor of Jamaica during the eighteenth century. Julian de Zulueta, a poor semiliterate rural Basque, went out to Cuba in the nineteenth century; entered the slave trade; and rose to be a wealthy mayor of Havana, a respectable member of the Spanish nobility, and an adviser to the monarchy of Spain. There was always some degree of initial snobbery, some inevitable snickering, and some understandable unease at accepting new members to the group, but in time all of this could be overcome.

Lady Nugent found it convenient to act "like an invalid, to keep up the character I have politically adopted" on meeting a group of French refugee ladies in Spanish Town until she could clarify their social status and determine "what ladies to receive." Because she was a bit of a prude and an official transient in the Jamaican society, she probably deliberately exaggerated social distance to bolster her husband's position. It is hardly likely that the other white elite ladies would have gone to such extremes to display rank with foreign women of their own color. Within the Caribbean context, color by itself was a ticket of admission.

The mutually reinforcing cleavages of race and color for the minority whites can hardly be overestimated in the Caribbean. Auguste Lacour, writing of Guadeloupe society in the middle of the nineteenth century, described with cutting precision the ranks within the local society as a whole and the congealing effect of color:

> Although the island counted among itself a number of the titled nobility, especially younger sons who had come out to the place in pursuit of their fortune, the nobility was not constituted as in France. Within the white group, the nobility did not exist. The only privilege of the nobility was being entitled to a seat in the *Conseil Supérieur*, and the exemption from the head tax for a fixed number of slaves. What constituted the nobility was not parchment, but color. To the white group, to individuals of the European race, were exclusively reserved all public, lucrative and honorific functions.

Color, therefore, delineated the boundaries of caste and highlighted the distinctions between "we" and "they." To a certain extent, it mitigated the potential class divisions within the white sector, especially after the Haitian Revolution demonstrated the ultimate consequences of placing class interests above racial solidarity. Race, color, and bondage were fundamental ingredients in white thoughts about their precarious world in the Caribbean. Unfortunately, it was sometimes the only thing they thought about—besides markets and profits.

Race, color, and legal status did not, however, preclude some relationships across caste lines. The masters could no more live without their slaves than the slaves could live without their masters. Each group, the free and the enslaved, the masters and the slaves, the Africans and the Europeans, adjusted to life in the tropical world as best they could. And this adjustment included an adjustment to each other. The monopoly of power exercised by the white sector on the plantations, in politics, in law, and in the export economy was more apparent than real. In two ways, the structure that the whites created was both fragile and contradictory. In the first place, the whites' economic success at all levels depended largely on factors entirely outside their control—including the supply of slaves, the price of sugar, and the fortuitous consistency of climate. In the second place, the white master class defined slaves as property but were forced to use them as persons of intelligence and self-will. Whatever the white masters may have confessed about the subordinate nature of their slaves, they encountered in their everyday dealings with them an uncomfortable, unmistakable humanity.

Alongside the continuous proliferation of laws establishing the sanctity of private property in Africans and the vast literature deploring the inherent inhumanity or subhumanity of slaves went an elaborate system of police-protection measures fully conceding the basic humanity of the slaves. The plantation was an artificial construct, but slaves were people. Slaves, after all, demonstrated equally all the qualities of the whites. They could work as hard, administer as efficiently, speak the languages as well, think as subtly, scheme as cunningly, inflict revenge as maliciously, love as passionately, fight as bravely, and subvert society as totally. Other forms of property—land, cattle, equipment, and buildings—could not respond as creatively to their circumstances. Slaves had a life, mind, and culture of their own that induced them to make the appropriate survival response to the situation in which they found themselves.

The exigencies of production, profit, and social order required substantial white supervision of nonwhite society. But this supervision could not take the form of unrelenting coercion or uninterrupted regulation. The white sector delegated authority, recognized cultural differences, encouraged divisions of rank, and employed all types of incentives to minimize the simultaneous disaffection of the majority of the slave sector. The numerical weakness of the master class provided an agent for upward social mobility. The fact that in most territories the whites could not even provide sufficient women for the adequate sexual satisfaction of the males meant that caste-confined relations, even at the most domestic level, had to be relaxed. Slave plantation society, then, held an ideal about race, class, color, and condition that was far removed from the operational reality of day-to-day living.

The practical operations of work and living in the slave society produced a number of contradictions, some of which proved quite dysfunctional to the system. At one level, ideal social stratification clashed with inescapable mobility. This clash produced explosive pressures of class, color, race, and status. The legal divisions of slave and free were the most sharply defined concepts of status established by the slave society. The society maintained the intrinsic nature of slavery by declaring that the offspring of any slave remained slaves, regardless of the status of one parent who might be free. At the same time, the slave society held freedom as the highest ideal and provided a number of ways in which the status could be achieved by those who were slaves. Slaves could buy their freedom on their own initiative. Masters could independently grant freedom to their slaves for satisfactory service or for private religious motives. Free parents could purchase the freedom of their offspring. Society granted freedom to slaves who fought bravely against foreign invaders or exposed conspiracies among their fellow slaves or had legitimate complaints of excessive cruelty and inhumanity against their masters. Freedom was also granted for idiosyncratic reasons. The Spanish normally granted freedom to foreign-owned slaves escaping from non-Catholic adversarial states to their own territories, provided that they claimed they were fleeing from religious persecution. This practice offered incentives for British and Dutch Caribbean slaves who were fleeing their Protestant masters but offered cold comfort for nominally Catholic French slaves. Superannuated slaves owned by the Spanish and French monarchs were granted freedom after what was considered a lifetime of royal service, and the French government manumitted slaves who had served seven or more years as drummers for the military troops. During the Ten Years' War (1868–1878) in Cuba, the Spanish government declared slaves of the insurgents to be free, while retaining in slavery those whose masters had loyally supported the Crown.

The slave system was not inflexible. Theoretically, individuals could move upward within the class structure and laterally across the caste divisions. The unskilled field slave acquiring a technical skill could assume a higher status. Slaves polishing their command of English, Spanish, French, Dutch, or Swedish could become part of the respected domestic staff of the plantation great house or the city residence, improving both their status and their value. Or field slaves could work their way into urban jobbing gangs, gaining social and occupational mobility and a better opportunity for eventual self-purchase. On the contiguous, overlapping, and frequently ill-defined boundaries of race and status, some "passing" could occur. Urban skilled slaves could successfully run away and become free. Free light-complexioned mulattoes could pass as white (and undoubtedly some wealthy ones did), legitimating their new status by judicious bribes, calculated marriages, or socially acceptable conduct. Even within the upper stratum, newcomers with money and temerity could break into the ranks of the socially privileged, as did Henry Morgan in Jamaica and Julian Zulueta in Cuba. The slave society, in short, was similar to any other society faced with widely fluctuating economic and demographic conditions and rapidly changing social norms. The dynamism had internal as well as external sources of stimulation.

Nevertheless, the fluidity of the structure, especially at the free level, engendered the type of internal class and caste friction that contributed to social instability and made the slave society a potentially revolutionary complex. During the nineteenth century, the Caribbean slave society was equally one of ferment and strife. Its potential strengths generated its inherent weaknesses. A divided society, it was simultaneously a divisive society. Tensions existed at all levels. Tensions existed between free and slave as well as within the free groups along lines of color and class. The most potentially explosive were tensions between free and slave and among the white groups. Between slave and free, the tensions took the forms of slave revolts, conspiracies, and subversions with various degrees of success. In French Saint-Domingue, the slave revolt destroyed the colony. In Cuba, most enduring of the Caribbean slave societies, the white group split basically between Spanish-born *peninsulares* and Cuban-born *criollos*. *Criollo* versus *peninsular* antagonism manifested itself in a number of conspiracies throughout the century, flared unsuccessfully during the Ten Years' War, and finally broke the last vestiges of the Spanish-American imperial connection in 1898. In 1788, the rift between *grands blancs* and *petits blancs* on Saint-Domingue—the most extreme case of intracaste antagonism anywhere in the Caribbean—opened the floodgates of revolution, with permanent reversals for French ambitions and the French dream of empire in the Amercas. In Jamaica, the political incompatibiilty between rural whites and urban whites contributed to the constitutional surrender of representative-assembly government after the Morant Bay uprising in 1865.

Class antagonisms paled against the force of racial distrust. The recurring slave revolts and the constant preoccupation with the possibility of slave revolts exacerbated the antagonistic racial divisions in every slave society. The increased exploitation of slaves at the very period when the institution of slavery was undergoing relentless international moral and intellectual attack—and in some cases physical dismantlement—coincided with the increased nineteenth-century awareness of ethnicity, ethnocentricity, and nationalism. The Caribbean societies, too, felt the winds of political change in the nineteenth century and began to articulate—although nowhere as strongly as in Cuba and on the neighboring mainland—a heightened sense of self-consciousness. Their sense of nation, however, clashed with their reality. Cultural, ethnic, and economic diversity appeared patently undesirable to adherents of social engineering who were infatuated with the current ideas of the other emergent nations.

This steady political awakening before the middle of the nineteenth century in the Caribbean coincided with the development of a lively local literature, drama, and art. While much that was written about the region came from the pens of foreigners, local writers increasingly expressed their ideas about their world. A distinct Caribbean civic culture, rooted in the diverse popular experiences of the various territories, was slowly maturing and beginning to compete with the adopted metropolitan cultures that remained the ideals of the elites. Aided by the expanding presence of the printing press after the eighteenth century and a growing literate readership for newspapers, books, and pamphlets, the various territories produced a vigorous and perceptive type of literature. This literature fell into three overlapping categories: political analyses, histories, and scientific publications designed to advocate political change and enhance the political position of the local elites; publications determined to defend or to attack slavery; and imaginative literature drawing heavily on stylized versions of local customs and manners. In one way or another, the various writings of such authors as José Agustín Caballero (1762–1825), Francisco Arango y Parreño (1765–1837), Félix Varela y Morales (1788–1853), José Antonio Saco (1797–1879), José de la Luz y Caballero (1800–1862), and Domingo del Monte y Aponte in Cuba; Eugenio María de Hostos (1839–1903) in Puerto Rico; or Richard Hill (1795–1872) in Jamaica all served these purposes. It was almost impossible to write about politics or culture during the nineteenth century without somehow contemplating the role of slavery and its enduring impact on the society in the Caribbean.

The anonymously published *Marly* (1828), a novel about Jamaican society, and the Cuban antislavery book *Francisco* (1837) by Anselmo Suárez y Romero discussed politics as well as the ways in which slavery affected social mores and revealed new local perspectives on the region. Along with the increasing acceptance of local dances, religious customs, music, and plays, the Caribbean Creole elites were, consciously or unconsciously, moving away from their own metropolitan ideals while fostering closer links between the elites and the masses.

SUGGESTED READINGS

Armstrong, Douglas V. *The Old Village and the Great House: An Archaeological and Historical Examination of Drax Hall Plantation St. Ann's Bay, Jamaica.* Urbana: University of Illinois Press, 1990.

Beckles, Hilary McD. *White Servitude and Black Slavery in Barbados, 1627–1715.* Knoxville: University of Tennessee Press, 1989.

Beckles, Hilary McD., ed. *Inside Slavery: Process and Legacy in the Caribbean Experience.* Mona, Jamaica: Canoe Press, 1996.

Bennett, J. Harry. *Bondsmen and Bishops: Slavery and Apprenticeship on the Codrington Plantations of Barbados, 1710–1838.* Berkeley: University of California Press, 1958.

Burnard, Trevor. *Mastery, Tyranny, and Desire: Thomas Thistlewood and His Slaves in the Anglo-Jamaican World*. Chapel Hill: University of North Carolina Press, 2004.

Dunn, Richard S. *Sugar and Slaves: The Rise of the Planter Class in the English West Indies, 1624–1713*. Chapel Hill: University of North Carolina Press, 1972.

Garrigus, John D. *Before Haiti: Race and Citizenship in French Saint-Domingue*. New York: Palgrave Macmillan, 2006.

Hall, Gwendolyn Midlo. *Social Control in Slave Plantation Societies: A Comparison of St. Domingue and Cuba*. Baltimore, Md.: Johns Hopkins University Press, 1971.

Higman, B. W. *Jamaica Surveyed: Plantation Maps and the Plans of the Eighteenth and Nineteenth Centuries*. Kingston: Institute of Jamaica, 1988.

Higman, B. W. *Montpelier, Jamaica: A Plantation Community in Slavery and Freedom, 1739–1912*. Mona, Jamaica: University of the West Indies Press, 1998.

Instituto de Historia de Cuba. *Historia de Cuba La Colonia: evolución socioeconómica y formación nacional de los orígenes hasta 1867*. Havana: Editora Política, 1994.

King, Stewart R. *Blue Coat or Powdered Wig: Free People of Color in Pre-Revolutionary Saint Domingue*. Athens: University of Georgia Press, 2001.

Knight, Franklin W. *Slave Society in Cuba During the Nineteenth Century*. Madison: University of Wisconsin Press, 1970.

Knight, Franklin W., ed. *General History of the Caribbean. Volume III: The Slave Societies of the Caribbean*. Paris and London: UNESCO and Macmillan, 1997.

Ramos Mattei, Andres, ed. *Azúcar y esclavitud*. San Juan: University of Puerto Rico Press, 1982.

Scarano, Francisco A. *Sugar and Slavery in Puerto Rico: The Plantation Economy of Ponce, 1800–1850*. Madison: University of Wisconsin Press, 1984.

Shepherd, Verene, and Beckles, Hilary McD., eds. *Caribbean Slavery in the Atlantic World: A Student Reader*. Kingston, Jamaica: Ian Randle, 2000.

Smith, S. D. *Slavery, Family and Gentry Capitalism in the British Atlantic: The World of the Lascelles, 1648–1834*. Cambridge, England: Cambridge University Press, 2006.

Turley, David. *Slavery*. Oxford, England: Blackwell, 2000.

CHAPTER 6

Imperial Fragmentation and Colonial Social Reconstruction, 1793–1886

Lord Bathurst [might consider] the propriety of communicating to the Governors of the several West Indies colonies that in the future no grants will be made to escheated slaves; but that all such persons will be emancipated; with the exception, first, of the aged, secondly, of the incurably diseased, thirdly, of the profligate, and fourthly of those whose ignorance is such as to prevent their earning their own subsistence.
—JAMES STEPHEN TO ROBERT HORTON, May 30, 1823

The old order changeth yielding place to new,
And God fulfills Himself in many ways,
Lest One good custom should corrupt the world.
—ALFRED LORD TENNYSON, *Morte d'Arthur*, 1842

Throughout the Caribbean, the nineteenth century represented a long period of social disintegration and reconstruction. Slowly and with considerable difficulty, the aging structure of the rigid, cruel, plantation slave societies yielded to the impatient emergence of a new set of polyglot societies of free, but distinctly not equal, peoples. The Caribbean experienced concurrently the same basic transformations that had characterized the societies of Western Europe and the mainland Americas. It was a time of turmoil, a time of change. It began with the determined declaration of the British North Americans in 1776 to rid themselves of their imperial bonds. It continued through the turbulent final decades of the nineteenth century. Everywhere societies were on the move, altering long-standing political and economic orders. Some historians have called this period the "Age of the Democratic Revolutions." In many ways, this is a misleading appellation. While there was much that was revolutionary, there was little that was truly democratic. Nevertheless, the changes were impressive and portentous. New configurations and new relationships weakened and sometimes dissolved the distinguishing bonds of empire, creating new political states. Nowhere was this more true than throughout the Americas. From the British empire emerged the republic of the United States of America in 1783. The French empire yielded Haiti in 1804. The Spanish empire produced a proliferation of restless states from Mexico to Argentina between 1810 and 1824, while the Portuguese empire, with a little prodding from the English, recognized Brazil as a coequal kingdom to Portugal in 1815 and granted it full independence in 1822. Haiti conquered the neighboring Spanish colony of Santo Domingo in 1822, only to lose it in 1844. Santo Domingo, finding a second course of Spanish colonialism no better than the first, opted for full independence in 1865. With the possible exception of Haiti, political reconstruction in the Caribbean had immediate meaning for only a small, privileged sector of the society. These political changes took place at the macrolevel of the state, and in most cases did not affect the daily lives of the vast majority of the people, the workers and peasants.

But at the local level, significant changes were also taking place. Within the Caribbean, by far the most important development was the growth of a predominantly Creole, inward-looking, and primarily peasant group of free workers evaluating on its own terms the burdensome legacy of slavery. Formerly excluded from meaningful participation in the political and cultural life of Caribbean communities, this sector suddenly became, throughout most of the region, the majority. As such, this group could no longer be benignly neglected. With freedom, these former slaves and "unappropriated people" proceeded to fashion their cultures and their societies in more positive ways than they could have done under the conditions and inherent restraints of the slave system. In French Saint-Domingue, the ex-slaves fought stubbornly under Toussaint Louverture to democratize their society far more than their metropolitan colleagues were prepared to do during the Revolution. They removed all disabilities of color, race, or place of birth from qualifications of citizenship in their new constitution promulgated in 1801. Elsewhere, the quest was to participate in the various territorial institutions and sensitize them to the urgent needs and expanding presence of the Afro-Caribbean sector of the population.

Colonialism had spread a common culture across wide areas but had not successfully imposed a cohesive common identity. Puerto Ricans thought of themselves as Spanish colonists who were different from the Cubans. Jamaicans shared much in common with Barbadians but felt distinctly different. Naturally, each Caribbean colony exhibited certain unique characteristics reflecting the variations in physical size, topography, economic development, population density, and composition; the "critical mass" of its dominant stratum; and even the peculiar course of its historical evolution.

Regional variation is not peculiar, however, to the Caribbean. Within any state, regardless of size, this sense of local consciousness often appears, coexisting with the larger identity. Regional or insular characteristics warped but never entirely broke the suggested commonalities that resulted from the special effects of slavery, the plantation system, and colonialism in the Caribbean. Without any doubt, the experience of slavery was the most pervasive single influence that affected the major Caribbean societies during the nineteenth century. The problem for local authorities rested less in its existence and control than in how to control its inevitable demise. Slavery, as David Brion Davis suggested, was a basic problem in Western culture. The Caribbean slave societies, therefore, evolved and disintegrated, consonant with factors that emanated both from their respective imperial systems and from factors produced locally. The combination of these external and internal factors explains the timing of the sequential stages of maturation, decline, and disintegration. Cuba and Puerto Rico did not have an identical experience with slavery and the plantation system during the nineteenth century, although within the narrow confines of the sugar industry, much was similar. The British colonies of Barbados, Jamaica, Trinidad, and Guiana all manifested significant variations in the postabolition period. The same observation could be made for the Dutch colonies of Curaçao and Surinam (now Suriname).

The timing of the abolition of slavery and the way it was carried out reflected both the political power of the metropolis in international affairs and the social, economic, and demographic conditions within each colony during the course of the nineteenth century. Yet the abolition of slavery represented merely one phase— albeit the final one—in the disintegration of the Caribbean slave society, as well as only one phase in the slow evolution of Caribbean society and the growth of Caribbean nationhood. The degree to which the majority of Caribbean communities had internalized slavery meant that they could never develop the type of social cohesion that was characteristic of mainland settler societies.

Settler societies, as we have already argued, represented the deliberate intention to re-create miniatures of the metropolis, with a definite symbiotic relationship. The colonists went out to occupy, settle, reproduce themselves, and produce whatever the land yielded in abundance. The colony became their *patria chica*, the region to which they eventually owed allegiance and with which they gradually forged an identity. But this does not indicate that all settler societies were identical copies of one another or that they were mirror images of their metropolitan societies. Indeed, Nicholas Canny and Anthony Pagden, in their excellent book *Colonial Identity in the Atlantic World, 1500–1800,* amply demonstrated that "the means by which the settler communities of the Atlantic world came to form, fabricate, or shape their identities were…highly individual ones," and, they asserted, "where you were very largely determined who you were." Likewise, Jack P. Greene cogently and perceptively argued for significant variations among the English settlements in the Americas in *Pursuits of Happiness: The Social Development of Early Modern British Colonies and the Formation of American Culture.* Settlers, regardless of their social status, consciously bore some ideal of the society they strove to construct— and the ideal was drawn from their home countries.

On the other hand, the overriding preoccupation of the exploitation, or non-settler, colonies was the crass emphasis on the organization of labor and the construction of a community geared to the maximum production of tropical staples or, in cases like British Honduras and British Guiana, timber for both the imperial and the international markets. The European components of the true exploitation societies viewed residence as a temporary sojourn to be endured and viewed their local communities as temporary political and economic extensions of the metropolises. With few exceptions, there were little or no feelings of identity or of community interest, since there could be no hope of re-creating the cultural ideals of the metropolises.

These two contrasting goals of the settler and the exploitation societies were neither clearly articulated nor distinctly separated at any time. In retrospect, it is easy to see that some colonies fell into one category, some into another, and some into both. But it was often a matter of timing. One or the other consideration superseded, or the two coexisted uneasily among the elites, as they did in Curaçao during the eighteenth century and in Cuba and Puerto Rico during the nineteenth century. Barbados, which originated as a settlement colony in the early seventeenth century, rapidly converted itself into an exploitation slave society by the end of the century. By the end of the eighteenth century, many other colonies—Jamaica, Guadeloupe, Martinique, Saint-Domingue, Trinidad—had settler components among their European exploiters. By then the European Creoles in these colonies were not considered as represensative of European culture as those who stayed at home. More important, in most colonies—especially the non-Hispanic Caribbean colonies—the European Creoles failed to maintain a large enough numerical group to sustain a viable subculture. The relatively small sizes of the white, politically dominant minorities—proportionally less than 20 percent in 1800 everywhere except in the Bahamas, Bermuda, Cuba, Puerto Rico, and Santo Domingo—simply could not develop separate identities that were confident and strong enough to impose themselves unilaterally on the rest of their societies. For the few whites in Barbados or Jamaica who spoke of those places as their homelands, the assertions had a hollow, contrived ring. This situation eventually affected the operation of the slave system and helped accomplish the disintegration of the slave society.

The colonial status was an important factor in the Caribbean. Unlike the circumstances in the United States, where slavery matured under the auspices of an independent, though sharply bifurcated nation-state, Caribbean slave societies always required the military, psychological, and economic support of the metropolises. The colonial status, therefore, made a difference in the timing of maturation, as well as in the abolition of the Caribbean slave systems. Colonies, by virtue of their subordinate status, could not operate independently of the metropolises. Crucial decisions concerning the colonies were resolved outside the area, in the metropolitan decision-making bodies. The problem of slavery was one such issue. A general emancipation of slaves independent of the whims of the metropolis involved reconsideration of the political status of the colony (as the situation in Saint-Domingue in 1794 made abundantly clear). For this reason, abolition assumed paramount importance in the internal fortunes and affairs of the European metropolitan powers.

The dismantling of the Caribbean slave systems can therefore be approached from two angles: the metropolitan dimension and the local perspective. Neither can be fully understood without the other. Slavery was, after all, a very complex system, and both a symbiosis and a dialectic continuously influenced the relations between masters and slaves.

The metropolitan dimension reveals itself most clearly in three interrelated facets of imperial life: politics, international economics, and the realm of ideas. These three facets intersected randomly across and within the various imperial systems, with differential impact on both settler and exploitation societies. Nevertheless, from the center, decisions tended to be made at high general levels without concern for the nuances of local or imperial variations. Imperial systems found it easier to act on general principles than on a plethora of individual cases. When the British Parliament legislated on the issue of slavery, it did not seriously consider that the circumstances in a relatively large colony like Jamaica varied from those in a small colony like Antigua. The French muted the enormous differences between Saint-Domingue and Martinique. The Dutch equated the conditions in Surinam (now Suriname) and Curaçao. The Spanish reluctantly conceded that Puerto Rico and Cuba varied considerably, thanks to the indecisive ten-year civil war in the latter colony.

With the exception of the unusual case of French Saint-Domingue, the abolition of slavery in the colonies followed concerted attacks on the institution at the political level in the metropolises. The process by which abolition took place began with general attacks on the nature of slavery as part of the tendency toward rationalism in the later half of the eighteenth century. This was followed by attacks on the slave trade and attempts from the center to ameliorate the material conditions of the slaves. Finally, there were attacks on the institution of slavery itself, with emancipation coming in some cases deliberately and in other cases precipitately. In almost all cases, the actual end of slavery, while not entirely unexpected, came surprisingly and untidily.

Changes in the general attitude toward slavery were reflected graphically in English court rulings throughout the eighteenth century. In 1729, the English attorney general and the solicitor general issued a strong opinion endorsing the perpetuity of the condition of slavery. "A slave," they wrote, "by coming from the West Indies, either with or without his master, to Great Britain or Ireland, doth not become free; and that his master's property or right in him is not thereby determined or varied; and that baptism doth not bestow freedom on him, nor make any alteration in his temporal condition in these kingdoms... [and] the master may legally compel him to return to the plantations."

By the 1770s, both public opinion and legal attitudes in Great Britain appeared to have made an abrupt about-face. In the famous ruling of Lord Chief Justice Mansfield on June 22, 1772, the detained intransit slave, James Somerset, was declared to be a free man. Somerset had been living in England with his master, a Jamaican plantation owner named Charles Stewart, for three years when he was encouraged to desert his service by antislavery supporters. Mansfield declared that the state of slavery was "of such a nature that it is incapable of being introduced for any reasons moral or political.... It's so odious, that nothing can be suffered to support it, but positive law." Six years later, in the case of *Joseph*

Knight vs. Wedderburn, a court in Scotland reinforced the opinion of *Somerset vs. Stewart.* "The state of slavery is not recognized by the laws of this kingdom," it declared, "and is inconsistent with the principles thereof; and the regulations in Jamaica, concerning slaves, do not extend to this kingdom . . . [and] that perpetual service, without wages, is slavery." These legal opinions complemented frequently articulated religious and philosophical antislavery positions and affected both the governing elites in the metropolis and an increasingly vocal majority of simple rural and urban folk. Not surprisingly, therefore, the cause of the Caribbean slaves became intrinsically connected with domestic political and economic discussions concerning political change in the metropolis.

In the 1780s and 1790s, the antislavery movement became organized with the formal creation of antislavery societies throughout England and France. These societies, through their representatives in Parliament in England and the Estates General and National Assembly in France, insisted that modifications of the colonial slave system be considered an essential requirement of colonial reform.

But it is only fair to point out that the majority of the opponents of slavery in the metropolises saw the institution more as "an aspect of commercial enterprise rather than as a central moral and human problem." The French antislavery society, the Société des Amis des Noirs, given the revolutionary situation, was far more successful in its advocacy of reform than any of its fellow associations, and indeed, the French did abolish slavery temporarily in 1793. Although Napoleon reinstituted slavery in Martinique and Guadeloupe, the situation in Saint-Dominigue moved out of his control, and his failure there was the prelude to greater failures to come. The British, however, did abolish the slave trade in 1808 and initiated an international campaign to terminate the trade everywhere. The slave trade to the Caribbean finally petered out by 1870.

Meanwhile, the institution of Caribbean slavery fell apart. The British government legally abolished slavery throughout its colonies in 1834, predicating its demise on a transitional period of enforced apprenticeship that terminated prematurely in 1838. The French and the Danes abolished slavery in 1848, and the Dutch, in 1863. The Spanish government abolished slavery in Puerto Rico in 1873 and in Cuba in 1886. With the abolition in Cuba, legal slavery ceased in the Caribbean.

With the exception of the Spanish Caribbean colonies, the movement toward the abolition of slavery followed a predictable, almost symmetrical course. As far as it can be ascertained, the gradual weakening of the economic importance of the colonies undermined their political influence within the structure of metropolitan decision making. The central decision-making apparatus capitulated before the combined pressures of political reformers, imperial free traders, and humanitarian idealists. In all cases, the parliaments tried to reconcile what they perceived as the divergent interests of metropolises and colonies, of colonial slave owners versus domestic political and economic pressure groups. The ones who got shortchanged in the deliberations were the slaves and ex-slaves.

One important observation that is often overlooked in the histories of abolition from the metropolitan viewpoint is that concern for the slaves—the real victims of the brutal system of slavery—was an incidental part of official policy. The fleeting references to recognition and reparation for the slaves never made an impact when the time for emancipation arrived. Concerns for commerce and property prevailed over those for justice and humanity. Yet the home governments and, above all, the advocates of abolition cannot be accused of calculated malice or unconscious hypocrisy. Metropolitan abolitionists were convinced that they were acting in the best interests of the slaves. Many were convinced that the material conditions of Caribbean slaves were superior to those of English workers but that their eternal servitude was unnatural, illegal, and unacceptable. Moreover, political decision making resulted from the brokering of conflicting pressure groups in the parliaments. The slaves and the vast majority of the Afro-Caribbean population had no way of participating directly in imperial politics. Representation on their behalf came from several groups with other, often more specific, interests in mind. When slaves became restless, rebellious, and destructive of people and property, they attracted the attention of a far wider audience than their immediate masters.

The British imperial system provided the first metropolitan-directed abolition movement. The abolitionists in England drew their strength from three areas: the religious community, the British working classes, and the imperialists and free traders—those supporting unrestricted trade and an expanding empire. In the colonies, the nonconformist churches—especially the Baptists, Moravians, and Methodists—advocated, with certain qualifications, the abolition of slavery. But they were really fighting for their institutional survival in the colonies and a bit of the evangelical action. The truth is that without the Afro-Caribbean population, most of which was in a highly coercive form of slavery, the nonconformist churches would have no clients for their services. Their natural constituency in the British Isles—the working classes—had a rather narrow equivalent in the colonies where most occupations were handled by slaves.

The British inclination toward emancipation coincided with a period when British industry and the English economy were no longer narrowly Atlantic and subservient to the domineering interests of their staple-producing West Indies.

Great Britain, at the beginning of the nineteenth century, was moving away from a predominantly trading nation to a complex economy based on finance, manufacturing, and trade. British capital and British manufactured goods were no longer traded mainly within the empire. The sugar industry illustrated this growing universality of English commercial activity. British West Indian sugar producers, once the main suppliers of raw sugar to the British market, were by the 1830s competing on that market with sugar produced in India, Mauritius, Cuba, Brazil, Singapore, Java, and the Philippines. They were competing not only with other slave-labor-produced sugar, but with an increasing amount of free-labor-produced sugar. The exporters of refined sugar faced the additional competition of a rising beet-sugar production, both in the United States and in Continental Europe. West Indian production was becoming increasingly noncompetitive, both within the imperial system and in the international market, owing to its low technological development and correspondingly high production costs. Sugar consumers came to resent the imperial preference that kept prices high and the economic and political importance of the small, tightly knit group of West Indian merchants and planters. This political and economic decline was near its nadir when the British Parliament moved to abolish slavery in 1833–1834.

The economic factor cannot be easily overlooked in the process of abolition. The English, French, Danish, and Dutch abolition movements coincided with the period of perceived economic stabilization or decline in the respective imperial possessions. Sugar exports from Jamaica, the largest of the British islands, remained fairly constant between 1821 and 1832. The median export figure of about 82,000 hogsheads then was considerably lower than the median figure for the period between 1799 and 1820. Sugar and rum production in the entire West Indies had declined between 1815 and 1833. A similar situation existed in Martinique, Guadeloupe, and Surinam (now Suriname). In those cases, production either remained constant or fell slightly, while the price of sugar plunged considerably. Overall, the situation varied from island to island or from colony to colony, but the predominant trend was toward fewer, though more productive, estates and the diversification of products.

The great number of estates that were sold or deeply indebted to outside merchants and bankers reflected the serious crisis of the Caribbean export economies. Fifty percent of the 151 sugar estates on the small island of St. Croix were in the hands of creditors in 1841. The dismal plight of the sugar economy in St. Croix found resonant parallels throughout the small colonies, especially the island colonies. But the situation was also true for the larger producers. In Jamaica, some 50 percent of the 775 sugar estates operating in 1772 had abandoned production by the end of the century. When the English slave trade was abolished in 1808, many estates could no longer recoup their operating expenses, much less repay their creditors. As a result, some 100 estates had simply been abandoned, while another 100 faced debt claims that jeopardized their continuation. From the viewpoint of sugar producers, the colonies faced considerable difficulties. If colonists did not sell their products, they could not buy imported manufactured goods. Metropolitan exports to these colonies, therefore, tended to decline prior to emancipation. Imports in the British Caribbean fell by nearly 25 percent between 1821 and 1833. French exports to Martinique fell by nearly 30 percent between 1841 and 1848, while those to Guadeloupe dropped by about 33 percent. The economic figures emphasize only one aspect of the metropolitan-colonial relationship, but they clearly underlined the declining economic importance of the Caribbean colonies to the industrializing countries of Europe. Obviously the non-Hispanic Caribbean was at the end of an economic cycle in the early nineteenth century. Except for Cuba and Puerto Rico, the staple export market was in a stage of crisis, and this reduced economic confidence in the region and its producers. Such perception might have been as important as the reality to the metropolitan decision makers who were contemplating the future of slavery in their colonies.

Unlike the British, French, Danish, and Dutch Caribbean, the Spanish Caribbean was just beginning to enter the sugar revolutions during the early nineteenth century. In Puerto Rico, sugar exports increased from about 838 tons in 1812 to 14,126 tons in 1830 and to more than 52,000 tons in 1850. In Cuba, the technological revolution after 1838 slowly transformed the sugar industry into a modern complex based on steam, railroads, and extensive *ingenios*. By 1868, Cuba, with an annual production of nearly 750,000 tons, could almost singlehandedly satisfy the world cane-sugar market demand. Yet the changing world sugar market and the mounting problems for all cane-sugar producers could be deduced from the figures for beet-sugar production, which in 1868 exceeded Cuban cane-sugar production.

Unfortunately for the Cuban and Puerto Rican sugar producers, Spain lagged far behind the other European metropolises and the United States in industrialization. It could not supply its colonies with the required manufactured consumer items or with the essential new technical equipment for efficient sugar making, much less provide a suitable market for the rapidly increasing quantity of tropical products. In addition, domestic political turbulence rendered Spain incapable of exerting the political and administrative control the colonial settler element desired over the restless slaves. Metropolitan influence in the Spanish Caribbean slave societies during the nineteenth century failed to rival that in the non-Hispanic Caribbean. Despite metropolitan opposition, therefore, Puerto Rico abolished slavery in 1873 at the request of the colonists—a request voiced as early as 1812. Spanish attempts to mediate in Cuban affairs were continually frustrated between the 1850s and the final abolition of slavery in 1886. What is more, both Cuba and Puerto Rico gradually gravitated away from the economic sphere of Spain.

Cuba was undoubtedly unique in the Caribbean experience. By the middle of the nineteenth century, Cuba was a prominent contributor to the Spanish treasury, accounting for almost 25 percent of Spain's revenues. The island provided the principal market for Spanish flour shipped from Bilbao and Santander, textiles from Barcelona, and wine and olive oil from Málaga, Seville, and Cádiz. The Spanish merchant community was clearly not in a position to antagonize their best customers by supporting the abolitionist movement that developed in Spain in the late 1860s. What is more, the slave owners owed the merchants a lot of money, and attacking slavery merely threatened to impoverish the owners and destroy their ability to repay their obligations. The Spanish merchants apparently had no faith in the purchasing power of ex-slaves. Above all, they shrewdly calculated that the termination of slavery would probably coincide with the end of the imperial connection and the diminution of their major export market. While merchants and shippers in England and France sought the abolition of the slave trade and the expansion of free trade, Spanish merchants and shippers supported restricted trade and the continuation of slavery.

That the Spanish should find themselves diametrically opposite to the rest of Western Europe on the issue of slavery sprung almost entirely from imperial economic and political considerations. The economic and political power of the planter class in Cuba was inordinately strong within the context of the Spanish imperial system. It was tantamount to the influence of the West India Interest within the British Parliament before 1776 or of the French chambers of commerce before the loss of Saint-Domingue. Emancipation would hardly have presented the same perspective to the English Parliament and public had they not lost their cotton-producing North American colonies or to the French had they not lost their rich colony of Saint-Domingue.

Economic considerations became inextricably bound up with political action as the British sought to pressure other participants to end the slave trade after 1808. The campaign was a long one. Spain accepted £400,000 in 1818 and agreed to end the Africa-Antilles trade within two years. But Cuban sugar production required African workers, and the Antillean slave trade continued until 1865. The French slave trade continued until the 1830s, and only in the 1850s did the vigorous Brazilian slave trade cease. The abolition of the slave trade was the necessary prerequisite for the general emancipation of the Caribbean slaves. Pressure to end the trade—which was largely international—was more easily and successfully applied than pressure to abolish slavery, which was considered an internal affair. Cuban slave owners in the nineteenth century were in a far stronger political position than British and French Caribbean slave owners to thwart metropolitan attempts to emancipate their slaves.

The dismantling of the Caribbean slave society during the nineteenth century reflected not merely political and economic considerations, but a new intellectual awareness about the nature of man and society. Such ideas had always accompanied the controversy over slavery, with humanists, theologians, and philosophers dividing almost equally on both sides of the issue—despite the overwhelming general acceptance of the institution itself. As secular thought moved in the direction of social engineering—most classically expressed or implied in the theories of Comtian positivism, social Darwinism, and Marxism—hostility to the institution increased, especially among nonintellectuals. But condemnation of the institution did little to increase sympathy for the slaves. Europeans expressed concern with the plantation society and the socioeconomic complex of slavery mainly because of its relation to their own domestic affairs. Slavery was therefore viewed in relation to social and technological goals: as an anachronism to the positivists who felt it inhibited the advent of the metaphysical stage of human development, a sign of fundamental weakness to the Darwinists, or a tool of the bourgeoisie to the Marxists. In its own way, each theory included strong elements of ethnocentricity and racism. But the important point is that all these theories increased the general antislavery sentiment in the metropolises and contributed to the greater agitation that mobilized the metropolitan mobs. Despite being Europocentric and reformist, abolitionist pressures from metropolitan social theorists undermined the position of slavery in the colonies by including it in their demands for domestic social and political reform. Not surprisingly, therefore, British abolition came in the wake of the great Reform Bill of 1832, and the French abolition came with the revolution of 1848. Abolition was partially a by-product of social theories emanating from the metropolises.

In the colonies, on the other hand, abolition and emancipation involved fundamental social problems affecting economic values, social positions, and political reconstruction and realignment. It was not, as in the metropolises, a tangential, theoretical issue. Moreau de Saint-Méry, the Caribbean Creole, demonstrated with abundant clarity this revolutionary social awareness when he declared in 1791 that extending the "Rights of Man" to the mulattoes in the French colonies would ultimately extend power to the most numerous. "For if once the slaves suspect," he wrote, "that there is a power other than their masters which holds the final disposition of their fates; if they once see the mulattoes have invoked this power and by its aid have become our equals—then France must renounce all hope of preserving her colonies." This prophecy applied not only to his homeland of Martinique, but to the larger neighboring colony of Saint-Domingue. His declaration revealed the enormous social tensions under which the colonial slave society endured and betrayed signs of its inherent self-destructiveness.

The social tension resulted from the nature of the slave society, for, with the exception of Bermuda, Cuba, and Puerto Rico, it presented the spectacle of a relatively small minority of whites dominating a large mass of black and mixed persons. Race, ethnicity, and color were facts of everyday life, the indelible determinants of status and condition. In most colonies this precarious numerical position contributed to a feeling of being beseiged among the whites. On the eve of the revolution in 1789, the white population of Saint-Domingue amounted to only 8 percent of the total, while Guadeloupe had only 12 percent whites. At the time of emancipation in Jamaica, the European sector of the population amounted to only about 4 percent of the island's total. In Barbados, the proportion of whites was just 15 percent. Antigua had slightly less than 6 percent whites. In 1830, Curaçao had a white population of slightly less than 25 percent, compared with 45 percent slaves. In plantation-dominant Surinam (now Suriname), the white population—of whom approximately one-half were Jews—amounted to just about 4 percent of the total population.

In every colony, the minority white population lived in fear of the legitimate aspirations of the free mixed and enslaved groups. Where the whites were not only few in number but also isolated on coercively managed plantations, the fear was even greater. Where elements of the settler groups existed, however, the situation was somewhat different. In Cuba, the white population was nearly 60 percent of the total in 1870. In Puerto Rico, the white population was about 51 percent. In both, too, fairly large mixed populations had predated the colonies' conversions to exploitation plantation societies. Time had fashioned a strong local sentiment and self-consciousness among these whites, and their attitudes toward their lands were not unlike elsewhere on the mainland where white majorities existed. Cuban whites, in particular, tended to identify politically with the United States, especially the southern slave owners of the early nineteenth century.

Throughout the Caribbean, the white population, regardless of size, dominated the administrative machinery of the local government, the militia, and the established churches. But in no two imperial spheres were colonial administrations the same, and even within each group, there were significant variations. Political control ranged from being very strong in the British colonies—especially in Barbados and Jamaica with their local planter-controlled legislatures—to weak in the Spanish islands that were theoretically administered from the metropolis. The Spanish colonial administration, notorious for its strong authoritarianism in the sixteenth and seventeenth centuries, succumbed in practice to the rule of local Creoles and *peninsulares* in Cuba and Puerto Rico in the nineteenth century. From their control of the town councils and the militias, the local whites were able to delay the implementation of abolition measures and to obstruct the evolution of an entirely free, multiracial society. Yet dependence on the metropolis, as Moreau de Saint-Méry pointed out, made the colonial whites extremely vulnerable. The problem of slavery affected politics as well as society and economics.

All Caribbean societies were afflicted with revolutionary discontent during the nineteenth century, and this discontent permeated all the social classes. As indicated in Chapter 5, the white classes never represented a homogeneous group, even in those situations where they constituted a very small minority of the population. While skin color provided a certain status indication, it proved insufficient to bond the conflicting class divisions. So the whites remained a faction-ridden, mutedly contentious group whose convenient unity was barely maintained against the twin dangers of class conflict and caste hostility. The divisions between Creoles and European expatriates was an ancient social one that had, by the nineteenth century, become somewhat anachronistic. Throughout the Caribbean expatriates no longer dominated the economy. The increasing sentiments of regional self-consciousness among the Creoles challenged the notion that birth in the metropolis provided inherent advantages for life in the tropics. Indeed, from the end of the eighteenth century, locally born whites throughout the region were referring with pride to themselves as Creoles or Americans or designating themselves by where they lived. The imperial system, however, continued to distinguish those born in the metropolis from those born overseas and virtually to exclude locals from high administrative positions. This preference accentuated the social distance between the two major white groups in the colonies. Ironically, although the *grands blancs* of Saint-Domingue behaved like a true nobility in the tropics, their representatives to the French Estates General after 1789 fraternized and voted with their metropolitan social equivalent, the Third Estate. Nevertheless, it must be conceded that the Third Estate had a number of the other two estates within its ranks.

Colonial life was curious. The white social classes in the plantation-dominant zones of the Caribbean colonies derived their social position from their relationship to plantation-export production and their cultural affinity to what they considered the prevailing behavioral norms of their respective metropolises. Yet each new generation found itself further away from the metropolitan culture and more involved in the scarring competition for status and office. While slavery indicated a major distinction in rank, the abolition of slavery jeopardized the accepted—and to the whites the acceptable—social distinctions between the various groups of men and women. One asset of the slave society to the white classes, therefore, was the ability to disguise social class differences by emphasizing racial caste solidarity. But racial solidarity, in the absence of a sufficient mass of individuals, still left the group vulnerable to interracial interaction and inadequate to fulfill all the occupational demands of the community.

Colonial governors invariably found that the white Creoles knew more about the day-to-day operational procedures of government and were more adept at local politics than the often disease-prone metropolitan recruits. Attempts at political and social cohesion, however, were frequently frustrated by the differences of political philosophy and regional origins of the members of the white elite. Scotsmen, Irishmen, and Welshmen did not necessarily behave more fraternally as individual representatives of metropolitan Great Britain in the far-flung reaches of empire. Basques, Catalans, and Galicians formed clubs that reinforced their *patriachiquismo* in the overseas Spanish colonies in a manner that might have been more exaggerated than in Iberia. And the political consequences of war changed colonies from one imperial sphere to another, so that after 1763, for example, generations of solidly elitist French in St. Lucia, Dominica, and St. Vincent found the newly arrived English treating them with undeserved suspicion and contempt. The same attendant snobbery followed the transfer of Spanish Trinidad to the English in 1797. Elite divisions based on religion and culture were not as marked as class divisions within the white group. Metropolitan white travelers to the Caribbean colonies, reflecting the views of the resident planter class, painted a dismal picture of lower-class dissolution, dissipation, and despair, not unlike the description generalized by Edward Long of Jamaica.

Long's negative picture was generally valid for all nonsettler colonies. The miserable condition of the poor whites, however, was brought on not by hereditary social class origins, but by the necessities of the plantation culture with its limited social activities, large subordinated masses, and extreme sexual imbalance among both white and black. For the plantation colonies themselves offered little to the lower class of whites except the dubious distinction of being regarded as socially superior to all nonwhites.

In the settler colonies of Cuba and Puerto Rico and in the veritable commercial marts, such as Curaçao or Guadeloupe, the situation was different. The lower-class whites or Creoles were not necessarily inferior to the upper-class whites. Indeed, they were often more economically successful and much more attached to the colony that was generating a life of its own. Cuba and Puerto Rico continued the traditional Hispanic strife—though considerably mitigated—of the Spanish-American mainland colonies' imperial rivalry between Creoles and *peninsulares*. But more crucial during the nineteenth century was the combined white slave-owner–sugar-producer resentment to the commercial and political policies of the mother countries. As long as slavery existed as a necessary form of labor recruitment and organization on the sugar estates, the whites supported

their metropolises, whose military might was needed in any possible confrontation of the races. The Spanish government exploited this situation of fear for a
very long time.

In economic success, as in decline, the colonial white classes would have been
an extremely restless, if not a revolutionary, group. The metropolitan attacks on
slavery did not help their precarious situation, since such attacks exposed both
their economic and social weaknesses. By threatening the bonds between colonial
and metropolitan whites, the dispute over slavery opened opportunities for slave
revolts. Most Europeans, overseas in the colonies as well as at home, admitted that
slavery was necessary for the survival of the colonies, especially after the destruction of Saint-Domingue. Thus, self-preservation tended to mitigate the mutual
suspicion and hostility within the white sector.

Still, white attitudes toward slavery took different courses in settler and nonsettler colonies during the nineteenth century. In some colonies, such as Puerto
Rico and Curaçao, slave owning was not a significant social index for the white
person. White and nonwhite slave owners did not feel especially threatened by
revengeful ex-slaves. The relative poverty of those colonies seemed to have an
efficacious equalizing effect on all the population, free and nonfree. In Cuba, the
large slave owners of the western part of the island fought abolition doggedly for
nearly fifty years. They brought in all the intellectually bankrupt arguments that
the nonsettler colonies had made familiar in the history of slavery: threats to legal
property rights, economic decline, threats to "civilization," and racial incompatibility. They never succeeded in developing an original, rational argument—as had
their North American colleagues—establishing slavery as a positive social good.
Instead, they merely played the game halfheartedly to gain time to develop a large
enough population and the mechanical technology that would adjust the imbalance between the high labor demands of sugar making and a low labor pool.

The racial fear of the nonsettler whites was more realistic, not only because
they were numerically outnumbered by discontented slaves and free persons of
color, but because the intercaste divisions of the society were under such a tremendous strain. It was the impatient demands of the free persons of color on Saint-
Domingue that opened the floodgates of revolution in the colony and eventually
led to the overthrow of all the whites and free persons of color. The free colored
people had legitimate grievances—such as the legal status of mulattoes—that they
wanted redressed. But these demands of the mulattoes ran counter to the white
grievances that emphasized a greater colonial autonomy and further restriction in
the privileges granted nonwhites. The outbreak of fighting in the colony, in which
both free groups employed their slaves as soldiers, was the ignition for an all-out
assault on the entire structure of the plantation system. The slaves eventually won
the multidimensional war and set up their own independent republic—the second
attempt at political engineering in the hemisphere.

The situation in Saint-Domingue was not duplicated elsewhere. The whites
employed obstructionist tactics, but they could not prevent successful nonwhite
penetration of the occupational and economic sectors. By 1832, nonwhites had

even gained some political abilities in the British Caribbean. The decline of the sugar industry in some places, like Jamaica, further weakened the resistance of the local whites to the demand of prosperous blacks for increased participation in politics and the economy. The rights to vote and to sit in the local assemblies, won just before the abolition of slavery, placed the political power of the whites in jeopardy. That they held on to the power and privileges based on their skin color for so much longer derived not from the dynamics of the local situation but from the operation of imperial politics.

The conduct of the white upper strata of exploitation plantation colonies during the twilight of slavery provides a good insight into the nature of the colonial elite. The Caribbean slave society was an artificial and novel construct in the history of European imperialism. The stratification based on occupation, race, and color created fundamental cleavages that could be removed only by the disintegration of the productive system and a reconstitution of the social elements. In most exploitation colonies, the whites never considered the place as a proper substitute for home. They behaved as exiles in the tropics, longing to get back to the societies from which they had come. Whenever they could, they escaped. And the problem of absenteeism was a chronic one in the British Caribbean. Since such whites tended not to see themselves as part of societies distinct from and independent of their mother countries, they were forced to defend their existence along a set of rules laid down by the Europeans and designed for an ethnically homogeneous society. Slavery was no longer an integral part of European society, and so it did not feature in their institutional arrangements. Europeans in slave colonies therefore had to supplement these arrangements and constantly remind their metropolitan cousins that life in the tropics was a world apart.

In the late eighteenth century, when the system of slavery was under vigorous attack from the Europeans, the Caribbean slave owners in the British colonies thought that by agreeing to some amelioration in the condition of their slaves they could retain the status quo and elude the abolition of the system. That plan failed—as did their relations in the international sugar market to which they felt irrevocably tied. Finally in the nineteenth century, they accepted compensation for their slaves and felt relieved to recover some of the fiscal expenditure with which to face the uncertain economic future. With the exception of Cuba, all the other Caribbean slave societies were intellectually bankrupt at the end of the slavery period. Everywhere the elites were in trouble—politically, economically, socially, and intellectually—and the metropolises were not very sympathetic to their plight.

The collapse of the superstructure of the slave system was not unrelated to the aggressive erosive forces from below. The slaves had never accepted the institution as a satisfactory medium of salvation. Nor, regardless of the belief of their masters, had they acquiesced in it fully. The long history of the Maroons in all the colonies bore eloquent testimony to the unquenchable will to be free that permeated every slaveholding society. After the example of Saint-Domingue and the Maroon wars, the restlessness of the slaves throughout the region increased the discomfort of the whites. In almost every colony, the slaves felt, with some justification, that the local whites were deliberately obstructing the course of emancipation. They also erroneously felt, especially when the agitation for complete abolition intensified after the 1830s, that they had already been set free by metropolitan orders. Violence accompanied the end of slavery in Cuba, St. Croix, Martinique, Guadeloupe, Demerara, and Jamaica. The slaves made it clear that they meant to emancipate themselves, by force if necessary.

But even without the forceful pressure of the slaves, Caribbean slavery would eventually destroy itself. Not only did it bear the seeds of potential self-destruction in open racial violence and sabotage, but it also failed to establish—as in the United States—a philosophy that could successfully counteract the increasing doubts of humanitarians, economists, and politicians in the home countries. In retrospect, it is quite easy to see that the process of abolition gathered tremendous momentum during the first three decades of the nineteenth century. But at the time, some of the most outspoken abolitionists, such as William Wilberforce and José Antonio Saco, thought that the final act of emancipation would take place in the distant future.

Abolition depended on the coincidence of the two erosive elements of external politico-economic reservations and internal caste and class antagonisms. Despite the overwhelming majority of slaves and their penchant for revolt, only in Saint-Domingue (Haiti) did successful revolt result in the termination of the system of slavery. In Puerto Rico, the upper strata realized that slavery was not the only method of human subordination and labor organization. Moreover, with the growing awareness of capital manipulation and the new sophistication in cost accounting, it was readily seen that a system of slavery required balancing convenience and cost. Slaveholders throughout the Caribbean paid an unduly heavy cost for the dubious convenience of having their workers precisely when and where they wanted them.

The rise of industrial capitalism proved an enemy of any social system that was inefficient as a mode of labor production or relatively inflexible in rational planning and cost accounting. It was never a simple case of slavery creating capitalism, which, in turn, destroyed its creator. As an integral part of international capitalism, plantation producers had to be responsive to the whims of their suppliers of capital, laborers, and markets. Rising costs of supplies and falling prices for commodities created severe problems for producers. While the price structure fluctuated, world overproduction—real or imagined—tended to drive the prices for sugar, coffee, cacao, and rum below production costs in the British West Indies. According to Lowell Ragatz, between 1822 and 1833 British Caribbean muscovado prices on the London market averaged only about thirty shillings per hundredweight, while production costs were estimated at more than twenty-four shillings. Additional transportation costs and import duties meant that the Caribbean producers were selling their product below cost. Sugar was the main commercial commodity, but the downward price spiral of sugar found a parallel in the other tropical crops as well. Coffee prices fluctuated from about

117 to 145 shillings per hundredweight in 1822, to between 42 and 83 shillings per hundredweight in 1830, and to between 75 and 94 shillings per hundredweight in 1833. Rum prices in 1830 were estimated to be two shillings and sixpence per gallon below production cost. Of course, these were crude calculations, and neither producers nor marketers could calculate the true production cost of their product at that time.

Caribbean producers faced certain fixed costs, and the wild gyrations of prices returned an unsteady income that left them incapable of making the capital expenditures necessary to maintain their equipment; ameliorate the condition of their slaves; or repair damages done by fire, earthquakes, hurricanes, floods, and other natural disasters. From Anguilla to Jamaica, the export economy found itself in straitened circumstances, and an increasing number of estates succumbed to foreclosures for debt payment.

Moreover, it was a situation that fed on itself. The plantation producers often worked on credit, and with the restrictions of credit in uncertain times, they found themselves in particular difficulties. But capital investment to increase efficiency, particularly in the quality of sugar that was produced, did not necessarily bring encouragement and rewards from their European and North American purchasers. The vacuum-pan process that produced a higher-grade sugar than muscovado threatened the metropolitan refiners and further jeopardized the rationality of mercantilistic restrictions. By the early 1840s, the Cubans were beginning to use the vacuum-pan process, but the benefits did not accrue to the British Caribbean producers until after 1845, when Parliament removed the surtax on "improved" sugar shipped from the colonies.

The economic zigzags of the nineteenth century could not obscure the fact that the plantation economy of the non-Hispanic Caribbean was sliding agonizingly down the road to obsolescence and impoverishment. The tragedy was not that production had declined on the main estates—for with the notable exception of Jamaica, sugar production stabilized or slightly increased after 1838—but that the Caribbean area needed to produce far more sugar at far lower prices to survive economically with an overall expanding world production not only of cane sugar but also of beet sugar. The British and French Antillean producers were, like all commodity exporters, at a market disadvantage, since they did not monopolize the supply of their product. Moreover, after emancipation the political power of the fabled West India Interest collapsed, removing the previous lobby for imperial protection offered to the British Caribbean producers on the English sugar market.

By the 1830s, the trauma of Haiti had manifested itself everywhere throughout the plantation Caribbean. In Cuba as well as British Guiana, planters dolefully predicted that a general emancipation of the slaves would result in the utter destruction of their so-called white civilization, the slaughter of the white inhabitants, and the further catastrophic reduction of the colonies to "rack and ruin." Emancipation came in the 1830s and 1840s in the British and French colonies, respectively, and nothing of the sort happened.

Apologists for the planter class in the British Antilles kept blaming the economic uncertainty in the region on the lack of industry among the Afro-Caribbean population, even after the abolition of slavery in 1834 and the termination of the disastrous apprenticeship system in 1838. Absentee planters, like Alexander Barclay of Jamaica, and un–self-conscious racists, like Thomas Babington Macaulay and Alexander Postlethwaite in England—as well as later historians who have repeated their misinformed biases about Caribbean society—simply did not understand the situation. They all believed that the ex-slaves were exhibiting some congenital defect and would not work, as though they wished to substantiate their previous outrageous convictions that the whip produced the most efficacious incentive to African labor.

Recent research has proved these assertions false. In only a few cases did the ex-slaves desert the plantations permanently. Planters and their supporters regarded the export economy as the only viable economy and so advocated the coercion and regimentation of the free black population under conditions not far removed from slavery. In some colonies, especially along the frontiers of Surinam (now Suriname), Trinidad, and Guiana, East Indians were introduced to bolster the servile plantation labor force and to provide a major stimulus to the expansion of the plantation system after the middle of the nineteenth century.

The theory that the black people of the Caribbean were either lazy or inept—or that the societies had collapsed, and the local economies were ruined after emancipation—was both malicious and unjust. A manifestation of the myopic, European ethnocentric view of the Caribbean, such observations were far removed from the reality of its dual economic structure and multiracial, multicultural complexity. Caribbean postslavery societies were not ruined but in a state of flux.

The everyday world for the vast majority of the Antillean population after the abolition of slavery was far from synonymous with the fortunes of sugar prices on the export market. Declines in the price of sugar affected them adversely but did not indicate the end of their economic existence. The internal economy based on small, diversified farming and local marketing, long practiced by slaves and ex-slaves, survived vigorously until a series of natural disasters in the 1850s, along with the machinations of the colonial system, dealt them a severe blow. Reversal, however, did not indicate annihilation, and the peasant economy regained its strength and flourished toward the end of the century.

The temporary demise of the sugar-export economy indeed signaled a new day for the African and Afro-Caribbean peoples. At the very time that the Europeans complained of "rack and ruin," the Caribbean colonies witnessed the most dynamic growth of a free peasantry. In land-abundant territories, such as Cuba, Puerto Rico, and the Dominican Republic, small farming expanded rapidly. In the former British sugar colonies, abandoned estate land became available. The dramatic decline in land prices beginning in the 1820s afforded the purchase of numerous estates at bargain prices. Both the affluent free colored and the frugal ex-slave populations took advantage of this circumstance. Where they could, the ex-slaves formed cooperatives, often under the guidance of religious leaders, and bought estates. Where they could not find the cash, they simply occupied available vacant lands and continued the cultivation of some of the many food crops that the planters and the colonial governments had imported during the eighteenth century to supplement the diet of the slaves.

In the British Caribbean, the establishment of these "free villages," as they were called, was a deliberate act, assisted by the stipendiary magistrates who were sent out from England to oversee the reconstitution of the new societies and to provide legal assistance to the ex-slaves against the powerful opposition of the planter-dominated local assemblies. The success of the free-village structure, however, depended on the peculiarities of geography, managerial personnel, and the fortuitous nature of local politics.

In larger territories like Jamaica, Trinidad, and Guiana, where there was ample uncultivated and unpossessed land, the industrious example of the Maroon communities had acted as a powerful magnet for the servile thousands working on the sugar plantations. After emancipation, a large proportion of the ex-slaves settled in free villages and formed the foundation of an agricultural peasantry, relating with, but largely independent of, the sugar estates. In Jamaica, black freeholders increased from 2,014 in 1838 to approximately 7,800 in 1840, to more than 20,000 in 1845, and to about 50,000 by 1859. In St. Vincent, some 8,209 persons built their own houses between 1838 and 1857 and bought and brought under cultivation more than 12,000 acres of land between 1845 and 1857. In Antigua, 67 free villages with a total of 5,187 houses and 15,644 inhabitants were established between 1833 and 1858. The situation was similar in Guiana, where land acquisition by ex-slaves was one of the most remarkable examples of West Indian industry. In 1838, the 15,000 ex-slaves were virtually landless. By 1842, more than 1,000 black families had already purchased over 7,000 acres of prime coastal land, valued at more than $100,000. By 1848, the Afro-Guyanese population had bought more than 400 estates and built more than 10,000 houses for themselves.

The capital investment to buy estates and build houses represented the ready availability of substantial amounts of cash among the nonwhite population at a time when currency was relatively scarce. This cash was certainly not under the control of the planting classes and was not directly derived from exporting sugar and sugar products to Great Britain. It was frugally collected and wisely invested by a new community that viewed the region as its permanent home. But the enormous expenditure on land immediately after emancipation also indicated that Caribbean slaves had had considerable amounts of cash, despite the fact that the large sums paid by the European mother countries as "compensation" money after emancipation went not to the ex-slaves but to their former masters.

Small peasant farming diversified the agricultural exports of the islands. New products, such as coconuts, arrowroot, beeswax, and honey, became important cash crops of these peasant farmers, and they became virtually self-sufficient in ground provisions. At the same time, the peasant farmers boosted the production of sugarcane, tobacco, coffee, cacao, limes, and rice.

The new communities and the new crops did not break the strong reliance on the production of sugar for the economic mainstay of the Caribbean region. To a large extent, sugar still remained "king." Part of its attraction was the large profit still to be made from sugar where soils were fresh and fertile, as in Cuba, Puerto Rico, Trinidad, and Guiana. The new producers had the advantage of adopting more efficient new technology, such as the system of *colonos* and *centrales* in Cuba, where independent cane farmers supplied their crop to huge complex mills that had greater grinding and sugar-producing facilities than they could satisfy from their own fields. In Cuba, too, railroads accelerated the transportation of canes and shattered the conventionally restricting radius of the plantation. With railroads and the new mills, the boundaries of the *central* virtually disappeared.

To find adequate labor, the region began to import Asians and other foreigners to work on the plantations rather than attempting to attract the free lower classes with higher wages. Between 1847 and 1871, the Cubans imported more than 100,000 Chinese as well as Mayo, Yaqui, and Mayan prisoners of war as laborers to augment their slave forces on the sugar estates. Between 1838 and 1917, nearly half a million East Indians came to the Caribbean to work on plantations—British Guiana imported 238,000; Trinidad, 145,000; Guadeloupe, 39,000; Surinam (now Suriname), 34,000; Jamaica, 21,500; Martinique, more than 6,748; Grenada, 2,570; St. Vincent, 1,820; and St. Lucia, 1,550. British Guiana imported 14,002 Chinese between 1853 and 1879, while Guadeloupe brought in 500 between 1854 and 1887, and Martinique introduced 500 in 1859 alone. But the Caribbean was not discriminating geographically in its search for laborers, bringing them from Ireland, Germany, Portgual, Spain, the Madeiras, West Africa, and Japan, as well as India and China. The importation of these contract, or indentured, laborers required huge sums of money to pay the daily wage of one shilling and sixpence (in the British colonies) and to provide all those services of housing and medical attention that the estates had been accustomed to supplying their nonfree workers. Only the most promising colonies could afford large-scale, subsidized labor importation. British Guiana invested £360,655 on the importation of about 50,000 laborers from Africa, India, Madeira, and the West Indian islands between 1841 and 1847. The high mortality rates and repatriation costs were discouraging at first. Eventually the immigration scheme succeeded. Land was sold to the East Indians, reindenture was made more attractive, and after 1898, the incentive of the automatic, paid return passage was abolished.

Asian indentured labor provided the mainstay of the sugar industry in Cuba, Trinidad, and Guiana, permitting expansion during the nineteenth century. But crucial variations in the scale of production developed. In 1792, the most efficient producers in the region yielded an annual average of about 30 tons per factory. By 1894, the yield had increased some fifty times to about 2,635 tons per factory, with the largest producers, Central Constancia, in Cuba producing a harvest of 19,500 tons of sugar—about the yield of the entire neighboring island of Jamaica. Cuba produced more than all the other Caribbean islands combined, with a greater yield of sugar per acre of cane and a larger average acreage of sugarcane per mill. What is more, Cuba was attracting hundreds of thousands of Spaniards to the island who went into *colono* sugarcane growing. In 1894, the Cubans produced about one-third of all the world's cane sugar and about one-eighth of the combined total of cane and beet sugar traded internationally. But that also was a year in which more sugar was produced from beet than from cane.

Nevertheless, the Caribbean continued to emphasize cane sugar production, placing all sorts of obstructions on landowning by peasant farmers and on the cultivation of other competing crops. At a time when the British colonies were lavishing money on the importation of Asians, their laborers emigrated to the sugar plantations in Cuba, the canal construction in Panama, the banana plantations in Costa Rica, and to all forms of manual labor in the United States. In 1865, on the eve of the Morant Bay riots in Jamaica, some poor people from the parish of St. Ann, plagued by disease and near starvation, petitioned Queen Victoria of England for permission to cultivate peasant crops on unused land belonging to the crown. The queen refused, encouraging them instead to work "steadily and continuously, at the times when their labor is wanted, and for as long as it is wanted... and thereby render the plantations productive." It was precisely such political insensitivity that discouraged the productivity of the peasants and hardened the class antagonisms that exploded at Morant Bay. The English government simply did not recognize that a new society was slowly being reconstituted after the abolition of slavery. The old order was changing, slowly but inexorably.

Whites in the Caribbean did not fully accept the changing reality of the new postslavery conditions. Blacks had to struggle steadily and continuously to secure their rights and to force the local elites to alter the anachronistic priorities established by slavery and the plantation. As long as sugar remained "king," all social goals were subordinated to boosting production. Little positive incentive was given to develop the arts, to inculcate a sense of national identity that was faithful to the plurality of peoples, or to encourage diversity in agricultural production. Toward the end of the nineteenth century, the island of Trinidad spent more money encouraging destitute East Indians to migrate to Trinidad, more money on medical attention for plantation laborers, and far more money on prisons and police services than on education. Plantation society in the Caribbean everywhere subordinated people to profits.

Until the middle of the twentieth century, the masses remained excluded from meaningful participation in their societies everywhere except in Haiti. The abolition of slavery and the political changes during the nineteenth century did not reverse the outward-looking, centrifugal forces of Caribbean societies. Those forces prevailed through it all, dividing and divisive. But one change was unmistakable: the caste structure had collapsed, forever baring the conflicts of race, color, and class and sowing the seeds of a Caribbean nationalism.

With the weakening or collapse of the overarching imperial command, each Caribbean territory began to operate more independently than before, emphasizing

local needs and local objectives rather than regional or imperial ones. The traditions of culture and imperial administration grew weaker against the local forces
of self-assertion. The would-be nationalism was fragmented, frustrated, and fragile. But it was there in embryonic form, delayed but not denied. This nationalism
was a product of the pecular history of the region.

The Caribbean colonies established in the seventeenth and eighteenth centuries were never, in any way, watertight compartments of the various European
imperial spheres. The theoretical bases of these cumbersome administrative
structures supported the myth that each American imperial unit was largely
self-contained and dependent on the mother country. Of course, the centraliz-
ing of communications through the metropolises tended to reinforce the importance of the connection between center and periphery while minimizing the
common features of the colonies. Control rested at the center. The European
masters controlled virtually all aspects of the colonial society: religion, manners,
commerce, transportation, marketing, manpower, production, and social order.
The overseas colonies complemented—or ought to have complemented—in an
asymmetrical way, the societies and the economies of the mother countries. This
complementarity engendered a reciprocal interdependence between colony and
metropolis.

Part of this myth led to the assumption that the Caribbean and other New
World colonies were overseas extensions of European metropolises. As such, the
colonists would reflect, to a greater or lesser degree, the social and political attributes of the mother countries. The early theories of empire, therefore, prescribed
laws that homogenized overseas colonies and minimized the individuality of place
and time. In practice, it was generally conceded that that was not the case. Even
in the centralized Spanish-American empire, local bureaucrats were allowed some
measure of independence, and in some measures it was accepted that the local
town councils could determine the best interests of the colonists. Over time, the
descendants of those Europeans who went out to the Americas developed a range
of identities that undermined the notion of a common sense of nationalism coin-
cident with the imperial boundaries. In short, Englishmen in Barbados began to
view themselves differently from Englishmen in Massachusetts or New York or
Maryland or Virginia. This might not have been surprising. More surprising was
that they also began to see themselves differently from Englishmen in Jamaica or
the Leeward Islands. Variations in local environment produced variations in the
way local colonists eventually viewed themselves and their world. The fabric of
English culture assumed new forms.

By the late eighteenth century, attitudes as well as identities began to change.
Along with a heightened awareness of self came a sharper definition of interests.
The political and economic interests that were articulated in the colonies came to
clash more frequently with those developed at the center of an empire. Differences
eventually led to divisions; and divisions, to the political fragmentation of empire
toward the end of eighteenth century.

This fragmentation began with the political emancipation of the British North American colonists in 1776–1783 and continued through the prolonged after-effects of the French Revolution that started in 1789. The American Revolution gave rise to the novel political entity called the United States of America. But it is debatable whether the creation of the new state reflected the reality of a strong sense of nationalism among the schismatic colonists in 1776. That nationalism had to be painfully forged in the years afterward. Similarly, the French Revolution gave birth to the independent state of Haiti in 1804, leaving the Haitians to estab-lish the basis for their nationalism in the turbulent times of the nineteenth cen-tury. Yet political independence was not the general aim of the great majority of colonists. Instead, the colonists wanted greater liberty to take action at the local level.

European imperialism could not create a common sense of identity in the Caribbean. Instead, the environment, the nature of the colonial economies, the nature of the relationships to the metropolises, and even accidental circumstances combined to accentuate the schismatic tendencies of Caribbean societies by the 1790s. The political changes, then, were in some ways reflections of the separate consciousnesses that developed during the eighteenth century.

The overall environment of the Caribbean determined the physical size of the community that could be readily maintained, although population growth was not merely a consequence of that environment. Geographic size and location, especially in the days of sailing ships, were of inordinate importance. A large land area more readily supported a relatively larger critical mass of people, and that larger critical mass facilitated the development of a complex social order. The ini-tial impetus for European settlement was to establish a better life, which meant maximum returns from minimum effort—getting rich easily or quickly, or both. Adequate quantities of fertile land for growing food and producing agricultural staples for export were attractive. Commerce was the engine of wealth, and com-merce in the eighteenth century meant tropical staple export.

The great majority of the islands of the Caribbean are too small to support any permanent settlements. The smaller of the permanently inhabited islands—the Bahamas, the Caymans, the Turks and Caicos, and the Virgin Islands, and others like Nevis, Montserrat, Marie Galante, Desirade, St. Martin, St. Eustatius, Saba, Carriacou, and Tobago—lacked the expanses of fertile land required to produce sugar, cotton, tobacco, indigo, or spices competitively. At one time or another, the communities on these islands tried to produce the commodities that could be sold on the international market. But they could not sustain the quantity or the quality of production to attract investors, credit, new immigrants, and cheap labor or to maintain the perception that there men could, despite the hazards of life, "grow rich as all men desire to do."

Perceptions often dominated reality in the eighteenth century, as they have always done. The general perception that the Caribbean islands constituted a highly perilous zone for living was not, in the context of the times, exaggerated. Part of the reason the Europeans were anxious to escape from Europe was that they found life in Europe to be "nasty, brutish and short." The average Englishman had a life expectancy at the beginning of the eighteenth century of about thirty-five years. The average mainland colonists had a bit better life expectancy than this, probably feeding the illusion that life in the Americas was better than life in Europe. But the life expectancy of anyone born in the Caribbean was lower than that of Europeans or the mainland colonists. "Englishmen who moved to the Caribbean," wrote Richard Dunn, "shortened their life expectancy significantly." It is not surprising that the conventional wisdom at the time thought of the Caribbean as a hostile environment and those who survived there as part of a mysterious other world. By the nineteenth century, however, the tables were turned. Caribbean whites began to consider themselves as superior to metropolitan whites, hardier survivors of a challenging frontier experience. But they could successfully convert this self-consciousness into a nationalism only if they could find a way to incorporate the various segments of color, race, and condition. That was the principal challenge of the nineteenth and twentieth centuries.

SUGGESTED READINGS

Andrews, George Reid. *Afro-Latin America, 1800–2000*. New York: Oxford University Press, 2004.

Carrington, Selwyn H. H. *The Sugar Industry and the Abolition of the Slave Trade, 1775–1810*. Gainesville: University of Florida Press, 2002.

Eltis, David, and Walvin, James, eds. *The Abolition of the Atlantic Slave Trade: Origins and Effects in Europe, Africa, and the Americas*. Madison: University of Wisconsin Press, 1981.

Gaspar, David Barry. *Bondmen and Rebels: A Study of Master-Slave Relations in Antigua*. Baltimore, Md.: Johns Hopkins University Press, 1985.

Green, William A. *British Slave Emancipation: The Sugar Colonies and the Great Experiment, 1830–1865*. Oxford, England: Clarendon Press, 1976.

Hochschild, Adam. *Bury the Chains: Prophets and Rebels in the Fight to Free an Empire's Slaves*. Boston: Houghton Mifflin, 2005.

Instituto de Historia. *Historia de Cuba: Las Luchas por la independencia nacional y las transformaciones estructurales, 1868–1898*. Havana: Editora Política, 1996.

Moore, Brian L., and Johnson, Michele A. *Neither Led nor Driven: Contesting British Cultural Imperialism in Jamaica, 1865–1920*. Mona, Jamaica: University of the West Indies Press, 2004.

Pérotin-Dumon, Anne. *Etre patriotique sous les tropiques: La Guadeloupe, la colonisation et la révolution (1789–1794)*. Basse-Terre: Societe d'histoire de la Guadeloupe, 1985.

Pérotin-Dumon, Anne. *La ville aux Iles, la ville dans L'île: Basse-Terre et Pointe-à-Pitre, Guadeloupe, 1650–1820*. Paris: Karthala, 2000.

Ragatz, Lowell J. *The Fall of the Planter Class in the British Caribbean, 1763–1833*. Reprinted. New York: Octagon Books, 1971.

Scott, Rebecca J. *Slave Emancipation in Cuba: The Transition to Free Labor, 1860–1899*. Princeton, N.J.: Princeton University Press, 1985.

Thompson, Alvin O. *Unprofitable Servants: Crown Slaves in Berbice, Guyana, 1803–1831*. Mona, Jamaica: University of the West Indies Press, 2002.

Viotti da Costa, Emilia. *Crowns of Glory, Tears of Blood: The Demerara Slave Rebellion of 1823*. New York: Oxford University Press, 1994.

Williams, Eric. *Capitalism and Slavery*. With a new introduction by Colin A. Palmer. Chapel Hill: University of North Carolina Press, 1994.

Wise, Steven M. *Though the Heavens May Fall: The Landmark Trial that Led to the End of Human Slavery*. Cambridge, Mass.: Da Capo Press, 2005.

CHAPTER 7

Caribbean Nation Building 1
Haiti and the Dominican Republic

France has finally learned; the people suffer, but they will not
go backwards...
> —Unsigned letter from Saint-Domingue, ca. 1792

Nèg ap trahi nèg depi nam Guinée [From Time Immemorial in
Guinea, every man betrays his neighbor].
> —FRANÇOIS DUVALIER's favorite aphorism,
> quoted in R. B. Heinl and N. G. Heinl, *Written in Blood*

The imperial fragmentation and colonial social reconstruction of the nineteenth century were manifestations of a long, difficult process of nation building in the Caribbean. The process comprised two aspects that were often confused. One aspect was the creation of new political states. That was dramatic, militaristic, heroic, and sensational. New states resulted from civil wars for political independence in British North America, French Saint-Domingue, and the Spanish-American mainland. British North America became the United States of America. French Saint-Domingue called itself, after an indigenous chiefdom, Haiti. The viceregal administrations of Spanish America fragmented and refragmented during the first decades of the nineteenth century. New Spain became Mexico and the United Provinces of Central America (that later dissolved into a number of separate states in 1839). New Granada produced Colombia, Venezuela, and Ecuador. (Later Colombia lost Panama.) The Viceroyalty of Peru gave way to Chile, Bolivia, and Peru. The Viceroyalty of Río de la Plata splintered and eventually became Argentina, Uruguay, and Paraguay. Portugal, with British prodding, created a new state in Brazil without either civil war or revolution. But the successful proclamation of these new states did not necessarily confirm the presence of a coherent national sentiment within the defined geographic boundaries of the state. Nation building was to be the tedious, tortuous preoccupation of the long nineteenth century.

Nowhere was nation building more tedious, prolonged, and tortuous than in the Caribbean. The process has been going on for nearly two centuries. Yet the very ideas that gave impetus to moves on the mainland to create independent

138

states also prevailed at the same time throughout the Caribbean. It began with the spontaneous and unheralded independence of Haiti in 1804. It accommodated several fits and starts in the Dominican Republic between 1821 and 1865 and continues unabated in the early decades of the twenty-first century. With the exception of Cuba, the sequence of evolution has been the creation of the state followed by the bonding of the nation. Both have been extremely difficult ventures.

From the independence of Haiti in the early nineteenth century to the newly articulated demands in Aruba and Montserrat in the late twentieth century, there lies an unbroken connection in the quest for territorial freedom and independence unleashed during the turbulence of the eighteenth-century world. Throughout the Atlantic world, newly emergent groups relentlessly clamored to be heard, to be free, and to be given political independence. In some places the success was remarkable. In France in 1789, a revolution popularized the rights of bourgeois man, decapitated the king, and shattered forever the conventional mystique of a semidivine monarchy in the crumbling dust of the Bastille. Between 1812 and 1822, the Spanish tried to institutionalize constitutional monarchy and failed—but the nature of the Spanish monarchy was forever altered. In Great Britain in 1832, an intimidated Parliament quickly unleashed reform to forestall violent revolution, eliminated the notoriously unrepresentative "rotten" boroughs, and in two steps extended the electoral franchise. The French Revolution and the general restlessness that gripped most of Europe also had its American counterpart.

In Europe a wide consortium of groups reestablished their alliances within national states, the states conforming more or less to national groups. In the Americas, states were carved from the former imperial domains as the ebb tide of imperialism and colonialism retreated inexorably from Yorktown on the lower Chesapeake Bay to Ayacucho high in the Peruvian Andes. More than the creation of new political entities was at stake. People were changing their attitudes toward the land, toward society, toward authority, and toward each other. All these changes seemed awfully portentous at the time, given the novelty of political engineering.

The famous revolutions of the late eighteenth and nineteenth centuries created new political forms and undoubtedly brought about unprecedented political changes. Yet the degree to which these significant changes reflected an equally profound change in the social basis of political power remains questionable. Very few of the new leaders in these new states had ideas that were incompatible with the *status quo ante*. The masses, who made possible the decisive military victory over the English metropolitan forces at Yorktown or helped defeat the Spanish imperial army at Ayacucho, derived little tangible political, social, or economic reward for their gallant efforts and considerable sacrifice. The long wars of independence that gave birth to the United States of America and the numerous Spanish-American mainland republics from Mexico to Argentina were successful mutinies, complicated by the overtones of civil wars. They were not unqualified revolutionary changes.

The history of social revolution in the Western Hemisphere starts not with Lexington and Bunker Hill in British North America in 1775, but less auspiciously in the French tropical colony of Saint-Domingue in the Caribbean. The North

American and Latin American wars of independence were political events, almost devoid of significant restructuring of the social classes. Although intrinsically connected with the events in metropolitan France as well as the United States, the Haitian Revolution sought not merely political independence for the state, but the personal freedom of the more than 80 percent of the inhabitants who were slaves. To accomplish this goal, the revolution had to be, as its metropolitan correspondent, both radical and destructive. The Haitians were forced to destroy the entire colonial socioeconomic structure that was the raison d'être for their imperial importance, and in destroying the institution of slavery, they unwittingly agreed to terminate their connection to the entire international superstructure that perpetuated slavery and the plantation economy. That was an incalculable price for freedom and independence.

The implications for the entire Caribbean—and slaveholding societies everywhere—were astonishing. From Boston to Buenos Aires, slave owners trembled at the consequences for themselves and their world. Haiti, the second independent state in the Western Hemisphere, was politically quarantined, maligned by many, assisted by few. France, understandably, grudgingly granted diplomatic recognition in stages between 1825 and 1837. Only after sixty years did the United States of America offer formal diplomatic ties. Haiti remained poor in material terms, but its people remained strong, free, and fiercely independent.

The logical starting point for revolution in the Caribbean in the eighteenth century rested in metropolitan France and what the French in 1789 called, with gallic subtlety, their "period of troubles." In 1789, the French monarch, Louis XVI, summoned the Estates General, the antiquated association of nobles, clergy, and commoners and inadvertently initiated the French Revolution. That was the simple, unsuspected beginning. The French king, being bankrupt, thought that he would make a deal with his parliamentary representatives: immediate fiscal relief for potential political reform. A revolution resulted from that simple monarchical pecuniary embarrassment at a time when France ranked among the richest countries in Europe. To the surprise of the metropolis, the colonists wanted a part of that deal.

The year 1789 proved in many ways to be a cataclysmic year. It began inauspiciously enough. The king in simple and sublime wishfulness called the parliament, the Estates General, to Versailles to enact fiscal reform. By May 1789 when the representatives came together, the question of fiscal reform could not be separated from wider and more far-reaching questions of fundamental political and social reform for France.

The year became one of the most memorable in French history. By the end of the year, political factions had emerged; the Third Estate had declared itself a National Assembly (June 17, 1789) and vowed on the tennis court not to disband until it had given France a new constitution. The monarch inadvertently recognized the National Assembly by ordering the nobles and clergy to join it. Soon rioting in Paris figuratively destroyed the reality of the French monarchy when it literally destroyed the Bastille on July 14. In August, the last vestiges of French feudalism were annihilated, and in early October, the Paris mob, led by women, dragged the king from Versailles to Paris with the National Assembly meekly following. Neither France nor the Americas would ever be the same again.

The most noteworthy event of that noteworthy year took place on August 26, 1789. Then the French National Assembly adopted the Declaration of the Rights of Man and of the Citizen that in 1791 became the preamble to the French constitution. From the Caribbean point of view, this was the single most important event in the initial phases of the Revolution. It raised, among other things, the question of political definition at three interrelated levels.

The first attempts at definition revolved around nationality devoid of race or social class. Who were Frenchmen? Should they be exclusively "males"? Were they to be residents of France? Or could Frenchmen lose their "Frenchness" by overseas residence and foreign birth? Should genealogy be the only sound basis for group ascription? Next came the questions concerning citizenship. By what basis did one become a citizen? Should citizenship be based on property or on "nationality," however defined? Could citizenship be differentiated from race and culture, or was it merely a convenient socioeconomic political category? Finally, questions concerning the state or, more precisely, where sovereignty ought to reside in the nation, emerged. What was France? Was it a monarchy? Or a democracy? Or a republic? And what did these words mean in political discourse?

These problems were enormously complicated by the existence of the French overseas empire and the nature and peculiar reality of French imperialism in the eighteenth century. For the great number of ordinary Frenchmen in France in 1789, the two most difficult and unfamiliar concepts were slavery and the notion of ethnic identity. Yet definitions of "man" and "citizen" became inextricably involved in these concepts, and resolving them brought into sharp focus the reality of the plural society overseas and the profound problem of slavery. And they occupied much of the debates in Paris.

The Rights of Man spoke of "liberty, equality and fraternity" and the "inalienable rights" of citizens. These rights were then defined as freedom of religion, freedom of speech, freedom of the press, equality before the law, protection from arbitrary arrest, and protection of property. These rights represented the sum of civil rights that a number of contemporary Americans hold dear for themselves but find difficult to extend to some of their fellow citizens who do not share their color, ethnicity, religion, cultural heritage, or geographic origin.

The phrase "inalienable rights" came from the second paragraph of the Declaration of Independence of the United States of America, which spoke of "unalienable Rights," a phrase copied from the Declaration of the Rights of Virginia, written by George Mason (1725–1792) in 1776. Mason, of course, had refused to sign the Declaration of Independence because it did not unequivocally oppose slavery or incorporate explicitly individual human rights. The Bill of Rights of the United States was approved at the first session of the First Congress on September 25, 1789, and presented to the various states for their ratification. By the end of the year, Maryland, New Jersey, and North Carolina had ratified ten of the twelve submitted articles. Frenchmen were familiar with the American discussions of the Bill of Rights. And free French colonials saw an opportunity to use the same logic to establish some rights of their own.

The Bill of Rights for the United States was eventually ratified in 1791—the same year as the first French constitution. The issue of slavery and ethnic identification formed an integral part of these rights in France. In the Atlantic world, slavery and ethnic identification constituted, perhaps, the most important issues.

The political revolution that began in 1776 in the newly declared United States of America opened a floodgate of reform and change that, in many respects, are still simmering in the contemporary Caribbean. The ardent aspirations embodied in the then-popular slogans of the "rights of man"—man here merely a generic term for all humans—and "liberty, equality and fraternity" are as relevant to today's world as they were in 1789. The trouble with slogans, of course, is that they have a beautiful capacity to obfuscate and soothe. Great rallying cries are not good blueprints for collective action. Ideal for divided oppositions, they are difficult and dangerous for political implementation. Nowhere was this more evident than in France and French Saint-Domingue in 1789. At times, it seemed as though France and its colonies were divided by a common language.

Yet both the potential difficulty and the political value of slogans were understood very well in 1789 by a broad assortment of people. The political problem of France in 1789 was akin to trying to make omelets without breaking eggs. In the reshuffling of the old order, some groups were apprehensive about their possible losses—as well they had reason to be.

Consider the narrow self-interest conveyed in the selection of the following letter from the good citizens of Nantes in late 1789. Nantes had been a prosperous French town, and to a great measure, its prosperity rested on the wealth accumulated from the transatlantic commerce of humans. Its citizens wanted liberty from unfair taxation and free trade but not abolition of the slave trade that condemned millions of Africans to exile and untimely death.

> Our city has passed from the most perfect tranquillity to the most violent agitation. This situation, which could have the most disastrous results, has been caused by the rumours aroused by several letters from our city, to the effect that Messieurs de Mirabeau, Chapelier, de La Rochefoucald, de Lameth and Barnave have joined to *bring about a discussion in the National Assembly on the abolition of the slave trade* [Emphasis added]; assured of the approval of the entire clergy and of a large part of the other members, it has been announced that their motion would be accepted and that the abolition of the commerce would be decreed. This disastrous decree, if ever it is pronounced, will bring total ruin to our commerce and to our port cities, the loss of our colonies, bankruptcy, uprisings against the decrees of the National Assembly, anarchy, and all the horrors which follow it. France was to have been regenerated [by the Revolution], and she will be forever lost.

Nowhere was this general apprehension of the new order more poignantly expressed than in the words of Bryan Edwards, the wealthy British West Indian planter and member of the English Parliament, when he described the tragic events in France to his fellow parliamentarians in 1798. "The time in which we live," he said, "will constitute an awful period in the history of the world; for a spirit of subversion is gone forth, which sets at nought the wisdom of our ancestors and the lessons of experience." Bryan Edwards, an apt spokesman for the comfortable classes, knew quite a bit about change. His world, after all, was a bit larger than that of some of his fellow Englishmen. Intelligent and perceptive, his words and deeds conveyed the thoughts of a white, bourgeois, Anglo-Saxon of the late eighteenth century, and his worldview was the constrained worldview of that small group. He would have fitted in quite comfortably in Philadelphia in 1776. His sentiments resonated throughout the Caribbean at the time. In 1791, Edwards was in Jamaica when the white colonists from the French colony of Saint-Domingue sent an urgent secret mission to the governor of Jamaica, General Adam Williamson, requesting assistance should the National Assembly, as they suspected, declare the emancipation of their slaves or should they prove incapable of defeating the massive revolt taking place on the Plaine du Nord. Officially the Jamaican governor remained benevolently neutral, but he encouraged white support and solidarity with fellow Caribbean slaveholders. In this way, Edwards found himself a volunteer in the French colony, then in the throes of a raging civil war.

Edwards's ethnocentric justification of the governor's action, as he wrote in the preface to his book, *An Historical Survey of the French Colony in the Island of St. Domingo*, first published in 1797 in London, reflected the fear that the events in Saint-Domingue were beginning to instill in the region:

> Superior to national prejudice, [Governor Williamson] felt, as a man and a Christian ought to feel, for the calamities of his fellow men; and he saw, in its full extent, the danger to which every island in the West Indies would be exposed from such an example, if *the triumph of savage anarchy over all order and government should be complete* [Emphasis added].

In viewing the prospect of the abolition of slavery in the neighboring colony as "the triumph of savage anarchy over all order and government," Edwards was, of course, viewing the events from the perspective of the American slaveholding and plantation propertied classes. He had, quite understandably, been more than a bit upset at the reports that Dr. Samuel Johnson (1709–1784) had raised toasts in London to "A speedy rebellion of the negroes of Jamaica, and success to them!" Even worse, Johnson had pontificated that resistance was always justifiable where force was the substitute of right and that the commission of a civil crime was not possible in a state of slavery. Thoughts such as these, charmingly engaging in the comfortable atmosphere of an English pub, were not designed to give slave-owning colonials in the Caribbean great peace of mind, for force, actual or implied, remained the principal agent for controlling the large numbers of plantation slaves. But Caribbean slaves did not need to hear the revolutionary slogans of "liberty, equality and fraternity" or "the rights of man" to plot their freedom. Slave revolts were endemic in every slave society, and the quest for freedom was never far from the minds of a great many slaves.

Yet the Haitian revolution—the only truly "democratic" revolution in the period that R. R. Palmer called "the Age of the Democratic Revolutions"—occurred not because conditions in French Saint-Domingue were inherently more volatile than elsewhere in the tropical American world but merely because of its accidental connection to France. The Haitian Revolution was the inadvertent stepchild of the French Revolution, the frightful culmination of the expectant fears of the good citizens of Nantes and of the group of Caribbean property owners represented by the planter Bryan Edwards.

The Haitian Revolution, like its metropolitan parallel, began with the calling of the Estates General in May 1789. At the time, few in France thought that the decree applied to the colonies. Designed to resolve the economic dispute between the French king and his Assembly of Notables, the affair quickly spread to engulf all Frenchmen. Frenchmen in the colonies mistakenly thought that they could participate in the political discussion in the metropolis without drastically altering their caste and class relations. For in 1789, those in the colonies who first declared themselves to be Frenchmen were the *grands blancs* elite. They had more to lose than they expected when they selfishly and audaciously fished in the disturbed political waters of the mother country. All colonial *grands blancs* were at risk, but none more so than in the prosperous colony of Saint-Domingue.

The French colony of Saint-Domingue in 1789 represented the epitome of the successful exploitation slave society in the tropical American world. In 1789, Saint-Domingue had a total population of about 500,000, of whom about 80 percent were slaves. The envy of every empire, it supplied about 66 percent of all French tropical produce and accounted for approximately 33 percent of all French foreign trade. Martinique and Guadeloupe each had total island populations of about 100,000 in 1789—of whom only about 20 percent were free. Frenchmen like the good citizens of Nantes and the other French Atlantic port cities of La Rochelle and Bordeaux supplied the African slaves, bought the fruits of their labor, and provided the domestic necessities of the overseas colonists, but they did not fully understand the volatile plantation world of the Caribbean and the subtle ways in which their societies operated.

As Medéric-Louis-Élie Moreau de Saint-Méry (1750–1819) tried to explain somewhat belatedly in the turbulent days in Paris, the tropical plantation colony was a strange and complex world. In Saint-Domingue, a white population of less than 25,000 psychological transients dominated the social pyramid that included, besides themselves, an intermediate, subordinate stratum of approximately 25,000 free, mainly miscegenated persons called the *gens de couleur*, and a vast, depressed, denigrated, overworked servile group of African and Afro-Caribbean (or Creole) slaves. In the other French colonies, the numbers were less, but the proportions were about the same. And the demographic profile was familiar across the Caribbean world wherever the great staple plantations dominated the landscape or gave economic and political significance to the territory.

This plantation world was quite removed from the social structure of metropolitan France. In France, the relatively homogeneous ethnicity allowed for the convenient and commonly accepted divisions of social "estates." By contrast, the colonies were culturally and ethnically plural. Rather than "estates," the colonies, as I noted before, had "castes": whites, free persons of color, and slaves. Each segment was subdivided—but not by common denominators. The whites were subdivided into *grands blancs* and *petits blancs*, the free persons of color into mulattoes and blacks, and the slaves into Creoles (or locally born) and *bozales* (or imported individuals). The whites were legally divided basically by wealth and their relationship to plantation production. The free persons of color were divided basically by observable skin color and other attributes of phenotype. The slaves were divided both by geographic locations of birth as well as by occupations. No coherent basic characteristics provided the foundations for internal class stratification in the Caribbean plantation world. Caste and class antagonisms everywhere combined to create a quite explosive situation in the colony. And since Saint-Domingue was the Crown Jewel of this world, it should not have been surprising that conditions there made divisions sharper and more reciprocally irritable than elsewhere in the Caribbean.

Saint-Domingue had more in common with the American world from Baltimore to Bahía than it did with the French world from Bordeaux to Boulogne. The cohesive force was the regimented slave plantation producing its annual harvests of sugar, cotton, indigo, and coffee and the various subsidiary activities related with that production. Groups and classes derived their social positions from their relation to the plantation structure—more than 8,000 plantations and more than 450,000 slaves. The society matured in consonance with the economic fortunes of the export commodities and the role of the local economy in the wider capitalist structure of the metropolis.

In 1789, the colonial sugar producers thought of themselves as a new nobility. Business was very good. In 1788, Saint-Domingue alone imported more than 29,000 slaves—between one-third and one-half of all the slaves sold throughout the Americas. The sugar producers—especially those absentees living in France—came to see themselves as the only genuine spokespersons for the colony. But they could not have been more mistaken. They were a social elite and an economically successful class but, within the realm of the French empire, a political nonentity.

Saint-Domingue in 1789 was not a unified colony, and it was not administered as a single unit. Geography, topography, and agriculture had coincided to define the western part of the island of Hispaniola (ceded by the Spanish to the French at the Treaty of Ryswick in 1697) into three centrifugal administrative provinces.

The first unit comprised the fertile northern plains, the Plaine du Nord, with large sugar plantations and the prosperous city of Le Cap Français, generally called Le Cap, the capital both of the North Province as well as the entire colony. The vast majority of slaves lived in North Province and were separated from the rest of the colony by the high range of mountains called the Massif. North Province was the stronghold of the *grands blancs*. Owing to its overwhelming economic importance, it was erroneously assumed to be typical of the entire colony. It clearly was not.

The second administrative unit was called West Province, although it lay due south of North Province and in the center of the colony. It was broken into two valleys: to the north, the Artibonite Valley, centering on the small town of Saint-Marc, and to the south, the Cul-de-Sac, centering on Port-au-Prince. In this part of the colony, the estates tended to be smaller, the crops more varied, and the population scattered about in a number of small towns. West Province was the stronghold of the *petits blancs*.

Finally, there was South Province. With its rugged terrain, small villages, and low population density; mixed marriages; and coffee, indigo, and cotton culture, this narrow peninsula, plunging westward far out into the Caribbean Sea toward Jamaica, was the stronghold of a dynamic, wealthy, free colored population and home of the celebrated Julien Raimond. Raimond left the colony in 1784 to petition for improved civil rights for the free coloreds and was extremely influential in the debates over citizenship in the French National Assembly.

South Province's participation in the French Revolution differed from that of the other two provinces. The free coloreds were initially excluded from the provincial assemblies drafting the *cahiers des doléances*, thereby increasing the caste tensions within the province. By 1791, in the midst of the debate over citizenship and with the revolt of the slaves in North Province already under way, fighting broke out in the South between whites—mainly *petits blancs*—and free coloreds. By 1792, the South was under the control of André Rigaud (1761–1811), a free colored appointed by the newly arrived revolutionary commissioners in an attempt to mediate the intrafree fighting and eventually reestablish control over the slaves. The plan failed, and the South remained loosely under the control of Rigaud, Alexander Pétion (1770–1818), and other free coloreds until the campaign of Toussaint Louverture (1743–1803) subordinated them in 1799. (In 1806, the South, again under Pétion, revolted against the new political state of Haiti and remained independent until 1818.)

Not surprising, the problem in the colony really began in earnest in 1789 over the question of precisely who constituted the proper representatives of the free population. The choice was a complex one, with selection among the wealthy absentee whites, wealthy whites resident in the colonies, all whites regardless of wealth, or all the wealthy regardless of color (as the free coloreds wanted). Each sector of the free colonial population accepted and adopted the current slogans of the Revolution to win support in France but particularized and emphasized only such connotations as applied to their own selfish cause or their narrow colonial interests.

Grands blancs saw liberty as greater colonial autonomy, especially in economic matters. Wanting an end to the detested *exclusif*, the mercantilistic trade within the empire, they advocated free trade and were willing to pay handsomely for this. Naturally, they emphasized liberty. *Petits blancs* wanted equality of all whites, not just landed proprietors, as well as loosened administrative control. To this sector

equality and liberty had special resonance—in that order. To these French equivalents of "red necks," there was no question about their being equal to free persons
of color. *Gens de couleur* focused on equality and fraternity with the whites, claiming they already fulfilled all the qualifications to make them active citizens—and
were more qualified than a substantial number of the white aspirants, especially
the hostile *petits blancs*. The *gens de couleur* gained the support of the vocal metropolitan Société des Amis des Noirs, the French antislavery society.

For their part, the whites, especially sensitive to the colonial situation and
prodded by the conservative, planter-based Club Massiac in France, feared that
political and social acceptance of any nonwhite group would undermine not only
the system of slavery, but the social dominance enjoyed by colonial whites. But not
far from their minds was the impact that any alteration in the system would have
on imperial property, wealth, and commerce. The failure of the colonial whites to
form a permanent alliance along either race or status lines ultimately proved disastrous for the colony and themselves.

The armed revolt in the colony began within the white group, by *grands blancs*,
especially in the north, reacting violently against the *petits blancs*–controlled
Colonial Assembly at St. Marc in West Province, which took upon itself the task of
writing a constitution for the entire colony in 1790. This constitution established
residence as the sole basis for citizenship, eliminating qualifications of race, property, and metropolitan birth. As such, it had interpreted the tennis-court oath as
legitimating *petits blancs* rather than the wealthy planters as the proper representatives of the colony—even though, curiously enough, all the colonial French whites
had joined the Third Estate at Versailles.

Both white groups armed their slaves and prepared for war in the name of the
metropolitan Revolution and presumably against the monarch. When the French
National Assembly ratified the May Decree of 1791 that enfranchised the propertied mulattoes, the whites in the colonies temporarily forgot their class differences
and forged an uneasy alliance to forestall what they perceived as the more feared
revolutionary threat of racial equality. By this act, the Revolution in France and
that of the colonies diverged. In France, the Revolution became a civil war. In
Saint-Domnigue, the civil war became a race war—or at least a war along ethnic
lines. That was the situation as it prevailed through 1791.

The white revolt in the colony was the beginning of the end of white rule.
Once the superordinate group had resorted to violence on that scale, there was
no way the revolt could be contained within class or caste sectors. Violence begat
greater violence. Once the moral authority, cohesion, and vigilence of the free
slave owners were challenged or had eroded—as they had for the two years that
the slaves saw (and helped) their masters kill one another wantonly—the slaves
grasped their opportunity to be free. For two years they had fought intermittently
on the side of some free faction or another, shouting liberty, equality, and fraternity. In August 1791, the slaves on the Plaine du Nord began to fight for their own
liberty, equality, and fraternity, and within a year, Saint-Domingue experienced a
slave revolt unprecedented in the annals of slavery.

Between 1792 and 1802, chaos prevailed throughout Saint-Domingue. At one time, as many as six warring parties were in the field simultaneously fighting for often conflicting ends: the slaves; the free persons of color; the *petits blancs*; the *grands blancs*; invading Spanish and English troops; and the French military, comprised of 21,900 troops (including 6,000 blacks in segregated black companies), all assisted by some 7,000 colonial militia (including free coloreds). In this situation, alliances were fleeting and numerous. As the killing increased, power slowly gravitated to the majority of ex-slaves—declared free by the abolition decree of the National Convention in France on February 5, 1794 (the same body that had executed the king and queen the year before)—led by the able Toussaint Louverture.

Ironically, the victory of the slaves was a victory for colonialism—and the Revolution in France. For it was the leftward drift of the Revolution that abolished slavery, and it was the implacable zeal of the Jacobin commissioner, Léger Felicité Sonthonax, to eradicate all elements of royalism in the colonies that facilitated the ultimate supremacy of the majority blacks—led by Toussaint Louverture—over the whites and free coloreds (although the victory over the free coloreds was never complete). Finally in 1797, Toussaint established his hegemony. He expelled Sonthonax and the invading British expeditionary forces, routed the free-colored opposition in the south, took the war into neighboring Santo Domingo, and gave the colony a new constitution. As a reward, he named himself governor-general for life. At this point, the revolution in the colony of Saint-Domingue was complete—two years before its metropolitan counterpart. A new society and a new polity were created—much to the discomfort of metropolitan France.

Between 1800 and 1802, Toussaint tried to rebuild the largely destroyed economy of Saint-Domingue. Hundreds of estates had been sacked and burned in the nearly ten years of civil war. Tens of thousands of individuals had lost thier lives. The magnificent irrigation system of the Cul-de-Sac collapsed from lack of maintenance and as a result of the torrential rains of the fall of 1800. Famine and lawlessness stalked the land. But Toussaint restored commercial relations with Great Britain and the United States, slowly began to feed his people, restored the operation of the sugar and coffee estates, and terminated the wanton massacre of white and colored persons. Although he pledged his loyalty to France, Toussaint acted with the independence of the dictator he had declared himself to be. For a brief time, it appeared that peace would return to Saint-Domingue.

All would perhaps have gone well had things remained at that. But a semi-independent Saint-Domingue with a free black population ran counter to the concept of "colony" to Europeans. In 1799, Napoleon Bonaparte (1769–1821) returned to France with his grandiose dreams of reestablishing a viable French-American empire and restoring slavery. His sentiments toward Africans in general and to his loyal governor-general in particular were extremely uncomplimentary. He referred to them as "utterly uncivilized men who did not know what a colony was, what France was." In 1802, he sent his brother-in-law, General Charles-Victor-Emmanuel Leclerc (1772–1802), with some 10,000 troops to, as he put it, "Rid us of these gilded Africans." Leclerc subdued the colony but did not fulfill his mission. Napoleon's dreams slowly faded as Leclerc, and most of the troops, died, largely from the ravages of yellow fever. Napoleon deceived and kidnapped Toussaint, exiling him to an early death in France. But the strong sense of freedom and independence achieved after 1794 could not be destroyed without also destroying the colony as it used to be. And this is precisely what Jean-Jacques Dessalines (1758–1806) did when he declared the independence of Haiti in 1804. The old order gave place to a new society of free and equal citizens.

The perfidious exile of Toussaint Louverture generated a widespread desperate resistance against which no French army could have prevailed. Henri Christophe (1767–1820) and Jean-Jacques Dessalines directed a resistance movement that was monumental in its savagery and destruction, since neither French nor Haitians gave any quarter. The thoroughness of the struggle between 1802 and 1804—either for imperial reconquest or in desperate self-defense—virtually precluded any easy reconstruction period for the newly emergent state and left an insuperable legacy of poverty, ruin, and social division. The fires that forged the birth of the state and the advent of Haitian nationalism unleashed such essentially disintegrative socioeconomic forces that no leader after 1804 found the situation manageable. Individual freedom and national prosperity became incompatible for the masses, and this fact provided a severe restriction for the diplomatic option of any successful commander against the French.

To Bryan Edwards, the destruction of the colony set at naught the wisdom of his ancestors and the lessons of experience. To the Haitian masses, however, that wisdom and those lessons were incompatible with their personal liberty. Their freedom took precedence over the prosperity of any new political state. So after 1802, they fought tenaciously to sweep away all vestiges of the old order of French government, white superiority, and plantation commerce. No study has yet examined this important aspect of the Haitian Revolution. But the assumption may be made that if a substantial proportion of the masses who formed the armies of the blacks and the mulattoes in Haiti sensed this incompatibility between freedom and prosperity, then the local leadership of Louverture, Dessalines, and Christophe was popular only to the degree that it identified with the trend of the majority or generalized an appeal that projected their sympathies as unequivocally antislavery, anti-French, antiwhite, and antiplantation. Dessalines's attacks upon the whites and mulattoes after 1802—in sharp contradistinction to those of Sonthonax earlier—could possibly have been this type of response, rather than any callous genocidal measure born of an intrinsic racial hatred. Only a violence superior to that of the slave masters could have secured the goals of the popular (that is, black) revolution in the colony, and such violence required little leadership or coordination. Once the masses began to act more from an interest in their own freedom than from any concern for their collective welfare and the prosperity of the emergent state—and this partially accounts for the widespread, spontaneous resistance to the French after 1802—then it seems that neither Toussaint nor anyone else could have significantly affected the future course of Haitian independence.

In the neighboring French Caribbean islands of Martinique and Guadeloupe, the origins and first acts of revolution were similar to the initial developments in Saint-Domingue. But their denouements were quite different. The explanations reside in geography, scale, and the vicissitudes of war.

In Martinique, the white planters allied themselves with the English (who sent a fleet out to the Caribbean in 1793) and easily put down the slave revolt, reversing the declaration of emancipation and restoring the working routine of the plantations. There it was a victory for royalism. At the Peace of Amiens in 1801, the island was restored to Napoleon, only to be recaptured by the British after the outbreak of war in 1803.

Things were a little different in Guadeloupe. There, the English (in alliance with the royalist planters) captured the island in 1793. Then the Jacobin commissioner, Victor Hugues, arrived with a French fleet, recaptured the island, and emancipated the slaves in the name of the Revolution. The white planters were defeated and purged of their royalism by simply killing them. Hugues also took the battle to St. Vincent, St. Lucia, and Grenada, allying himself with the local Caribs. By 1799, when he was appointed governor of French Guiana, Hugues had trimmed his political radicalism to fit the conservative winds of change in the metropolis. Slavery was virtually restored, and the colony was subdued. Full restoration of slavery, however, came only in 1802 under the new governor, General Antoine Richepance, at a tremendous loss of lives as hundreds of ex-slaves chose suicide rather than reenslavement. But by 1802, the remnants of the French planter class in Guadeloupe, no doubt cognizant of affairs in Saint-Domingue, had virtually abandoned any expectation of a restored planter colony in the Americas. In so doing, they may have been unconsciously anticipating the actions of Napoleon Bonaparte, who in 1803 sold Louisiana and put the French imperial interest in the Americas on permanent hold.

The French Revolution and events in Saint-Domingue had far-reaching effects on the subsequent course of Latin American and Caribbean history and on the pattern of state engineering in three generally interrelated ways: political, economic, and social.

Politically, the Revolution resulted in the establishment of the second independent state in the Western Hemisphere: Haiti, in 1804. Yet Haiti did not become the example to be emulated among political aspirants in Latin America and the Caribbean. It was not directly responsible for the independence movement on the mainland, and its attempt to incorporate neighboring Santo Domingo failed after 1844. Santo Domingo eventually became the second Caribbean state to gain its political independence in 1864.

The slave revolt in Saint-Domingue had repercussions among all neighboring slaveholding societies. News from Saint-Domingue in 1791 led to persistent social and political unrest throughout the region. Slaves in all the Guianas were unusually restless in 1795. In Jamaica, the Second Maroon War broke out in 1795–1796. Between 1795 and 1797, slaves and Maroons fought Europeans in Dominica, St. Lucia, and St. Vincent. Julien Fedon and his brother, Jean Fedon, led many free coloreds in a massive revolt against British rule on Grenada in 1795. It may be significant that all the leaders of this revolt were born outside Grenada and resented the increased discrimination against free non-European property holders in the 1790s. In Colombia, Venezuela, and Surinam (now Suriname), the Maroon wars flared again in 1797–1798. And until 1810, both the British and the French found their black military regiments extremely restless, rebellious, and unwilling to fight against individuals of their own color.

Although the French state reversed itself and reinstituted slavery in Martinique and Guadeloupe, the system of slavery in the Caribbean—at least in the non-Hispanic Caribbean—never recovered its economic vitality. A free Haiti became the foreboding alternative to the widespread use of coerced people. With the Saint-Domingue slave market effectively closed, Great Britain moved success-fully for the abolition of their slave trade in 1808 and eventually for the abolition of slavery throughout the British West Indies in 1834.

France recognized the independence of Haiti in 1825, and the United States (which pioneered the creation of politically new states in the Americas in 1776) extended diplomatic recognition in 1862. Indeed, the political example of Haiti was not deemed worthy of emulation by the aspiring new states during the nine-teenth century, and it became the counterpoint of the United States. Everywhere in the Americas, slave owners feared that any diminution in vigilance would result in their slaves creating another "Haiti." Throughout Latin America and the Caribbean, the suspicion of African and indigenous peoples increased, and the fear of popular revolt sharpened the antagonism toward this sector of the popu-lation. In some ways, therefore, the revolutionary experience of Haiti accentuated the growing identity based on ethnicity that was already an integral part of the political discourse of the age of the French Revolution.

The economic impact of the revolution was equally widespread. Locally, it reduced the wealthiest colony in the world to poverty—dispersing, demoting, or destroying the families that controlled production and wealth. Haiti moved from being a plantation-dominated economy to a peasant-style economy with enormous long-term economic consequences for individuals as well as the new state.

The physical destruction of Haiti stimulated coffee and sugar production else-where in the Caribbean, and the agricultural expansion of Cuba, the Guianas, and Trinidad resulted directly from the transfer of slaves, technology, and cultivation techniques to these territories. Despite his awareness of the inherent risks of slave-plantation-based production, the elimination of Haitian production meant to the Cuban Creole Francisco Arango y Parreño that "the moment of our happiness has arrived." Cuba quickly replaced Saint-Domingue as the world's leading sugar producer, although it was very careful not to allow the servile population to exceed the free population. Indeed, because of the tragic example of Haiti, historians have had wonderfully rich demographic data on Cuban society during the nineteenth century, since the officials frequently checked the island's population to ensure white numerical superiority.

But the collapse of French overseas sugar making, combined with the French involvement in the Continental wars and the resultant naval blockade of France, led to increased sugar prices as sugar—along with other food items—became scarce in France, further contributing to urban riots. Napoleon's response was to develop the beet-sugar industry that, in half a century, overtook cane sugar as the sweetener of choice. With the exception of mass producers of cane sugar like Cuba, small sugar producers would never again experience the production of wealth that made the eighteenth century legendary.

The social consequences of the revolution were enormous. As in all civil wars, the most obvious physical consequence was the dislocation that drove masses of migrant groups of destitute colonists far afield, with most concentrating in Jamaica, Cuba, Venezuela, Trinidad, Colombia, and Mexico. Some colonists even migrated to New Orleans, Louisiana; Charleston, South Carolina; Baltimore, Maryland; Philadelphia, Pennsylvania; New York; and Boston. The penchant for Caribbean migration was already illustrated at the time of the Haitian Revolution. Of course, a great many did not survive to run away.

But there were also profound psychological consequences. The Haitian Revolution shattered the myth—at least within the tropical Caribbean—that slavery was a benevolent form of African salvation or an effective method of labor organization. After Haiti, social control became increasingly more difficult and more expensive in every slave society—although no dominant group lost total control as had the slave owners in Saint-Domingue. Whites became more conscious of their ethnic differences, and so did the nonwhites. In nonsettler societies, whites slowly lost the confidence to govern.

Haitian military success in forging a state from a slave society indicated the enormous potential of ex-slaves. Napoleon was reported to have dismissed accounts of African and Afro-Caribbean military skills as certainly no match for "civilized Frenchmen." Those "civilized Frenchmen" had presumably amply demonstrated their military efficiency at guillotining one another in France. But Saint-Domingue was truly another world, and Napoleon's military genius, if not his own example, should have made him realize that great men are produced by the challenges of the moment. Genius requires opportunity, and the revolution produced opportunities in abundance. The Haitian Revolution produced an astonishing number of outstanding military leaders, such as Toussaint Louverture, Charles Belair, Jean-Jacques Dessalines, Henri Christophe, André Rigaud, Alexander Pétion, Jean François, Moise, and Biassou. Louverture, Moise, Dessalines, and Biassou were born in slavery, but their minds remained unfettered, and when the opportunity presented itself in war, they distinguished themselves as gifted leaders of men. With the possible exception of Louverture and Rigaud, the Haitian leaders produced in the conflict were men of war, not men of peace—and their military experience did not serve them well in civilian situations.

Unfortunately, their military and political success also reinforced the negative stereotypes that Europeans had of Africans. In Latin America and the Caribbean,

Haitian success accentuated the latent fears that some whites and some free coloreds had of blacks in general. This white fear commingled with suspicion reached alarming proportions in Cuba in 1843 and accounted for a massive genocidal murder of slaves and free persons of color in the regions around Matanzas and Cárdenas when the authorities thought they had discovered a conspiracy to abolish slavery.

The Haitian Revolution may be seen both as a revolution within a revolution and as a revolution in its own right. As a revolution within a revolution, it illustrated the practical difficulty of assuming that a slave society in an overseas territory could be a linear political and social extension of the metropolis. In this, the members of the Club Massiac were more accurate than the Société des Amis des Noirs. They had warned in 1789 that Saint-Domingue was a world apart and had to be so treated. That is why the civil war in France became a race and ethnic war in Saint-Domingue.

As a revolution in its own right, the Haitian case represented the first complete social revolution in modern history. If we accept a revolution as a complete change in the social basis of political power (which allows us to make a meaningful distinction between a revolution and a simple coup d'état), then no greater change could be manifest than the slaves becoming the masters of their destinies within a free state. Compared with this, the "revolutions" of 1776 in British North America and those of mainland Spanish America between 1810 and 1824 were mere reshufflings of the political elites—the ruling classes before remained essentially the ruling classes afterward, although the personnel might have been slightly altered in the process. Neither in the United States nor in France did revolutions produce truly democratic societies.

But the revolution in Haiti is also a case study of the arrogance of power. The tragic mistake that all the upper classes made—and it was common among the French administrators, the *grands blancs,* the *petits blancs,* the free colored supporters of Julien Raimond, André Rigaud and Alexander Pétion, the English invaders, and the Spanish invaders—was to underestimate the intelligence, sensitivity, and feelings of self-worth of the majority black populations. All assumed that black slaves should be the "hewers of wood and drawers of water" indefinitely, that somehow freedom and social esteem were the special preserve of the wealthy, nonblack upper classes. In the final analysis—and they all paid an inordinately high price for this—they underestimated the sacrifice that black men were willing to pay to obtain or maintain their freedom. The willingness to pay the ultimate sacrifice for one's freedom knows no distinctions of race, color, or class. In the French Revolution whites who were willing to die for their liberty and equality simply could not understand that blacks could be similarly moved—and in the case of slaves, moved in an even more meaningful way. In a myopic definition of self-interest, the white Frenchmen elevated ethnic preference over their own material well-being and physical survival and learned that power and status can be both subjective and fleeting. From the recognition of their self-worth sprang the collective sensibility of their new nationalism.

But there were incalculable practical costs for the establishment of Haiti. The relocation costs for the thousands of refugees dispersed during the revolutionary turmoil was enormous. And the society paid collectively as well. Altogether, the population of the colony of Saint-Domingue might have been reduced by one-half to one-third of what it was in 1791. Bryan Edwards claimed that 300,000 perished between 1790 and 1796, which would have been about 60 percent of the population in 1789.

The physical destruction was enormous. It occurred in two phases. The first took place between 1796 and 1798 when the British occupied sections of the Môle, West Province, and North Province. The defensive, "scorched-earth" policy was designed as part of the expulsion of the occupiers who were as busy trading as they were fighting. The second, more serious phase came after 1802, and it was extended to secure and maintain the independence of Haiti against French imperial schemes.

The English lost about fifteen thousand troops to death, desertion, and discharge during their ill-fated occupation of Saint-Domingue. Altogether, their campaign in the Caribbean may have cost about fifty thousand casualties—about a half of whom would have died. That was probably fewer than in their European campaign that was being waged at the time. The British learned a lot about tropical diseases—especially yellow fever and malaria—useful information for their future wars. But they also learned that they could effectively use black regiments, and after the French wars, those troops became a standard feature of the British military in the Caribbean. Of course, the Spanish and the French had been using black regiments for centuries before the English made this self-serving discovery.

Obviously the French paid the highest price of all. They lost their most important colony, a severe blow to the national economy. By losing Saint-Domingue, the French lost their last chance to retain a viable American empire, although that would not have been immediately obvious. More important, the ten thousand troops that Napoleon sent with Leclerc in 1802—reinforced by several thousands later—represented the finest the French could field at that time. Their loss in Saint-Domingue, it may be argued, weakened the French in the later Peninsular War and might have been felt all the way to Waterloo. The tragic road to Waterloo, then, may have begun among the treacherous paths of Saint-Domingue.

The Haitian Revolution had repercussions throughout the entire Atlantic World, and it permanently altered the balance of political power in the Western World. It profoundly affected political developments in its metropolis, France, as well as in England, the United States, and the Spanish imperial world.

For almost a century, the success of the revolution created, in the words of Kenneth Ramchand and Anthony Maingot, "a terrified consciousness" among the white population along the Atlantic coast from Boston to Buenos Aires. The whites lost their self-confidence, as well as the belief in an automatic superiority over all nonwhites, and would use the phrase, "Remember Haiti" as a sort of artificially enforced group solidarity like circling wagons on the prairie.

Among nonwhites the reaction was also notable. Maroon communities all around the Caribbean reasserted their autonomy and engaged in new wars with the European powers. Free nonwhites took inspiration from the egalitarian and democratic nature of the Haitian constitutions that placed an emphasis on human dignity and genuine equality before the law, as well as the elimination of privileges based on skin color. In many ways the Haitian Revolution was the first step in the long, slow process of the disintegration of the inhumane system of the slave trade and slavery. It took almost a century to dismantle the slavery complex in the Americas. Yet the Haitian Revolution was a blow from which the system could never fully recover.

Perhaps nowhere was the impact more profound that in France. The imprudent decision of Napoleon Bonaparte to reverse the abolition of slavery in the colonies and to subdue Toussaint Louverture led to a disastrous colonial war in Saint-Domingue that ended with the independence of the colony and the permanent loss of the wealthiest possession in the French sphere. The French lost more than forty thousand of their best trained troops, and this loss possibly affected their military performance in the Peninsula Campaign after 1808, as well as the broader European wars leading up the debacle at Waterloo. With the fiasco in Saint-Domingue, Napoleon abandoned the idea of a French American idea (although the French were reluctant to bury the notion) and sold the immense Louisiana Territory to the United States in 1804. This acquisition converted the United States into a continental power with frontiers on both Atlantic and Pacific Oceans.

The devastation of Haitian agriculture after 1791 stimulated sugar and coffee expansion elsewhere in the Caribbean, especially in Cuba, Puerto Rico, Trinidad, the Guianas, and Jamaica. This expansion was sometimes aided by Haitian refugees. Meanwhile, in Haiti agriculture became increasing nonplantation, focusing on a subsistence pattern that would greatly undermine the chances for a vibrant national economy during the nineteenth century.

The Haitian Revolution also changed the world of sugar. The Continental Blockade of the Europeans against France in 1805 forced Napoleon to develop beet sugar as a substitute for cane sugar. By the middle of the nineteenth century, beet sugar had captured nearly one-half of the world sugar market, breaking a monopoly that had lasted for more than six hundred years. For dedicated Caribbean sugar producers, things would never again be the same as they were in the halcyon sugar days of the eighteenth century.

Finally there was the relationship with Simón Bolívar, the George Washington of the South American independence wars. In 1815, after his stay in Jamaica, Bolívar visited Alexander Pétion, the president of the Southern Republic of Haiti, who provided arms and troops to continue his campaign to expel the Spanish from the mainland. Bolívar did not admire the openly egalitarian nature of Haitian governments, but he did promise to abolish slavery wherever on the mainland that he was successful, and he kept his word.

In the final analysis, the establishment of the independent state of Haiti represented a monumental step forward, not just for black people, but for black power in the Caribbean. It irreparably weakened the foundation of the slave system and held a faint beacon of hope for the forces of non-European nationalism throughout the Americas. Haiti represented a harsh choice between human dignity and material well-being. Haitians opted for independence in 1804, not because they did not appreciate the advantages of wealth and power, but because they would rather be free men in a free land. They took the French revolutionary slogans more seriously than the French themselves. That they could not project their achievements across a broader landscape does not diminish the magnitude of their achievement at that time and in that place. Haiti might not have been an admirable model of state formation for the neighboring Latin American states at the beginning of the nineteenth century since it represented potential social chaos. But, like the French Revolutionaries in 1789, the Latin Americans probably did not fully understand the enigma that was Haiti. And many of the later problems of the mainland states were already manifest in microcosm in that early Caribbean state in the early nineteenth century.

The declaration of Haitian independence in 1804 represented a victory for the popular forces, tantamount to a victory of the ideas of Emiliano Zapata and Zapatismo in the Mexican Revolution a century later. The former slaves and descendants of slaves took over the government and tentatively sought to establish their independence in a hostile world. It was not easy. Civil war between blacks in the north under Henri Christophe (until his suicide in 1820) and mulattoes in the south under Alexander Pétion divided the society, while the gradual proliferation of small peasant holdings undermined the national economy. After about 1810, plantation products declined precipitously. Sugar exports fell from 141,089,831 pounds in 1789 to 18,535,112 pounds in 1801, to 600,000 pounds in 1821, and to 16,199 pounds in 1836. In 1842, Haiti exported only 6,000 pounds of sugar. Sugar clearly is most optimally produced on large-scale farms—a lesson repeated in the Caribbean from Toussaint Louverture to Fidel Castro. Coffee exports fell gradually from 76,835,219 pounds in 1789 to 32,189,784 pounds in 1826 and then climbed to 37,622,672 pounds in 1836. Coffee production remained the main economic enterprise throughout the nineteenth century. Cacao exports became erratic, but declined slightly from 758,628 pounds in 1789 to 550,484 pounds in 1836. Cotton exports fell from more than 7 million pounds in 1789 to a little more than 600,000 pounds in 1826 but increased to more than 1 million pounds ten years later. Indigo ceased to be an export commodity. Clearly in the agricultural restructuring that followed the Haitian Revolution, highland crops fared better than lowland crops, and peasant crops survived far better than capitalist, plantation ones.

The emphasis on peasant production led to a great diversification of the Haitian agricultural production. Crops that could be grown successfully on small plots and commodities that could be produced with individual effort or very little labor increased at the expense of the former tropical staples. This was the case with saltpeter, logwood, mahogany, tobacco, hides, gum, ginger, beeswax, honey, coconuts, bananas, castor oil, and reed cane mats. Production of ground provision for domestic consumption also increased, as did the semibarter arrangements of the internal marketing system.

Peasant production, however, did not prove attractive to international entrepreneurs. John MacGregor described Haiti through his commercially biased British lens in 1846 in a fashion typical of the visitors of the nineteenth century:

> From the day on which Christophe expired, down to the present day, a period of twenty-six years, neither industry, nor improvement, nor energetic administration, nor the extension of the education of the people, nor any progress in the march of civilization, appears in the agricultural, manufacturing, commercial, moral, social, or political condition of the republic of Haiti. The climate, the soil and the pastures, yield almost without culture, sufficient merely to feed a people, too indolent to work for comfort and luxuries.

But other visitors remarked how peaceful the new kingdom was, how relatively free from crime and contention were its residents under the first three heads of state, Jean-Pierre Boyer (1818–1843), Faustin Soulouque (1847–1859), and Nicholas-Fabre Geffrard (1859–1867). The rivalry and vicious political infighting of the elites did not appear to filter down to the masses, at least not until the economic situation for the state had deteriorated after the middle of the nineteenth century. But as politics became a profession, its practitioners recruited an ever-increasing number of peasants into private armies geared toward political activity. Eventually these private armies evolved into the *cacos*, designed to protect private landlords as well as to plunder the countryside.

Without a strong political and economic infrastructure, the essentially adequate peasant production could not be harnessed efficaciously for the general good. Haiti was to become a permanent case study in the debilitating limitations of a peasant economy. Nearly two centuries of political independence have not altered the slide to isolation, poverty, and abandonment of the tropical state that was once the richest colony in the world. By the end of the nineteenth century, Haiti had become the poorest state in the Americas.

But Haiti after independence found itself beset with as many internal as external problems. The most complex internal problem was probably the question of color. The problem throughout the nineteenth century was not only between blacks and mulattoes, but between those who had a long, free lineage and those who had recently arrived at that status as a result of the revolution. Sorting out the color problem was made extremely difficult since it was deliberately politicized. The first constitution of the free Haiti tried to erase the color question by stating that all residents of the republic, regardless of their origin, were "black." This converted color into a matter of politics, not pigment, and involuntarily designated as equally black all mulattoes and whites (especially Germans and Poles) who had fought against the French. Moreover, the constitution declared that whites were forbidden to own or acquire land or any other property. Opposing the constitutional designation, therefore, brought with it potential economic penalties. But the definitions of color remained fluid, subjective, and sometimes whimsical, plaguing social and political relations until the present.

In 1859, Haiti changed from a monarchy to a republic. But the authority of the central government became increasingly restricted to the capital, Port-au-Prince, and in the countryside something close to anarchy prevailed. Dependent on the fluctuations of the world coffee market and the benevolence of foreign powers, Haiti eventually found itself occupied by the United States military in 1915. The occupation dissolved the political institutions, which were not re-formed until 1930, and controlled the customs receipts until 1947. It failed, however, to stifle Haitian nationalism and, if anything, might even have revitalized it. Despite their promise to reform the political system, the Americans did little to stabilize local politics, and on their departure very little had really changed in Haitian life. In 1957, François "Papa Doc" Duvalier, a physician and folklorist who had taken some public health courses at the University of Michigan, handily won an army-supervised presidential election by appealing to nationalism, racism, and an impenetrable mysticism masquerading as voodoo. He was popular, having been an active player in politics since the 1930s, and his election capped a year of uncertainty. More than that, Duvalier claimed that he had ended "mulatto" rule, referring to his predecessors Paul Magloire (1950–1956) and Dumarsais Estimé (1946–1950). Within two years, he had consolidated his position by eliminating his opponents, real and imagined, and had defeated an invasion in the south. Creating a private army of thugs, the infamous Tonton Macoutes, Duvalier skillfully exploited the anticommunist backlash of the Cuban revolution to eliminate internal opposition and gave the state a new constitution in 1964 that declared him president for life. In 1971, shortly before his death, another constitutional change gave the president the power to name his successor (subject to ratification by the electorate), and he named his only son, Jean-Claude.

In 1985, Jean-Claude Duvalier held a referendum that supported his claim to be president for life with 99.98 percent of the votes in favor. It proved to be a short political life. Though less dictatorial and sadistic than his father, Jean-Claude "Baby Doc" Duvalier was overthrown in February 1986 amid rising economic, political, and social discontent. Political power quickly reverted to the army. The twenty-nine-year dynasty had not accomplished much for the majority of the population. Haiti remained the poorest country in the Western Hemisphere with an annual per capita income of less than $400, an employment rate of only 60 percent of the labor force, and an illiteracy rate well above 80 percent of its nearly 9 million people. Although more than 70 percent of the population lives by agriculture, farming accounts for less than 40 percent of the gross domestic product, and poor Haitians emigrate in large numbers to wherever they can find legal or illegal employment.

The post-Duvalier period has not seen any significant improvement in the Haitian political or economic condition. The army, often with outside support, remains the power behind the throne. In 1991 it ousted the first democratically elected president after the Duvaliers, the Salesian priest Jean Bertrande Aristide (born 1953), who headed a popular movement called Fanmi Lavalas (Floodtide Family). By 2004 Aristide had served as president on three occasions, but then an international consortium, including France, Canada, and the United States, engineered his ouster. He sojourned in the Central African Republic and Jamaica before settling with his retinue in South Africa, where he occasionally sends sermons back to Haiti and expresses a desire to return. Aristide remains very popular in Haiti.

During the past twenty years, Haiti has received substantial aid from international sources. But the chronic weakness of its institutions frustrates every effort to improve the daily lives of its growing population. Aid from the United States alone between 1990 and 2010 amounted to roughly $4 billion dollars, with little evidence of infrastructural change. Other international agencies, such as the World Bank and the International Monetary Fund, have experienced the same results with their efforts in Haiti. This lamentable weakness of the political system was demonstrated when a massive earthquake struck Haiti on January 12, 2010, causing extensive damage especially in the cities of Port-au-Prince, Léogane, Petit-Goáve, and Jacmel. The disaster killed more than 230,000 persons, injured more than 300,000, and left more than 1 million homeless. Altogether more than 250,000 residences and some 30,000 commercial buildings were destroyed, including almost all the most important public buildings of the capital city. The government of President Rene Préval (b. 1943) remained paralyzed for months afterward, while several international agencies and foreign governments assumed control of humanitarian aid for the population of approximately 9 million.

Haitian history and nationalism have been closely tied to the affairs of its neighbor, the Dominican Republic, which shares the eastern two-thirds of the island of Hispaniola. In both states, some sharply contrasting circumstances of the period deeply affected the manner in which the symbols of nationalism thrived or failed to thrive. Haiti developed from a colony that was the center of a dynamic French empire, with a predominantly black population (albeit slaves) and a vibrant economy (albeit plantation based). In the process of creating the new state, Haiti destroyed its white elite and promoted its African heritage as the proud, homogenizing symbol of the new state, a beacon for all black Americans. The colony of Santo Domingo, on the other hand, constituted a peripheral part of a Spanish empire that was falling apart in the early nineteenth century. Its small population was about equally divided between Spanish and Creoles, mestizos and blacks. The miscegenated Creoles controlled political leadership, promoted Hispanic ideals, and pretended that theirs was a "white" society threatened by a "black" neighbor. With an economy about evenly mixed among grazing, tobacco farming, and sugar production, and sharply divided regionally (parallel to the geographic zones of Saint-Domingue), the new Dominican Republic had considerable difficulty in creating a homogeneous state and nation. Unlike Haiti, its economy developed during the nineteenth century in concert with immigrant entrepreneurs colluding with a small number of local landowning and business families. Nevertheless, some comparisons accompanied those contrasts. In both states, weak administrative centers, struggling economies, and the continual external threats helped the military caudillos to emerge, and militaristic politics became a major occupation as well as a conduit for economic and social upward mobility.

In 1795, Spain ceded its colony of Santo Domingo to France at the Treaty of Basle. The colony's population was very small, compared to the prosperous French sector, perhaps no more than 100,000 inhabitants—equally divided among whites, free coloreds, and slaves—in an area 1½ times the western part. Toussaint Louverture conquered the territory in 1800 and freed the slaves. After 1804, the eastern part was considered an essential factor in the defense of Haiti. But the French were expelled in 1808, and Spanish colonialism was fitfully reestablished. This situation lasted until 1821. The following year, the Haitians, under Jean-Pierre Boyer, again reconquered the eastern part of the island and held it until 1844, when the Dominicans successfully expelled the Haitians and established an unstable republic under Pedro Santana (1801–1864). Plagued by persistent attacks from Haiti, as well as by interminable conspiracies within, Santana successfully petitioned to have the republic declared a province of Spain in 1861—with himself as governor. But Spain, consumed with its own internal problems, found the heterogeneous province virtually ungovernable and abandoned it in 1865 (after Santana's death) to his rival, Buenaventura Báez (1810–1884), who unsuccessfully sought to have it annexed to the United States. Until 1882, political chaos prevailed, with the presidency frequently revolving among caudillos supported by one or the other of the personalist political factions called *rojos*, "reds" (followers of Báez); *azules*, "blues" (followers of Santana); or *verdes*, "greens" (splinter factions of the two between 1873 and 1876 led by then-president González). The theme was a familiar one in the politics of Latin America: regional *caciques* converting themselves into national caudillos.

From 1882 to 1899, the country was dominated by Ulises Heureaux (1845–1899), a ruthless dictator from the north, who imposed a Napoleonic political authoritarianism and a socially conscious modernizing program of internal reforms. Like Francisco Franco in post–civil-war Spain, Heureaux brought a repressive order and stability to affairs that facilitated speculative economic ventures, promoted a commercial middle class, and encouraged a large number of immigrants to enter the republic. He expanded education, industry, and internal communications and improved both the army and the bureaucracy. Heureaux elevated the practice—later developed to a high art by Rafael Trujillo Molina (1891–1961)—of treating the state as a private domain and removing the distinction between private and public functions. Political power rested on paid armies. At the time of his assassination in 1899, military expenditure accounted for more than 70 percent of the national budget. What was good for the military politicians was not necessarily equally good for the state and its citizens, and by the end of the century, the Dominican Republic found itself, like its neighbor, onerously indebted to foreigners and teetering at the edge of bankruptcy. After 1905, the United States began to take an active interest in the Dominican Republic and Haiti, partly for private commercial reasons, partly for strategic reasons, and partly to counter the threat of the establishment of a German foothold in the Americas. Finally in 1916, the United States sent in the Marines to occupy the Dominican Republic, impose order, and supervise the collection of customs. The Marines were withdrawn in 1924 amid concerted opposition in the country, but the control of the customs lasted until 1941. The occupation accomplished considerable reorganization of the political, social, and economic life of the Dominican Republic, although not always in accord with the goals of the occupying power. At the same time that the Marines were imposing order, a powerful anti-American sentiment stimulated a new xenophobic nationalism that temporarily brought together the wealthy and the poor, the rural and the urban, the guerrilla opponents and the respectable classes into a recalcitrant opposition to foreign military rule. The creation of the National Guard to replace and depoliticize the military produced, promoted, and projected into power Rafael Leónidas Trujillo Molina, the "Little Caesar of the Caribbean," who in 1930 overthrew the elected president, Horacio Vasquez (1860–1936), and monopolized power until his assassination in 1961. Like Duvalier in Haiti—or his fellow National Guard creations, Anastasio Somoza García (1896–1956) in Nicaragua and Fulgencio Batista Zaldívar (1901–1973) in Cuba—Trujillo completely dominated the state in every way, providing a modicum of social and economic reforms at the expense of human and political rights.

The near simultaneous military occupations of Haiti and the Dominican Republic represented a new attempt by the United States not only to "spread the American dream," but finally to put meaning into the dormant nineteenth-century proclamations of the Monroe Doctrine and Manifest Destiny. A reluctant imperialist, the United States wanted hegemonic power in a dependent hemisphere. Converting the Caribbean into an "American Mediterranean," then, remained a central feature of U.S. thought and action. But U.S. plans, goals, and ideology were incoherent, inconsistent, and unintelligently pursued. Above all the nation demonstrated a remarkable incapacity to differentiate between its own short-term and long-term advantages. And it never attempted to understand the complex world of the Caribbean. The U.S. concept of race proved cruder, more bipolar, and more divisive. Racism permeated U.S. foreign policy, which helps to explain why its attitude toward Haiti diverged from that toward the Dominican Republic. A Department of State official confessed as much in a memo written in 1921:

> It is well to distinguish at once between the Dominicans and the Haitians. The former, while in many ways not advanced far enough for the highest type of self-government, yet have a preponderance of white blood and culture. The Haitians on the other hand are negro for the most part, and, barring a very few highly educated politicians, are almost in a state of savagery and complete ignorance. The two situations thus demand different treatment. In Haiti it is necessary to have as complete a rule by Americans as possible. This sort of control will be required for a long period of time, until the general average of education and enlightenment

can be raised. In the Dominican Republic, on the other hand, I think that we should endeavor rather to counsel than control.

As in Cuba and Puerto Rico earlier, the U.S. military government concentrated its attention on education, public health, and public order based on the new National Guard. The rationale was that attention to the material conditions would constitute the basis of a more democratic society. In the end, while the occupation failed to alter significantly political or social culture, it did boost nationalism and provide the new political powers with better instruments of mass control.

After his rise to power in 1930, Trujillo skillfully manipulated the rhetoric of the Americans to serve his own internal political purposes and to mollify all types of opposition. In 1937, Trujillo, in an action that he described as "deafricanizing the country and restoring Catholic values," savagely murdered about thirty thousand Haitians, most of whom worked as cane cutters along the border with Haiti. International mediation prevented a full-scale war between the two states, but the attacks produced a favorable backlash for Trujillo in his own country. Until the 1960s, contrary to appearances, Trujillo would promote the Dominican Republic as a white Hispanic society. Nevertheless, black immigrant workers from Haiti and the neighboring British Antilles continued to constitute the workforce on sugar estates in the Dominican Republic.

By the end of his ruthlessly efficient but suffocatingly tyrannical rule, Trujillo had modernized the economy of the state and had greatly strengthened the army without much change in the political or social culture. The chaotic aftermath ended with another military occupation by the United States in 1965. Unlike the first occupation in 1916, the unilateral invasion "to defend American lives and property" was quickly replaced by international forces operating under the auspices of the Organization of American States. A mediated settlement facilitated the holding of peaceful and free elections in 1966 that were won by the prolific writer and political chamaleon Joaquín Balaguer (1906–2002), who had served as Trujillo's president in 1961 and had been exiled the following year. Balaguer served as president three times: 1960–1962, 1966–1978, and 1986–1996. His administrations witnessed gradual improvements in the economy and significant expansion of the social and political rights of women. Accusations of fraud in the 1994 elections resulted in widespread political unrest, and Balaguer surrendered the office of president two years later to Leonel Fernández (born 1953), who would later be reelected in 2004 after the constitution removed the single-term restriction. By that time the Dominican Republic had made significant strides toward rebuilding a strong civil society, enormously enhancing the role of women, and broadening common respect for the diverse groups within the state.

The political structure has been democratized to the extent that a number of parties openly compete, and the state administrative structure remains in the hands of civilians. In the post-Trujillo era, the Dominican Republic has undergone tremendous transformation, not the least of which has been the change from a quasi-private fiefdom to a national state. The army has accepted, sometimes reluc-tantly, the results of the national voting and allowed the presidents to serve out their terms of office. The Dominican Republic in the late 1980s, therefore, joined the rest of the Caribbean (except Cuba and Suriname) in the practice of a mod-ern political culture based on free, competitive, regularly held elections. Regular elections, however, do not provide the full test of the maturity of the nation-state. Political stability remains precarious as long as basic economic expectations are unfulfilled. In this sense, the challenges to Caribbean nationalism derive equally from internal as well as external sources.

SUGGESTED READINGS

Bell, Madison Smartt. *All Souls' Rising: A Novel*. New York: Penguin, 1995.

Bell, Madison Smartt. *Master of the Crossroads: A Novel*. New York: Penguin, 2000.

Bell, Madison Smartt. *The Stone that the Builder Refused: A Novel*. New York: Pantheon, 2004.

Bell, Madison Smartt. *Toussaint Louverture: A Biography*. New York: Pantheon Books, 2007.

Calder, Bruce J. *The Impact of Intervention: The Dominican Republic During the U.S. Occupation of 1916–1924*. Austin: University of Texas Press, 1988.

Cassá, Roberto. *Movimiento obrero y lucha socialista en la República Dominicana (desde los orígines hasta 1960)*. Santo Domingo: Fundación Cultural Dominicana, 1990.

Dore y Cabral, Carlos. *Reforma agraria y luchas sociales en la República Dominicana, 1966–1978*. Santo Domingo: Editora Taller, 1981.

Dubois, Laurent. *A Colony of Citizens: Revolution and Slave Emancipation in the French Caribbean, 1787–1804*. Chapel Hill: University of North Carolina Press, 2004.

Dubois, Laurent. *Avengers of the New World: The Story of the Haitian Revolution*. Cambridge, Mass.: Harvard University Press, 2004.

Dubois, Laurent, and Garrigus, John D. *Slave Revolution in the Caribbean, 1798–1804: A Brief History with Documents*. Boston: Bedford St. Martin's, 2006.

Dupuy, Alex. *Haiti in the World Economy: Class, Race, and Underdevelopment Since 1700*. Boulder Colo.: Westview Press, 1989.

Esteban Deive, Carlos. *Las emigraciones dominicanas a Cuba (1795–1808)*. Santo Domingo: Fundación Cultura Dominicana, 1989.

Fick, Carolyn E. *The Making of Haiti: The Saint Domingue Revolution from Below*. Knoxville: University of Tennessee Press, 1990.

Gaspar, Daid Barry, and Geggus, David Patrick, eds. *A Turbulent Time: The French Revolution and the Greater Caribbean*. Bloomington: Indiana University Press, 1997.

González-Ripoll, María Dolores *et al.*, eds. *El Rumor de Haiti en Cuba: temor, raza y rebeldía, 1789–1844*. Madrid: Consejo Superior de Investigaciones Cientificas, 2004.

Guerrero Cano, María Magdalena. *Sociedad Politica e Iglesia en el Santo Domingo Colonial, 1861–1865*. Santo Domingo: Academia Dominicana de Historia, 2010.

Knight, Franklin W. "The Haitian Revolution and the Notion of Human Rights." *Journal of the Historical Society*, 5 (Fall 2005): 391–416.

Martínez-Vergne, Teresita. *Nation and Citizen in the Dominican Republic, 1880–1916*. Chapel Hill: University of North Carolina Press, 2005.

Peguero, Valentina. *The Militarization of the Culture of the Dominican Republic from the Captains General to General Trujillo.* Lincoln: University of Nebraska Press, 2004.

Plummer, Brenda Gayle. *Haiti and the United States: The Psychological Moment.* Athens: University of Georgia Press, 1992.

Pons, Frank Moya. *The Dominican Republic: A National History.* New Rochelle, N.Y.: Hispaniola Books, 1995.

Popkin, Jeremy D. *Facing Racial Revolution: Eyewitness Accounts of the Haitian Insurrection.* Chicago: University of Chicago Press, 2007.

Roorda, Eric Paul. *The Dictator Next Door: The Good Neighbor Policy and the Trujillo Regime in the Dominican Republic, 1930–1945.* Durham, N.C.: Duke University Press, 1998.

San Miguel, Pedro. *La isla imaginada: historia, identidad y utopia en la Española.* San Juan: La Trinitaria, 1997.

Santamaría García, Antonio, and Naranjo Orovio, Consuelo, eds. *Más allá del azúcar: Política, diversificación y prácticas económicas en Cuba, 1878–1930.* Madrid: Doce Calles, 2009.

Smith, Matthew J. *Red and Black in Haiti: Radicalism, Conflict, and Political Change, 1934–1957.* Chapel Hill: University of North Carolina Press, 2009.

Turits, Richard Lee. *Foundations of Despotism: Peasants, the Trujillo Regime, and Modernity in Dominican History.* Stanford, Calif.: Stanford University Press, 2003.

CHAPTER 8

Caribbean Nation Building 2
Cuba, 1868–2010

> Cuba could easily provide for a population three times as great
> as it now has, so there is no excuse for the abject poverty of a
> single one of its present inhabitants. The markets should be
> overflowing with produce, pantries should be full, all hands
> should be working. This is not an inconceivable thought. What
> is inconceivable is that anyone should go to bed hungry, that
> children should die for lack of medical attention.... What is
> inconceivable is that the majority of our rural people are now
> living in worse circumstances than were the Indians Columbus
> discovered in the fairest land that human eyes had ever seen.
> —Fidel Castro, *History Will Absolve Me*, October 16, 1953

> We are a fighting people, setbacks have not got the better of us,
> and we have come through some difficult times. We won when
> we were just a handful. Today we are millions, and no external
> or internal force, no objective or subjective conditions can hold
> back our victorious march to the future.
> —Fidel Castro, Armed-Forces-Day speech, December 5, 1988

By the middle of the nineteenth century, Cubans had already begun to manifest a rebellious sense of national identity more precocious than any found
elsewhere in the Caribbean and perhaps in the Americas. It is not easy to explain
why Cubans should have been so politically self-conscious at the beginning of the
eighteenth century, but Cuba's historical experience varied slightly from that of the
other Caribbean colonies. Geography was a major factor. Cuba was a large island,
the largest in the Caribbean—although size had little to do with its early colonization. It was bountifully endowed with gently rolling, fertile, cultivable land; dense
hardwood forests; and fine harbors, making it immensely habitable. That was
not considered an asset until the late eighteenth-century agricultural revolution.
Cuba's early importance derived from its perfect strategic location when maritime transportation depended on ships driven by sail. After the Spanish imperial
reorganization in 1585, Cuba became an important nodal point in the transatlantic
communication network. The excellent harbor at Havana provided a convenient

collection point for the protected galleons sailing back from the New World. Soon Havana was preeminent among the notorious fortified Spanish-American cities, including San Juan in Puerto Rico, San Juan de Ulloa in Mexico, and Cartagena in New Granada. Military fortifications and expanding administrative functions infused importance to the city and stimulated its gradual prosperity. Cuba was a major beneficiary of the late eighteenth-century administrative and economic reforms of Charles III (king 1759–1788). By the eighteenth century, the island had already possessed a critical mass of settlers, that is, a large enough population base to fulfill all the complex occupational functions of the community and a coherent culture, albeit heavily concentrated around Havana in the west and Santiago de Cuba in the east. As John McNeill showed in *Atlantic Empires of France and Spain*, "Cuban society reflected Spanish society a good deal more than did most parts of Spanish America." A diversified white population included peasants and landless laborers; artisans, construction workers, shopkeepers, import and export merchants, prostitutes, butchers, salters, stevedores, ditchdiggers, tailors; a bureaucratic class serving city, colony, and empire; a professional class of officers in the army and navy, lawyers, doctors, chemists, priests, scribes, ships' captains, and university professors. Rounding out the population were a growing number of slaves and a small but expanding landed aristocracy and nobility.

The island underwent a tremendous population explosion and frenzied economic development after 1750. Under the impetus of an impressive annual subsidy (until 1808) from Mexico, a series of free-trade agreements (beginning in 1776), and the aggressive penetration of North American merchants into the Cuban trade, the overall transformation was phenomenal. The population increased from 160,512 in 1757 to 272,000 in 1790 and reached more than 1,300,000 in 1860. By 1899, the population had reached 1,631,687. Between 1790 and 1860, the fastest-growing segment of the population was that of the slaves, imported legally and illegally from Africa and needed to boost production on the sugar plantations then taking advantage of the collapse in Saint-Domingue. By 1840, nonwhites outnumbered whites by a small number. At that time, the original settler society had already been severely strained by a series of sugar revolutions but, unlike Jamaica or Barbados, had not been totally converted into a plantation and slave structure. Mindful of the situation in Haiti, the Cubans actively reduced the number of nonwhites by restricted immigration—eventually ending the slave trade—and wanton slaughter (as after the *La Escalera* conspiracy of 1843 in Matanzas). After 1860, the greater increase in the population occurred among the white sector. Between 1860 and 1920, more than 600,000 Spaniards migrated to the island, increasing the proportion of whites in the population, shattering the stereotypes of occupation and race, but, surprisingly, not diluting the nationalist sensibility on the island.

The city of Havana grew physically and almost doubled its population by the end of the eighteenth century. A measure of this transformation may be gauged from the fact that Havana was by 1790 the largest American port city—and third in population size after Mexico City and Lima in the hemisphere. With a population of 51,307 in 1792, Havana far exceeded in size its Caribbean rivals: Cap Français

(15,000), Kingston (23,508), and Port-au-Prince (6,200). But Havana also substantially surpassed its competitors or trading partners on the mainland. At about the same time, Boston had a population of 18,038. New York had 33,131 inhabitants. Philadelphia, whose traders did most of their business with Havana, had a population of 42,444. Vera Cruz, the main Caribbean export city of Mexico, had a population of about 15,000; Rio de Janeiro, 38,707; and Buenos Aires, roughly 30,000. Even excluding the 17,000 slaves, Havana was a big and important city at the end of the eighteenth century, ranking among the most prominent anywhere in the Americas. What was more, Havana had a university (established in 1728) and a dynamic cultural life.

Modern Cuban history may be divided into three periods: the late colonial period, ending in 1898; the period of republican independence between 1902 and 1959; and the Castro revolution that replaced it after 1959.

During the nineteenth century, the Cuban sugar industry achieved monumental success. Although it relied considerably upon slave labor—and African slaves continued to be imported in large numbers until the late 1860s—it also incorporated a variety of free laborers, drawn from Europe, Asia, and Mexico. In addition, it was an innovative society. The first sugar revolutions at the end of the eighteenth century restructured land use and concentrated production on sugarcane growing, milling, and boiling. The process resembled the conventional structure of production that had been in existence for centuries, uniting in a single labor-intensive frenzy the combined complementary tasks of agriculture and manufacturing. Given the technological constraints at the time, much duplication was inevitable, and the maximum unit of production remained around three hundred metric tons per year per unit. After that, the producer duplicated the entire structure in a semiautonomous unit. In that way, one owner had many estates, each a virtual carbon copy of the others. Most sugar estates at the end of the eighteenth century produced closer to thirty tons of sugar per harvest.

By 1840, however, a new series of technological revolutions overtook the sugar industry, making it the most mechanized and efficient in the world, employing steam-powered mills, vacuum-drying vats, and narrow-gauge railroads to boost productivity and production enormously. These technological innovations destroyed the old formula for sugar production and engineered a voracious expansion of the industry eastward from Havana, expelling or absorbing small landholders, eliminating subsistence farming, and converting the island's famous and extensive hardwood forests of pines, mahogany, cedar, and lignum vitae into unbroken fields of sugarcane. The output per mill was impressive, increasing from about 30 tons per mill in 1790 to 72 tons per mill in 1830, to 120 tons in 1840, to 300 tons in 1860, to 500 tons in 1870, to 1,330 tons in 1890. Equally significant is the already high average production of the sixty-four mechanized mills in 1860: an average of 1,176 tons per mill. By the 1860s, the sugar industry accounted for 83 percent of all exports, and with an annual harvest of more than 500,000 tons of sugar, Cuba alone produced nearly a third of all cane sugar traded on the world market. Higher production indicated a smaller number of sugar factories and increased productivity. Even before the arrival of United Fruit Company, a pattern of concentrated landholding was apparent. In 1857, *ingenio* Santa Susana had 11,000 acres with 1,700 in cane, 866 slaves, and a harvest of 2,700 tons. *Ingenio* Alava, owned by Miguel Aldama, had approximately half its 5,000 acres in cane and produced more than 3,500 tons of cane with a labor force including 600 slaves. By the 1880s, the construction of *centrales* (central factories) indicated the separation of the industrial from the agricultural process in sugar manufacturing and further augmented productive efficiency. By 1894, as Eric Williams noted in his study, *From Columbus to Castro,* "Cuba produced more than fifty times as much [sugar] as Jamaica exported, ten times as much as British Guiana, four times as much as the French West Indies." In the twentieth century, corporate enterprises boosted production even more.

The sugar revolutions fundamentally altered the structure of Cuban society and economy, creating a new, rich class of slave owners who used their wealth to augment their political power and social status. The small landed aristocracy in the middle of the eighteenth century moved enthusiastically into sugar production and commerce. The elite comprised families, such as the Arango y Parreño, de las Casas, Montalvo, O'Farrill, Calvo de la Puerta, Peñalver, Beltrán de Santa Cruz, Barreto, Zayas Bazán, Mateo Pedroso, Herreras, Nuñez del Castillo, Recio de Oquendo, and Kindelán, some of whom had established residence in Cuba in the sixteenth century. These families demonstrated the common eighteenth-century pattern, especially of mainland settler families, of intermarriage and overlapping participation in the church, bureaucracy, economy, and military. By 1790, Cuba boasted a titled nobility of twenty persons, a fourfold increase over the number in 1760. The titled nobility ranked at the top of the elite. Beginning in the 1790s, an increasing number of the elite took advantage of the penurious state of the Spanish treasury to purchase supernumerary captaincies and colonelcies in the regular army and militia. Indeed, by 1800, Cubans held a majority of the offices in the local garrison in Havana, a majority of the colonelcies, and a majority of positions in municipal government. The Cuban elite was unusually cosmopolitan. It not only established conjugal links with distinguished families all along the Atlantic seaboard from Massachusetts to the Río de la Plata, but fraternized with the metropolitan elite, sending members to the Spanish court and even placing offspring in the highly select Royal College of Nobles. Gonzalo O'Farrill (1754–1831), born in Havana, rose to be lieutenant-general of the Spanish army and minister of war. A Cuban, Joaquín Beltrán de Santa Cruz y Cárdenas, spent seven years at the Spanish court and returned to Cuba as the Conde de Santa Cruz de Mopos, a brigadier in the regular army and the subinspector-general of the army in Cuba—unique achievements for a Creole in the Spanish empire.

The individual achievements of the Cuban Creole elite were not, in the great majority of cases, unique in the history of the Caribbean or of the mainland colonies. What appears exceptional in the Cuban case, however, is the relatively large size, cohesiveness, and self-confidence of this group. While political astuteness encouraged the Cuban settler elite to support the Spanish government, the elite identified increasingly with their homeland—and by the beginning of the nineteenth century, that homeland was unmistakably Cuba. Then the aristocracy came to concentrate more on landed investment while retaining dominance over the merchant community in the Consulado. Nowhere else in the Caribbean was this the case. When the Spanish government was no longer required to support slavery at the end of the century, the Cuban elite abandoned Spain and supported the cause of independence. Their imperial loyalty derived from the convenience of self-interest.

By the middle of the nineteenth century, the Cuban sugar society was already a volatile mixture of constricting feudalism cum modern technologically advanced capitalism. It was international in its connections. The society needed workers from Africa; food from Spain and North America; machinery and technicians from England, France, Germany, and North America; and markets in North America, England, and Spain. With commerce expanding, Havana became an important international port of call, above all for North American merchant traders. The number of North American–registered ships calling at Havana increased from 150 in 1790 to 1,886 in 1852. By 1877, more than 82 percent of Cuban exports went to the United States, while only 6 percent went to Spain. Clearly, Spain no longer served as the economic metropolis for the island. The mercantile interests of the colony and those of the metropolis inevitably began to diverge.

Changing economic interests had some effect on political opinions. Throughout the century, the island produced a steady number of articulate spokesmen and activists who advocated its independence: Félix Varela y Morales (1788–1853), José Antonio Saco (1797–1879), Carlos Manuel de Céspedes (1819–1874), Francisco Aguilera (1821–1877), Ignacio Agramonte (1841–1873), Enrique José Varona (1849–1933), and José Martí (1853–1895). In the 1820s and 1830s, Spain had to suppress a number of conspiracies that were designed to unite Cuba with the centrifugal forces on the mainland. In the 1840s and 1850s, a number of filibuster expeditions supported by proslavery forces in the southern United States tried to wrest the island forcefully from Spain. At the official level, the United States government tried unsuccessfully to purchase the island. Nevertheless, the issue of slavery divided the elite, and Spain managed to extend an uneasy control throughout the century, exiling dissidents and hanging conspirators, while undulating between promises of reform and disappointing displays of performance. Cuban nationalism, still in its infancy, suffered the vitiating effects of race, class, color, and occupational discrimination.

By the 1860s, the centrifugal factions had become strong and broad based. Spain promised political autonomy and Cuban participation in the metropolitan Cortes in 1867. The following year, a domestic military revolt toppled the Spanish monarchy, and almost a month later, on October 10, 1868, Carlos Manuel de Céspedes and thirty-six nationalist companions declared against Spanish colonial rule in their famous *Grito de Yara* (Yara Declaration) that heralded the first war of Cuban political independence. The war lasted ten years and ended in a stalemate, reflecting the deep internal divisions politically, socially, and economically in the island. The rich sugar producers of the western part of the island and the vast majority of their slaves supported the metropolis. The insurgent nationalists rallied a motley variety of supporters: reformists willing to live within the Spanish empire, advocates of total independence, small- and middle-level landowners who objected to increased taxes, abolitionists seeking the abolition of slavery, small slaveholders who enjoyed amicable relations with their slaves and had nothing much to lose, annexationists proposing incorporation into the United States with an eye to reconciling their politics with their economics, and peasants and shop-keepers from the eastern part of the island who derived no tangible benefits from the colonial government and were more indifferent than committed. They formed elusive guerrilla bands and fought doggedly against the Spanish army and its coali-tion of wealthy volunteers in a series of indecisive campaigns across the eastern half of the island from Camagüey to Oriente. At the Pact of Zanjón in 1878, Spain, quite exhausted by the war, again promised major political and economic reforms: a general amnesty for all insurgents and unconditional emancipation for all African slaves and Asian indentured workers participating in the rebel armies. But a num-ber of nationalist leaders including Antonio Maceo (1845–1896) refused to accept the Spanish conditions of surrender and left the island to continue preparations for a renewed struggle for total independence. The Ten Years' War sounded the death knell for slavery, and in 1886 Cuba became the last Caribbean country—and second to last (with Brazil last) in the Americas—to abolish that despicable system of human suffering and exploitation.

In the 1890s, political and economic crisis in the island increased. Four fac-tions clamored for attention: those who were satisfied with the status quo, those who wanted a sort of dominion status (like that recently bestowed on Canada by Great Britain) within the Spanish empire, those who wanted annexation to the United States, and those who wanted unqualified independence. The disparate organizations operating both inside and outside the island were coordinated and magnificently mobilized by the brilliant poet and propagandist, José Martí. But economic conditions in the period after the Ten Years' War were miserable for the vast majority of Cubans. During the 1880s, capital was scarce. Interest rates on credit soared, sometimes to 30 percent per year, beyond the reach of modest producers. Sugar prices declined as competition increased, leading to a number of bank failures. Employment opportunities in government, in the shipyards, in businesses, and in cigar factories plummeted. Wages fell, and the cost of living rose. Cuba experienced broad-scale social and economic unrest at the moment when the political system in the metropolis found itself least able to attend to colo-nial affairs. Conditions improved during the early 1890s, but by then the Cuban Revolutionary party of José Martí had forged a broad coalition with the single goal of fighting for the independence of Cuba.

On February 24, 1895, a second war of independence broke out, and it quickly became a far more total war with far more serious consequences than the first. Geographically, the war covered the entire island and, thanks to the tireless organi-zation of Martí, spanned all groups and classes. Spain deployed more than 200,000 troops. Both sides killed civilians and burned sugar estates, coffee plantations, and towns, waging war without quarter. Approximately 10 percent of the population died or were exiled. The economy was shattered. By 1898, commercial activity had virtually come to a standstill. Sugar production dropped from more than 1,500,000 tons in 1894 to less than 200,000 tons in 1897. The United States, with investments exceeding $50,000,000 in Cuba and trade with twice that amount, became concerned and excited. After a mysterious explosion aboard a visiting warship, the USS *Maine*, the United States entered the war against Spain on April 25, 1898. By August, Spain had signed a peace protocol in Washington that ended hostilities, and with the signing of the Treaty of Paris on December 10, 1898, the Spanish empire in the Americas came to an inglorious end. Unfortunately for the Cubans, it did not result in their political independence.

Instead, victorious Cuba found itself occupied by the military forces of the United States. The U.S. occupation was a mixed blessing. It brought peace, though it increased the level of popular discontent and dissatisfaction by disbanding the Cuban army. It built a number of schools but imposed an inadequate American-style educational system on the island. It busily built roads, paved the streets of Havana, repaired and extended the telephone system, started sewer works, and extended public sanitation. But the major beneficiaries of most of the renovation and new construction were U.S. contractors and entrepreneurs. The occupation restored the economy but at the price of establishing a U.S. hegemony. It institutionalized politics but disfranchised Cubans. Only about 30 percent of adult males qualified to vote in the elections of 1900 that created the first government of a free Cuba. Moreover, the Platt Amendment (1901), reluctantly accepted by the Cubans, conferred on the United States the right to dictate all international agreements, to regulate the local economy, to intervene in domestic political affairs—"for the welfare of the people, politically, mentally and morally" as General Leonard Wood declared—and to establish a naval station at Guantánamo Bay on the southeastern coast of the island.

Tomás Estrada Palma (1835–1908), a veteran of the Ten Years' War who had succeeded Martí as leader of the independence movement, assumed office as the first elected president of Cuba on May 20, 1902. An unabashed annexationist, Estrada Palma proved to be the wrong man at the wrong time. Vain, weak, incompetent, and greedy, he could not stand up to the United States or to the increasing domestic political factions. U.S. economic interest expanded by leaps and bounds. Hundreds of thousands of acres of prime sugar and tobacco land passed into North American ownership. By 1905, more than thirteen thousand North Americans had acquired land in Cuba. Foreigners controlled iron and copper mines, the railroad companies, the utilities, shipping companies, and banks. In 1911, North Americans had capital investments amounting to more than $200 million, compared with British investments of $60 million, French investments of $12 million, and German investments of $4.5 million. Cubans were finding it difficult to compete in their own country. Latifundism grew in the twentieth century like mushrooms on compost. By 1959, large local and foreign corporations controlled 75 percent of the best arable lands in Cuba. The United Fruit Company owned 93,000 acres. The Punta Alegre Company owned 112,000 acres and leased a further 43,000 acres. The Vertientes-Camagüey Company owned or leased 800,000 acres. The Cuban Atlantic Sugar Company had 400,000 acres, and its rival, the Cuban-American Sugar Company, had 500,000 acres. The Manatí Sugar Company owned or leased 237,000 acres, most of which were cultivated in sugarcane. Julio Lobo, the world's largest sugar vendor, owned or otherwise controlled 1 million acres. The Administración de Negocios Azucareros, owned by the heirs of the Spaniard Lureano Falla Gutiérrez, had 300,000 acres. The name "Cuba" almost became synonymous with "sugar."

The political stability that the United States ardently sought to serve its strategic purposes and as a guarantee for its investments proved elusive from the very beginning. Estrada Palma rigged the presidential elections in 1905 and won a Pyrrhic victory. Immediately he faced a revolt of the losing Liberals and was driven from office the following year. The result was a second military occupation by the United States beginning in October 1906. This occupation was less offensive and more indirect than the first. Charles Magoon (1861–1920), a lawyer who had been governor of the Panama Canal Zone, assumed the position of provisional governor of Cuba. The Cuban constitution remained in force, and the Cuban flag continued to fly (alongside the American flag) from public buildings. Assisted by a civilian advisory commission, Magoon revised the electoral procedure, broadened the franchise, and held elections that returned the Liberals to office. José Miguel Gómez (1858–1921) took office on January 28, 1909, and supervised an economic boom that accentuated the gulf in Cuban society between the "haves" and the "have-nots." The "haves" comprised a small group of foreigners and local bourgeoisie. The others constituted an amorphous congregation of dispossessed, unemployed, itinerant workers; seasonal immigrants; and frustrated politicians—in general, the lower classes of all races.

Between 1902 and 1959, Cuban politics, despite a record of frequent elections, could hardly be described as an exercise in democratic process. It consisted of graft, corruption, malfeasance, administrative incompetence, and blatant social insensitivity to the lower orders, especially the Afro-Cubans. It was government that operated in the shadow of the political and economic interest groups of the United States. Cubans became adept at playing the United States card to serve their interests, but it was a most difficult and unpredictable game. In the long run, it did not serve to enhance the political maturity of the Cubans or the political interests of the United States or the cause of peace and prosperity. Social unrest was endemic. The pattern set by Gómez was followed by his regularly elected successors, Mario García Menocal (served 1913–1921), Alfredo Zayas (1921–1925), Gerardo Machado (1925–1933), Fulgencio Batista (1940–1944 and 1952–1959), Ramon Grau San Martin (1944–1948), and Carlos Prío Socarrás (1948–1952). All used public office to serve private ends and showed scant respect for human rights. Machado and Batista were the most notorious, employing military force, selective assassinations, and constitutional manipulations to gain and keep office. Political corruption extended to the lowest ranks of government. One-fifth of the candidates in the 1922 elections had criminal records, and a frequent occupation of the legislatures was the passage of amnesty bills exonerating members of the government from past criminal actions. Besides general amnesties, presidential pardons were abusively abundant, further enhancing the power of the presidency. Between 1933—when he overthrew Machado with the connivance of the United States—and 1959—when having lost that base of support he abandoned the country—Batista was the most powerful politician in Cuba. But presidential power rested on brute force, not on the legitimacy of popular support. In 1912, a group of aspiring middle-class Afro-Cubans led by Evaristo Estenoz and Pedro Ivonet organized themselves to secure better jobs, to obtain access to the political patronage system, and to protest the 1911 Morua law aimed at eliminating political associations based on color and race. The response of the government was swift and brutal, resulting in the loss of more than three thousand Afro-Cuban lives, mainly in Oriente Province. That effectively destroyed the Afro-Cuban political aspirations to use the process. Thereafter, a modified version of U.S. racism colored race relations in Cuba. In 1917, having lost the elections, the Liberals resorted to revolt as they had successfully done in 1906. The Americans sent military units into Camagüey and Oriente and, to the surprise of the Liberals, supported the conservative government of Menocal and defused the protest. But there was no consistent pattern to U.S. intervention in Cuban political affairs. In 1933, the United States intervened on the side of the opposition, abruptly ending the Machado dictatorship.

In the meantime, the economy of the island was integrated with the mainland. Cubans used U.S. currency, bought U.S. commodities, and sold virtually all their products in the U.S. market. Sugar, despite wild fluctuations, was the principal money earner. But the income from sugar was augmented by a vigorous tourist business promoted by luxury hotels, gambling casinos, and brothels catering to every vice. Havana gained prominence during the years of the legally enforced alcohol prohibition in the United States (1919–1933) as the place for easy booze, willing bedmates, and indiscriminate betting. The island exuded an air of prosperity, but it was superficial, restricted to a small circle of politicians, their families and cronies, and their foreign patrons. The recurring cycles of boom in the 1920s, 1940s, and 1950s did not penetrate much below the upper classes or beyond the suburbs of Havana and Santiago.

For the majority of Cubans in the 1950s, life was brutally miserable and often miserably short. Unemployment and underemployment were rife, especially in the sugar zones. Public services were appallingly inadequate and, even worse, unevenly distributed. Greater Havana, with 17 percent of the Cuban population, had 60 percent of the dentists, 66 percent of the chemists, 60 percent of the nurses, and a disproportionate share of everything. But even in Havana, the contrast between the affluent of Miramar, Vedado, and El Country Club and the poor of Old Havana and Pogolotti was remarkable. Still, the contrast between urban and rural Cuba remained astonishing. Rural Cuba in 1958 was a world apart. Only 9 percent of rural homes had electricity, compared with 87 percent in the cities.

Well over 90 percent of rural Cubans did not regularly drink milk or eat fish, meat, or bread, despite living in a country with one of the most highly developed cattle industries in the Americas. Rural illiteracy was four times that of urban areas. The city of Havana boasted a ratio of 1 doctor for every 220 persons, but that fell off to 1 for 2,423 in rural Oriente. Although the national per capita income of $353 in 1958 was among the highest in all Latin America and the Caribbean, the average rural worker made merely $91 per year. Workers' incomes declined relatively and absolutely between 1951 and 1955, although overall conditions in 1958 were slightly better than in 1955. Moreover, with government income lavished on an excessive bureaucracy and the army, there was little flexibility for setting priorities.

Economic discontent was not a major factor in the unforeseen collapse of the Batista dictatorship in 1959. For more than fifty years, Cubans had endured illegitimate governments, corrupt politicians, and a system apparently incapable of regenerating itself. The tug-of-war between Washington and Havana produced a succession of political jugglers whose main goal was to play their game as long as they could. The opposition remained fragmented by class, by political orientation, by geography, and by goals. In 1933, a glimmer of hope appeared with the end of the Machado dictatorship and the attempt at substantial political reforms. That proved short-lived. A promising constitution promulgated in 1940 offered effective suffrage and no reelection, but Batista's coup d'état in 1952 turned the clock back beyond 1933. The dozens of frustrated groups that sprung up after 1952 all declared themselves, in common with the rhetoric in Latin America at that time, to be revolutionaries. No consensus existed in Cuba in the 1950s on what precisely constituted a revolution, although the precedent of Mexico in 1910 and the contemporary evolving situation in Bolivia were suggestive references. What all the various organizations in Cuba agreed on, however, was that no revolution could begin without first getting rid of Batista, by ballot if possible or by force if necessary. Since balloting was impracticable, violence and force became the instruments of political discourse. A faction led by Fidel Castro (b. 1926) attacked the Moncada military barracks in Santiago de Cuba on July 26, 1953—the centenary of Martí's birth—giving lasting significance and a catchy appellation to a suicidal fiasco. Castro, after serving a brief prison term, was amnestied and left the country for exile in Mexico, vowing to return. He did so in 1956, arriving on the yacht, *Granma*, with about eighty sympathizers, including the Argentine doctor Ernesto "Che" Guevara (1928–1967), whose idealistic volunteer work in Guatemala had been abruptly interrupted by a U.S.–inspired coup d'état against the legitimate government of Jacobo Arbenz (1917–1971). Opposition to Batista was the political coagulant of the day. Since very few entertained the immediate possibility of change in 1959, no concrete programs existed when the 26th of July Movement assumed the government on January 1 of that year. The Batista government had collapsed totally and unexpectedly, and the rapidity of its demise left the opposition groups under a loose coalition of political aspirants controlled by the charismatic Fidel Castro and the idealistic, ideologically committed Ernesto "Che" Guevara.

The Castro revolution, despite its series of inauspicious starts, quickly established itself as nothing less than the evasive, discomfiting reconciliation of nation and state that had been energetically pursued since the early nineteenth century. The civil wars between 1868 and 1898 created a state, but at the expense of a unified and cohesive nation. After 1959, the alienated nation erratically found its home. And the unquestioned head of that home was the popular, loquacious Fidel Castro.

Like all previous revolutions, the Castro revolution was a confused, ambiguous progression of pragmatism and idealism. Unlike most previous revolutions, the level of violence was minimal, partly because most opponents chose to emigrate rather than fight. Most observers and participants anticipated the calling of early elections to legitimate the government of the victorious 26th of July Movement. In the first flush of victory, Castro himself spoke often of an early return to the constitution of 1940. But by the spring of 1959, Guevara was ominously stating that the people wanted "revolution first; elections later." Ad hoc government by "guerrillas in power" became the order of the day. But in 1959, very few regretted the departure of the tyrant Batista.

In retrospect, it is easy to delineate a series of changes, or overlapping phases, through which the revolution passed: the liquidation of capitalist enterprises and the introduction of socialist models between 1959 and 1963, a period of flux between 1963 and 1965, a period of radicalization at home and abroad between 1966 and 1970, a period of political evaluation and institutionalization at home and military activism abroad between 1970 and 1979, and retreat and consolidation after 1980. Some of the changes were subtle, and some were abrupt and contradictory. Each major phase, in addition, had its own internal subdivisions. But the revolution tried to keep one major objective in mind and to pursue it narrowly to the end. The turning points were determined partly by the exigencies of the revolution—its general principles of bringing social justice, dignity, and a strong sense of national purpose—and partly as a self-protective stance against external attacks and internal conspiracies. Defending the revolution always had the highest priority. But the revolution was not a passive, reactive revolution. It began with the ambitious goal of rectifying immediately the accumulated economic, political, and social grievances of a century, passing about 1,500 decrees in the first nine months. In the end, the revolutionaries achieved, by trial and error, the complete restructuring of Cuban society. But it is important to note that it worked in a conducive political climate and with a population with great expectations of the redemptive power of politics. As Jorge Dominguez wrote, "When the revolution came to power, government intervention in the social system was expected and acceptable as desirable. The Cuban revolution changed the characteristics of participation. All of it became politicized, nationalized, centralized. The government discouraged political indifference and began to harness political participation to transform society and to increase its own power and control."

The first three years were perhaps the most confused as the revolutionaries boldly sought, against great odds, to dismantle the capitalist state and to construct a socialist, centralized one. With breathtaking pace, the revolution instituted a series of measures that gave land to the landless, work to the unemployed, and higher wages to the employed and reduced rates to renters and the clients of public utilities. In March 1959, the government legally abolished discrimination wherever it existed publicly in hotels, restaurants, night clubs, country clubs, resorts, and beaches. All Cuban facilities were opened freely to all Cubans regardless of race, class, color, age, sex, or occupation. The lower orders of society—urban and rural workers, peasants, the unemployed, renters, consumers of all sorts, and Afro-Cubans—were the primary beneficiaries, and they immediately embraced the revolution enthusiastically. By the summer of 1959, the government was deliberately vague about whether its reform measures presaged a socialist revolution. But the speed and thoroughness of the reform measures were not designed to give local and foreign capitalists great peace of mind. Out went the remnants of the Batista army, the old political parties, labor unions, and professional and farmers' organizations. In came a set of new, aggressively enthusiastic institutions: the National Institute of Agrarian Reform (INRA) and the Cuban Institute of Cinematic Arts (ICEAC) in 1959; the Central Planning Board (JUCEPLAN), the Federation of Cuban Women (FMC), and the Committees for the Defense of the Revolution (CDR) in 1960; the National Association of Small Farmers (ANAP), the Revolutionary Armed Forces (FAR), the Ministry of the Interior (MININ), and the Integrated Revolutionary Organizations (ORI, reorganized in 1963) in 1961; and the Young Communist League (UJC) established in 1962.

The opposition to these reforms came from four not entirely unrelated sources, and although it came slowly and was uncoordinated, it came with incredible vehemence. One group of opponents were former comrades-in-arms against Batista who lost out in the reshuffling of power in 1959. Some of them left genuinely disappointed by the socialist rhetoric and blatant anti-Americanism of Castro's speeches as well as the indefinite delay in holding free elections. They left the country early, mainly for the United States, and organized from self-imposed exile the first anti-Castro community abroad. Another source of opposition comprised the property owners, local and foreign, whose rents were arbitrarily reduced or whose land had been appropriated by the Agrarian Reform Laws; the entrepreneurial classes; and the political organizers and trades union bosses who were gradually put out of business by the dismantling of the old patronage system. They were vocal in their protests, but through the first year and into the second, they tried unsuccessfully to work within the system, hoping for deliverance from abroad. Most of these local opponents were to leave shortly after the fiasco of the Bay of Pigs. The third source was the hierarchy of the Roman Catholic Church in Cuba. It supported the early reform and only started to express reservations late in 1959 when, despite Castro's vacillation over ideological direction, socialists and communists were gaining visible positions in the upper echelons of the revolutionary government and Cuba agreed to sell sugar to the Soviet Union. But like the other groups, the Catholics seriously underestimated the genuine popular support and political skill of the revolutionaries and, in the end, lost out. Finally, the fourth source resided in the official and private business interests in the United States. Their opposition was reflected in government attitude and action emanating from Washington. From the beginning, Cuban-American relations were made more complicated because the United States insisted on viewing Cuba through the opaque lens of its cold war-influenced geopolitical East-West diplomatic conflict. The revolution presented official Washington with a sharp dilemma. On the one hand, communist influence could not be allowed to expand in the Western Hemisphere, especially in what had been regarded since the turn of the century as "an American lake." On the other hand, it was not clear whether Castro and his group were communist sympathizers with a concrete blueprint or simply well-meaning political reformers bent on cleaning up a politically messy situation and therefore deserving the benefit of the doubt. Caught without a coherent policy, the government of the United States stumbled from one erratic tit-for-tat scheme to another. In response to the nationalization of hundreds of millions of dollars' worth of U.S. landed property by the National Institute for Agrarian Reform, Washington abruptly reduced the sugar quota in 1959. In early 1960, the Soviet Union offered Cuba petroleum at prices considerably below the then current world-market rates. The U.S. refineries—Standard Oil, Texaco, and Shell—refused to refine the oil, and the Cuban government responded by appropriating their Cuban assets in June 1960. Washington retaliated by canceling the sugar agreement with Cuba in July, abruptly terminating its most important market as well as its principal source of foreign exchange. In August, a variety of private U.S. enterprises were nationalized, including banks, sugar mills, and service stations. In October, the United States imposed a trade embargo on Cuba, forbidding the export of all nonmedicinal items. Almost immediately the Cubans expanded the expropriations to include all foreign property and a large number of designated Cuban businesses. In addition, a second urban reform law restricted ownership to no more than one urban residence, creating an immediate supply of state-owned residences with their occupants paying reduced rents. The government then agreed to compensate the owners of appropriated properties at the fixed rate of $350 per month. By the end of 1960, foreign investments in Cuba had been virtually eliminated, and the Cuban government ended up controlling about half the national economy. By January 1961, when the United States broke diplomatic relations, the Cubans had no option but to extend their commercial relations with the Soviet-bloc countries.

The United States, having played the economic pressure card and lost, abandoned the opportunity to negotiate meaningfully with the Cubans. In early 1960, the Eisenhower administration had approved a plan to overthrow the Castro government, using a slightly modified form of the familiar method used to overthrow the socialist government of Jacobo Arbenz in Guatemala in 1954. Cuban exiles were armed, trained in Nicaragua, and given logistical support to invade Cuba. The new Kennedy administration continued to support the military option in early 1961 but realized that simply overthrowing Castro by force was not the solution to the Cuban problem or to radical revolution in Latin America. Instead, in March 1961 President Kennedy announced a bold new Alliance for Progress at a meeting of the Organization of American States held at Punta del Este, Uruguay. With $500 million seed money from the United States, Kennedy tried to steal the thunder from the Cuban revolution by promising that his "vast cooperative effort, unparalleled in magnitude and nobility of purpose," would by the end of the decade produce a social and political metamorphosis throughout the region. "The standard of living of every American family will be on the rise, basic education will be available to all, hunger will be a forgotten experience, the need for massive outside help will have passed" as "free men working within a framework of democratic institutions" would make violent revolutions unnecessary. Then the United States president expressed the beguiling hope that Cuba and the Dominican Republic would "soon rejoin the society of free men." The president knew more than he implied. On April 17, 1961, some 1,300 Cuban anti-Castro exiles, armed and trained by the American Central Intelligence Agency, arrived from Nicaragua to an unfriendly reception at Playa Girón or the Bay of Pigs in south central Cuba. On May 30, a small group assassinated the dictator of the Dominican Republic, Rafael Trujillo.

The fiasco at Playa Girón was just another move in the political chess game between the United States and Cuba. But it was an important one. On May 1, Fidel, having easily rounded up and imprisoned the beleaguered pawns of the Central Intelligence Agency, emphatically announced that Cuba would be a socialist state. No internal opposition would be tolerated. There would be no room for neutrality, no patience for dissidents. One had to be for or against the revolution. More than 100,000 persons suspected of antigovernment activity were quickly imprisoned, although most were released after interrogation. Those who had expected the messiah to arrive with the invading army at Playa Girón lost all further hope. Thousands desperately abandoned Cuba for the United States, inadvertently strengthening the revolution by depleting the forces of resistance at home. Approximately 200,000 persons joined the exodus from Cuba in the first three years of the revolution, many, no doubt, thinking that they were undertaking a temporary sojourn. The emigration decimated the ranks of the wealthy and skilled, created a shortage among various important occupations, and weakened public administration. But it also cleared out the vast majority of the disaffected, making the counterrevolution powerless. After 1961, the revolution could no longer be overthrown from within. In January 1962, the United States voted for the expulsion of Cuba from the Organization of American States, but unlike the sanctions against the Dominican Republic in 1959, the trump card had already been played. Expulsion proved inconvenient diplomatically and an irritant but not a calamity and not unexpected. In October 1962, the United States discovered that the Soviet Union had begun to install ballistic missiles in Cuba. President Kennedy imposed a naval blockade around the island and negotiated the removal of the missiles in return for a guarantee that the United States would remove the blockade and refrain from invading the island. At the end of the year, Cuba exchanged the survivors of the Bay of Pigs for $53 million worth of medical supplies, drugs, and food.

The hostility of the United States forced the Cubans to move closer to the Soviet bloc. In 1960, Cuba and the Soviet Union reestablished full diplomatic relations, broken in 1952 as part of the cold-war fallout, and quickly thereafter the Soviet Union and its allies became the major market for Cuban exports, especially sugar. The Soviets generously supplied enormous quantities of military hardware, offered petroleum at bargain-basement rates, and extended low-interest loans as well as grants to help the faltering economy in the difficult throes of dislocation and transition. By the 1980s, the Soviet subsidy would be worth several billion dollars per year. The dominant Soviet role forced Cuba to support the Soviets in their dispute with China, although "Che" Guevara vocally admired the Maoist model of a virtually self-sufficient enclosed economy with its emphasis on moral rather than material incentives. This difference might partly explain the departure of Guevara in 1965, two years before his tragic death in the mountains of Bolivia. Disappointed by the denouement of the missile crisis, the Cubans retreated for a while and concentrated on domestic matters after 1962, but the outbreak of the Vietnam war and the invasion of the Dominican Republic encouraged a discreet move back into the Soviet orbit. Full integration into the socialist mainstream, however, did not come until after the failure of the vaunted 10 million-ton harvest in 1970. Soviet military and economic support were crucial for the revolution, especially in its early phase. Between 1961 and 1979, the Soviet Union supplied approximately 22 billion dollars in military and economic aid to Cuba and supplied about 98 percent of Cuban oil imports. Apart from the economic aid and war matériel, Nikita Khrushchev's (1894–1971) repeated declarations that he would retaliate for any attack on Cuba directed by the United States gave Washington serious cause for concern. Cuba-American relations could not be confined to a local bilateral issue but had potentially serious international ramifications. The Soviet Union effectively entered the geopolitics of the American hemisphere. Cuba–Soviet Union relations were complex, however. The Soviet Union benefited from having a political satellite conveniently close to the United States, but had the Cubans not demonstrated capable internal political strength, their usefulness would have been of limited value. Nor have the relations been entirely free of friction. Relations were strained between 1963 (partly as a result of the missile agreement done without Cuban input) and 1970 and again in the late 1980s when Mikhail Gorbachev's politically liberal introductions of *perestroika* and *glasnost* made the Cubans uncomfortable.

The revolution has continually had to balance domestic and international concerns equally. The domestic concerns were serious. Although internal political opposition diminished significantly by 1962, the economic problems increased. The distribution of resources produced an immediate amelioration of material conditions for the lowest sector of the population. The losers were those at the top, a substantial proportion of whom had left the island. But the challenge was in creating an economy of plenty that would maintain the new living standards and satisfy the raised expectations of the first year. That proved elusive. At first, there was an attempt to diversify the economy and reduce the inordinate reliance on sugar exports. The goal was to balance economic development between an agricultural sector with an agrarian revolution boosting the production of food crops, beef, pork, eggs and milk and a manufacturing sector replacing the shortfall created by the U.S. trade embargo. It did not work. In 1962, rationing of scarce commodities began, steadily increased, and by the end of the decade had been extended to basic, formerly abundant consumer items, such as cigars and sugar. Sugar output fell, but neither production nor productivity in other areas compensated for the decline. Constant mobilization for war, the ad hoc nature of decision making, and the shortage of competent technicians frustrated the attempt to create a brave new world for Cubans.

Between 1965 and 1970, the Cubans concentrated on domestic matters. Already the state had become extremely centralized, with power tightly held in the hands of Fidel Castro and a growing military under the command of his brother, Raul. The departure of Guevara allowed Castro to advocate openly the Chinese model of socialism, albeit with a strong modification to the Cuban circumstances. The government expanded appropriations of private property; extended the collectivization of agriculture; reorganized the Communist party; and, in light of the increasing scarcity of domestic goods, placed an emphasis on building a moral "New Man" indifferent to material incentives. By early 1968, Castro was boasting that Cuba was constructing the most orthodox communist society in the world. Mass mobilization increased, and a campaign against bureaucrats and bureaucracy resembled the chaos produced by the Cultural Revolution in China. Some unsuccessful attempts to export their brand of revolution—the concentrated *foco* (cell) of revolution—to the Dominican Republic, Guatemala, Argentina, Venezuela, and Bolivia ended in fiasco and alienated Cuba diplomatically from most of the rest of the hemisphere during the early and mid-1960s. The lofty rhetoric to create "One, many Vietnams" or make the "Andes the Sierra Maestra of Latin America" saw no follow-through in action but helped keep the revolutionary enthusiasm high on the island. In 1968, Castro announced that he had changed his mind on the economy. Rather than disparage monoculture and demote the production of sugar, he admitted that making sugar was the one area in which the Cubans could incomparably excel—and they were going to produce the unprecedented amount of 10 million tons of sugar in 1970. Sugar prices had been rising, and the calculation was that in the 1970s the trend would continue, bringing enormous financial benefits to the island. At about the same time, Cuba gave a qualified endorsement of the Soviet invasion of Czechoslovakia, thereby facilitating a rapprochement. It was a timely move. The 1970 harvest came in at 8.5 million tons, higher than ever before but far short of the symbolic target. The economic cost of the decline in nonsugar productivity and general dislocation was enormous and a serious blow to the idea of moral incentives. After 1970, Cuba abandoned Sino-Guevarist–style idealism for orthodox socialism, increasingly directed by the Soviet Union. In December 1970, a Cuban delegation headed by Carlos Rafael Rodríguez (b. 1913) went to Moscow and after some discussion established the Cuban-Soviet Commission of Economic Scientific and Technical Collaboration.

Under Soviet auspices, the 1970s saw the methodical orthodox institutionalization of the state. On the economic side, the Russians agreed to train Cuban scientists and to supervise the construction, renovation, and expansion of steel, fertilizer, and pharmaceutical plants; sugar factories; and electricity. The military received new supplies of the most modern planes, tanks, and naval vessels in the Soviet arsenal. In 1974, local and municipal political organizations (Poder Popular) were restructured in the province of Matanzas and extended later to the rest of the island. In 1975, the First Party Congress approved a new comprehensive Family Code that detailed the regulation of domestic life. The following year, a new constitution reorganized the national political structure, replacing the six previous provinces with fourteen administrative divisions: Pinar del Río, Havana, the city of Havana, Matanzas, Cienfuegos, Villa Clara, Sancti Spíritus, Ciego de Ávila, Camagüey, Las Tunas, Holguín, Granma, Santiago, and Guantánamo. The government was restructured along socialist lines, with a Council of Ministers headed by the president, Fidel Castro, and a legislative National Assembly. Creating new political institutions did nothing to diminish the influence and personal domination that Castro held over the island.

Orthodoxy in the 1970s paid handsome economic dividends. Fidel Castro paid two visits to the Soviet Union, reciprocated by top Soviet officials, including Premier Leonid Brezhnev. Partly as a result of the depressed conditions of the 1960s, the national economic growth rates between 1971 and 1976 were statistically impressive. Russian aid was munificent. The Soviet Union increased the price paid for sugar and nickel, increased technical aid, deferred payments of previous loans, suspended some interest, and agreed to increased Cuban sugar sales on the free market. But part of the improved economy had to do with the escalation of sugar prices between 1972 and 1974, peaking at the historic high of sixty-five cents per pound on the world market in November 1974. Although Cuba sold most of its sugar in the socialist countries at generous prices, it also sold an increasing proportion on the free market and benefited from the favorable trend. The Cubans miscalculated, however, that the price "would never drop below 16 or 17 cents per pound." By late 1976, the world sugar market price had fallen to nine cents and, by the early 1980s, hovered discouragingly at six cents—some eight cents below estimated production costs. Before the fall, substantial strides were made in education, housing, health care, and the overall quality of life. In the mid-1970s, with consumer lines shortening, the Cubans had good reason to believe that they had turned the corner. For one brief shining moment, it seemed that the good times had finally arrived, justifying the revolutionary sacrifices of a decade. Then, like the rest of the Americas, the economic aftereffects of OPEC II suddenly turned all hope to frustrating despair. Cuban export earnings fell rapidly, and even restricting imports could not alleviate the deteriorating economic situation. By 1976, Cuba was running serious trade deficits and borrowing money on the capitalist market. By 1979, only 40 million dollars could be raised, most of which went to retire short-term interest. The restrained expectations helped produce the general dissatisfaction and discontent that spurred more than 125,000 Cubans to abandon their country during the Mariel boatlift months of 1980.

The 1970s also saw significant changes in foreign policy. The international ambience changed in the late 1960s. In Latin America and the Caribbean, much, too, had changed since the heady, idealistic days of the 1960s when Cuba blithely promised to help any revolutionary group overthrow an imperialist government. Restricting reality replaced the unbridled ideals of the early 1960s. In 1967, "Che" Guevara died and with him the romantic notion of rural guerrilla *focos* spontaneously and gallantly subduing governments as advocated by the participants of a tricontinental congress held in Havana earlier that year. The domestic economy forced Cubans to look inward. The resources simply were not available for the indiscriminate support of disparate groups in desperate situations, and the quest to produce 10 million tons of sugar absorbed all their energies. Romantic revolution was not quite compatible with the new pragmatic orthodoxy of the 1970s. But external conditions facilitated the transition. By 1970, socialist governments— one civilian, one military—had come to power in Chile and Peru and had further reduced the diplomatic isolation of Cuba. That same year, Chile established commercial relations with Cuba. Slowly Cuba changed both its rhetoric and its attitude toward its Latin American neighbors and gradually reestablished diplomatic ties with a number of Latin American states. By 1975, despite hesitation by the Organization of American States, eleven Latin American and Caribbean countries independently resumed diplomatic and commercial relations with Cuba: Chile, Peru, Barbados, Jamaica, Guyana, Trinidad and Tobago, Argentina, Panama, the Bahamas, Colombia, and Venezuela. Without having formal diplomatic ties, Cuba had sent generous disaster assistance to the earthquake victims in Lima, Peru, in 1970, and Managua, Nicaragua, in 1972 (despite being antagonistic to the Somoza government). Disaster relief was also sent spontaneously to Jamaica, Grenada, Guatemala, Honduras, and Chile. This was followed by volunteer brigades of teachers, agronomists, doctors, and construction workers dispatched to Guyana, Jamaica, Suriname, and, after 1979, to Nicaragua and Grenada. In addition, Cuba offered more than ten thousand scholarships in medicine, engineering, agronomy, and other technical and vocational skills to students from Africa, Asia, Latin America, and the Caribbean. In 1977, Cuba and the United States established Interests Sections in Washington and Havana, but further normalization of relations foundered on the intransigent attitude of the United States toward Cuban involvement in Latin America and Africa.

In the 1970s, Cuba became an important player on the world scene. Nowhere was this more evident than in Africa and among other Third World countries. The Cuban involvement in Africa went back to the earliest ideological and idealistic days of the revolution, with modest military and technical assistance to the Algerian Liberation Front in 1960 and Ghana in 1961. In 1964–1965, "Che" Guevara toured Algeria, Ghana, Congo-Brazzaville, Guinea-Bissau, Mali, Dahomey, Tanzania, and the United Arab Republic. One result of the tour was Cuban assistance to the Popular Movement for the Liberation of Angola (MPLA), the Front for the Liberation of Mozambique (FRELIMO), and the African Party for the Independence of Portuguese Guinea and the Cape Verde Islands (PAIGC).

Also, in April 1965, Guevara escorted some two hundred Cuban fighters (later reinforced) to Congo-Brazzaville, where they accompanied the anti-Tsombe guerrillas until the end of the fighting in December. Although Guevara himself then left for Bolivia (where he was killed), the Cubans remained as part of military training missions to freedom fighters in Angola and Guinea-Bissau as well as to help President Sékou Touré (1922–1984) in Equatorial Guinea. These first Cuban initiatives suffered a setback with the coups d'état that overthrew Ben Bella in Algeria in 1965 and Kwame Nkrumah in Ghana in 1966.

The policy of the 1970s represented a slight modification and a major expansion of the 1960s policy. Cuba began to support friendly progressive governments encountering internal or external threats, downplaying the individuals, ideological groups, and revolutionary capture of the state. By 1975, Cuba had small military missions in Sierra Leone, Equatorial Guinea, Somalia, Algeria, Tanzania, South Yemen, Oman, and Syria. In 1975–1976, Cuba sent more than thirty thousand combat troops to prevent the annihilation of the MPLA and to help consolidate and maintain the Angolan government in power. In May 1977, Cuba sided with the Ethiopians against the Somalians in the Ogaden dispute—thereby leading to a break in Cuban-Somalian relations at the end of the year. In 1978, some seventeen thousand Cuban troops joined the Soviet Union in a campaign that ousted the Somalians from the Ogaden. Cuban support has been indispensable for Angolan security, and Cuban intervention represents a major factor in the politics of southern Africa. In 1989, the Cubans agreed to withdraw their troops from Angola by 1991 and participated prominently in the international agreement to establish the independence of Namibia. Partly as a result of its admired active involvement in Africa, Cuba hosted the Sixth Summit Meeting of Non-Aligned Countries in Havana in September 1979 and chaired the organization until its 1983 meeting.

The 1980s were tantalizing years for the Cubans. The sharp decline of commodity prices, rising interest rates, and rapid increase in industrial goods aggravated the domestic economic situation. A few years of plenty gave way to a decade of scarcity. Budget deficits appeared in 1980 and by 1982 totaled some 785 million dollars. Not only did the deficits continue throughout the decade, but trade deficits complicated the picture as natural disasters, crop diseases, and machinery breakdown reduced industrial output. Reduced spending in the dominant social economy contributed to the disruptive Mariel exodus in the late spring and early summer of 1980. Ironically, the majority of those who left during the Mariel exodus were the pampered products of the revolution, young men and women who had no experience of life before Fidel. In the late 1970s, the government moved to reduce the amount of free services and goods, implementing a modest charge (often optional) for previously gratuitous services, such as day care for infants, bus fares, and utilities. Malingering and other petty antisocial conduct increased, affecting production and morale. Shortages returned, and hard currency became very scarce. To compensate for inadequacies, parallel markets (where excess state-produced goods could be sold at fixed prices) and *mercados libres* (free peasant markets) were created in 1979, and small-scale private enterprise and entrepreneurship was encouraged. These were revoked in 1986 as disruptive to proper socialist development. By late 1987, Fidel Castro was exhorting Cubans to join a new revolutionary process of "rectification" against materialism, consumerism, individual enrichment, fraud, corruption, embezzlement, and poor performance. In a speech on October 8, 1987, commemorating Guevara's death, Fidel extolled: "We are rectifying all those things—and there are many—that strayed from revolutionary spirit, from revolutionary work, revolutionary virtue, revolutionary effort, revolutionary responsibility; all those things that strayed from the spirit of solidarity among people." Cuba had, indeed, traveled a long, weary way, but there was no rest in sight, no laurels to be garlanded. The monumental achievements of the revolution created an insatiable appetite for more. The revolution could never fulfill the expectations that it itself had engendered.

The popular disenchantment at home had parallels in international relations. Friction developed with Barbados in 1976 over the transshipment of military forces to aid Angola. The sabotage of a Cuban civilian airliner by anti-Cuban exiles in Caracas that year led to the suspension of diplomatic relations between Cuba and Venezuela from 1980 until 1989. The prestige of heading the nonaligned nations suffered a major setback when the Soviets invaded Afghanistan, a member state, in 1980. Cuban unwillingness to lead the condemnation of the invasion—an unpopular gesture among Third World nations—reinforced the opinion that Cuba was a Soviet satellite and not truly a nonaligned state. At the same time, Cuba's bid for membership in the Security Council of the United Nations, opposed by many Latin American and Caribbean states, failed. In 1980, Michael Manley, Fidel Castro's close friend, lost the elections in nearby Jamaica and was out of power for eight years. In 1982, Cuba championed the cause of Argentina against Great Britain in the Malvinas/Falkland Islands war that went badly for Argentina and worse for the Argentine military. In October 1983, an internal coup toppled and murdered Maurice Bishop in Grenada. This precipitated an invasion by United States troops that expelled the Cubans working on the Point Salines airport and ended the local, Castro-style experiment. Even in Nicaragua and El Salvador, the promises of the early 1980s did not shine with the same electrifying luster.

If the 1970s represented the best years of the revolution, the Mariel exodus in the spring of 1980 indicated that a new phase had begun in Cuba. Mariel was the symptom of serious national social and economic malaise. It was also the beginning of a gradually widening alienation with its chief benefactor, the Soviet Union, that would last until its collapse in 1991. It was the beginning, too, of a noticeable alienation of ordinary Cubans from their government. Castro hated the political and economic reforms of Mikhail Gorbachev (born 1931), especially the democratizing policies of *perestroika* (restructuring) and *glasnost* (opening) introduced after 1985. Moreover, during the 1980s, the Soviet Union replaced the extraordinarily generous five-year aid plans based on material exchanges based on need with annual plans calculated on cost-accounted, hard currency–based transactions. This meant that Cuba rapidly accumulated a growing balance-of-payments problem with the Soviet Union that would become a major stumbling block with Russia after 1991.

The precipitate collapse of the Soviet Union hit Cuba hard. Overnight Cuba lost almost its entire foreign trade, and the gross domestic product declined by one-third. Severe shortages occurred in all aspects of the economy, resulting in a marked deterioration in the quality of everyday life. Petroleum imports fell to about 10 percent of the pre-1990 total. The termination of energy supplies led to prolonged and widespread electricity blackouts, but equally important, Cuba lost a major source of income from its re-export of Soviet oil surplus. For a short time, the entire transportation, agricultural, and industrial systems remained paralyzed and food shortages reached critical proportions. In the first years, the average Cuban lost about nine kilos (roughly twenty pounds), and hunger and food deprivation affected a broad swath of the population. Social afflictions like malnutrition in children and suicides among the elderly became noticeable.

Fidel Castro declared the emergency a "Special Period in time of peace" and mobilized the country as though it was on war footing. The government and the population became extremely creative. Major emphasis was placed on food production. Collective, mechanized farming gave way to semi-independent cooperatives as well as old-fashioned individual and family manual operations. Sugar cane fields were cut up and distributed to farmers and urban refugees who were willing to create zones of self-sufficient food production. By 1996 free-market farmers were producing more than 75 percent of the foodstuffs consumed in the cities. In 1993 the government depenalized the holding of foreign currency and authorized private businesses. Transportation was reorganized, employing bicycles to replace cars and introducing the hideous converted tractor trailer buses called "camels" that could hold three hundred passengers. Horses and mules were attached to carriages and mobilized to boost transportation throughout the island. Everywhere family restaurants, called "*paladares*," sprung up spontaneously like mushrooms. They filled a temporary void, but by 2000 the government had extended tight control over *paladares*, considerably reducing their attractiveness both for owners and clients. During the Special Period, the government expanded the tourist industry, revamped the sugar industry, encouraged mixed private-public initiatives as well as Cuban-foreign enterprises, and broadened private sector employment. By 2009, private-sector employment represented about 22 percent of the labor force. Unemployment has been acknowledged as 1.7 percent of the labor force in 2009, probably a very low estimate.

By 2000 the revamped Cuban economy began to grow again. Some four hundred joint ventures poured more than U.S.$4.5 billion into the economy. More than 1.7 million tourists arrived on the island, providing a gross income of nearly 2 billion dollars. In 2007 Cuban government figures set the rate of growth at 7.5 percent, below that of India or China but far better than any other state in the Americas. Nevertheless, the structural economic problems of Cuba remained. The government tried to bring some order to the currency situation in 2004 by removing the U.S. dollar as a preferred unit and basing official transactions on two forms of the Cuban peso. One was a nonconvertible peso (CUP) used for domestic transactions and wages. The other was a Convertible Cuban Peso (CUC). The U.S. dollar ceased to be legal tender, and its use required a 10 percent conversion penalty. Meanwhile other foreign currencies, exchanged at arbitrary rates, remained exempt from the U.S. dollar conversion penalty. Since 1999 the Cuban economy has derived substantial assistance from Venezuela and Bolivia that exchange oil at favorable prices in return for corps of Cuban medical and other professional personnel. The People's Republic of China has also been investing heavily in Cuba, as elsewhere in Latin America and the Caribbean. Cuba survived the Special Period, but it became clear that although the socialist rhetoric remained dominant in official discourse, the revolution no longer had the resources and the will to maintain the old egalitarian welfare state of the 1970s and 1980s. In the new mixed economy, some folks would be left behind.

On July 31, 2006, Fidel Castro, after abdominal surgery, passed on to his brother, Raul, many of his official duties. Two years later, Fidel resigned as president of Cuba and was succeeded by Raul Castro. For a year or so, Raul removed many common irritating restrictions of daily life, such as restrictions on owning cell phones, computers, and domestic electrical appliances; patronizing local hotels; and having a title to one's residence. Yet celebrating the fiftieth anniversary of the revolution in 2009 was a somber affair. The revolution had made an unexpectedly successful transition, but much remained to be done. Nevertheless, the U.S. embargo remained in effect, and Washington's policy toward Cuba remained enigmatic. In March 2009, Raul purged his administration of most of the Fidel-appointed holdovers, including some talented and experienced technocrats. An increase in pensions brought monthly income to slightly more than nine dollars per month. Basic food items, however, remained scarce, and housing and transportation continued to generate major widespread discontent.

The achievements of the Cuban revolution lie not merely in the prosaic compilation of comparative statistical information—houses, schools, and hospitals built; doctors, teachers, agronomists, and technicians trained; communications and utilities provided; roads, factories, and farms constructed; the number of men in arms—or the discussion of human costs in death, exile, and alienation. The achievements of the revolution transcend the mere introduction of a socialist society and a socialist economy. The success of the revolution also lies in the tremendous infusion it gave to Cuban and Caribbean nationalism. The Cubans demonstrated that race, color, class, and limited natural resources do not constitute insuperable handicaps to the creation of an independent, just, and equitable society. The revolution instilled national pride and a sense of regional identification in those Cubans who remained and struggled and survived to construct a society in which equality of opportunity became truly an operational inalienable right. Equality of opportunity unleashed tremendous creative energy that manifested itself in all aspects of Cuban life: organization, literature, the creative arts, sports, diplomacy, and construction. The revolution did not create a paradise, but what it accomplished against such odds is truly impressive. Not all Cubans are well fed, well housed, well cared for, and well educated. But the overwhelming majority of Cubans currently enjoy facilities and opportunities that before 1959 remained the preserve of the privileged few. The national government has a legitimacy, popularity, and international respectability never before experienced in the history of the republic. Cuban advice and assistance are accepted in countries where once both were despised and detested. Only Washington hosts more diplomatic missions than Havana in the Americas.

Across the Caribbean, the revolution still holds magnetic appeal to young, progressive, idealistic political aspirants. As nationalism finds wider roots throughout the ministates of the Caribbean, the Cuban model of ethnic pluralism and economic development is an attractive option for local leaders trying to mold social cohesion within the confines of a fragile state. But the Cuban appeal has waned considerably, overtaken by events in Eastern Europe and Nicaragua.

By 2010 the Cuban revolution had managed to demonstrate that it was no longer synonymous with Fidel Castro, although his pervasive influence remained like a gigantic shadow over every action of his brother, Raul. The revolution continues to demonstrate a remarkable flexibility and pragmatism, defying the frequent predictions of its premature demise. The more Cuba changes, the more it seems to become like any other neighboring Caribbean state. This observation illustrates the inherent unpredictability of the process of revolution wherever it occurs.

SUGGESTED READINGS

Balboa Navarro, Imilcy. *Los brazos necesarios: inmigración, colonización y trabajo libre en Cuba, 1878–1898.* Valencia: Fundación Instituto de Historia Social, 2000.

Bardach, Ann Louise. *Without Fidel: A Death Foretold in Miami, Havana, and Washington.* New York: Scribner, 2009.

Bretos, Miguel A. *Matanzas: The Cuba Nobody Knows.* Gainesville: University Press of Florida, 2010.

Cluster, Dick, and Hernández, Rafael. *The History of Havana.* New York: Palgrave Macmillan, 2006.

de la Fuente, Alejandro. *A Nation for All: Race, Inequality, and Politics in Twentieth-Century Cuba.* Chapel Hill: University of North Carolina Press, 2001.

Díaz-Briquets, Sergio. *The Health Revolution in Cuba.* Austin: University of Texas Press, 1983.

Dreke, Víctor. *From the Escambray to the Congo: In the Whirlwind of the Cuban Revolution.* New York: Pathfinder Press, 2002.

Dye, Alan. *Cuban Sugar in the Age of Mass Production: Technology and the Economics of the Sugar Central, 1899–1929.* Stanford, Calif.: Stanford University Press, 1998.

English, T. J. *Havana Nocturne: How the Mob Owned Cuba…and then Lost It to the Revolution.* New York: Morrow, 2008.

Geyer, Georgia Anne. *Guerrilla Prince: The Untold Story of Fidel Castro.* Boston: Little Brown, 1991.

Gjelten, Tom. *Bacardi and the Long Fight for Cuba: The Biography of a Cause.* New York: Viking, 2008.

Gleijeses, Piero. *Conflicting Missions: Havana, Washington, and Africa, 1959–1976*. Chapel Hill: University of North Carolina Press, 2002.

Gott, Richard. *Cuba: A New History*. New Haven, Conn.: Yale University Press, 2004.

Helg, Aline. *Our Rightful Share: The Afro-Cuban Struggle for Equality, 1886–1912*. Chapel Hill: University of North Carolina Press, 1995.

Iglesias García, Fe. *Del Central al Ingenio*. Rio Piedras: University of Puerto Rico Press, 1998.

McAvoy, Muriel. *Sugar Baron: Manuel Rionda and the Fortunes of Pre-Castro Cuba*. Gainesville: University Press of Florida, 2003.

McGillivray, Gillian. *Blazing Cane: Sugar Communities, Class, and State Formation in Cuba, 1868–1959*. Durham, N.C.: Duke University Press, 2009.

Moreno, Francisco José. *Before Fidel: The Cuba I Remember*. Austin: University of Texas Press, 2007.

Moses, Catherine. *Real Life in Castro's Cuba*. Wilmington, Del.: Scholarly Resources Press, 2000.

Pérez, Louis A., Jr. *To Die in Cuba: Suicide and Society*. Chapel Hill: University of North Carolina Press, 2005.

Pérez, Louis A., Jr. *Cuba Between Reform and Revolution*. New York: Oxford University Press, 1988.

Pérez, Louis A., Jr. *Winds of Change: Hurricanes and the Transformation of Nineteenth Century Cuba*. Chapel Hill: University of North Carolina Press, 2001.

Pérez-Stable, Marifeli. *The Cuban Revolution: Origins, Course, Legacy*. New York: Oxford University Press, 1999.

Sawyer, Mark Q. *Racial Politics in Post-Revolutionary Cuba*. New York: Cambridge University Press, 2006.

Scarpaci, Joseph, Segre, Roberto, and Coyula, Mario. *Havana: Two Faces of the Antillean Metropolis*. rev. ed. Chapel Hill: University of North Carolina Press, 2002.

Schoultz, Lars. *That Infernal Little Republic: The United States and the Cuban Revolution*. Chapel Hill: University of North Carolina Press, 2009.

Smith, Wayne S. *The Closest of Enemies: A Personal and Diplomatic History of the Castro Years*. New York: Norton, 1987.

Sweig, Julia E. *Cuba: What Everyone Needs to Know*. New York: Oxford University Press, 2009.

Tone, John Lawrence. *War and Genocide in Cuba, 1895–1898*. Chapel Hill: University of North Carolina Press, 2006.

Whiteford, Linda M., and Branch, Laurence G. *Primary Health Care in Cuba: The Other Revolution*. New York: Rowman & Littlefield, 2008.

Yun, Lisa. *The Coolie Speaks: Chinese Indentured Laborers and African Slaves in Cuba*. Philadelphia: Temple University Press, 2008.

Zanetti, Oscar, and García, Alejandro. *Sugar and Railroads: A Cuban History, 1837–1958*. Translated by Franklin W. Knight and Mary Todd. Chapel Hill: University of North Carolina Press, 1987.

CHAPTER 9

Caribbean Nation Building 3
Puerto Rico and the Ambivalent Identity

But the sentiment of independence is real enough among
young fellows and the common people, and it only awaits to be
organized by a politician with some poetry in his make-up.
>—LUIS MUÑOZ MARÍN, 1925, quoted in Roberta Johnson,
>*Puerto Rico: Commonwealth or Colony?*

The Puerto Rican does not have an easy patria as others do.
Ours is difficult, but good. The identity of a people is affirmed
by growing with the times, rather than by disappearing with
the times.

>—LUIS MUÑOZ MARÍN, quoted in Kal Wagenheim,
>*Puerto Rico: A Profile*

The slow emergence of Puerto Rican nationhood resulted, as elsewhere in the Caribbean, from the fortuitous conjunction of external and internal forces. It was a classic victim of circumstance. In order to understand the historical process of development, one must constantly bear in mind the prevailing domestic social and economic conditions as well as the general political context of the times. Although the fourth largest of the Caribbean islands, Puerto Rico was always overshadowed within the Spanish empire, first by Santo Domingo and then by Cuba. Its population growth and economic development were more similar to the smaller islands than to the mainstream islands like Cuba or Jamaica. Yet it tried consistently to chart its future amid the frustrating handicaps of poor timing, poor chances, and poor manpower.

The nineteenth century saw Spain's imperial sunset in America, and this situation provided the opening for the growth of Puerto Rican self-consciousness, just as it did in the case of Cuba. Until the late eighteenth century, Puerto Rico had been a sleepy outpost of empire, with an impregnable fortress around San Juan and scattered rural settlements of highly miscegenated inhabitants throughout the island. The economy depended on smuggling, trading of hides, and dried meat, timber, and foodstuffs. The administrative costs were subsidized by the infrequent arrivals of the *situado*, the annual subvention from Mexico that ceased after 1808. In 1765, the island had only about forty-five thousand inhabitants. The nature of the economy may be deduced from the proportional utility of the land area being used. Only about 18 percent of the land at that time was cultivated, mainly in provisions, and 82 percent was devoted to cattle pastures. Even more interesting, the useful land was overwhelmingly divided into small plots. Of the cultivated land, 67 percent was in small plots, some of which were far too small for the profitable pursuit of commercial agriculture. By the time of the French Revolution, the population had increased to around 100,000. The relatively rapid increase in the later part of the eighteenth century indicated the attention paid to agriculture at that time and the consequences of the active reforms of Marshall Alejandro O'Reilly (1725–1794), the Dublin-born fortifications expert who joined the Spanish army at the tender age of ten. O'Reilly had served with distinction in Spain and Cuba (and was to serve later in Louisiana), and his mission in Puerto Rico was both to secure the defense of the island and to make it economically self-sustaining. Declaring that the inhabitants of the island were the poorest of the king's vassals in all the Americas, O'Reilly sought to rectify the situation. If small St. Croix could be economically rewarding to Denmark, then, he reasoned, Puerto Rico had immense potential. That meant, in the thinking of the late eighteenth century, more people and more intensive cultivation. To a great extent, he succeeded. By 1815, the population had doubled to more than 220,000 and by 1846 was estimated at 443,000, including some 51,000 slaves and 175,000 free blacks and mulattoes. Although a minor colony, Puerto Rico was not immune from the irresistible forces of change unleashed by the Enlightenment, the American Revolution, and the French Revolution. It, too, participated in the heady movement for political and administrative reform that followed the Napoleonic invasion of Spain and the decapitation of the Spanish monarchy in 1808 with such profound consequences for the Spanish-American empire.

The first stirring of local political reform came with the short-lived Spanish constitution of 1812 that converted Cuba and Puerto Rico into the equivalent of internal provinces of Spain and authorized election of representatives to the Cortes. In addition, the organizational structure of the island was redrawn, with the creation of many more town councils and a Provincial Council with limited advisory powers to the governor. At that time, the Puerto Rican representatives tried to have slavery abolished but failed to persuade the determined interests of the Cuban representatives. But Puerto Ricans, like their Cuban colleagues, were beginning to articulate views that set them apart from their metropolitan peers. They defined themselves as "Americans" and felt that they had more in common with other colonists in the Americas than with Spain. This differentiated self-interest would color the conflict not only with the Spanish administration, but continually with their Cuban colleagues.

The economic revitalization of the island got a new stimulus under the direction of Alejandro Ramírez, the first intendant, who took office in 1813. Foreign immigration was encouraged; free trade was extended; taxes were reorganized; and major incentives were given to the cultivation of export crops, especially sugar, tobacco, cotton, and coffee. The area under cultivation of sugarcane increased from 5,054 *cuerdas* in 1813 to 16,149 in 1834 (1 *cuerda* = 0.97 acres). Initially, all forms of cultivation increased, but gradually the trend clearly shifted, first to sugar-cane cultivation and then, after about 1850, to coffee. In 1830, Puerto Rico had approximately twice the area devoted to subsistence crops—plantains, bananas, maize, rice, sweet potatoes, yams, and other tubers—than to export crops. By that time, commerce had assumed great importance, increasing in worth from at most 269,000 pesos in 1813 to more than 7 million pesos in 1835. By 1862, subsistence agriculture and export agriculture were almost equal. In 1866, the legal Puerto Rican foreign trade was valued at approximately 18 million pesos. But by 1896, coffee acreage alone far exceeded that of subsistence agriculture, the second major form of land cultivation. Of course, the Americans would revitalize sugar production.

By 1821, the Spanish flag had been replaced on the mainland. Spain lost the vast area from Texas and California in the north to Chile and Argentina in the south. It sold Florida to the United States in 1819 and administered Santo Domingo fitfully between 1803 and 1821 and again from 1861 to 1863. Puerto Rico and Cuba represented the full measure of the once great Spanish-American empire and gained more bureaucratic attention than previously. Yet the histories of both colonies were only vaguely similar during the period of the nineteenth century when high profits and economic prosperity accompanied the disgraceful perpetuation of the slave society in the Caribbean.

Puerto Rico, like Cuba, also experienced sugar revolutions during the nineteenth century. But neither the scale of sugar production nor the demographic consequences of the sugar revolutions were as pronounced in Puerto Rico. In Puerto Rico, the sugar revolutions began after 1800 and by 1850 had just about run their course. By the peak productive years for sugar at the middle of the nineteenth century, Puerto Rico exported about fifty-two thousand tons of sugar, mainly to the United States, Spain, Great Britain, and France. To facilitate the expansion of agriculture, the island depended on a combination of slave and free labor, boost-ing the importation of African slaves and implementing laws to compel landless peasants to engage in virtually forced labor on the plantations. The slave trade ended in the mid-1840s when the slave population peaked at around fifty-one thousand—a modest 15 percent of the total number of inhabitants on the island at that time. Not surprising, that was also the period of the most slave revolts and conspiracies, with disturbances in Ponce, Guánica, San Germán, Isabela, Vega Baja, Toa Baja, Naguabo, and Juana Díaz. By 1860, slaves made up only 7.1 percent of the island's 600,000 inhabitants, Nevertheless, in the sugar zones, slaves formed an indispensable labor force. While slaves continued to be the most viable form of labor in the plantation zones, the Puerto Rican sugar industry always employed free immigrants from Spain and the Canary Islands, as well as free wage laborers from among the large, local peasant population. The concentration on sugar was localized in three major enclaves around Guayama, Ponce, and Mayagüez, with smaller enclaves centered in Patillas, Yauco, San Germán, Añasco, Arecibo, Vega Baja, Río Piedras, Trujillo, Loíza, and Fajardo.

As in the case of Cuba, the political reforms that were promised by the metropolis in the 1830s, 1840s, and 1850s did not materialize, and frustrations built up in the colonies. By 1865, the colonial question assumed great importance in Madrid. Spain remained the only slave-owning power in the Caribbean, and the moral support of slavery eroded considerably with the loss of the South in the American Civil War. A Spanish abolitionist society, led by the Puerto Rican Julio Vizcarrondo, was agitating for the immediate end of slavery in Cuba and Puerto Rico. Spanish domestic politics was at this time quite unstable and unpredictable, aggravated by the unpopularity of Queen Isabel II. But Spain was also preoccupied with the increase in Creole political restlessness overseas, especially after the short, unhappy experience with Santo Domingo, which regained its independence in 1863 after just two years of renewed Spanish government. In November 1865, Antonio Cánovas del Castillo, the foreign minister, called for elected representatives from Cuba and Puerto Rico to advise the Spanish government on proposed new reforms for the overseas colonies. Puerto Rico elected six representatives to the Madrid commission, and their suggestions included the abolition of slavery, reduction of taxes, and freedom of trade and of the press—in short, the civil rights of peninsular Spaniards.

Talks of political reform got out of control in the colony, however, and a number of liberal intellectuals and small farmers began to agitate for political and economic change. On April 27, 1867, a riot broke out in Puerto Rico among members of the artillery who were seeking better pay and shorter terms of service. The governor had the leaders executed, but in his paranoia he also rounded up a number of liberal spokespersons whom he suspected of conspiring against Spanish rule and ordered them into exile in Spain. Ramón Emeterio Betances (1827–1898) and Segundo Ruíz Belvis (1829–1867), rather than reporting to Madrid as ordered, headed for New York, where they joined a fledgling revolutionary group that advocated complete independence for Cuba and Puerto Rico. Ruíz Belvis died in Chile while seeking support for the Antillean cause, but Betances—like José Martí—traveled widely, exhorting the overthrow of Spanish rule in Puerto Rico. The culmination of their conspiratorial effort was the abortive uprising, the Grito de Lares, on September 23, 1868. It is possible that the rebels knew about similar conspiracies in Cuba and in Spain, where five days earlier, on September 18, Generals Juan Prim and Francisco Serrano "pronounced" against the queen and ushered in what their supporters called *la revolución gloriosa* (the glorious revolution).

Lares, a mountainous, coffee-producing municipality, was the site of one of many of the Betances-organized clubs that had promised to fight for liberty or die in the cause. Newly organized as a municipality in 1832, Lares was a rapidly growing area with considerable friction between Creoles and immigrants, mostly Spaniards. The hardy coffee growers were losing their land to the invading merchants, and economic discontent probably led some to join the rebels. While the leaders of the rebel conspiracy may have held the same lofty ideas of the political rights of man as Betances, most of their followers found more tangible, more immediate reasons in the economic disadvantages and social discrimination of the colonial situation. The conspiracy that produced the ill-timed and ill-fated revolt at Lares was poorly planned, poorly executed, and plagued by misfortune. The authorities accidentally learned about the conspiracy in advance, forcing a rapid alteration in the plans—advancing the starting date by a week. Some of the local leaders wavered until the last moment, unsure that they had either the will or the military supplies to defeat the Spanish army. In the end, the republic they declared at Lares lasted less than twenty-four hours. Their organizer, Betances, was also having his share of troubles. He lost his munitions in the Dominican Republic and his ship in St. Thomas. In any case, he would have arrived too late. By September 29, the original date for the uprising, it was all over, save the memories and the legal recriminations.

The "glorious revolution" in Spain was not so viewed in the Caribbean colonies. But it did accomplish the abolition of slavery in Puerto Rico, the abolition of the pass laws, and extended representation to the Cortes. On March 22, 1873, the last 31,635 slaves in Puerto Rico received their emancipation. Forced to work for their masters for three years, they only won full civil rights five years later. But neither slavery nor its abolition produced the profound social and economic dislocations of Cuba or Jamaica.

The civil war in Cuba and the highly unsettled political conditions in Spain precluded any coherent policy toward the colony, although the elusive consensus among the local elite was for some reform in the commercial and political structure. But although the elite was relatively small in Puerto Rico, it was sharply divided over the proper course of political reforms. In 1870, the more conservative sector, mainly centered in San Juan, organized itself loosely as a political party, calling itself the Liberal Conservative Party. But the name continually changed, according to the leadership, and after 1873, it called itself the Unconditional Spanish Party (Partido Incondicional Español). While the Unconditional Spanish Party supported economic reforms and the reduction of some forms of taxation, it vehemently resisted political reform, declaring that such would ruin the island's economy and produce another revolution as in Haiti. What was good for San Juan was not necessarily good for the rest of the island, and the Creoles in Ponce and the other cities joined together in a loose coalition calling themselves the Liberal Reform Party (Partido Liberal Reformista). The Liberals advocated the restoration of provincial status to Puerto Rico and the extension of the Spanish constitution to the island. The Spanish government manifested a marked preference for elected representatives who were wealthy and who supported the continued colonial status without significant reform. Liberal aspirations, however, suffered a sharp decline when the Spanish republic was overthrown in 1874, and Alfonso XII and the Bourbons returned to power. The return of conservatism in Spain and the continuing war in Cuba were inauspicious moments for political reform in the colonies.

The sense of local identity—Puerto Rican *patriachiquismo*—was vitiated by the nature of society in general and especially of the elite. During the nineteenth century, the population had increased threefold, from slightly more than 300,000 in 1828 to nearly a million in 1899. A substantial proportion of this increase derived from immigration, rather than a natural increase of the native population. Immigrants, mainly from Spain, controlled the bureaucracy, the Church, commerce, moneylending, and the profitable export trade in sugar, coffee, cotton, tobacco, and hides. But immigrants also came from Germany, Italy, Corsica, the Canary Islands, the United States, Great Britain, and the mainland Spanish-speaking states. The small elite sent its sons abroad for an education, mainly to Spain, France, Germany, and the United States. Some of these sons studied abroad on scholarships—among them, the later patriots, José Julian Acosta (1825–1891) and Roman Baldorioty de Castro (1823–1899). Under the republican government in Spain, some attention was given to intellectual life in the colonies, with the reorganization of secondary education in Puerto Rico in 1873 and the establishment of the Puerto Rican Atheneum in San Juan in 1876. In the 1880s and 1890s, the island experienced the expansion of libraries, theaters, and literary societies, catering mostly to the elite, but more and more attracting workers and peasants also. The majority of the population remained illiterate and excluded from meaningful political participation by virtue of not having the vote. But their gradual incorporation into the social and economic activities of the elite led to their politicization, accompanied by a noticeable increase in the overall sense of solidarity and insular identity. This insular identity was propagated through a number of small newspapers that circulated in various towns throughout the island: *La Crónica* and *La Democracia* in Ponce, *La Abeja* in Humacao, *La Patria* in Mayagüez, and *El Buscapie* in San Juan. By the early 1890s, these newspapers favored a sort of autonomy status within the Spanish system and the extension to Puerto Rico of the political and civil rights prevailing in the various provinces of the peninsula.

Spain granted Puerto Rico major domestic autonomy in 1897. It was a shrewd political move, but one that resulted from the political weakness of the metropolis. Since it was granted without prior approval of the Cortes, it was of dubious constitutional merit. The autonomy that the island won was the hard work of Roman Baldorioty de Castro and Luis Muñoz Rivera (1859–1916), who was then the passionate, articulate, young editor of *La Democracia* in Ponce. Both in Spain and in Puerto Rico, opinion was sharply divided over the issue of the constitutionality of the grant. The autonomist charter created in Puerto Rico a government headed by a governor-general; a bicameral parliament with a house of representatives and an administrative council; a provincial assembly; a municipal government; and a representational delegation of sixteen deputies and three senators in the Spanish Cortes. The franchise was extended to all literate males aged twenty-five and older who were not otherwise disbarred (such as the military in active service, criminals, and mental incompetents). The island could impose its own import duties, establish commercial relations with foreign states, and make any laws not specifically reserved to the Spanish Cortes. In sum, these were precisely the conditions that the Puerto Rican elite had been, in one way or the other, pleading and negotiating for since 1867. With a great deal of compromise, the charter was put into effect in early 1898 after elections in which Muñoz Rivera emerged as the dominant politician.

Unfortunately, 1897 was a very bad year to win any type of colonial concessions from war-weary Spain. Although the island of Puerto Rico did not formally declare war and was not directly engaged in the fighting, war came to Puerto Rico nevertheless. Its hard-won political concessions were quickly and brutally overtaken by events. With incredibly unfortunate coincidence, the new autonomist government was scheduled to take over in May 1898, the very month in which the American navy bombarded San Juan. In July, American troops landed at Guánica and quickly fanned out over the island. In Ponce, long a seat of autonomy supporters, the Americans were received enthusiastically. General Nelson Miles, the invading commander, declared that the Americans had come to Puerto Rico to bring protection of property, peace, and prosperity "and to bestow upon you the immunities and blessings of the liberal institutions of our government...to give to all within the control of its military and naval forces the advantages and blessings of enlightened civilization." The experiment in autonomy wilted like cut flowers on a hot tropical pavement. At the Treaty of Paris in December 1898, Spain weakly ceded Puerto Rico, Cuba, and the Philippines to the United States—so that they could more effectively spread their dream of an American hemisphere—and agreed to pay $20 million of war reparations. America emerged after the war as a major world power.

American knowledge of Puerto Rico in 1898 was abysmally poor. One writer admitted that Americans knew more "about Japan or Madagascar" than about Puerto Rico. Then as now, they confused matronyms and patronyms—not to mention their embarrassing ignorance of common social graces—and insisted on referring to individuals by the improper surname. Luis Muñoz Rivera was invariably referred to as "Mr. Rivera," rather than by the correct abbreviated form, "Mr. Muñoz." The island endured two years of military government before the Foraker Act of 1900 instituted a civilian government in Puerto Rico that restored a new form of colonialism. The military government operated similarly to that in Cuba. It began under a strict martinet, an ethnocentric and self-righteous egotist named Brigadier General Guy V. Henry. That established the ground rules that colored the Puerto Rican—United States relationship for nearly half a century. The policy was what was good for the Americans should be excellent for the Puerto Ricans. Henry saw his mission as saving the Puerto Ricans from themselves and the legacy of Spanish vices by establishing an efficient political system, improving the general sanitation of the island, and facilitating the process of Americanization by teaching English and inculcating all aspects of American culture. And, incidentally, he thought that by granting franchises personally to Americans, he could remove graft and corruption among Puerto Ricans.

The highly unpopular Foraker Act established a quasi-republican form of government in which the governor, the Cabinet, and all judges of the island's Supreme Court were appointed by the president of the United States, while Puerto Ricans elected a lower house of delegates of thirty-five members. An elected resident commissioner in Washington reported to the United States Congress, but had no vote. Free trade with the mainland was established, but the entire tariff system was merged immediately with that of the more powerful United States of America. Puerto Rico after 1900 assumed a status similar to that of the District of Columbia in the government of the United States. It could be heard, but it had no vote, even on matters pertaining to its own interests.

Muñoz Rivera did not accept the political derogation of the status of Puerto Rico lightly. He incorporated his own Federalist Party into an umbrella organization called the Union de Puerto Rico and in 1910 was elected the resident commissioner to the United States Congress in Washington. There he campaigned ceaselessly for a plebiscite to determine the status of Puerto Rico among statehood, independence, or autonomy. Through skillful diplomacy, the Puerto Ricans finally persuaded the United States Congress to pass the Jones Act of 1917, which provided a bill of rights for Puerto Rico, conceded United States citizenship for residents of the island, and instituted popularly elected houses of the legislature. Moreover, the governor of Puerto Rico was granted more latitude in appointing his Cabinet.

The political victory of the Puerto Ricans was fundamentally a Pyrrhic one. The social and economic price proved costly, damaging, and permanent in the long run. Puerto Ricans found themselves relegated to second-class citizens in their own land, denigrated by the influx of a new people holding a different somatic-norm image from theirs and arrogantly contemptuous of their culture and their legacy. North American ingenuity rapidly destroyed the relatively diversified peasant economy and replaced it with seemingly endless fields of sugarcane owned or controlled by such large absentee North American enterprises as the South Porto Rico Sugar Company, incorporated in New Jersey in 1900; the Fajardo Sugar Company, incorporated in New York in 1905; and the Central Aguirre Supar Company, organized under Massachusetts trust laws in 1905. By 1915, large stretches of the landscape were converted to tasseled fields of sugarcane punctuated by efficient central factories and connected by ribbons of conveniently located highways and railroads. By 1930, sugarcane fields accounted for approximately 40 percent of all cultivated land, and sugar, 66 percent of the value of all agricultural production. The statistical picture of the island looked rosy. The elimination of endemic and epidemic diseases and the improvement in public health reduced death rates, especially among the predominantly rural population. Harbors were improved. Trade flourished, with most of it going to the United States. Irrigation works greatly improved agricultural productivity. For a few dazzling years, Puerto Ricans enjoyed a chimerical euphoria of an economic success that disguised the malignant and painful side effects of their continuing colonialism. Then the bottom fell out of the sugar market, and the international economic depression of the 1930s hit savagely at every monocultural exporter. Between 1930 and 1932, the gross national product of the island plunged, dragging the per capita income down from $122 to $86. Poverty, disease, and malnutrition were rampant. By 1933, about 65 percent of the labor force was unemployed. Like everywhere else in the

Caribbean, Puerto Ricans began to reexamine the bases of their society and of the economy and the liabilities of dependence. Like people in other Caribbean countries, Puerto Ricans sought to make political action the engineer of social change.

The lean years spawned intensive, often radical political activity by younger men, often bilingual, who had a clear idea of what they wanted for their country. One such young man was Pedro Albizu Campos (1891–1965). Albizu Campos and his Nationalist Party sought independence and a radical restructuring of the economic bases of the society. All over the island at political rallies marked by violence and fiery oratory, he pointed out that Puerto Ricans needed complete control of their affairs if they were to attack successfully the problems of overpopulation, illiteracy, unemployment, underemployment, and a dismally low adult life expectancy of forty-six years. The Nationalists repeatedly attacked the legality of the status of the island and the violation of its laws, especially the 500-acre limit placed on landholdings in 1900. By 1917, some 477 holdings already exceeded this amount. But their message bore no fruit in the 1934 elections, and so the party increased its emphasis on violence as one way of getting rid of the American presence. After all, violence had achieved that end during the occupations of Haiti and the Dominican Republic. Albizu Campos was imprisoned for conspiring against the United States in 1937 and would spend the following twenty years in and out of prison. His party waned. But his message did not die, and the *independentistas* would remain a small but vocal component of Puerto Rican politics.

Between 1938 and 1964, Puerto Rico experienced the charismatic, innovative, and effervescent influence of Luis Muñoz Marín (1898–1980), son of Luis Muñoz Rivera. Muñoz Marín was a politician with much more than "some poetry in his make-up." A gifted poet and journalist in two languages, he had a strong sense of destiny and an infectious sympathy for the impoverished rural Puerto Rican, the *jíbaro*. Deploring what he graphically described as "a land of beggars and millionaires, of flattering statistics and distressing realities," he finally returned from the United States, where he had lived since childhood, to Puerto Rico in 1931 and committed himself to politics full time. The greatest politician the island produced, he virtually engineered its complete political, social, and economic transformation singlehandedly under "Operation Bootstrap." In the 1930s, Muñoz Marín possessed tremendous political assets: a highly recognized political name, a nationalist tradition, wit, charm, eloquence, and friendship or familiarity with leading U.S. politicians, including the new president, Franklin D. Roosevelt. Muñoz Marín was a nationalist with a difference: as Arturo Morales Carrión observed in *Puerto Rico: A Political and Cultural History,* he saw the United States not as the enemy, but as a misguided, ill-informed, potentially benevolent friend. In the contentious and factious world of Puerto Rican politics at the time, this view isolated him.

The 1930s proved a period of severe changes for Puerto Rico. The Great Depression set the watermark in the economy. The population had doubled between 1900 and 1940, and about 40 percent of the population was younger than fifteen years at the end of that period. The island was predominantly rural, with 70 percent of the population living in villages and small towns. Yet fully

80 percent of the rural folk were landless. Agriculture was the main employment of 44.7 percent of the rural population, but the sugar industry had virtually collapsed, compounding the employment problems of the rural folk. The island also had a small, progressive middling class of businessmen, merchants, and landowners subordinated to a smaller American expatriate community inflexibly practicing the racial and residential exclusivity familiar on the mainland. Politics was also undergoing a generational transfer. Political warriors of the pre-depression era were passing from the scene. By 1940, Antonio Barceló (d. 1938) of the Liberal Party, Santiago Iglesias (d. 1939) of the Socialist Party, and Rafael Martínez Nadal of the Republican Union Party were dead or lay dying, and the parties were scrambling their leadership and arranging new coalitions. It was a time of political flux. At first Muñoz Marín joined forces with the Liberal Party but was expelled in 1937. On July 22, 1938, he founded the Popular Democratic Party, with its symbol of the straw-hatted *jíbaro* and its slogan (pointedly reminiscent of Emiliano Zapata, the agrarian populist of the Mexican revolution) *Pan, Tierra y Libertad* (Bread, Land, and Liberty). Emphasizing social and economic reform, rather than political status, Muñoz Marín and his followers took the issue to the voters in the elections of 1940. Repeating that it sought to ameliorate the economic conditions of the island within the status quo, the Popular Democratic Party managed to win enough votes to form a coalition government in 1940 and handily won reelection in 1944. And for the first time in the history of Puerto Rico, a politician fulfilled his pre-election promises. Large estates were broken up, land was provided for the landless, education for the illiterate was provided, and plans were established for rural electrification and industrialization. In 1948, Luis Muñoz Marín became the first Puerto Rican to be elected governor. Reelected in 1952, 1956, and 1960, his achievements were manifold. He converted the island economy from being overwhelmingly agricultural to industrial. He vigorously attacked the previously intractable problems of housing, health, and education. He boosted the per capita income from a modest $121 in 1940 to $900 in 1965. And he created the Associated Free State, or Commonwealth, that has considerably defused—though not resolved—the issue of status.

The modification of the political relationship of Puerto Rico and the United States resembled the status that Puerto Rico had achieved on the eve of the Spanish-American War. Public Law 600 of 1950, approved by the president of the United States, allowed Puerto Rico the right to write its own constitution, which comfortably won approval in a referendum in 1951, thereby creating the *Estado Libre Asociado* (Associated Free State, or Commonwealth), inaugurated on July 25 of the following year. This relationship gave Puerto Rico complete autonomy in internal matters and continued the equal use of citizenship and federal services of the United States. Puerto Ricans finally assumed full control of the judiciary as well as the legislature. On paper, the relationship looked impressive enough to warrant a United Nations General Assembly resolution in 1953 that "the people of the Commonwealth of Puerto Rico have been invested with attributes of political sovereignty." The commonwealth status was a popular but not a unanimous selection in Puerto Rico. A referendum held in 1967 to fore-stall U.N. action on Puerto Rico indicated that 60 percent of the voters preferred the commonwealth status, 39 percent wanted statehood, and less than 1 percent wished complete independence. The appeal of the status quo lies in its comfort-able, convenient, "better the devil you know" familiarity. But it is also a practi-cal implementation of the curious state of "inbetweenity" and ambivalence that permeates and inhibits the full expression of a national sentiment.

Concurrent with the modification of the political status came a reorganiza-tion of the economic structure of the island under an economic development program called Fomento, or "Operation Bootstrap." Based on rapid industrializa-tion and consistent emigration, "Bootstrap" produced some impressive gross eco-nomic statistics that, like the data for Saint-Domingue in 1789, Mexico in 1910, or Cuba in 1958, could be read in different ways. Modest reform and reorganiza-tion had been carried on since the depression as economic relief and wartime support measures. After 1949, a structured program was designed to thoroughly revolutionize Puerto Rican society. Between 1948 and 1965, about 1,027 new manufacturing plants were opened on the island, producing a variety of export items: yogurt, petrochemicals, pharmaceuticals, appliances, and textiles. The government offered a number of incentives to mainland enterprises to relocate. Buildings were constructed and leased for ten years to the occupier, who could at the end of the period either relocate or purchase them. Workers were trained at Puerto Rican government expense. Corporations were granted ten years' tax holi-days, and, through the Puerto Rican Government Development Bank, businesses could borrow money for machinery at attractively low interest rates. By 1960, Puerto Rican–made brassieres and electric shavers accounted for 25 percent of the mainland market. Between 1948 and 1965, net income from manufacturing increased from $58 million to $449 million, a value-added increase of some 20 percent. By 1960, Fomento-sponsored factories had created more than 41,500 new jobs, and the labor force on the island had increased absolutely from 663,000 in 1948 to 769,000 in 1965. During the same period, employment in agricul-ture declined from 36.3 percent of the labor force to 17 percent. Overall, wages increased, nearly doubling in agriculture and increasing sevenfold in manufac-turing. The average annual salary rose from $433 in 1940 to $2,753 in 1970. The annual gross national product increased from $651 million in 1948 to nearly $9 billion in 1979. The island changed from a predominantly rural society in 1940 (66.7 percent rural) to an overwhelmingly urban one (76.6 percent) in 1960. Even more, the difference in conditions between urban and rural life had been largely eliminated by 1989.

Economic transformation did not resolve all the basic problems of Puerto Rico, and it created some new and unexpected ones. "Operation Bootstrap" cre-ated new jobs but, owing to an enormous population increase, failed to reduce significantly the unemployment rate. In 1965, about 14 percent of the labor force was unemployed—about the same as the rate in 1987. One study revealed that rather than making inroads in the rural unemployed, "Bootstrap" hired the formerly rurally employed. More than two-thirds of a sample of 1,045 factory workers admitted that they had been employed full time before joining the factory but left former rural jobs for higher wages. Escalating wage scales projected Puerto Rican workers among the best paid in all Latin America and the Caribbean but also fueled a veritably insatiable appetite for consumer items and food imported from abroad. In 1977, it was estimated that Puerto Rican imports alone accounted for 153,000 jobs and $3.47 billion in gross income to the economy of the United States. After 1970, more than 50 percent of the income generated by Puerto Rican industry was repatriated, and an increasing number of incentive-started manufacturing plants were packing up and leaving for new locations, rather than renewing their leases, purchasing their plants, or continuing operations elsewhere on the island. Modernization and development, therefore, accentuated the economic dependence of Puerto Rico on the United States—an aspect overlooked by those who sought to transfer the Puerto Rican model of economic development elsewhere.

Like the rest of the region, Puerto Rico experienced "the revolution of rising expectations" in the decades of the 1950s and 1960s. The overall modernization of the society (especially the new emphasis given to education) resulted in a pronounced increase in mobility (especially the quest for new economic opportunities). People moved in droves from the countryside to the towns and from the towns to the United States seeking new economic opportunities. Most of the migrants were young and among the better educated. Emigration from the island increased from an annual average of about 1,000 people in the 1930s to 20,000 in the 1940s and to 40,000 in the 1950s. In 1953, 70,000 Puerto Ricans migrated to the United States. Between 1950 and 1959, some 430,000 had relocated outside their native island, and by 1970, the population on the mainland had reached 1.5 million, creating a new variant of the Puerto Rican nationalist: the diaspora community in the United States.

The association between Puerto Rico and the United States has been unique, a fact that continually frustrates the colonial committee of the United Nations. The island's economy is totally integrated into that of the U.S. Mainland. Since 1917 Puerto Ricans have been recognized as legal citizens of the United States, although with a peculiar form of citizenship circumscribed in a number of ways. The island has, like the District of Columbia, a nonvoting delegate in the U.S. Congress, who partakes in the regular affairs of Congress, although his or her vote may not determine the result of any issue. Puerto Ricans on the island have the right to join Mainland political parties and participate in their primaries. Nevertheless, they may not vote in presidential elections unless they are registered residents in one of the fifty states. Island residents pay the U.S. social security tax but not the federal income tax. Although Puerto Ricans pay social security tax, they are excluded from Supplemental Security Income and receive reduced Medicaid funding. From time to time, the federal government or the U.S. Supreme Court has specifically clarified the Puerto Rican situation. For example, in November 1992, President

George H. W. Bush issued a memorandum requiring all heads of federal agencies and executive branch departments to consider Puerto Rico as though it were a state.

Concerns about the political status of Puerto Rico have not been confined solely to the island's residents, who express their opinions in frequent non-binding referenda. Since the 1990s, the Congress and presidents of the United States have formed committees and task forces to look into the status issue. Presidential task forces in 2005 and 2007 reiterated the unilateral power of the Congress to alter the status of Puerto Rico. These task forces also reasserted the ultimate authority of Congress on any of possibly four future options for the commonwealth. These options are continuation of the commonwealth status quo, modification of the status quo, statehood, and independence. In April 2010 the U.S. Congress approved a measure for federal intervention into the process of periodic referenda to resolve the issue. The measure was sent on to the Senate, where the Senate Committee on Energy and Resources started to gather evidence and hold hearings in May 2010.

U.S. colonialism before 1952, associated statehood since then, and unstinted largesse after 1900 have not genuinely revolutionized society and politics. The goal since 1900—at least from the perspective of Washington—was twofold. The first goal, a political one, was to make Puerto Rico a type of Anglo-Saxon society like Texas or California, "a sovereign state within the Union." The second, a cultural one, was to eradicate the Hispanic legacy on the island. Both were, of course, interrelated. And both so far have failed to a certain degree. "Operation Bootstrap" undoubtedly introduced many positive changes to Puerto Rico and even converted Puerto Rico into the envied half sibling of the other Caribbean states before 1959. Few in those halcyon days bothered to look beneath the astounding figures of economic expansion and growth or made the distinction between quantitatively more and qualitatively better. But after the 1970s, it became increasingly clear that more and different did not automatically amount to a better quality of life for Puerto Ricans. Although Puerto Rico's average per capita income ranks among the highest in the Caribbean, it falls below the poorest state in the United States. In 1976, more than 50 percent of all Puerto Rican families depended on supplementary federal food stamps, and in that depressed year unemployment reached nearly 40 percent of the labor force. While increasing the income of all the population, "Operation Bootstrap" has not achieved anything approaching equity by reducing the historical gap between the "haves" and the "have-nots." In 1953, it was calculated that the poorer 45 percent of Puerto Ricans shared a mere 18 percent of the total national income. In 1970, despite the rapid expansion of material culture and material needs, that same 45 percent shared only 16 percent of the total Puerto Rican income. Associated statehood for forty years has made Puerto Rico somewhat different in degree, but certainly not basically different from the neighboring states of the Caribbean. Perpetuating ambivalence has not resolved some of the problems of identity. Puerto Rico at the end of the twentieth century remained quite Caribbean and quite Third World. In some aspects, it remains an attractive regional model, but not as desirably so as it once appeared in the 1950s and 1960s.

The Puerto Rican economy performs in tandem with that of the United States, and while basic insular economic data do not compare favorably with those of the Mainland, the island does well by Caribbean standards. After federal transfer funds, the single largest contribution to the gross domestic product comes from the approximately 5 million tourists who visit the island. In 2007 it was estimated that the median household income in Puerto Rico was US$17,741. The unemployment rates climbed to 15.9 percent in January 2010, reflecting the adverse economic situation on the Mainland. As a result, the government has been forced into draconian measures to close the widening budget deficit, including massive layoffs and punishing new taxes. These measures met strenuous resistance from a broad sector of the population. But one thing is certain: Puerto Rico has surprisingly held its own against great odds.

SUGGESTED READINGS

Ayala, César J. *American Sugar Kingdom: The Plantation Economy of the Spanish Caribbean, 1898–1934.* Chapel Hill: University of North Carolina Press, 1999.

Ayala, César J., and Bernabe, Rafael. *Puerto Rico in the American Century: A History Since 1898.* Chapel Hill: University of North Carolina Press, 2007.

Baralt, Guillermo A. *Buena Vista: Life and Work on a Puerto Rican Hacienda, 1833–1904.* Translated by Andrew Hurley. Chapel Hill: University of North Carolina Press, 1999.

Bergad, Laird W. *Coffee and the Growth of Agrarian Capitalism in Nineteenth-Century Puerto Rico.* Princeton, N.J.: Princeton University Press, 1983.

Blanco, Tomás. *El perjuicio racial en Puerto Rico.* Rio Piedras, Puerto Rico: Ediciones Huracán, 1985.

Cabán, Pedro A. *Constructing a Colonial People: Puerto Rico and the United States, 1898–1932.* Boulder, Colo.: Westview Press, 1999.

Carr, Raymond. *Puerto Rico: A Colonial Experiment.* New York: Vintage, 1984.

Clark, Truman R. *Puerto Rico and the United States, 1917–1933.* Pittsburgh, Pa.: University of Pittsburgh Press, 1975.

Dietz, James L. *Economic History of Puerto Rico: Institutional Change and Capitalist Development.* Princeton, N.J.: Princeton University Press, 1986.

Duany, Jorge. *The Puerto Rican Nation on the Move: Identities on the Island and in the United States.* Chapel Hill: University of North Carolina Press, 2002.

Figueroa, Luis A. *Sugar, Slavery, and Freedom in Nineteenth Century Puerto Rico.* Chapel Hill: University of North Carolina Press, 2005.

Flores, Juan. ed. *Divided Arrival: Narratives of the Puerto Rican Migration, 1920–1950.* 2nd ed. New York: Centro de Estudios Puertorriqueños, Hunter College, 1998.

Guerra, Lillian. *Popular Expression and National Identity in Puerto Rico: The Struggle for Self, Community, and Nation.* Gainesville: University Press of Florida, 1998.

Heine, Jorge. *The Last Cacique: Leadership and Politics in a Puerto Rican City.* Pittsburgh, Pa.: University of Pittsburgh Press, 1993.

Johnson, Roberta Ann. *Puerto Rico: Commonwealth or Colony?* New York: Praeger, 1980.

Kinsbruner, Jay. *Not of Pure Blood: The Free People of Color and Racial Prejudice in Nineteenth-Century Puerto Rico*. Durham, N.C.: Duke University Press, 1996.

Lewis, Gordon K. *Puerto Rico: Freedom and Power in the Caribbean*. New edition with an introduction by Anthony Maingot. Kingston, Jamaica: Ian Randle, 2004.

Martínez-Vergne, Teresita. *Capitalism in Colonial Puerto Rico: Central San Vicente in the Late Nineteenth Century*. Gainesville: University of Florida Press, 1992.

Martínez-Vergne, Teresita. *Shaping the Discourse on Space: Charity and Its Wards in Nineteenth-Century Puerto Rico*. Austin: University of Texas Press, 1999.

Morales Carrión, Arturo. *Puerto Rico and the Non-Hispanic Caribbean: A Study in the Decline of Spanish Exclusivism*. Rio Piedras: University of Puerto Rico, 1974.

Morales Carrión, Arturo. *Historia del Pueblo de Puerto Rico: Desde sus Orígines hasta el siglo XVIII*. San Juan: Edición Cordillera, 1980.

Morales Carrión, Arturo. *Puerto Rico: A Political and Cultural History*. New York: Norton, 1983.

Moscoso, Francisco. *Clases, Revolución y Libertad: Estudios sobre el Grito de Lares de 1868*. Rio Piedras: University of Puerto Rico, 2006.

Picó, Fernando. *Amargo Café (los pequeños y medianos caficultores de Utuado en la segunda mitad del siglo xix)* Rio Piedras, Puerto Rico: Huracán, 1985.

Picó, Fernando. *Historia general de Puerto Rico*. Rio Piedras, Puerto Rico: Huracán, 1986.

Picó, Fernando. *1898: La Guerra después de la guerra*. Rio Piedras, Puerto Rico: Huracán, 1987.

Picó, Fernando. *Puerto Rico 1898: The War After the War*. Translated by Sylvia Korwek and Psique Arana Guzmán. Princeton, N.J.: Markus Wiener, 1987.

Picó, Fernando. *History of Puerto Rico: A Panorama of Its People*. Princeton, N.J.: Markus Wiener, 2006.

Picó, Fernando. *Puerto Rico Inside and Out: Changes and Continuities*. Princeton, N.J.: Markus Wiener, 2008.

Silvestrini, Blanca G., and Luque de Sánchez, María Dolores. *Historia de Puerto Rico: Trayectoria de un pueblo*. San Juan: Cultural Puertorriqueña, 1987.

Silvestrini de Pacheco, Blanca. *Los trabajadores puertorriqueños y el Partido Socialista (1932–1940)*. Rio Piedras: University of Puerto Rico, 1979.

Silvestrini de Pacheco, Blanca. *Violencia y criminalidad en Puerto Rico, 1898–1973*. Rio Piedras: Universidad de Puerto Rico, 1980.

Suárez Findlay, Eileen. *Imposing Decency: The Politics of Sexuality and Race in Puerto Rico, 1870–1920*. Durham, N.C.: Duke University Press, 1999.

CHAPTER 10

Caribbean Nation Building 4
The Commonwealth Caribbean

And I shall remember the long hard years of the modern
beginning and that it was the little people, the poor, the humble, and the seeming weak who first began to blow on the still
living but small and hidden flame of freedom and blew till it
soared like a torch and all the land began to light up around
us. . . . So out of the past far away and the past near at hand is
born the present, in which a people coming to maturity and
nationhood can look back and give praise, look around and
give thanks, look forward with prayer and in humility but with
confidence and strength.

—NORMAN W. MANLEY, chief minister of Jamaica,
in a broadcast on November 10, 1957

The century between 1850 and 1950 saw a quiet, subtle change overcome those
formerly glorious, valuable, and distinguished colonial possessions in the
British Caribbean. Unlike France and Spain, England was still at the floodtide of
empire, the center of gravity of which had moved away from the Caribbean. No
longer important in imperial terms, the Caribbean retained a nostalgic charm and
curiosity like a grand old family suddenly *venido a menos* (existing in reduced
circumstances). From the metropolitan point of view, they became charges—albeit charges that still provided some economic benefits and a ready outlet for the
bureaucratic and administrative mediocrities crying out for some recognition at
home. Along the spectrum of empire at the end of the nineteenth century, the
British West Indies ranked enigmatically somewhere between the established
settler colonies moving inexorably to Dominion status—such as Canada, India,
Australia, and New Zealand—and the variegated, recently acquired African colonies, administratively incorporated but still largely unknown. The colonial political systems, in general, did not provide viable avenues for the careful cultivation
and creative fertilization of sentiments of national consciousness and collective
self-respect. Official imperial attitudes wavered between maudlin paternalism and
exasperated contempt. With few exceptions—most notably John Jacob Thomas of
Trinidad, author of two outstanding, if undeservedly unknown, books, *The Theory*

and Practice of Creole Grammar and *Froudacity: West Indian Fables by James Anthony Froude*—West Indian elites succumbed to the alien notions of European social Darwinism, dissipating their energies in commercial pursuits and social climbing. To excel according to the criteria of the mother country's culture became the ultimate achievement. The British Caribbean elite became adept at imitation, at what the writer V. S. Naipaul called, "Mimic Men."

Below the elite, among the lower orders of society, however, a strong sense of ethnic identity and attachment to the land developed. Their resistance to conform to relegated stereotypes forced them to adopt political strategies that were designed to change both the condition of their daily lives and the nature of the colonial state that inhibited their independence. But, like elsewhere in the region, confusion existed regarding society and state, undermining the growth of nationalism. No consensus existed among the intelligentsia concerning the exact nature of an appropriate state for such diverse peoples scattered across thousands of miles of sea on sparsely populated islands of various sizes and even more sparsely inhabited continental enclaves. Both in Great Britain and in the West Indies, there was small, vocal support for a federation of the British islands and the two mainland territories of British Honduras and British Guiana. The ideas derived from the nineteenth-century preoccupation with efficiency. The British officials were looking for some way to reduce the administrative costs and the embarrassment of small, nonwhite colonies that seemed economically unviable. There were also some hesitant steps taken toward confederation. In 1871, the Leeward Islands Confederation was constituted. An attempt to incorporate with Canada failed, but the talk of a federation of some sort continually haunted discussions about the political future of the English-speaking Caribbean. While individuals from the region often participated in these discussions, the most serious proposals emanated from a regular series of reports issued periodically by visiting delegations sponsored by the British Parliament: the Royal Commission Report of 1882, the Royal Commission Report of 1897, the Major Wood Report of 1922, and the Royal Commission Report of 1938. After 1920, a number of shared organizations or common associations lent some practical experience to the idea of confederation. By the 1950s, the British West Indies had common regional participation in labor unions, trade and commerce, legal associations, a Civil Service Federation, cricket teams, the Imperial College of Tropical Agriculture (situated in Trinidad but serving the entire British Empire), the West Indian Meteorological Service, and the University College of the West Indies. All these associations, while they did foster some regional consciousness, were weaker than their local units and portrayed less of a coherent view of the West Indies than their names and functions suggested. More often than not, they were out of touch with the masses locally and regionally.

The network of empire partly insulated the British West Indies from the magnetic force of North American invasion at the turn of the century. The West Indies were therefore spared the military occupation and administration that mobilized and coordinated cross-class opposition in Haiti, Cuba, and the

Dominican Republic. External threat sharpened national consciousness in those French-speaking and Spanish-speaking parts of the Caribbean, while the English-speaking parts tended to support gradualist, reformist, evolutionary patterns of political development.

Serious thought about political independence tended to founder on the harsh reality of limited natural resources. Apart from the agricultural potential, the natural resources of the Commonwealth Caribbean—as the British West Indies is more properly called—are extremely limited. Jamaica and Guyana have extensive deposits of bauxite, some of which is mined and processed locally into alumina and sold to the United States. In addition, Jamaica has large quantities of gypsum. Trinidad has limited supplies of petroleum and larger quantities of pitch and natural gas. Guyana has gold, emeralds, and bauxite. Small, noncommercially viable deposits of manganese, lead, copper, and zinc are found throughout most of the islands. But most of the territories possess nothing more valuable than beautiful beaches, marvelously variegated seas, and a pleasant climate conducive to the promotion of international tourism. Industrialization, therefore, varies from territory to territory. Agriculture is playing a declining role in economic activity. The sugar industry, which was the mainstay of the Caribbean economies, has fallen on hard times. Neither production nor productivity has been competitive for the past century. Although in Barbados, Guyana, and Jamaica the labor force in sugar (and in agriculture in general) still forms the major sector of the employed labor force, the contribution that sugar makes of the gross national products of these islands has steadily declined. Barbados, Guyana, and Jamaica have kept their sugar industries going against all odds, but they have steadily reduced their dependence on sugar exports and have diversified their economies. For example, in 1946 Barbados had fifty-two sugar factories, producing nearly 100,000 tons of sugar and employing more than 25,000 persons during crop time. By 1980, the number of factories had declined to eight, although production had increased, and the number employed was slightly less than 9,000. The proportion of the gross domestic product contributed by sugar and sugar products declined from 37.8 percent in 1946 to 10.9 percent in 1980. By 2010 sugar and sugar products represented a greatly reduced proportion of the Barbadian gross domestic product. A number of sugar estates were converted into golf sporting facilities, and the government was successfully transitioning into a mixed economy based on manufacturing, high technology, tourism, and off-shore financial management.

With sugar and bananas no longer prominent Caribbean exports, the region has been desperately trying to diversify the economic base. Doing so has been extremely difficult in the face of global competition and the insuperable handicaps of scarce natural resources and limited physical size as well as population base. Moreover, with the exception of the Bahamas and Trinidad and Tobago, the generally high unemployment figures have proved stubbornly intractable. While more states have been trying to wean themselves from the strong dependence on the United States, it has not been easy to do so. The United States still controls a significant proportion of the Commonwealth Caribbean foreign trade and provides significant foreign assistance to the region. Nevertheless, Canada, the European Union, and China have been expanding their economic contacts across the region.

The Commonwealth Caribbean political culture reflects the diverse ways in which these islands were brought into the British empire and administered as well as the dominant political views in London at the time of their incorporation. Some of these traditions can still be observed in the operation of contemporary politics in the region. Three patterns emerged, corresponding to the older colonies settled or acquired before the eighteenth century; the colonies taken during the Seven Years' War (1756–1763) and ceded by France in 1784; and the newer colonies, conquered at the end of the eighteenth century or early nineteenth century.

In the first group of colonies settled or acquired before the eighteenth century, Barbados, the Bahamas, the Leeward Islands, and Jamaica resulted from early attempts to found settlement colonies. Like the mainland North American colonies (and Bermuda), these territories had representative assemblies that were based on the bicameral system of the mother country. Each colony had a governor who represented the monarch, an appointed upper house, and an elected lower house. The electoral franchise, however, was extremely restricted, vested in a few wealthy male property holders among the small minority of the free population. Power was divided between the governor who executed the laws and the Assembly that made them. But the Assembly retained the right to pass all money bills— including the pay for the governor—and used this right to effectively obstruct legislation or simply control the new officials.

These older colonies also had an effective system of local government based on parish vestries. The vestries were elected annually by the freeholders and met frequently to levy local revenues for the maintenance of the poor, the support of the clergy, the conservation of roads, and other local business such as the licensing of teachers. These functions were not far removed from those of the municipal councils in Cuba, Puerto Rico, and Spanish Santo Domingo.

Dominica, Grenada, St. Vincent, and Tobago were brought into the British empire between 1763 and 1814. They were referred to as "ceded islands" and also had assemblies, which functioned sometimes like those in the older territories. Grenada and the Grenadines were captured during the Seven Years' War (1756–1763) and were ceded by France at the end of the war. St. Vincent was acquired as part of the settlement of 1783 between France and England. Tobago, Dominica, and St. Lucia, won during the Napoleonic wars, were ceded in 1803, 1805, and 1814, respectively. But the small size of the free landholding population in these islands vitiated the functions of these assemblies and precluded the development of a viable system of local government such as occurred in Jamaica and Barbados. The British administered them under two units: the British Leeward Islands (St. Kitts, Nevis, Barbuda, Anguilla, Antigua, and Montserrat), to which Dominica was attached from 1871 to 1940, and the British Windward Islands of St. Lucia, St. Vincent, and Grenada (and including Dominica between 1940 and 1956).

When Trinidad, St. Lucia, and British Guiana were brought into the empire in 1797 and 1814, respectively, the British government, cognizant of the difficulty it had with the various local planters' assemblies, vested the royal governors with virtually autocratic powers. That was known as Crown Colony government. At the same time, it retained the previous Spanish, French, and Dutch forms of government, gradually altering them through time. No sustained attempt was made to foster local government in these newer colonies, although the leading cities—Port of Spain, Castries, and Georgetown—had municipal councils. Perhaps, as a result, the practice of a strong grassroots democracy failed to develop early in the latter territories.

Colonial acquisition and administration were not neatly and easily accomplished. St. Lucia changed colonial status about fourteen times and was administered as a British Crown Colony between 1814 and 1871 when it joined the Leeward Islands group. Tobago changed imperial masters more than a dozen times before finally being acquired by Britain in 1802—a position ratified by the French in 1814—and experienced many forms of administration before being confirmed as a ward of Trinidad in 1889. The Bahamas were irregularly colonized by the English beginning in 1629, had a representative assembly in 1728, got a population boost from the fleeing mainland royalists with their slaves after 1776, and settled into a dull routine as a minor Crown Colony until the granting of complete internal self-government in January 1964. The British Virgin Islands were first sighted by Francis Drake in 1595, were annexed by Britain in 1672, entered the sugar revolutions with the rest of the region, and faded economically during the nineteenth century. Between 1871 and 1956, they formed part of the British Leeward Islands administration and, having opted not to join the West Indies Federation, became a Crown Colony. The Cayman Islands were erratically settled by Englishmen and until 1848 were administered by the Bahamas. After a short period of legislative government (1848–1863), they reverted to the administration of Jamaica until 1962 when they became a Crown Colony.

The postemancipation period placed great strains on the anachronistic representative system. Designed originally for colonies of Englishmen, they were no longer representative of the majority of citizens but merely of a small, atavistic minority of the oligarchy. Sometimes these oligarchies were too small to provide the necessary administrative apparatus, which explains the shifting nature of colonial government in some of the smaller islands and the constant quest of the English government to reduce the costs of their government. The power of the purse that the planter class once astutely wielded declined along with the value of the export economy, denying to the assemblies their former intimidatory power over governors. The British government had always been uneasy about the colonial representative assemblies, especially when an increasing number of non-Europeans were gaining eligibility while the black masses were denied the right to vote and to serve. In Jamaica, just before the collapse of the system in 1865, the Assembly had 49 members representing 23 constituencies and elected by 1,457 voters. Only

1,903 registered voters existed in a population of 400,000—nearly half of whom were adult males.

The Morant Bay Rebellion of October 1865 in Jamaica rang the death knell for the old representative assemblies as they had traditionally existed. The "rebellion" was really a protest of rural black peasants in the southeastern parish of St. Thomas. The conflict had unmistakable racial and religious overtones, pitting George William Gordon (1821–1865), a leading member of the urban party of Merchants and Free Persons of Color, and Paul Bogle (ca. 1802–1865), a popular preacher in the Native Baptist Church, against the custos (the senior vestryman), a German immigrant named Baron Maximilian von Ketelholdt; the rector of the established Church, the Reverend S. H. Cooke; and the governor of the island, Edward John Eyre, a hostile, incompetent administrator of limited intelligence but long service in minor colonial posts. Gordon and Bogle were Baptists, and Gordon had been a member of the local St. Thomas-in-the-East vestry—until he was disbarred by the governor—as well as a member of the Jamaica Assembly from 1844 to 1849 and reelected in 1863. The original demonstrators were protesting unjust arrests at the courthouse in Morant Bay when, failing to obey an order to disperse, they were fired on by the militia, who killed seven of the protesters. The crowd then rioted, burning the courthouse and killing fourteen vestrymen, one of whom was black. Bogle and Gordon, arrested in Kingston, were tried by court-martial in Morant Bay and hanged. In 1965, the Jamaican government—an independent and representative entity—declared the two to be the island's first "National Heroes." Altogether, Governor Eyre ordered nearly five hundred peasants executed, six hundred brutally flogged, and one thousand houses burned by the troops and the Maroons, the descendants of former runaway slaves with whom the government had a legal treaty. In December, the Jamaica Assembly abolished itself, making way for Crown Colony government. The act was the final gesture of the old planter oligarchy that did not wish to share political power in a democratic way with the newly emergent groups.

In the constitutional reorganization of the British Caribbean in the later part of the nineteenth century, only Barbados managed to retain its representative Assembly. Jamaica, the Windward Islands, and British Guiana joined Trinidad as colonies administered fully by the Crown, while the Leeward Islands experimented with a federal system. With periodical adjustments, Crown Colony government endured until the middle of the twentieth century. Despite its paternalistic rhetoric and many practical reforms in the social, educational, and economic arenas, it retarded political development in the West Indies by consistently denying the legitimacy of political organizations while elevating the opinions of selected individuals. By so doing, it narrowed rather than broadened the social base of political power.

The limited political opportunities offered by service in the various municipal councils and parish vestries emphasized the inadequacies of the system of appointed councils in which social considerations overrode merit as the primary basis for selection. Appointed members had no political constituency—the basis on which they were chosen—and therefore no responsibility to the majority of people. Opposition to the Crown Colony system of government, therefore, came more from these local authorities than from the larger territorial bodies.

One curious aspect of the predominantly exploitation societies in the Caribbean was the inability of the whites to supply enough manpower for the bureaucracy and the professions. This persistent deficiency resulted in the opportunity for educated members of the lower orders of society to move into the professions; attain respectability; and, in some cases, achieve modest wealth. Normally a secondary education was sufficient to gain employment as a teacher, journalist, or minor civil servant or an apprenticeship in law or medicine. Throughout the British West Indies, then, the key to upward mobility for the black and colored classes rested in their educational levels. Before the middle of the nineteenth century, education throughout the English-speaking Caribbean consisted of three types: (1) education abroad on one's private initiative, (2) education in the islands in exclusive schools designed for the local whites who lacked the resources for a foreign education, and (3) education for the academically able of the intermediate group of nonwhites.

The wealthy planters generally sent their children abroad, mainly to England, but a surprisingly large proportion went to study in British North America. As early as 1720, Judah Morris, a Jew born in Jamaica, was lecturer in Hebrew at Harvard College. Alexander Hamilton, born in Nevis in 1755, attended King's College (later Columbia University), where his political tracts attracted the attention of George Washington. Hamilton served Washington and his new country with distinction, eventually becoming the first secretary of the treasury of the United States. Other students attended colleges like the College of William and Mary and the College of Philadelphia. The indigent whites attended a number of local grammar schools founded by charitable bequests in the eighteenth century, such as Codrington College and Harrison College in Barbados and Wolmer's, Rousea's, Beckford and Smith's, and Manning's schools in Jamaica. Slaves and their offspring were given religious instruction but not much more. Indeed, a law in Barbados in 1797 made it illegal to teach reading and writing to slaves. Early in the nineteenth century, the endowment from the Mico Trust—originally established in 1670 to redeem Christian slaves in the Barbary States of North Africa—opened a series of schools for blacks and free colored pupils throughout the Caribbean and three teacher-training colleges—Mico in Antigua and Jamaica and Codrington in Barbados. These teacher-training colleges offered the highest level of education locally and reflected the goals set by the metropolis for the region. Cuban nationalism derived great impetus from its local university after 1728, but tertiary education arrived in the British West Indies only in 1949.

After 1870, there was a minirevolution in public education throughout the Caribbean. This minirevolution coincided with the establishment of free, compulsory, public elementary education in England and in individual states of the United States. A system of free public primary education and limited secondary education became generally available in every territory, and an organized system of teacher training with established standards for examinations was established.

But the main thrust of public education in the nineteenth and early twentieth centuries did not come from the local governments. Rather, it came from the various competing denominations. The Church of England, the Baptists, the Moravians, the Wesleyans, the Presbyterians, and the Jesuits operated vast systems of elementary and secondary schools. At the end of the nineteenth century, the churches virtually monopolized elementary education in Jamaica, Barbados, and Guiana and ran a majority of the primary schools in Trinidad, Grenada, and Antigua. The most outstanding secondary schools—St. George's College, Kingston College, Jamaica College, Calabar High School, and the York Castle High School in Jamaica; Harrison College, Codrington College, The Lodge School, and the Queens College in Barbados; Queen's College, St. Mary's, and Naparima in Trinidad; and the Queen's College of Guyana—plus the principal grammar schools in the Bahamas, Antigua, St. Kitts, and Grenada owe their origins to religious denominations. Each territory had a board of education that supervised both the government and the denominational schools. Government assistance to the denominational schools gradually increased until, by the middle of the twentieth century, governments had gained control over all levels of education. Although public education was far from perfect—most colonies still spent more on prisons than on schools—it fired the ambitions of the urban poor. In the British Caribbean, primary and secondary education provided powerful levers for politicization.

Based on the British system—even to the use of British textbooks and the sitting of British tests—the colonial Caribbean educational system was never modified to local circumstances. Indeed, the point was conveyed in a cryptic comment by C. L. R. James (1901–1989) in his magnificent, semiautobiographical treatise, *Beyond a Boundary*. "When I left school I was an educated person," wrote James, "but I had educated myself into a member of the British middle class." Eric Williams (1911–1981), a contemporary of James in Trinidad, was even more blunt in his book, *Inward Hunger: The Education of a Prime Minister:*

> The purpose of the secondary school in Trinidad was to ensure the Anglicanisation of the colony. It consciously took the English public school as its model. The external examinations of Oxford and Cambridge, in which Trinidad was the first colony to participate, strengthened the prevailing English influence.... The secondary curriculum was indistinguishable from that of an English public school....Queen's Royal College and St. Mary's College were not only English grammar schools in the tropics, they were also excellent grammar schools.

Nevertheless, regardless of its biases and shortcomings, this secondary education system created a cadre of leaders throughout the region whose strong sense of local identity and acute knowledge of English political institutions served the region well in the twentieth century.

Education produced two groups in the British West Indies. The first identified closely with the British system—especially with the Fabian Society of radical thinkers within the newly formed British Labour Party—and sought political reforms through the conventional parliamentary channels. The most ardent representatives of this group were individuals in the local legislatures, such as Sandy Cox and J. A. G. Smith in Jamaica, T. Albert Marryshow in Grenada, D. M. Hutson in British Guiana, or Andrew A. Cipriani in Trinidad. Although they did not depend on the masses for political support (since the masses did not yet have the vote), they knew how to incorporate the masses into political action and joined the municipal and parish councils in urging a reduction in the privileges of the old planter classes and more local representation in local affairs. They also advocated legal recognition of the fledgling trade union movement in the Caribbean.

The second group was more populist, more independent, and more inspired by a semimillennial spiritual return to Africa. From this group came individuals, such as John J. Thomas (ca. 1840–1889), the articulate sociolinguist and formidable literary opponent of James Anthony Froude; Claude MacKay (1890–1948); H. S. Williams (b. 1869), founder of the Pan-African Association in London in 1897; George Padmore, born Malcolm Nurse around 1910 and later the gray eminence of Kwame Nkrumah of Ghana; Richard B. Moore (1893–1978); W. A. Domingo (1889–1968); and Marcus Mosiah Garvey (1887–1940), founder of the Universal Negro Improvement Association in Jamaica (1914) and Harlem (1916). Thomas, Williams, and Padmore came from Trinidad, although the latter two were sons of Barbadian immigrants; MacKay, Garvey, and Domingo, from Jamaica; and Moore, from Barbados.

Outside these organizational types were a number of individuals from all the colonies who had served abroad in the First World War in the West India regiments. Some of these individuals were of African birth and after the war were given land and pensions in several territories where they formed the nucleus of an early pan-Caribbean movement. Their war experiences left them critical of the British government and of British society, and they joined the radical elements of the nonwhite, restless, middle classes in agitating for political reforms to bring self-government to the Caribbean colonies.

It was the political agitation of these groups that laid the groundwork for the generation of politicians who later dismantled colonialism in the British Caribbean after the Second World War: Norman Manley and Alexander Bustamante in Jamaica; Robert Bradshaw in St. Kitts; Vere Bird, Sr., in Antigua; Eric Matthew Gairy in Grenada; Grantley Adams in Barbados; and Uriah Butler, Albert Gomes, and Eric Williams in Trinidad.

The political agitation that periodically enveloped the English Caribbean had roots in the dismal economic situation. Low wages, high unemployment, high inflation, and an inflexible, insensitive colonial administration fueled the passions of discontent that frequently erupted into general riots. The colonial government had placed its faith in sugar and the large staple-producing plantation. Sugar was not doing well economically, and it remained the chief barometer of the general economic conditions of the Caribbean. Increased productivity in Jamaica, Barbados, Trinidad, and British Guiana could not mask the insoluble difficulties of unstable prices and unreliable marketing. Until 1884, a large number of small or marginal producers continued to supply the British market. But the increased dumping of European-produced beet sugar, particularly from Germany, forced sugar prices down on the London market. British Guiana sugar, considered the best on the market, fell from twenty-six shillings per hundredweight (112 pounds) to fifteen shillings, and general muscovado fell from twenty shillings to thirteen shillings per hundredweight in one year. The impact fell swiftly across the Caribbean, eliminating a number of smaller producers and forcing the larger producers to modernize or abandon production. A number modernized. In Grenada, sugar production fell 60 percent during 1883–1884. Two years later, about two-thirds of the area under sugarcane cultivation in St. Vincent had been abandoned. In Jamaica, a number of sugar estates were put on the market. Some estate owners went into bankruptcy or simply abandoned cultivation. Jamaica maintained production levels only by increasing productivity on larger, more efficient sugar estates. By 1900, the more efficient producers had installed better mills to increase the quantity of juice extracted from the sugarcane and used the centrifugal process of crystal separation to improve the general appearance and quality of their sugar. But in the industry as a whole, technical improvements were introduced slowly, and too often the response to increased production costs or decreased profits was simply to lower wages arbitrarily. Unemployment was rife; underemployment was rampant. Many of the smaller islands abandoned sugar production altogether. The reduction of British Antillean sugar estates from about 2,200 in 1838 to about 800 in 1890 released more land for peasant agriculture. Peasant farms, therefore, competed for labor with the estates. Both complained about a shortage of labor. But the shortage was more fiction than fact. Most of the presumed shortage could be attributed to low wages. Wages on sugar estates were one-quarter to one-half of those paid on Cuban sugar estates in the same period. Not surprisingly, a large number of West Indians emigrated for economic reasons to Venezuela, Panama, Costa Rica, Nicaragua, Guatemala, Cuba, Mexico, and the United States. When these economic opportunities ended with the Great Depression, the returning migrants and the frustrated laborers erupted in violent discontent throughout the region from 1935 to 1938.

Nationalism and class consciousness increased tremendously in the years between 1919 and 1939, the tantalizing interwar years. Like the Bolivian Indians after the wars in the Gran Chaco, the West Indians who returned to the Caribbean after service in Europe in the First World War were changed men. They agitated for political and social change for their home communities. And their agitation coincided with a number of other factors that together contributed to hastening the untimely end of European colonialism in the Caribbean. These factors were—besides the experience and aroused self-consciousness of the war years—the Harlem Renaissance and the Universal Negro Improvement Association of Marcus Garvey; the economic impact of the great worldwide depression beginning in 1929; the crisis of the West Indian sugar industry; and the termination of accessible outlets for West Indian emigration, especially to Panama, Cuba, and the United States.

All these factors were related and increased in acuteness as time passed. Political and economic conditions facilitated the success of William Alexander Bustamante's (1884–1977) Jamaica Labour Party in 1944, when only fifteen years before, in 1929, Marcus Garvey's People's Political Party had failed to make any appreciable impact on the formal political system of Jamaica. The difference was that in 1944 the colonial system had collapsed, and the masses had the vote. Power moved, indirectly, to the people. The Harlem Renaissance involved a number of expatriate West Indians—Claude McKay, Marcus Garvey, W. A. Domingo, and Richard B. Moore—who were articulate, involved, politically organized, and determined to promote the Caribbean political agenda at international meetings. They supported a more vigorous local press by contributing fiery letters and provocative articles and began the literary shift away from the Eurocentric romanticism of the nineteenth century to a type of work focusing on the realities of Caribbean society and the plight of the masses. This incipient nationalism found expression in the poetry of Thomas Henry MacDermott, who wrote under the pen name "Tom Redcam" (1870–1933); in journals such as the *Jamaica Post, Jamaica Times,* the *Jamaica Advocate, Focus,* and *Public Opinion* in Jamaica, *Bim* in Barbados, *Trinidad* and the *Beacon* in Trinidad, and *Kyk-over-al* in British Guiana; in novels such as W. Adolphe Roberts's (1886–1962) *Brave Mardi Gras* and *The Single Star,* Alfred Mendes's (b. 1897) *Pitch Lake* and *Black Faunus,* and C. L. R. James's *Minty Alley;* and in histories such as James's *The Black Jacobins* and A. H. Mahoney's *After England, We.* The new authors created, with great difficulty, the closest works the English-speaking Caribbean had ever had to a popular literature designed for the masses without patronizing them.

From 1919 to 1929, labor discontent erupted in riots throughout the Caribbean. Each was followed by a British commission of inquiry that toured the area; diagnosed, as best it could, the source of the grievances; and prescribed, often with British Fabian social consciousness, palliatives parading as reforms. The procedure was not new, and neither were the recommendations. But the 1930s were very serious years producing a difference both in degree and in kind. The Great Depression hit hard at the local export economies. Sugar prices fell. Wages almost disappeared; the familiar escape valve of emigration for work rapidly closed as Panama, Cuba, and the United States suddenly found black Caribbean laborers dispensable and undesirable. Between 1935 and 1938, labor unrest raced through the Caribbean like a canepiece fire on a windy day. In 1935, the sugar workers in St. Kitts and British Guiana went on strike, followed by a coal strike in St. Lucia and a strike against an increase in customs duties in St. Vincent. In 1937, the oilfield workers in Trinidad went on a strike that widened into a general strike and eventually merged into widespread labor unrest in Barbados, St. Lucia, British Guiana, and Jamaica. The common suffering of the workers created more regional solidarity than the common institutions of the governments. In 1938, Jamaican dock workers refused to work without better pay and better working conditions. In a society that lived by importing and exporting, the dock workers' strike was quickly felt throughout the land. The colonial authorities panicked. Military

reinforcements rushed to the colonies to support the local law enforcement officers. Order was restored at a cost of 115 workers and their supporters wounded,
29 dead, and considerable property damage. Labor unions sprang up like mush-
rooms to channel the workers' discontent: the Jamaica Tradesmen and Workers
Union, Jamaica United Clerks Association, and the Bustamante Industrial Trades
Union in Jamaica; the Oilfield Workers Trade Union, All Trinidad Sugar Estates
and Factory Workers Trade Union, and the Federated Workers Trade Union in
Trinidad; the Barbados Workers Union and National Union of Public Workers in
Barbados; British Guiana Labour Union, Seamen's Union, and Transport Workers
Union in British Guiana; and the General Workers Union of British Honduras.
These unions worked closely with social organizations and, with the change in
constitutional status, rapidly spawned political parties that rushed to take advan-
tage of electoral reforms that were extended piecemeal throughout the region after
1944. Within a short time, each territory had a more-or-less established two-party
system, and a number of able, popular, eminent politicians: Norman Manley and
Alexander Bustamante in Jamaica; Robert Bradshaw in St. Kitts; Eric Matthew
Gairy in Grenada; Grantley Adams in Barbados; Uriah Butler, Albert Gomes, and
Eric Williams in Trinidad; Cheddi Jagan and Forbes Burnham in British Guiana;
and George Price in British Honduras. These were a part of the generation that
ushered in the political independence of the 1960s.

The riots of the 1930s brought swift political changes. But the conditions that
precipitated the explosions had been building slowly for more than half a century. The long period of direct and modified Crown Colony government after
the unfortunate Morant Bay disturbances of 1865 produced two political tendencies throughout the English Antilles. The first, to which allusion has already been
made, was a strengthening of the executive power in the hands of the governor.
While this undoubtedly made administration easier for the governors, it had some
negative consequences for the social basis of political power and political development. As Carl Campbell so eloquently put it, "[Crown Colony government] sought
constantly to increase the area of government and decrease the area of politics."
Campbell was, of course, describing the situation in Trinidad in the middle of the
nineteenth century. But his portrayal would have been apt for any English colony at the beginning of the twentieth century. Colonial governors were not inhibited by the threat of legislative-council vetoes of their decisions or by the type of
obstructionism that had characterized the assemblies before 1865. Colonial governors were responsible only to the secretary of state for the colonies in England. By
appointing members to the legislature who were socially compatible with the goals
of empire, the governors reduced the range of experience and advice available to
them. But they were not interested in local opinion and local advice. If they were,
they would not have stifled public opinion by consistently discouraging political
organizations and insisting that only individuals could express their views.

Not surprisingly, the dominant views of the local governments were those of
the planter classes, especially the older, more established planter classes. But by the
end of the nineteenth century, the planter class was not only a divided class but

was also being challenged by the popular classes. This created a series of recurring political crises among the governors, the legislatures, and the Colonial Office and led to some modest reforms in the system in the early twentieth century.

The dissolution of the caste structure of the Caribbean slave society—based on the confusing divisions of race, occupation, and status—after abolition gave rise to a new, more complex class society. The class divisions within the declining castes generated some new segments and some new strains. The planter class, which had never been homogeneous either within territories or across the English colonies, became even more variegated.

Coming to the fore in the nineteenth century was a new petty bourgeois class: merchants, successful estate owners (without the ancestry and the traditions of the older ones), and members of the professions and of the expanding managerial positions. This class was far more heterogeneous than the class it was surreptitiously displacing in economic and political affairs. In Jamaica, a very large number of Jews were given the franchise, and they participated actively in politics. This is remarkable because Jews obtained equality in Jamaica and sat in the local House of Assembly long before they secured such privileges in Britain. In Barbados, a small number of free persons of color and Jews moved up, but the resilience of the planter aristocracy inhibited the opening of opportunities found elsewhere. In Trinidad, the white elites included English, French, Scots, and Spanish, and the division along Catholic and Protestant lines was as great as along political and social lines. In British Guiana, the elite included Dutch, French, and English planters and merchants. While governors might prefer the older planter families, especially those of English ancestry, the new reality was inescapable, and gradually the appointments to high political office reflected the social arrival of these new men. Although they tended toward political conservatism, it was a less rigid conservatism than had prevailed for centuries in the Caribbean.

The retention of political control by the small, predominantly planter and merchant elites until the 1940s should not obscure the increasing social and political democratization of the Caribbean societies. The roots of this process of social and political democracy derived from four sources: economic diversification, which opened up economic opportunities; the expanded educational system, which produced a new professional class; the dynamic expansion of organized religion; and the rise of labor unions. While not of equal weight, they all collectively contributed to the formation of that strong tradition of democratic government that has characterized the English Caribbean during the twentieth century.

Expanded economic opportunities certainly helped create a new, broader-based middle class throughout the English Caribbean between 1880 and 1937. Much of this middle class was non-European—formerly from the free colored community of the days of slavery, reinforced by the more industrious East Indians and other new immigrant groups of the late nineteenth and early twentieth centuries (such as Jews, Lebanese, Syrians, and Portuguese). The prosperous black and colored middle class, then, has as long an antecedent in the Caribbean as has the white planter class. And their contribution to the denouement of the Haitian revolution is well known. This aspiring bourgeois class expanded significantly during the postslavery period.

The lower ranks of the civil service had always provided an opening for non-white talent, since in the typical exploitation colony sufficient Europeans could not be found to fill all vacancies. In the larger islands, local groups provided the required manpower. In the other areas, intercolonial immigrants were hired. The police forces in Trinidad and British Guiana were composed mainly of immigrants from Barbados, for example, although the senior officers were always European. Bridget Brereton pointed out that in 1892 only 47 of 506 policemen in Trinidad were local (9.3 percent), with 292 men coming from Barbados (57.7 percent) and 137 from the other islands (27 percent).

New exports—such as rice, bananas, limes, cacao, nutmeg, and arrowroot—provided the means for a few to join the economic middle classes and their off-spring—aided by an elementary or secondary education—to rise even higher. In British Guiana and British Honduras, lumbering provided sporadic economic opportunities. From time to time, the furniture industries of England and North America or local building and renovation demanded wallaba, crabwood, mahogany, greenheart, simarupa, cedar, silverballi, and bulletwood. Later in the 1920s and 1930s, the aircraft industries used hardwood for making airplane propellers. Guyanese greenheart was used in dock and canal construction throughout the British Isles as well as in Holland, France, and Argentina, and wallaba for roofing shingles was periodically popular throughout the Caribbean. Rice cultivation, while primarily a peasant activity in Trinidad and Guyana, did, nevertheless, help propel a number of their black, East Indian, and Chinese producers into the ranks of the middle class. Wealth, of course, was not enough to endow middle-class status, but it often facilitated the upward social mobility of the sons of peasants, who with the requisite education could aspire to full status.

Education, however, was the great social elevator of the English-Caribbean masses. From the middle of the nineteenth century, public education, initially under denominational sponsorship but gradually falling under state auspices (as I indicated earlier), expanded rapidly. A primary education with some knowledge of languages was useful in commercial concerns, since most of the English-Caribbean states conducted much of their commerce with the neighboring Spanish countries. A secondary education was helpful in getting into the lower ranks of the bureaucracy and essential for entering the professions. A system of scholarships enabled the children of the lower orders with the necessary abilities to move into secondary schools and thus into the professions. The number was never large, but the stream was constant; the practice was of such historic traditions that the competition for these places was fierce. Studying for these scholarships was more than an individual effort—it was a family enterprise. Moreover, by the early decades of the twentieth century, this process of academic selection and rigorous preparation for the examinations set in England—and uniform for both English and non-English students—was controlled by predominantly black schoolmasters, the foundation of the emerging "certificated masses." Walter Rodney wrote: "The rise of the middle class can only be effectively chronicled and analyzed in relationship to the schools.... The position of headmaster of a primary school must be viewed as constituting the cornerstone of the black and brown middle class." Eric Williams, a distinguished product of the system wrote, "If there was a difference between the English public school and its Trinidadian imitation, it was this, that the Trinidad school provided a more thorough preparation for the university than the average English school, partly because the students stayed to the age of twenty rather than eighteen and took a higher examination, partly also because it was not even the cream of the crop, but the top individual from Trinidad, who found himself competing with a large number of English students of varying ability." The fact that village primary-school headmasters were also lay preachers and intellectuals and quasi-legal arbiters of the community increased their importance both socially and politically. The village schoolmaster remains a potent force in the politics of the English-speaking Caribbean.

The history of the churches molding the intellect and the political sophistication of the masses started in the nineteenth century. The churches' dominance in the system of education has already been discussed. Their role was, and remains, an important one in the history of the Caribbean. But what is interesting is that the churches have managed to be both politically revolutionary and conservative, avant-garde and reactionary, depending both on the issues involved and on the type of denomination.

While the mainstream churches—mainly the Anglican and the Roman Catholic denominations—accompanied the expansion of imperialism with the expressed desire to convert "the heathens," their close identity with the established order was a severe handicap to their effective incorporation of the lower orders of society. They were especially ineffective with the Hindus and Muslims from India. So what early religious conversion took place was most effectively accomplished by such nonconformist groups as the Baptists, Methodists, Moravians, Presbyterians, and Quakers. These essentially evangelical sects originated in the metropolitan countries with a mass or working-class urban clientele in mind. Their strongest converts were among the poorer classes. But in the Caribbean, they were faced with a rather anomalous situation: the hostility or indifference of the planters and the established churches and no class equivalent to the poor urban European working class. They had either to work among the slaves and free nonwhites or to surrender their advocacy. They chose the former and so came into direct confrontation with the local elites. Nonconformist missionaries, white and nonwhite, remain some of the unsung heroes in the struggle for the disintegration of the Caribbean slave systems.

The nonconformist churches enjoyed phenomenal success among the nonwhites until the late nineteenth century. But they paid a price. Their practice and their preaching became syncretized with the rival Afro-Caribbean religions, such as Kumina and Myal. When social practice blocked the upward mobility within the hierarchy of the churches of the nonwhite members, they flocked to form their own congregations, much as occurred throughout the United States. Some of these congregations moved into a succcession of charismatic religions, beginning with the rise of Pocomania in the 1880s and moving to Bedwardism in the early twentieth century and Rastafarianism in the 1930s. All these religions espoused trances, public confessions, dreams, spirit possession, and exotic dancing. Marcus Garvey successfully tapped this popular religious tradition to provide support for his political cause. The churches provided experience in mass mobilization and grassroots organization. But more important, they provided the psychological support for the black masses and gave them comfort and a self-confidence rare among their color, class, and condition.

Political experience came most immediately and directly from the difficult growth of labor organizations throughout the Caribbean. The tendency toward trades unionization derived from the plethora of mutual aid and benevolent societies among the Afro-Caribbean population that existed from the period of slavery. Without the vote and without a representative voice in the corridors of power, the lower classes used these societies for their mutual social and economic assistance. To obtain political leverage, the working and employed classes had only two recourses: the general strike and the riot.

From time to time, some of these strikes were widespread enough to bring the plight of the masses to the attention of the Colonial Office and forced significant changes in the constitutional order.

Of such magnitude were the so-called Water Riots of Trinidad in 1903. These riots began as a middle-class dissatisfaction with the colonial government's attempt to install water meters and reduce wastage. The municipal Ratepayers Association, a solidly middle-class organization, appealed to the working and unemployed classes of the city of Port of Spain. An excited mob assembled outside the legislative council's office, and the end result was an altercation in which sixteen people were killed and forty-three injured by reckless police shootings. The office of the legislature was burned to the ground. After the usual official inquiry, the Colonial Office gradually agreed to the insistent demands of a number of middle- and working-class organizations for the restoration of an elected city council. This council was put in place between 1914 and 1918.

Other such riots occurred in Demerara, British Guiana, in 1905. Starting as a localized dispute over wages by some stevedores in Georgetown, the disturbances quickly spread to sugar-field workers, factory workers, domestics, bakers, and porters, engulfing an ever-widening area beyond the city limits. The causes of the riots were essentially economic, and the workers—as opposed to their middle-class sympathizers—lacked any organizational structure. Nevertheless, the governor of the colony called out the military forces and put down the disturbances with the loss of seven lives and a score of seriously injured. The rioters failed to achieve their economic goals, but for a few days, the riots brought together a great number of the middle and lower classes and left a legacy of middle-class leadership of some elements of the working classes that would give some impetus to the development of a trade union movement. The coincidence of these riots throughout the English Caribbean created an impression in Britain that the political administration of the colonies required greater attention—an impression that was reinforced with each commission report issued thereafter.

Between 1880 and 1920, the Caribbean witnessed a proliferation of organizations, despite the marked coolness of the authorities to them. A number of these organizations represented such middle-class workers as teachers, banana growers, coconut growers, cocoa farmers, cane farmers, rice farmers, lime growers, and arrowroot growers. Sometimes, as in the cases of the Reformist Association in British Guiana and the Ratepayers Association in Trinidad, they had overtly middle-class political aspirations: a widening of the political franchise to allow more of their members access to political office. But more and more workers were forming their own associations of fledgling unions and agitating for improvement in their wages and working conditions. And, as in the cases of the 1905 riots in British Guiana and the Water Riots in Trinidad, the two sets of organizations worked in concert—though the martyrs to the cause were singularly from the working and unemployed classes. One reason why the two sets of organizations—middle class and working class—could work in concert was their common determination that political reform of the unjust and anachronistic colonial administrative system was the major element in achieving their divergent goals. They realized that historically the governors had worked with a small and unrepresentative segment of the old planter class to make the political instruments serve their narrow economic ends. To the middle classes and the workers—and, to a certain extent, to the masses of urban unemployed—social and economic justice would be possible only if they themselves controlled the political machinery, and there were only two ways to gain access to the political machinery—through persuasion or by force.

To a great degree, this conviction still remains among the populations of the Caribbean. It was given further authenticity when the English Labour Party, and especially the Fabian wing of the party, expressed a sympathy with this view. But the Fabians did more. They actively sought to guide these fledgling political associations along a path of "responsible reform," thereby hoping to avert revolutionary changes. After the First World War, the Fabians grew more influential—as did the British Labour Party—in British politics. The experience both of the Boer War and of the First World War strengthened the anti-imperialists within Britain and shattered the self-confidence to rule far-flung colonies of diverse peoples. There was even less enthusiasm for colonial domination when the administrative costs exceeded the economic returns. The result of this metropolitan ambivalence about empire was a sincere attempt to rule constitutionally and openly. British critics of colonial rule expressed their opinions freely, and even the government Blue Books produced annually on each colony contained shortcomings of bureaucrats and policies.

But talking about West Indian problems was not the same as doing something about the problems. And by the 1930s, it was clear that British colonial policy was intellectually bankrupt. Through the 1920s and the 1930s, the British labor unions had sought to guide and encourage the formation of West Indian affiliates. As a result, unionization was common throughout the region, and many of them were formally or informally affiliated with the British Trade Union Congress. Nevertheless, it must be pointed out that trade unions in the Caribbean have relatively few dues-payers among their memberships. Membership indicates active participation rather than financial support.

The results of Fabian tutelage and reformist policies appeared to fail when workers broke out in spontaneous demonstrations throughout the English-Caribbean region, beginning in St. Kitts in 1935 and culminating in Jamaica and Guiana in 1938. A hastily despatched royal commission, dominated by Fabians and chaired by Lord Moyne (hence the Moyne Commission), toured the region and reported on the dismal conditions with strong recommendations for significant political reform. The Moyne Commission noted the increased politicization of workers in the region, derived from the war experiences of West Indian soldiers, the spread of elementary education, and the influence of industrial labor unrest in the United States. But after the riots, the union of the middle classes and the workers was formalized. The British government extended the franchise to all adults over the age of twenty-one and set about building the apparatus for modified self-government with greater local participation.

In this way, Jamaica came to hold the first general elections under universal adult suffrage in 1944, and the other territories followed soon thereafter. The alliance of professionals and labor leaders easily captured the state apparatus from the old combination of planters and bureaucrats. Thus, in most colonies a very close bond developed between the political parties and the workers' unions, most of which were highly personal instruments. In Jamaica, the Jamaica Labour Party drew its basic support from the Bustamante Industrial Trade Unions, both of which were tightly controlled by Bustamante. Its rival, the Peoples National Party, was at first affiliated with the Trades Union Council and after the purge of the radicals in 1951 created the National Workers' Union—the popular base that catapulted Michael Manley to political eminence. In Barbados, the Barbados Labour Party depended in the early days on the mass base of the members of the Barbados Workers' Union. Likewise, labor unions formed the catalyst for the successful political parties of George Price in British Honduras, Vere Bird in Antigua, Robert Bradshaw in St. Kitts, Eric Gairy in Grenada, and Cheddi Jagan in British Guiana. The notable exception was Eric Williams in Trinidad. His People's National Movement, established in 1956, succeeded despite a constant struggle against a sharply divided collection of strong unions.

After the Second World War and until the late 1960s, a sort of honeymoon existed between the political parties and the labor unions. Expanding domestic economies allowed substantial concessions of benefits to workers, whose real wages increased significantly as unionization flourished. But the increase in wages coincided with the noticeable expansion of the local economies and significant growth in the gross domestic product after the Second World War. That was not to be the case beyond the late 1960s.

As part of its decision to push modified self-government, the British authorities revived the old idea of a regional confederation. The idea had floated about the Colonial Office since the later part of the nineteenth century, but was given new vitality with a regional conference held at Montego Bay, Jamaica, in 1947. The British, as usual, were interested in administrative efficiency and bureaucratic centralization. The West Indians talked about political independence. A compromise was worked out. The West Indian Meteorological Services and the University of the West Indies (as a college of London University) were set up, and plans were made for the creation of a political federation that would unite the various territories and eventually culminate with the political independence of the region. These new regional organizations joined others already in existence, such as the Caribbean Union of Teachers, established in 1935; the Associated Chambers of Commerce, organized in 1917; and the Caribbean Labour Congress, inaugurated in 1945.

The federation began inauspiciously with the leading politicians in Jamaica—Norman Manley (then premier) and Alexander Bustamante—and in Trinidad—Eric Williams—refusing to stand as candidates in the federal elections. As the leading politicians of some of the most important participating units, their reluctance to become directly involved diminished the prestige and weakened the appeal of the larger political unit. Moreover, it condemned the larger unit to be politically weaker than some of its component parts. This uneasy federation of ten territories (excluding British Guiana and British Honduras) lasted from 1957 to 1961, when Jamaica opted to leave. Doomed from the start by lukewarm popular support, the federation quickly foundered because of the uncompromising insular interests, especially of the principal participants, Trinidad and Jamaica. The former would not accept unrestricted freedom of movement; the latter would not accept a binding Customs Union. But personalities and domestic politics overshadowed the decision to hold a referendum in Jamaica in 1961 to decide the advisability of continued participation. On September 19, 1961, about 54 percent of the Jamaican electorate voted to end their involvement in the federation. It was the lowest popular vote in any Jamaican election, but the government accepted the decision and initiated the plans to request complete independence for the state. Attempts by Trinidad and Barbados to salvage the federation after the withdrawal of Jamaica failed. Beginning in 1962, Jamaica and Trinidad began the parade toward Anglophone-Caribbean political independence. Barbados and Guyana gained their independence in 1966; the Bahamas in 1973; Grenada in 1974; Dominica in 1978; St. Lucia, St. Vincent, and the Grenadines in 1979; Belize, Antigua, and Barbuda in 1981; and St. Kitts-Nevis in 1983. Montserrat, the British Virgin Islands, the Cayman Islands, and the Turks and Caicos Islands remained British Crown Colonies in 1989 with limited internal self-government, while Anguilla, having broken away unilaterally from St. Kitts-Nevis in 1967, became an associated state of Great Britain in 1976. With some of these colonies discussing the prospect of independence, the proliferation of ministates in the Caribbean has definitely not ended.

Since the Second World War, the sense of self and the sentiment of nationalism have intensified throughout the Caribbean. Political independence has greatly fostered this nationalist sentiment. In the Bahamas, Jamaica, Barbados, and Guyana, strong two-party political systems have developed, and the performances of third parties have been dismal in elections.

Trinidad has a multiparty system, which was dominated between 1956 and 1987 by the People's National Movement, first under the leadership of Eric Williams (party leader, 1956–1981) and then George Chambers (party leader, 1981–1987). Politics in Trinidad and Tobago after 1986 became more competitive among the political parties. The National Alliance for Reconstruction, led by A. N. R. Robinson, won the elections that year. Patrick Manning and the People's National Movement won the elections in 1991 and 2001. Basdeo Panday of the United National Congress formed the government in 1995, and Kamla Persad-Bissessar led to power a coalition of the United National Congress and the People's Partnership in May 2010. Both in Trinidad and in Guyana, ethnic politics constitute a part of the political equation, as Hindu and Muslim East Indians form coalitions with black Trinidadians and Guyanese.

In the smaller islands, a number of factors have coincided to make dual-party, democratic politics a difficult achievement. In some cases, the populations are simply too small to provide the critical mass of diversity and anonymity. Familiar and kin relations make secret balloting and privacy elusive goals. History did not provide the large number of associations and cooperative organizations that were part and parcel of life in Jamaica, Barbados, Trinidad, or Guyana. As a result, political stability and coherence of the type found in the larger units have been elusive, and between 1979 and 1983 the government of Grenada was taken over by a band of young enthusiasts led by Maurice Bishop and Unison Whiteman, leaders of an opposition group called the New Jewel Movement. The People's Revolutionary Government, as the new government called itself, tried to create a new type of politics in the English Caribbean, modeled after the Cuban Revolution. The experiment ended prematurely in confusion. First, Bishop, a close friend of Fidel Castro, was overthrown, put under house arrest, and then executed by a faction led by Bernard Coard and army chief-of-staff Hudson Austin. A military occupation of the country by troops from the United States in October 1983 overthrew the rebels and restored electoral politics and, in general, the status quo ante. Ironically, the United States, having bitterly condemned the Bishop government's attempt to build a new airport at Point Salines on the southern tip of the island with Cuban and other international assistance, ended up finishing the airport after its conquest of the island. The Grenada experiment was the only successful transfer of political power in the independent Commonwealth Caribbean without the benefit of free elections—although some elections, especially those in Forbes Burham's Guyana, have been notoriously fraudulent.

With the exception of Trinidad and Guyana, where East Indians constitute the ethnic majorities, most of the rest of the Caribbean states have predominantly African-derived populations. Race, class, and color, however, do not constitute the mutually reinforcing cleavages found elsewhere; no regional political or social organization exists exclusively on the basis of race, class, or color. Overt forms of segregation and discrimination do not exist, and crude political appeals to race and color, such as was attempted by Marcus Garvey or his political disciples, have not been successful so far. Nevertheless, color consciousness permeates the societies. Despite the common official language, common institutions, and common historical experience, each island and state has its distinct set of characteristics. The local inflection of the English spoken in Jamaica varies significantly from that of Barbados or Trinidad or Guyana. Literacy rates vary from 70 percent plus in Jamaica and St. Lucia to 90 percent plus in Trinidad, Barbados, and the Bahamas. Barbados is one of the most thoroughly literate countries in the world.

The unavoidable heterogeneity of Caribbean populations has been a formidable but not an insuperable challenge to national integration. In a region where incessant biological mixture has occurred over centuries, any ethnic ideal clashes with the observed reality of everyday life. Nevertheless, ideals exist, often based on European models, which vary from the expressed rhetoric of the political majority that tries to emphasize the African cultural heritage. Yet politics and culture do not offer an easy solution to the delicate personal and familial problems of the pluralistic society. And at all levels of Caribbean societies, tensions operate between the centrifugal tendencies of state policies and ideals and the centripetal forces of beliefs, family, and kin. These tensions are exacerbated by the fragile political structures and even more fragile economic foundations on which a viable, cohesive nationalism must be forged among the Commonwealth-Caribbean peoples. The most urgent challenges for the new political leaders lie in satisfying the constantly rising expectations amid the painful reality of constantly shrinking resources. Moreover, the masses are losing their patience and enchantment with the current system of democratic politics.

Perhaps as a result, the area is extremely dynamic culturally, with a veritable explosion of local talent after the Second World War. Commonwealth-Caribbean poets and novelists of international caliber include A. J. Seymour, Martin Carter, Edgar Mittelholzer, and Wilson Harris from Guyana; Samuel Selvon, V. S. Naipaul, and Earl Lovelace from Trinidad; Derek Walcott from St. Lucia; George Lamming from Barbados; and Mervyn Morris, Vic Reid, John Hearne, Andrew Salkey, and Roger Mais from Jamaica. In painting and sculpture, the late Edna Manley was universally recognized. Commonwealth-Caribbean music—the calypso, the reggae, the ska, and the steelband orchestra—has captivated listeners around the world. Like the people themselves, all art forms in the Caribbean demonstrate an eclectic variety harmoniously combining elements of European, African, Asian, and indigenous American traditions. For the first time, the main cultural forms reflect the complex reality of the people and their history, not half-digested imitations of distant cultures.

By the last decade of the twentieth century, the Commonwealth Caribbean had reached the threshold of nationhood. Almost everywhere, the shape of the state was secure—although in some islands, far more so than in others. The quest of bonding together the nation was continuing with remarkable success. The vision carried by only a few at the beginning of the century was being spontaneously shared by the majority of the populations at the end of the century. The torch had passed from one generation to another. Caribbean peoples were beginning to come to grips with the daunting problems and limited prospects of political autonomy. Norman Manley, whom the *Daily Gleaner* of Jamaica described as "the embodiment of the spirit of the nation" and the "main architect of Jamaica today as a people, as a society, [and] as a nation," reflected sagely on his seventy-fifth birthday in 1968 in his farewell address to public service on the political and intellectual changing of the guard. "My generation," he declared, "had a distinct mission to perform. It was to create a national spirit with which we could identify ourselves as a people for the purpose of achieving political independence on the political plane." And, he continued, "I am convinced, deeply convinced, that the role of this generation is to proceed to the social and economic reform of Jamaica." Manley spoke not only for his fellow Jamaicans, but also for all the peoples of the Caribbean. The generation of leaders produced throughout the Caribbean in the first half of the twentieth century in many fields was, indeed, a most remarkable one.

Despite the considerable challenges to the Commonwealth Caribbean—most of which they share with the rest of the region as well as the entire hemisphere—many states have made significant progress in creatively mobilizing their human and natural resources to sustain or improve the daily conditions of life for the great majority of their population. The Bahamas, Barbados, St. Lucia, and Trinidad and Tobago are admirably well-administered states. The entire group has demonstrated a marked ambivalence toward cooperative action since the collapse of the ill-fated confederation in the early 1960s. Between 1965 and 1972, several Commonwealth-Caribbean states attempted to establish a common free trade area. In 1973 at the Treaty of Chaguaramas Barbados, Guyana, Jamaica, and Trinidad and Tobago created the Caribbean Community (CARICOM), which gradually expanded to include fifteen full members (Antigua and Barbuda, the Bahamas, Barbados, Belize, Dominica, Grenada, Guyana, Haiti, Jamaica, Montserrat, St. Kitts-Nevis, St. Lucia, Saint Vincent and the Grenadines, Suriname, and Trinidad and Tobago), five associate members (Anguilla, Bermuda, the British Virgin Islands, the Cayman Islands, and the Turks and Caicos Islands), and seven observers (Aruba, Colombia, the Dominican Republic, Mexico, the Netherlands Antilles, Puerto Rico, and Venezuela). CARICOM is not the only supranational organization in the Caribbean.

A number of former Leeward Islands states met in Basseterre, St. Kitts, in 1981 and constituted the Organization of Caribbean States (OECS), designed to foster economic coordination and mutual respect for human and legal rights, as well as assistance in natural disasters. Currently the secretariat is in Castries, St. Lucia, and the organization consists of seven member states (Antigua and Barbuda, Dominica, Grenada, Montserrat, Saint Kitts and Nevis, Saint Lucia, and St. Vincent and the Grenadines) and two associated states (Anguilla and the British Virgin Islands). As with CARICOM, other noncommonwealth countries, such as the U.S. Virgin Islands, Saba, and St. Martin, have also been discussing the possibility of joining the OECS.

Then in 1994 several Caribbean and non-Caribbean states came together in Cartagena, Colombia, to set up the Association of Caribbean States (ACS) with a secretariat in Port of Spain, Trinidad. Presently the ACS has twenty-five members and four associate members. In addition to the CARICOM representatives, Colombia, Costa Rica, Cuba, El Salvador, Guatemala, Honduras, Mexico, Nicaragua, Panama, and Venezuela are full members. Aruba, France, the Netherlands Antilles, and the Turks and Caicos Islands are associate members, while Argentina, Brazil, Canada, Chile, Ecuador, Egypt, Finland, India, Italy, Morocco, the Netherlands, Peru, Russia, Spain, South Korea, Turkey, the Ukraine, and the United Kingdom are observer states.

The proliferation of membership in supranational regional associations has not altered noticeably the overall effectiveness of the political or economic institutions of the Commonwealth Caribbean. There have been several overlapping committees and regular summit and committee meetings with the usual published reports and recommendations. Beyond that, the organizations appear more enthusiastic in their rhetoric than in their actions.

SUGGESTED READINGS

Bolland, O Nigel. *On the March: Labour Rebellions in the British Caribbean, 1934–39.* Kingston, Jamaica: Ian Randle, 1995.

Bolland, O Nigel. *The Politics of Labour in the British Caribbean: The Social Origins of Authoritarianism and Democracy in the Labour Movement.* Kingston, Jamaica: Ian Randle, 2001.

Bolland, O Nigel, compiler and editor, *The Birth of Caribbean Civilization: A Century of Ideas About Culture and Identity, Nation and Society.* Kingston, Jamaica: Ian Randle, 2004.

Brereton, Bridget. *A History of Modern Trinidad, 1783–1962.* Kingston, Jamaica: Heinemann Educational Books, 1981.

Brereton, Bridget, Martínez-Vergne, Teresita, Römer, René, and Silvestrini, Blanca G., eds. *General History of the Caribbean: Volume V. The Caribbean in the Twentieth Century.* Paris and London: UNESCO and Macmillan, 2004.

Bryan, Anthony T., ed. *The Caribbean: New Dynamics in Trade and Political Economy.* New Brunswick, N.J.: Transaction, 1995.

Bryan, Patrick E. *The Jamaican People 1880–1902: Race, Class and Social Control.* 2nd ed. Mona, Jamaica: University of the West Indies Press, 2000.

Bryan, Patrick E. *Edward Seaga and the Challenges of Modern Jamaica.* Mona, Jamaica: University of the West Indies Press, 2009.

Buffon, Alain. *Histoire du Crédit Agricole Mutuel de Guadeloupe.* Guadeloupe: Éditions Hervas, 1996.

Craton, Michael. *Pindling: The Life and Times of Lynden Oscar Pindling the First Prime Minister of the Bahamas, 1930–2000.* Oxford, England: Macmillan, 2002.

Dyde, Brian. *A History of Antigua: The Unsuspected Isle.* London: Macmillan Education, 2000.

Edie, Carlene J. *Democracy by Default: Dependency and Clientelism in Jamaica.* Kingston, Jamaica: Ian Randle, 1991.

Grossman, Lawrence. *The Political Ecology of Bananas: Contract Farming, Peasants, and Agrarian Change in the Eastern Caribbean.* Chapel Hill: University of North Carolina Press, 1998.

Levi, Darrell E. *Michael Manley: The Making of a Leader.* Athens: University of Georgia Press, 1990.

Lewis, Gordon K. *The Growth of the Modern West Indies.* New Edition with an introduction by Franklin W. Knight. Kingston, Jamaica: Ian Randle, 2004.

MacDonald, Scott B. *Trinidad and Tobago: Democracy and Development in the Caribbean.* New York: Praeger, 1986.

Maingot, Anthony P. *The United States and the Caribbean.* Boulder, Colo.: Westview Press, 1994.

Maingot, Anthony P., and Lozano, Wilfredo. *The United States and the Caribbean: Transforming Hegemony and Sovereignty.* New York: Routledge, 2005.

Manley, Michael. *Jamaica: Struggle in the Periphery.* London: Third World Media, 1982.

Munasinghe, Viranjini. *Callaloo or Tossed Salad? East Indians and the Cultural Politics of Identity in Trinidad.* Ithaca, N.Y.: Cornell University Press, 2001.

Neptune, Harvey R. *Caliban and the Yankees: Trinidad and the United States Occupation.* Chapel Hill: University of North Carolina Press, 2007.

Nettleford, Rex, ed. *Jamaica in Independence: Essays on the Early Years.* Kingston, Jamaica: Heinemann, 1989.

Oostindie, Gert, and Klinkers, Inge. *Decolonizing the Caribbean: Dutch Policies in a Comparative Perspective.* Amsterdam: Amsterdam University Press, 2003.

Palmer, Colin A. *Eric Williams and the Making of the Modern Caribbean.* Chapel Hill: University of North Carolina Press, 2006.

Palmer, Ransford W. *Caribbean Dependence on the United States Economy.* New York: Prager, 1979.

Palmer, Ransford W., ed. *The Repositioning of U.S.-Caribbean Relations in the New World Order.* Westport, Conn.: Praeger, 1997.

Payne, Anthony, and Sutton, Paul. *Charting Caribbean Development.* Gainesville: University Press of Florida, 2001.

Richardson, Bonham C. *Panama Money in Barbados, 1900–1920.* Knoxville: University of Tennessee Press, 1985.

Rodney, Walter. *A History of the Guyanese Working People, 1881–1905.* Baltimore, Md.: Johns Hopkins University Press, 1981.

Seecharan, Clem. *Sweetening Bitter Sugar: Jock Campbell the Booker Reformer in British Guiana, 1934–1966.* Kingston, Jamaica: Ian Randle, 2005.

Stephens, Evelyne Huber, and Stephens, John D. *Democratic Socialism in Jamaica: The Political Movement and Social Transformation in Dependent Capitalism.* Princeton, N.J.: Princeton University Press, 1986.

CHAPTER 11

State and Nationalism in the Contemporary Caribbean

I have travelled everywhere in your sea of the Caribbean...from
Haiti to Barbados, to Martinique and Guadeloupe, and I know
what I am speaking about.... You are all together, in the same
boat, sailing the same uncertain sea...citizenship and race
unimportant, feeble little labels compared to the message that
my spirit brings to me: that of the position and predicament
which History has imposed upon you.... I saw it first with the
dance...the merengue in Haiti, the beguine in Martinique
and today I hear, *de mon oreille morte*, the echo of calypsoes
from Trinidad, Jamaica, St. Lucia, Dominica and the legendary
Guiana.... It is no accident that the sea which separates your
lands makes no difference to the rhythm of your body.

—PÈRE LABAT, 1743

The quest to establish the state and the desire to mold the nation are bound up
inextricably with the Caribbean people's wish to exercise control over their
societies and their destinies. As completely artificial societies indelibly stamped
with the pervasive legacies of imperialism, colonialism, and slavery, the Caribbean
societies have had inordinate difficulty creating and maintaining a strong, cohesive
national sensibility. Some exist as precariously viable political entities in a milieu
of scarce resources and marginal administrative skills. The models of development
for other states and nations simply do not easily fit the Caribbean experience.

The long, tortuous struggle to dismantle imperialism, overcome colonialism,
and create independent states or forge cohesive nations has produced bittersweet
results throughout the Caribbean. At the beginning of the twenty-first century,
all the various Caribbean states find themselves in difficult situations. In many
cases, they have secured the existence of the state. In many areas, they have con-
clusively established a sort of collective identity, although they have not yet necessarily established a consensus on what represents the nation. Without doubt,
they have created an identity—or had one foisted upon them. But the confidence
that these goals—state, nationalism, identity—will provide the panacea for the
good life is waning. The dismantling of imperialism shattered the vague prospect

of a common regional nationalism, even among those communities not divided by language or culture. The fragmentation has endured well into the twenty-first century as the emergence of ministates shows no cessation with the desires of Montserrat and Aruba to seek their own independent status. The cruel current irony is that having struggled to throw off the asphyxiating bonds of imperialism and colonialism, the region finds both its stability and its viability threatened by a number of insidious forces. But before I examine them, it is worth looking at the fragmented region.

The Caribbean reality at the beginning of the twenty-first century is tantalizingly difficult to define. In many ways, it is a unique area: in its history, in its ethnic composition, and in its pattern of political evolution. The more than 40 million inhabitants scattered across hundreds of islands and the mainland enclaves of Belize, Guyana, Suriname, and French Guiana represent an eclectic blend of almost all the peoples and cultures of the world. The languages they have inherited they have made their own—enriching and re-forming them to express and reflect their individuality, their kaleidoscopic past, and their ethnic mosaic. The region is like a prism with light passing through—whatever enters is transformed. This leads to enormous imprecision in self-definition or even in how others may choose to view them—and a veritable nightmare for statisticians, demographers, and especially those obsessed with color and race. Nothing in the Caribbean is simple. Bipolar contrasts rarely exist. Things tend to be placed along a fluid spectrum, and the local speech richly reflects this graduated variety. Even the term *Caribbean* can be subject to various political and geographic definitions.

The ethnic amalgam that the people of the United States crudely and simply categorized as "black" or "white" was, at the very least, always tripartite in the Caribbean. Color and race were never simple watertight categories in themselves but rather characteristics that blended with others to produce changeable categories. Because their origins are so diverse, when the Caribbean peoples do designate themselves, they do so in confusing, sometimes hyphenated, blends, rather than in sharply distinguishable elements that are polarized as simply black or white, African, Asian, American Indian, or European.

No two censuses of the Jamaican government provide identical categories for racial designations of the population. In 1960, the categories were African, Afro-European, East Indian, Afro-East Indian, Chinese, European, Afro-Chinese, Syrian, and Other. Except for the category labeled, "Syrian," there was some obvious geographic logic to the designation. In 1970, however, the categories were changed to Negro-Black, Amerindian, East Indian, Portuguese, Chinese, White, Mixed, Syrian/Lebanese, Other, and Not Stated. Most census returns for the region do not provide the type of meticulous breakdown offered by the Jamaican example.

Indeed, most Caribbean census returns fail to designate race, although race, color, and class are powerful status indicators throughout the region. Fidel Castro's declaration that the Cubans were an "Afro-Latin people" reflected the reality but nevertheless shocked quite a few Cubans. People in the Caribbean prefer not to talk openly about race and color. This has not made either national sentiment or national identity easy and clear-cut. As Roberta Johnson stated in the particular context of the Puerto Rican situation, "patriotism is not loyalty to a polity [but] based on the feeling of being part of a people, of being Puerto Rican." As elsewhere, the Puerto Ricans are a mosaic of ethnic groups. Johnson went on to describe how Puerto Rican culture is a conglomerate of imports and that its institutions are all imported; yet there is a strong, romantic attachment to the island, especially among the diaspora community. To a greater or lesser degree, this has also been the situation for the rest of the Caribbean. The difficult task of the leaders of the politically independent states is to convert the "romantic attachment" into a coherent sense of national identity. With the exception of Cuba, Haiti, and the Dominican Republic, this has not yet been achieved.

Norman Manley, in a moving introduction written in 1965 to the popular nationalist novels of the Jamaican author Roger Mais, perceptively captivated the experiences as well as the challenges of political and intellectual leadership in the modern Caribbean:

> The new birth of Jamaica in 1938 did many things, but one thing stands out like a bright light: the National Movement brought with it a great upsurge of creative energy. We suddenly discovered that there was a place to which we belonged, and when the dead hand of colonialism was lifted a freedom of spirit was released and the desert flowered. Our best young men plunged deep into the lives of the people and came up with poems and paintings and with vivid and powerful books.
>
> It was a strange world they discovered; strange, most of all, in the fact that it was not a world where different cultures had blended into a single significant pattern, but a world divided and split in a manner as peculiar as it was deep-seated. It was not just a question of colour, nor yet of rich and poor; it was a matter of differences that involved widely different acceptances and rejections of values, different interpretations of reality, the use of identical words to express different concepts and understandings.

All these various differences to which Manley referred had to be harmonized before the foundation myths from which national identity draws its sustenance could be successfully inculcated among the public. Creating an independent state was one way to begin the process of harmonizing the various sentiments and attitudes that must eventually be synthesized in a national sentiment. That, therefore, was the work of the early nationalists. And a generalized consensus on the notion of the state became the essential foundation myth for individual groups of Caribbean peoples. Creating foundation myths, of course, required a common sense of the regional history, and transmitting it was far from easy. Having lost the great majority of its indigenous inhabitants, the various intrusive ethnic and cultural components of the modern Caribbean simply tried to appropriate and expand their views on the majority. Without controlling political power, that was not easily accomplished. Community, after all, has never been an integral part of the Caribbean experience. It should not be surprising, therefore, that the notion of nationalism should carry a variety of meanings throughout the Caribbean. It is part of the historical legacy of the region. The Caribbean peoples did not all arrive at a common point by a common route.

Indeed, politics as well as society throughout the Caribbean seem to move along a fluid spectrum. This was true of the initial settler and exploitation societies, and it remained true of the legacies they left in the Caribbean. While some of these territories retained some elements of their founding settler communities, many succumbed to the harsh, stultifying, denigrating experience of the exploitation plantation society based on slavery. Settler societies retained, in many cases, the institutional molds and cultural norms through which a variant nationalism found some guiding roots. Among some entities—in Bermuda, Cuba, the Dominican Republic, Puerto Rico, and Martinique—a critical mass of Europeans existed to staff these institutions and to provide cultural continuity and an elite consensus on cultural, if not political, matters. These descendants of Europeans tried to maintain and propagate a myth that their societies would eventually be the cultural microcosms of European societies. They reconstructed a sort of European polity but failed to infuse it with the type of legitimacy that ensured its vital continuity. The Europeanized cultural elite arrogantly thought that they would dominate political power forever, and the masses, through some vague Darwinist principle, would eventually fade away or acculturate upward. That did not work out, however, because the ethnic chauvinism of the nineteenth century lumped together all those not actually born in Europe as "inferior peoples." The new euphemism was "civilization," and it had strong connotations of the industrial society.

By the end of the nineteenth century, it was less easy to maintain the myth of white superiority in the exploitation colonies—although it was always tried. Certainly the resistance of the Black Caribs in Dominica, the defeat of the French soldiers in Haiti, and the various Maroon wars throughout the region had shattered the myth that whites in the Caribbean could militarily overpower nonwhites under any and all circumstances. But minority status merely reinforced among the local whites the prevailing European view that the Africans were savages at worst and "uncivilized" at best. Indeed, one result of the successful Haitian war of independence was precisely to decry the destruction of "civilization" in the former French colony.

In 1928, the numerically small, predominantly white Jamaican elite still pretended that they represented the sole repository of culture and spoke contemptuously of the overwhelming majority of the inhabitants in unabashedly racist terms. Consider the description of Jamaica that appeared in *Jamaica in 1928: A Handbook of Information for Visitors and Intending Residents with some Account of the Colony's History*, written by the English expatriate director of the Institute of Jamaica, Frank Cundall, and published by the West India Committee in London in 1928:

> The races inhabiting the West Indies today are a few native Indians (British, Scotch [sic], Irish and Welsh and their descendants), French, a few Creole (i.e., born in the West Indies), Spanish, Creole, negroes [sic], labourers from India, Chinese, who in Jamaica are rapidly developing as a trading class, and the Creole descendants of these Indians and Chinese, Portuguese, who originally came from

Madeira, a few Syrians, who came as traders, and a large number of mixed race of negro [sic] and European in varying shades, from Sambo (three-quarter black) to those in whom the strain is imperceptible, and a small number the result of connections between negroes [sic] and coolies, Indians and negroes [sic], and Europeans and Indians.... The Negro race has at present gone but a short way on the path to civilization. The individuals are still as children, childlike in their belief and faith. Once gain their confidence and they will trust implicitly.... Gratitude is, it is to be feared, not a strong point.

Two observations may be made about the foregoing statement. The first is that it betrayed a tendency still prevalent throughout the region to confuse ethnic and geographic terms. Race is therefore defined both in terms of geographic origin and color. The second observation is that in 1928 the white sector, represented by the director of the Institute of Jamaica, accounted for less than 5 percent of the population of the island. This 5 percent, however, controlled both the economic and the political structures. Only by drastically restructuring the social base of political power and by overthrowing the colonial elite could an open, democratic, and meritocratic society be created. Political change, then, assumed in the Caribbean a clearly messianic quality among the masses. The state would deliver justice and correct wrongs and reward the supporters of benevolent change. Political independence took on the qualities of secular messianism. The creation of the state had to take precedence over the formation of the nation, thereby imparting to Caribbean politics (much as elsewhere in Latin America) a particular quality—a penchant for the articulate, messianic, caudillo-type political leader.

Politically, the contemporary Caribbean community falls into three categories: nominally independent states, associated states, and dependencies. The criteria for this division of convenience are legal and political and do not reflect closely the reality of their power relations in world affairs since no Caribbean state is, or can become, absolutely independent. The independent, or sovereign, states are Antigua and Barbuda (1981), the Bahamas (1973), Barbados (1966), Belize (1981), Cuba (1902), Dominica (1978), the Dominican Republic (1865), Grenada (1974), Guyana (1966), Haiti (1804), Jamaica (1962), St. Kitts-Nevis (1983), St. Lucia (1977), St. Vincent and the Grenadines (1979), Suriname (1975), and Trinidad and Tobago (1962). Altogether, more than 28 million of the 32.5 million people of the Caribbean live in these nominally independent states, accounting for more than 86 percent of the total regional population. The associated states include Aruba and the Netherlands Antilles (Curaçao, Bonaire, Saba, St. Eustatius, and St. Martin), all self-governing states associated with the Netherlands; French Guiana, Guadeloupe, and Martinique, overseas departments of France; and Puerto Rico, an Associated Free State, or Commonwealth, associated with the United States of America. The associated states account for slightly more than 4 million people, or 13 percent of the regional population, although Puerto Rico alone accounts for more than 3 million of that subtotal. Finally, there are the dependencies of various sorts: Anguilla, Bermuda, the British Virgin Islands, the Cayman Islands, Montserrat, the Turks and Caicos Islands, and the U.S. Virgin Islands. With slightly more than 200,000 persons, these dependencies account for less than 1 percent of the regional population.

The linguistic divisions do not correspond neatly with the political fragmentation. There are four major language groups. Spanish is the major language in Cuba, Puerto Rico, and the Dominican Republic. Together these three states account for more than 61 percent of the regional population. English is the major language in Anguilla, Antigua and Barbuda, the Bahamas, Barbados, Belize, Bermuda, the British Virgin Islands, Dominica, Grenada, Guyana, Jamaica, Montserrat, St. Kitts, St. Lucia, St. Vincent and the Grenadines, Trinidad and Tobago, the Turks and Caicos Islands, and the U.S. Virgin Islands. Altogether these eighteen states and territories account for slightly more than 9 percent of the regional population (and a number less than the population of the Dominican Republic alone). French is the official language of the departments of French Guiana, Guadeloupe, Martinique, and Haiti. These units combined account for 20 percent of the Caribbean population—although Haiti alone accounts for 15 percent of that total. Dutch is one of the official languages of Aruba, the Netherlands Antilles, and Suriname, together accounting for slightly more than 2 percent of the regional population.

Further confusing the linguistic map, some units are bilingual or polylingual. Puerto Rico is officially bilingual in English and Spanish. English, Hindi, Javanese, and Sranan Togo are spoken in Suriname. English, Spanish, and Papiamento are included in the official languages of the Netherlands Antilles. Aruba includes Papiamento as one of its official languages. And a French-based Creole is widely spoken in Haiti and mutually intelligible in Guadeloupe, Martinique, St. Vincent, and St. Lucia. Language, of course, has little relevance to the political culture. Political, social, and economic patterns in the Caribbean seldom conform to the linguistic or cultural boundaries.

With the exception of Cuba, Haiti, and Suriname, the independent states all have free, open, and competitive elections at more or less regular intervals. Strong two-party systems exist in Jamaica, Puerto Rico, Barbados, and the Dominican Republic, and at least one dominant party exists in the others. Regardless of the system, the region has produced an unusual number of charismatic, caudillo-style politicians: George Price in Belize; Lynden Pindling in the Bahamas; Fulgencio Batista and Fidel Castro in Cuba; Alexander Bustamante, Norman Manley, Michael Manley, and Edward Seaga in Jamaica; François Duvalier and Jean-Claude Duvalier in Haiti; Luis Muñoz Marín in Puerto Rico; Rafael Trujillo, Joaquín Balaguer, and Juan Bosch in the Dominican Republic; Vere Bird in Antigua; Grantley Adams and Errol Barrow in Barbados; Eric Gairy and Maurice Bishop in Grenada; Eric Williams in Trinidad; and Forbes Burnham and Cheddi Jagan in Guyana. The appeal of the caudillo throughout the region should not be surprising. The colonial experience carried with it strong elements of authoritarian rule invested in governors, governors-general, and captains-general. The representative assemblies of the British territories until the middle of the twentieth century were oligarchic and, as far as the majority of the people were concerned, never truly represented their interests. The new nationalist politicians established their legitimacy by popular acceptance. They not only had to be popular, they also had to be populist.

But there is another aspect to the inordinate respect given to political leaders in the region. In the early modern period, the notion of the state, especially among the illiterate masses, was weak. In politicizing the masses, the nationalist politicians inculcated the belief that a renovated polity would redress the indignities, the marginality, and the neglect of the previous period. In common with most of Latin America and much of the Third World, politics and political participation in the Caribbean represented an operational means to a concrete end. The modern state was invested with the personal qualities of the great *patrón*, the priest, or the plantation owner. It was supposed to guide and nurture and protect. The caudillo represented the embodiment of the modern state and was expected to behave as a just mediator among classes, factions, groups, and interests. Political appeal, therefore, tended to run less along ideological lines than along personal lines. The politicized masses in Jamaica who promised in the 1940s to follow Bustamante until they died, the *jíbaros* who responded fanatically to the appeal of Muñoz Marín in Puerto Rico in the 1950s, and the revolutionaries who enthusiastically supported Fidel Castro in the 1960s were all confident that the promised political changes would also personally change their lives. That, in large measure, accounts for the political longevity of the ideologically opposed Juan Bosch and Joaquín Balaguer in the Dominican Republic. Both have accumulated such a large, strong contingent of followers who share their contrasting vision of the new society that younger politicians find it difficult to carve out a place in the system.

Indeed, the Caribbean masses tended to interpret the changes to their societies as the direct results of the benevolent or malevolent actions of their leaders. The charismatic leaders aroused, appealed to, and articulated the expectations of the masses but, in so doing, expressed the limits of charismatic leadership, for popular disappointment results in the immediate transfer of public affection and loyalty. This particular political environment also complicated the process of political succession, for whether or not the leaders fulfilled the expectations of the masses, the changes in the historical circumstances indicated that new political mobilization would have to be based on new strategies. The bitter economic experience of the 1970s was lethal for the practice of charismatic politics.

Charismatic, personalist political leadership in the Caribbean corresponded to a period of severe crisis in the political, economic, and social structures of the Caribbean. It was a transitional phase. In the 1920s and 1930s, the political systems all faced serious threats from the restless masses. Civil unrest was widespread. The intellectually bankrupt, socially myopic governors, administrators, and oligarchs had lost their confidence to rule. The Great Depression exposed the inherent inadequacy of agricultural-export economies to raise the total incomes of the local populations. Governments, even if they cared to, had difficulty finding sufficient revenue to serve the needs of the local populations. At the same time, these needs were increasing as the region experienced a general population explosion. The solution to these multiple problems was seen in a number of changes implemented during and after the Second World War. Governments sought to become more representative and more legitimate, with the expansion of the franchise and a broadening of the participant groups. Trade unions and political parties were legitimated and brought into the administrative process. The franchise was extended to all adults over the age of twenty-one. This, in effect, created a new alliance of upper-, middle-, and working-class participants who captured state power and redirected it to serve the goals of the alliance. To expand the economy, new development schemes were advocated, designed to expand employment resources. These schemes almost all centered on increased industrialization comparable to that taking place in Puerto Rico in the 1940s and 1950s under Muñoz Marín's tenure. The emphasis in those years was mainly on economic restructuring with a broader purpose: promoting national identity, national cohesion, and political and economic independence. Since foreigners supplied the capital for this development, it was commonly referred to as "industrialization by invitation." The new Caribbean leaders sought not only to expand the economic base, but to reorder the distribution of national wealth and to gain control over the ownership of national resources and the priorities of the state. In this way, political power became inseparable from economic control and social justice.

The years immediately following the Second World War saw an overall increase in world trade, and as trading nations, the Caribbean participated. The economies grew significantly for nearly two decades, and in some cases growth was impressive. The Puerto Rican experience has already been examined under "Operation Bootstrap." In other areas of the Caribbean, manufacturing-based industrialization also scored equally substantial gains. The case of Jamaica illustrates the trend. At the end of the war, agricultural products—sugar, rum, bananas, citrus, tobacco, ginger, pimento, coffee, and cocoa—represented the entire range of Jamaican exports. Between 1943 and 1951, the number of manufacturing plants in Jamaica increased from 365 to 627, and the workforce increased from 14,373 to 23,098. But the factories were small, employing relatively few individuals. The average factory employed 36.8 workers in 1951, compared with 39.4 in 1943. The same sort of expansion took place in Barbados and Trinidad.

In the 1950s, the extractive industries—bauxite in Jamaica, Haiti, the Dominican Republic, and Guyana and petroleum in Trinidad—and temporary price increases among the traditional agricultural exports boosted national production and productivity and reinforced the view that the economies were expanding. The regional developmental economists were delighted and self-congratulatory, but their emotional response was premature.

Like the Puerto Rican case under "Operation Bootstrap," things did not work out in the Caribbean in the long run quite as they had been planned. On the positive side, industrialization, especially import-substituting manufactures, did result in marked increases in the gross domestic products, with a beneficial impact on national and per capita incomes. A look at the changes in some available national per capita incomes between 1957 and 1980 illustrates the measure of economic growth. The Bahamas, Barbados, Puerto Rico, and Trinidad and Tobago were high performers. Using constant 1957 U.S. dollars, the per capita income of the Bahamas by 1980 had increased from $400 to $1,571; that of Barbados, from $200 to $1,571; that of Puerto Rico, from $563 to $1,433; and that of Trinidad and Tobago, from $423 to $2,080. Guyana, Haiti, Jamaica, and the Dominican Republic were moderate performers during the same period, with increments far short of their regional colleagues. Guyana increased its per capita income from $235 to $328; Jamaica, from $329 to $490; the Dominican Republic, from $239 to $543; and Haiti, from $105 to $138. Until the mid- to late 1960s, wages kept pace with the inflation rates, indicating that workers were, on the whole, better off in the 1960s than they were in the 1940s. Moreover, increased national incomes and locally determined national priorities had resulted in considerable public expenditure on the essential social services—education, public health care, roads, housing, and supplemental nutritional support. But even as the good times rolled along, the negatives loomed large; some could not have been foreseen.

In the first place, industrialization failed to accomplish the expected employment objectives. Despite heavy extraregional emigration—accounting for approximately 10 percent of the natural population increase during the period—industrial employment was proportionally no better in the 1960s than in the 1940s. Between 1950 and 1963, according to Jay Mandle, "Trinidad and Tobago's labor force increased by nearly 100,000, whereas jobs in the country's dominant sugar and petroleum sectors had declined over the same years by about 3,800." In Jamaica, some 13,000 new jobs were created by industrialization between 1956 and 1968, but the labor force had increased by 325,000 during the same period. Worse for the government and the economy, the sugar industry had eliminated about 10,000 jobs during those thirteen years. Nowhere in the Caribbean did industrialization provide the sustained volume of new jobs to take up the slack resulting from the decline in the agricultural sector. Puerto Rico achieved the most successful industrial-sector employment, with about 35 percent of its labor force employed in manufacturing by 1980. At the same time, the workforce in agriculture had shrunk to 3 percent. Cuba, the Dominican Republic, and Trinidad managed to peak at about 20 percent of their labor forces in industry, while the best that Jamaica could do by 1980 was 15.2 percent. And to complicate matters, the new industrial jobs were often taken by full-time workers who were previously employed in the agricultural sector. Only Haiti and the Dominican Republic continued to have 50 percent or more of the labor force in agriculture in 1980. While relatively higher industrial wages led to an increase in agricultural wages, the latter lagged so far behind that many lost any desire for work in agriculture. Agriculture declined as a contributory sector to the gross domestic products, forcing more people off the land and into the cities, thereby increasing the need for expenditures of the central governments on needy social services and police protection. In some cases, the expansion of tourism and other, mainly informal, economic activities offset the steep decline in agricultural employment and productivity. With the exception of Puerto Rico and Haiti, most Caribbean manufacturing is geared mainly to serve small domestic or limited regional markets. In any case, manufacturing seldom exceeded 25 percent of the gross domestic products in 2010, and the prevailing winds of globalization make industrial expansion difficult.

By the late 1970s, unemployment was a major problem throughout the Caribbean. The prospect was bleakest for the newly educated young people who where ready to join the labor market. The unfortunate situation in all the Caribbean states was that unemployment grew absolutely during the 1970s, and the standard of living declined for the population as a whole. Industrialization simply did not cope with the pressures of normal population increases. All the economic models of development that were pursued failed to resolve the problem of rising unemployment rates. With the exception of Cuba (where the unemployment rate in its socialist economy stood at 3.4 percent in 1980), by the end of the 1980s the unemployment figures ranged between 10 percent and 40 percent of the potential labor forces. These rates were generally higher than those normally prevailing before the implementation of the industrial schemes in the 1940s and after. By the 1970s, too, the relief valves provided by emigration, mainly to Europe, Canada, and the United States—or even intraregionally to Cuba, the Bahamas, the Dominican Republic, and Trinidad—had been legally closed off. Unemployment and underemployment were particularly rife among urban groups, thereby aggravating the social problems of political unrest, narcotics abuse, and narcotics trafficking. The construction of factories and housing estates on land formerly farmed, fallowed, or grazed produced a corollary of increased urban slums. Caribbean cities became the magnetic reservoir of the impoverished, the landless, the jobless, the politically powerless, the frustrated, and the marginal by all measures, much like the pattern elsewhere throughout Latin America.

Between the 1960s and the 1980s, the region experienced a roller-coaster economy that left it more vulnerable to international forces than it had ever been. The performance of the local economies fluctuated in tandem with international trade. The optimistic economic outlook of the 1960s gave way to pessimism in the 1980s. The general mood of rising expectations of the earlier period changed drastically to one of widespread disappointment and discontent.

Between 1961 and 1970, inflation rates in the region averaged a manageable 3.4 percent per annum, ranging from about 2 percent in the Dominican Republic to 6 percent in the Bahamas. The improved economic performances registered by Caribbean states were achieved largely by concentrating on exportable agricultural commodities, mining for raw materials shipped abroad, and import-substituting manufactures that prospered on finishing materials imported from abroad. Expanded economies allowed governments to achieve much and promise more.

During the 1960s, the generally expanding economies allowed for heavy investment in housing, education, and social services at both the public and private levels. Governments became the single largest employer of labor. In Puerto Rico, government employment accounted for 24 percent of the active labor force in 1985. In Jamaica, the government employed 18 percent of the active labor force, amounting to about 33 percent of all the wage earners in the country. The pattern

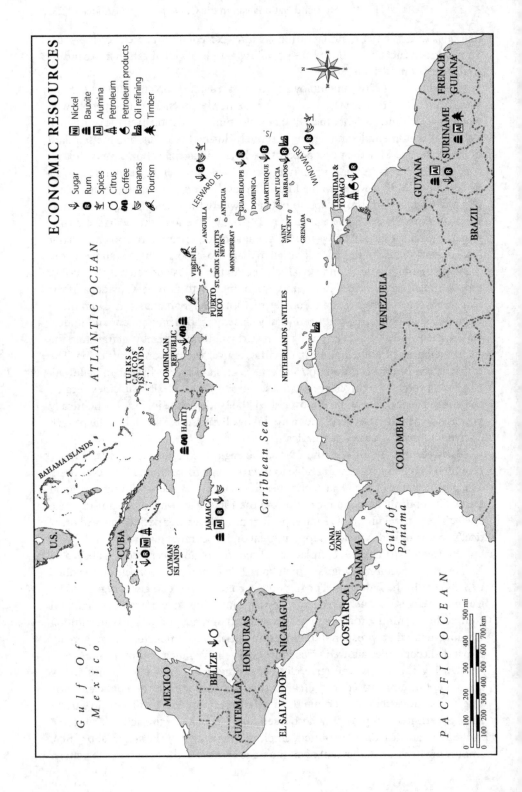

ECONOMIC RESOURCES

Nickel   **Sugar**
Bauxite   **Rum**
Alumina   **Spices**
Petroleum   **Citrus**
Petroleum products   **Coffee**
Oil refining   **Bananas**
Timber   **Tourism**

Gulf of Mexico

U.S.

ATLANTIC OCEAN

BAHAMA ISLANDS

CUBA

CAYMAN ISLANDS

JAMAICA

TURKS & CAICOS ISLANDS

DOMINICAN REPUBLIC

HAITI

MEXICO

BELIZE

GUATEMALA

HONDURAS

EL SALVADOR

NICARAGUA

COSTA RICA

PANAMA

CANAL ZONE

Gulf of Panama

Caribbean Sea

VIRGIN IS.

PUERTO RICO

ST. CROIX

ANGUILLA

ST. KITTS NEVIS

MONTSERRAT

ANTIGUA

LEEWARD IS.

GUADELOUPE

DOMINICA

MARTINIQUE

SAINT LUCIA

BARBADOS

SAINT VINCENT

GRENADA

WINDWARD IS.

NETHERLANDS ANTILLES

Curaçao

TRINIDAD & TOBAGO

COLOMBIA

VENEZUELA

GUYANA

SURINAME

FRENCH GUIANA

BRAZIL

PACIFIC OCEAN

0   100   200   300   400   500 mi
0   100   200   300   400   500   600   700 km

was the same in Trinidad, where the government employed one out of every three wage earners, and the total was about 20 percent of the active labor force. The concentration of employment in the service sector also reflected the expansion of the tourist and trading sectors. In 1986, employment in services accounted for 84 percent of the labor force in the Bahamas, 67 percent in Barbados, 59 percent in both the Dominican Republic and Trinidad and Tobago, 52 percent in Guyana, 49 percent in Jamaica, and 20 percent in Puerto Rico. The high public-sector employment frustrated attempts to reduce the overall size of the public sector in the difficult economic years of the early 1980s and increased the general level of disenchantment with some governments. The sharp decline in commodity prices and trade in the late 1970s resulted in sharp increases in inflation rates between 1980 and 1985. As major employers of labor and major actors in the economies, the governments had few options but to borrow heavily from abroad. By the 1980s, national indebtedness became a heavy burden, with substantial proportions of scarce hard currency channeled into interest payments.

Greater integration into international commerce inevitably meant greater economic dependence. Many governments borrowed lavishly from the available pool of money recycled from the petroleum-exporting states in the mid-1970s to fund schemes that failed to bear fruit. By the 1980s, repayment of interest on those loans absorbed sizable proportions of national incomes. But industrialization and urbanization also had other economic consequences for the region. Slowly the region began to consume what it did not produce. While most societies were self-sufficient in food before 1940, only Cuba remained so in 1988. Food imports ranged from 6 percent to 22 percent of all imports in the region, greatly compounding the urgent need for hard currencies by the local states. Part of the very high public and private indebtedness of the region in the late 1970s resulted from the food trade. Policies designed to reduce high external indebtedness by reducing imports had widespread effects throughout the Caribbean with severe political repercussions, such as the food riots in the Dominican Republic in 1984 that resulted in seventy persons killed, two hundred wounded, and more than four thousand arrested. The narrow economic base of the Caribbean countries renders them constantly vulnerable to fluctuations in international interest rates, as well as calculated attempts by internal and external forces to destabilize their sovereignty and their independence.

Economic problems obviously strongly influenced the political situation throughout the Caribbean. Politics and politicians have been judged more by their ability to respond creatively to the basic and immediate economic challenges than by their underlying ideology or political principles. But policies and politicians remain circumscribed within very narrow operational limits. Changing the basic economic constraints of the state is extremely difficult, as the Jamaica case proved in the 1970s and 1980s. Rhetoric and promises bear little relationship to practice and performance. Politics becomes more style than substance.

Despite Edward Seaga's constant criticism of former Prime Minister Michael Manley's "socialist" economic policies in Jamaica during the late 1970s, by the end of his term of office in the late 1980s, Seaga had not altered many of the basic thrusts of his predecessor. Jamaicans apparently voted in 1980 for better fiscal management, not fundamental ideological change. After nine years, the Jamaican economy was not manifestly in better shape than in 1980, with the International Monetary Fund establishing the policy guidelines. In 1989, Manley and the Peoples National Party returned to office, muting their longstanding criticism of the constraints of the fund. For his part, Manley's preelection promises held none of the former lofty language of "democratic socialism" and a "new economic order." Rather, his promise was an ambiguous consolation to "put people first." In much the same way, in 1959 "Che" Guevara and Fidel Castro promised that by following a socialist path, they would make Cuba the economic showplace of the Caribbean and Latin America. For a brief period, they even thought of reducing the dependence on sugar production. Yet in 1982, Cuba was producing more sugar than ever before and was lamely trying to implement a modified version of the Puerto Rican development model of the 1950s. The test of political efficiency rests in the reality and perceptions of economic performance.

Consciously or unconsciously, the contemporary Caribbean states follow three economic models of development. The Cuban socialist model is fully integrated with the Soviet and East-European economies and carries on a large portion of its commerce through barter arrangements. The second model is found in Puerto Rico, the French Antilles, Aruba, and the Netherlands Antilles. There the economies are extensions of larger, openly capitalist economies—the United States, France, and the Netherlands. The third group tries to operate as public-cum-private enterprise mixtures of the other two and is highly dependent on external aid—loans, grants, and special trading arrangements with the United States, Canada, or the European community. No ideal type has emerged from among these three generally accepted models of sociopolitical reconstruction— socialist Cuba with its highly centralized decision-making system; the integrated free-enterprise economies of Puerto Rico, the Netherlands Antilles, and the French Caribbean; or the mixed version of Jamaica, the Dominican Republic, and the others. No model is perfectly applicable on a regional basis. Some systems have generated more satisfactory results in some areas at the expense of others. But no Caribbean state has yet achieved an enviable degree of social and economic development.

For a short time, it was felt that the Cuban model provided a possible breakthrough. Its success in overcoming some pervasive Caribbean problems of public health, unemployment, illiteracy, and inequitable resource and wealth distribution influenced Jamaica (under Michael Manley's "democratic socialist society," 1972–1980) and Guyana (under Forbes Burnham's "cooperative socialist republic," 1970–1985), as well as the short-lived People's Revolutionary Government of Maurice Bishop in Grenada between 1979 and 1983. Not all Caribbean governments, however, found the Cuban model attractive. Both the government of Barbados under J. M. G. M. "Tom" Adams (1972–1985) and the government of Trinidad and Tobago under Eric Williams (1956–1981) were cautious and correct in their relations with Cuba. The governments of Eugenia Charles in Dominica, Milton Cato in St. Vincent, and Vere Bird in Antigua were consistently critical and sometimes deprecatory.

While the Cuban model undoubtedly removed the disconcerting discrepancy between the richest and poorest sectors of the society and provided a more equitable redistribution of resources, it was no more attractive and duplicable than the Puerto Rican model of the 1950s. It also had some pronounced handicaps. It has been implemented at a very high cost to individual liberties, and it was totally unacceptable to the United States of America. In the 1980s, other weaknesses appeared in the Cuban model. The major one was the inability to provide self-sustaining economic growth.

During the late 1970s, when the region was convulsing with the enormous economic consequences of the energy crises produced by sudden upward price changes ordered by the Organization of Petroleum Exporting Countries, Cuba was cushioned by its relationship to the Soviet Union. Cuba bought 97 percent of its petroleum needs from the Soviet Union at about one-third the going world price. It sold about 45 percent of its sugar to the Soviet bloc at prices that sometimes ranged as high as five times the world free-market price. It sold 75 percent of its nickel to the Soviet Union at guaranteed premium prices. And it periodically arranged low-interest loans and grants from the Soviet Union. Altogether, the direct and indirect economic subsidy to the Cubans amounted to between $3 billion and $4 billion per year, or approximately $300 for every Cuban citizen on the island. Despite this consistently high annual subsidy after the late 1970s, the Cuban overall economic situation was not significantly different from that of the rest of the region.

In 1980, largely for economic reasons, more than 125,000 Cubans opted to leave their country. The gross socialist product of the island fluctuated just like capitalist systems elsewhere, with a period of negative growth in the mid-1980s. The economy was no more diversified in 1989 than in 1970 or, for that matter, in 1959. Exports still fell far short of imports in value, creating a growing trade deficit throughout the 1980s. In 1982, the Cuban government declared a change in its laws to permit a modified version of the Puerto Rican-style incentive industrialization but by 1989 had made very little headway in attracting Western firms.

Cuba's per capita gross domestic product was not significantly different from that of the other Caribbean states. With a per capita gross domestic product of about $1,534, the Cuban economy might have been more buoyant than that of Haiti ($379), Guyana ($720), Jamaica ($1,047), and the Dominican Republic ($1,225)—it was less so than Trinidad and Tobago ($2,837), Barbados ($2,865), Guadeloupe ($3,151), Martinique ($3,717), Puerto Rico ($4,301), the Netherlands Antilles ($6,600), the Bahamas ($7,600), and Bermuda ($13,421). Unemployment, although relatively low by regional standards, began to attract attention in the late 1980s. Moreover, Cuba began to accumulate an increasing foreign debt with Western money lenders that surpassed $6 billion in 1988. Even before the unforeseen collapse of the Soviet Union in 1991, the Cuban economy began to demonstrate significant stresses. These stresses were enormously exacerbated during the Special Period. The recovery of the economy during the first decade of the twenty-first century has not eliminated the fundamental problems of asphyxiating state control. All these problems tended to overshadow the admirable accomplishments of which the Cubans were justifiably proud in other fields.

The fragmented postcolonial societies in the Caribbean produced a variety of inconsistent and unexpected situations. Colonial political traditions or imperial cultural legacies proved inadequate predictors of political history after independence. The Spanish empire produced the independent states of Cuba, the Dominican Republic, and Puerto Rico. All three followed separate courses after independence. Cuba first moved in the orbit of the United States from 1902 to 1959 and then became, for a time, an unorthodox member of the Soviet-bloc countries. In the late 1980s, Cuba, under a charismatic authoritarian government, was as orthodox a socialist state as any of Eastern Europe. Puerto Rico emerged from a form of colonialism under U.S. jurisdiction as an openly democratic polity, associated closely with the United States. Puerto Rican citizens are also citizens of the United States. The Dominican Republic has had an uneasy history. After a chaotic period, it endured the long dictatorship of the Trujillos. Between the overthrow of the Trujillo regime and the election of Leonel Fernández in 2004, the country experienced some turbulent economic times. But in 2010, the economy seemed to be slowly getting back on track with declines in inflation and some stability in currency exchange rates. Overall the Dominican Republic has come a long way from the struggling democracy that emerged in the 1960s.

The Dutch-Caribbean empire collapsed into Aruba, a would-be ministate seeking its own independence; the Netherlands Antilles, a precarious association enjoying a special relationship with the previous metropolis; and the Republic of Suriname. Both Aruba and the Netherlands Antilles are attractively cosmopolitan states. In the few months prior to the granting of independence to Suriname in 1975, about 40 percent of the population voluntarily emigrated to the Netherlands. Within five years, the political system had totally collapsed, and the country was under martial law between 1980 and 1988. Elections in that year did nothing to restore democracy or to diminish the power of the commander of the national army, Lieutenant-Colonel Desire Bouterse. Nevertheless, Bouterse managed to modify his authoritarian tendencies sufficiently to become popularly elected in 2010 as the president of Suriname. The expansion of bauxite production, along with the discovery of petroleum and gold, has considerably brightened the economic prospects of the country.

In 1946, Guadeloupe, Martinique, and French Guiana became overseas departments of France, legislatively and administratively on par with any other domestic French departments. The French Caribbean departments balance their budgets only with substantial preferential subventions from the central government. Together, the three departments exported bananas, pineapples, sugar, rum, petroleum products, shrimp, and timber in 1985 valued at $290 million and imported goods valued at nearly $2 billion. Despite substantial economic assistance—much like that of the United States to Puerto Rico—rumblings of centrifugal discontent sporadically disturb the political ambience of Guadeloupe. Although Martinique and Guadeloupe rank among Caribbean countries with a higher standard of living, occasional anti-French sentiments appear, more so in Guadeloupe than in Martinique. Part of the difference lies in the excellent public service in Martinique of Aimé Césaire (1913–2008), who was elected mayor of Fort de France in 1945 and served until 2001. Guadeloupe has shown more irredentist tendencies. In 1995 it became an observer in the Association of Caribbean States, and in 2009 it experienced prolonged civil unrest based on low wages, a rising cost of living, and perceived social inequality. Haiti, the other relic of French Caribbean colonialism, has been mired in political instability and irredeemable poverty for most of its independent history. The catastrophic earthquake of January 2010 brought a large number of international agencies to Haiti, all promising to assist the country to rebuild and modernize its political and economic institutions—and to stay as long as it took to get the job done.

The British Caribbean, with the largest number of political units, represents the most varied political legacy of colonialism. The confident expectation that the political systems after independence would imitate and perpetuate the "Westminster model" of Great Britain proved unwarranted. Of the twelve independent states that emerged after 1962, three—Dominica, Guyana, and Trinidad and Tobago—opted to become republics. Antigua and Barbuda, the Bahamas, Barbados, Belize, Grenada, Jamaica, St. Kitts-Nevis, St. Lucia, and St. Vincent and the Grenadines have remained constitutional monarchies, with the queen of England as the titular head of state. The queen is represented by a local governor-general. Some territories have demonstrated a consistent support of democratic principles; others have not. In some cases, a strong affiliation exists between the political parties and the trade unions. In Jamaica, both major parties, the Peoples National Party and the Jamaica Labour Party enjoy substantial trade union bases in the National Workers' Union and the Bustamante Industrial Trades Union, respectively. In Barbados, the Barbados Workers' Union is affiliated with the Democratic Labour Party. Eric Gairy's Grenada United Labour Party grew out of his trade union, the Grenada Manual and Mental Workers Union, that he organized in July 1950. Elsewhere, the experience has not been as commonplace. In Trinidad and Tobago as well as in Guyana, the dominant political parties—the People's National Movement in Trinidad and the People's National Congress in Guyana—have established their political dominance despite limited trade union affiliation. In the smaller islands, the combination of close family and community relations limits the scope of political mobilization, thereby inhibiting the proper development of party politics as practiced at Westminster or in the larger units. In a society where virtually everyone knows everyone else, secret balloting and objective evaluations are extremely impractical, if not impossible.

Organized workers, however, are not an essential prerequisite for party stability or political democracy. Indeed, they are poor indicators of the state of politics in any given territory. Both the intensity of organization and the proportion of the labor force organized in unions vary considerably throughout the region. Nor does a given union membership necessarily indicate the proportion of members who pay dues. In any case, the figures are quite unreliable. Cuba and Puerto Rico have the oldest registered trade unions within the Caribbean, with a history of formal organization going back to the beginning of the twentieth century. In both cases, the organized unions tend to be independent of the political parties. Trinidad and Tobago, with about one-half the population of Jamaica and one-sixth the population of the Dominican Republic, has approximately the same number of union members, but they are distributed in more individual unions than in either of those states. While unions may provide a convenient accessible constituency, they do not necessarily constitute a reliable base. Moreover, apart from Cuba, organized labor represents a diminishing fraction of the workers in any state, seldom exceeding 40 percent of the labor force. Where data are available, only Cuba, Jamaica, and Suriname show more than 40 percent of the labor force unionized. Barbados, Dominica, Grenada, and Trinidad and Tobago range between 30 percent and 39 percent, while Haiti and the Dominican Republic have less than 10 percent of their labor forces unionized. The potential political impact or worker organization, however, is muted in the Caribbean milieu, where consistent unemployment and underemployment have been pronounced features since the 1960s. In 1985, ten states reported unemployment figures in excess of 20 percent of their labor forces: Anguilla, the Bahamas, the Dominican Republic, Grenada, Guyana, Jamaica, Martinique, St. Kitts-Nevis, St. Vincent and the Grenadines, and Suriname. Nine states reported rates between 10 percent and 19 percent: Antigua and Barbuda, Barbados, Belize, Dominica, French Guiana, Haiti, the Netherlands Antilles, Puerto Rico, and Trinidad and Tobago. If the official data are to be accepted, general employment has improved across the Caribbean. At least the reported unemployment figures had come down sharply by 2010. Only Haiti, with 66 percent unemployment; Dominica, with 23 percent; and St. Lucia, with 20 percent appeared anomalous. Antigua and Barbuda, Barbados, the Dominican Republic, Jamaica, Puerto Rico, and St. Vincent and the Grenadines reported unemployment rates in excess of 10 percent of the labor force. Patterns of employment organization, then, appear to bear little relationship to the formal political systems and may be the result of accidental historical forces.

The history of the peoples of the Caribbean is one of continual struggle. It is not, however, a history of unrelieved despondence or crippling despair. Rather, Caribbean history looms rich with magnificent accomplishments against great odds as well as significant failures. But in great struggles, the goal is to win the long war, not surrender after the first defeat. Failures should not be confused with inability, nor should the lack of opportunity be equated with a lack of vision or a lack of will. A region that has produced leaders and thinkers of the caliber of Toussaint Louverture, José Martí, Fidel Castro, Marcus Garvey, Norman Manley, Alexander Bustamante, Eugenio María de Hostos, Luis Muñoz Marín, Arthur Lewis, Derek Walcott, Grantley Adams, Errol Barrow, George Lamming,

J. J. Thomas, George Padmore, C. L. R. James, Eric Williams, Cheddi Jagan, Martin Carter, Aimé Césaire, Edwidge Danticat, Forbes Burnham, and George Price has already established a distinguished tradition of men of vision and will. Moreover, in terms of both the state and the nation, they are all relatively new states and new societies. Only Haiti and the Dominican Republic have an independent history stretching back to the nineteenth century. All the other states are products of the twentieth century. And like the polities, the people are youthful. With the surges in the population during the middle decades of the twentieth century, by 1989 nearly 50 percent of the regional population was less than eighteen years of age. The Caribbean is a region of youthful vigor—and that may be its greatest asset.

The diverse challenges of the present and the future loom dauntingly large in the Caribbean. Natural disasters across the Caribbean arrive with monotonous predictability and often with catastrophic impact. Some states handle these disasters far better than do others, and regional cooperative action is always rapid and spontaneous. Calamity usually brings out the best in intraregional goodwill. In 2010 Cuba and the Dominican Republic instantly responded with massive medical and humanitarian aid to the earthquake in Haiti. But other challenges are harder to combat collectively. International narcotic trafficking has been insidiously undermining the administrative effectiveness of all states, and the solution has so far escaped local and regional governments. Political systems everywhere appear to be losing popular support, and political parties no longer demonstrate efficacious ways of mobilizing their mass support. Nowhere in the Caribbean has the manner of political succession been worked out satisfactorily, and it is remarkable how few states have shown signs of breakdown. The general economic problems also constitute a constant challenge. Globalization of commerce challenges the viability of sustained economic well-being at a time when aid from conventional benefactors seems scarce. Without doubt it will not be easy for small countries, such as those in the Caribbean, in the new millennium. Yet if the past is prologue, the Caribbean will meet each challenge with determination, resilience, and fortitude—and in most cases, success. While it will not be easy, most states will overcome their challenges. The new times demand new measures and new ideas as well as new men of clear vision and strong will. The historical circumstances of the region have always forced it to be a revolutionary society, not to destroy or disturb but to survive. The urgencies of the twenty-first century make that revolutionary tradition most appropriate. The old order has definitely changed, but what is new is not yet clear. Imported panaceas have merely produced false promises. Maybe the time has finally arrived to seek out bold local solutions for local problems. The survival of individual Caribbean sovereignty rests not in the continued pursuit of insular options, but in regional cooperation on a scale never before attempted. In cooperation lies future possibilities. What Père Labat observed in 1743 remains true: the Caribbean peoples "are all together, in the same boat, sailing on the same uncertain sea...citizenship and race unimportant." The time has never been more appropriate for the fragmented

Caribbean community to begin to think seriously and cooperatively about the welfare of their entire community.

SUGGESTED READINGS

Bardach, Ann Louise. *Without Fidel: A Death Foretold in Miami, Havana, and Washington.* New York: Scribner, 2009.

Brereton, Bridget, ed. *General History of the Caribbean: Volume V. The Caribbean in the Twentieth Century.* London: UNESCO/Macmillan, 2004.

Bryan, Patrick E. *Edward Seaga and the Challenges of Modern Jamaica.* Kingston, Jamaica: University of the West Indies Press, 2009.

Chamberlain, Mary. *Family Love in the Diaspora: Migration and the Anglo-Caribbean Experience.* Kingston, Jamaica: Ian Randle, 2006.

Craton, Michael. *Pindling: The Life and Times of the First Prime Minister of the Bahamas, 1930–2000.* Oxford, England: Macmillan, 2002.

Desch, Michael C., Domínguez, Jorge, and Serbín, Andrés, eds. *From Pirates to Drug Lords: The Post-Cold War Caribbean Security Environment.* Albany: State University of New York Press, 1998.

Diaz-Briquets, Sergio. *The Health Revolution in Cuba.* Austin: University of Texas Press, 1983.

Dupuy, Alex. *Haiti in the New World Order: The Limits of the Democratic Revolution.* Boulder, Colo.: Westview Press, 1997.

Gjelten, Tom. *Bacardi and the Long Fight for Cuba: The Biography of a Cause.* New York: Viking, 2008.

Gliejeses, Piero. *Conflicting Missions: Havana, Washington, and Africa, 1959–1976.* Chapel Hill: University of North Carolina Press, 2001.

Griffith, Ivelaw L., ed. *The Political Economy of Drugs in the Caribbean.* New York: St. Martin's Press, 2000.

Guerra, Lillian. *Popular Expression and National Identity in Puerto Rico: The Struggle for Self, Community, and Nation.* Gainesville: University Press of Florida, 1998.

Harriott, Anthony. *Organized Crime and Politics in Jamaica: Breaking the Nexus.* Kingston, Jamaica: University of the West Indies Press, 2008.

Henke, Holger, and Reno, Fred, ed. *Modern Political Culture in the Caribbean.* Kingston, Jamaica: University of the West Indies Press, 2003.

Hernández, Rafael. *Looking at Cuba: Essays on Culture and Civil Society.* Translated by Dick Cluster. Gainesville: University Press of Florida, 2007.

Higman, B. W. *Jamaican Food: History, Biology, Culture.* Kingston, Jamaica: University of the West Indies Press, 2008.

Higman, B. W. *A Concise History of the Caribbean.* New York: Cambridge University Press, 2011.

Howard, Michael. *The Economic Development of Barbados.* Kingston, Jamaica: University of the West Indies Press, 2006.

Knight, Franklin W., and Martínez-Vergne, Teresita, eds. *Contemporary Caribbean Cultures and Societies in a Global Context.* Chapel Hill: University of North Carolina Press, 2005.

Levi, Darrell. *Michael Manley: The Making of a Leader.* Athens: University of Georgia Press, 1990.

Manley, Michael. *Jamaica: Struggle in the Periphery.* London: Third World Media, 1982.

McAvoy, Muriel. *Sugar Baron: Manuel Rionda and the Fortunes of Pre-Castro Cuba.* Gainesville: University Press of Florida, 2003.

McGillivray, Gillian. *Blazing Cane: Sugar Communities, Class, and State Formation in Cuba, 1868–1959.* Durham, N.C.: Duke University Press, 2009.

Meeks, Brian. *Envisioning Caribbean Futures: Jamaican Perspectives.* Kingston, Jamaica: University of the West Indies Press, 2007.

Morales Domínguez, Esteban. *Desafíos de la problemática racial en Cuba.* Havana: Fundación Fernando Ortiz, 2007.

Palmer, Colin A. *Eric Williams and the Making of the Modern Caribbean.* Chapel Hill: University of North Carolina Press, 2006.

Palmer, Colin A. *The Politics of Power: Cheddi Jagan, Great Britain, the United States, and the Struggle for British Guiana.* Chapel Hill: University of North Carolina Press, 2011.

Payne, Anthony, and Sutton, Paul. *Charting Caribbean Development.* Gainesville: University Press of Florida, 2001.

Peguero, Valentina. *The Militarization of Culture in the Dominican Republic, from the Captains General to General Trujillo.* Lincoln: University of Nebraska Press, 2004.

Pérez-Stable, Marifeli. *The Cuban Revolution: Origins, Course, and Legacy.* New York: Oxford University Press, 1999.

Plaza, Dwaine E., and Henry, Frances, eds. *Returning to the Source: The Final Stage of the Caribbean Migration Circuit.* Kingston, Jamaica: University of the West Indies Press, 2006.

Rathbone, John Paul. *The Sugar King of Havana: The Rise and Fall of Julio Lobo, Cuba's Last Tycoon.* New York: Penguin Press, 2010.

Romberg, Raquel. *Witchcraft and Welfare: Spiritual Capital and the Business of Magic in Modern Puerto Rico.* Austin: University of Texas Press, 2003.

Schoultz, Lars. *That Infernal Little Cuban Republic: The United States and the Cuban Revolution.* Chapel Hill: University of North Carolina Press, 2009.

Swan, Quito. *Black Power in Bermuda: The Struggle for Decolonization.* New York: Palgrave Macmillan, 2009.

Warner-Lewis, Maureen. *Central Africa in the Caribbean: Transcending Time, Transforming Cultures.* Kingston, Jamaica: University of the West Indies Press, 2003.

Weintraub, Amelia Rosenberg. *Cuba in the Shadow of Change: Daily Life in the Twilight of the Revolution.* Gainesville: University Press of Florida, 2009.

Chronology

1492	October 12, Christopher Columbus, sailing under the Spanish flag, sights land somewhere in the Bahamas and thereby begins the integration of America, Europe, Africa, and Asia. The Atlantic world takes shape. October 28, Columbus lands along the Cuban coast. December 6, Columbus lands along the coast of Santo Domingo and after the wreck of his flagship, *Santa María,* establishes the first transient European settlement in the New World.
1493	Second voyage of Columbus. Between November 3 and 19, he sights a number of islands between Dominica and Puerto Rico, including Guadeloupe, Montserrat, and St. Kitts. On November 14, the first sea battle takes place in Caribbean waters between the Spanish *flotilla* and a group of Indian canoes.
1494	May 5, Jamaican north shore explored.
1498	Third voyage of Columbus. Visits Cuba. Discovers Grenada, St. Vincent, Trinidad, and the Guyana coastline. First gold rush on Santo Domingo.
1501	Nicolás de Ovando named governor of Santo Domingo, effectively revoking the original Columbus charter.
1502	April 3, Columbus's fourth and last voyage begins at Seville, and after a delay he lands at Martinique on June 15. Battered by storms, the fleet explores the islands and the coast from Honduras to Panama. Ovando arrives in Santo Domingo.
1503–04	Columbus sails through the Cayman Islands and is marooned on the north shore of Jamaica with 115 men. Casa de Contratación established at Seville to regulate shipping to the New World as well as to collect the "royal fifth" of gold, pearls, and trade goods. Spanish expansion to Puerto Rico begins.

1508   Juan Ponce de Léon officially settles Puerto Rico and finds gold. Reports that Indians on Hispaniola are rapidly diminishing.

1509–10   Juan de Esquivel settles Jamaica. First sugar mills started on Hispaniola.

1511   Diego de Velázquez settles Cuba. Council of the Indies established. Fray Antonio de Montesinos preaches sermon against the ill-treatment of Indians that converts an *encomendero* of Santo Domingo named Bartolomé de las Casas.

1512   Laws of Burgos, first European colonial charter, attempts to establish proper official relations between Spanish and non-Spanish society in the Americas.

1515   First exports of Caribbean sugar to Spain.

1516   Las Casas appointed Protector of Indians.

1518   August. Charles V grants permission for 4,000 African slaves to be sent to the Antilles to relieve the labor shortage, especially in the mines.

1519   Hernán Cortés sails from Cuba to conquer Mexico.

1542   New Laws of the Indies. Spanish begin convoy system to protect their silver fleet from pirates, privateers, and envious rival European powers.

1585   Challenges to Spanish hegemony lead to expansion of escorted *flotillas* and retrenchment to fortified, defensible enclaves.

1595   Spain begins formal grants of *asientos* to supply African slaves to the Indies.

1604   Spanish concede inability to monopolize the Americas at the Treaty of London. Dutch developing salt industry off Venezuelan coast.

1609   Spanish concede limitations of their American possessions at Truce of Antwerp. Bermuda settled.

1609–20   Attempts by English and Dutch to plant permanent colonies on periphery of Spanish possessions in eastern Antilles and Guiana. Dutch succeed in Essequibo in 1616.

1621   Dutch West India Company formally established.

1624   English settle Barbados and St. Kitts. Dutch settle Berbice.

1625   Dutchman Piet Heyn captures Spanish treasure fleet off Matanzas Bay, Cuba. Nevis settled by English.

1630–97   Age of buccaneers.

1630–40   Dutch establish themselves on Curaçao, Saba, St. Martin, St. Eustatius. English settle Antigua, Montserrat, St. Lucia. French settle Martinique and Guadeloupe.

1640   Population of Barbados estimated at 30,000.

1647   First Barbados sugar sent to England.

1648   Dutch and French divide island of St. Martin.

1649   First slave revolt on Barbados.

1651   British colonists settle Suriname.

1652   Navigation Ordinance attempts to implement mercantilism; leads to series of naval wars between English and Dutch. First Anglo-Dutch war.

1655   Jamaica captured from the Spanish. Ceded along with Cayman Islands in 1670.

1666–67 Second Anglo-Dutch war. Treaty of Breda (1667) gives Suriname to the Dutch in exchange for the Dutch colony on Manhattan Island, New York.

1672–78 Third Anglo-Dutch war. Royal Africa Company organized by the English.

1684   English Crown takes over Bermuda.

1685   French systematize their slave system by promulgation of the *Code Noir*.

1692   Earthquake destroys city of Port Royal, Jamaica.

1697   Spain cedes western Hispaniola to France at the Treaty of Ryswick.

1702   French Guinea Company gains the *asiento*.

1713   England exacts from France and Spain, a transfer of the *asiento* to a semi-official commercial front, the South Sea Company.

1728   University of Havana founded.

1734   First Maroon war in Jamaica.

1739   Spanish government suspends the South Sea Company's *asiento*, leading to War of Jenkin's Ear.

1739–63 Wars between European powers over Caribbean commerce and possessions. Capture of Havana by the English. French lose all possessions except Saint-Domingue during the period.

1740   Real Campañía Mercantil de la Habana, or Havana Company, formed to develop Cuban slave trade and agriculture.

1754   Moravian missions established in Jamaica.

1755   Barcelona Company chartered to trade with Puerto Rico and Santo Domingo.

1766–76 Expansion of free trade in the Caribbean.

1767   French Caribbean sugar exports exceed British.

1772   English chief justice, Lord Mansfield, declares slavery illegal in England.

1774   Cuban census estimates population at 171,620.

1778   Ackee fruit introduced to Jamaica from West Africa.

1783   Grenada ceded to British at Treaty of Versailles.

1788   Outbreak of the French Revolution. Société des Amis des Noirs founded in France.

1789   Cuba begins free trade in slaves. Methodists begin missions in Jamaica. Declaration of Rights of Man and the Citizen in France.

1791   Havana Economic Society formed by 27 Creoles. Slave revolt begins in Saint-Domingue.

1792   French National Assembly abolishes racial discrimination in determining citizenship.

1793   Breadfruit tree introduced to Jamaica from Tahiti. British navy captures Martinique, Guadeloupe, and St. Lucia.

1794   French National Assembly temporarily abolished slavery.

1795   Second Maroon war in Jamaica. Carib war in St. Vincent. Outbreak of Julien Fedon's 16-month rebellion in Grenada.

1797   Trinidad captured by the British.

1798   Toussaint Louverture establishes domination of ex-slaves in Saint-Domingue.

1799   Toussaint made governor-general of Saint-Domingue and captures Santo Domingo.

1800   Scottish Missionary Society begins work in Jamaica. As a result of the loss of Santo Domingo, *audiencia* transferred to Cuba, giving the island jurisdiction over Puerto Rico, Florida, and Louisiana.

1801   Toussaint announces the first constitution for Saint-Domingue.

1802   Napoleon decides to reconquer Saint-Domingue and kidnaps Toussaint.

1804   Jean-Jacques Dessalines declares the independence of Haiti. Denmark abolishes its transatlantic slave trade.

1808   Great Britain and the United States abolish the slave trade.

1811   British Parliament declares slave trading a felony.

1813   Sweden abolishes the slave trade.

1814   First English Baptist missions in Jamaica.

1815   End of Napoleonic wars. British purchase Demerara, Essequibo, and Berbice from the Dutch, consolidating them into British Guiana in 1831.

1816   Cuban sugar planters win the right to deal in real estate.

1817   Spain accepts £400,000 to abolish the slave trade after 1820.

1818   France and Holland agree to abolish the slave trade.

1821–23 Conspiracy called *Soles y Rayos de Bolívar* (Sons and Rays of Bolívar) in Cuba aimed at the abolition of slavery and independence.

1822–44 Haitian occupation of Santo Domingo.

1823   Grenada grants full citizenship to free nonwhites. Large slave revolts in British Guiana.

1827   British Parliament declares slave trading to be piracy and therefore punishable by death.

1828   Order in Council abolishes all civil and military distinctions based on race in Crown Colonies.

1831–32 Antimissionary riots in Barbados, Jamaica, and British Guiana. Jamaica and Barbados grant full citizenship to Jews and free nonwhites. Tax on munumission abolished in French Antilles, and free persons of color granted full citizenship.

1833   Emancipation Act passed by British Parliament initiating apprenticeship system in British Antilles effective 1834. Grande Anse slave revolt in Martinique. Compulsory registration of slaves in the French Antilles.

1834   Havana-Güines railroad begun. British Guiana imports laborers from Madeira. Antigua abolishes slavery without apprenticeship. Elected councils on restricted franchise begin in Martinique and Guadeloupe. French Society for the Abolition of Slavery founded to replace Amis des Noirs.

1836   Slavery declared illegal in France.

1838   Havana-Güines railroad completed. Slavery finally abolished in British Antilles.

1840   Codrington College completed in Barbados.

1844   Conspiracy of *La Escalera* discovered in Cuba.

1845   Jamaica opens second railroad in the Caribbean, from Kingston to Angels.

1846   Sweden abolishes slavery. Peasants revolt in Haiti. British Parliament removes preferential tariffs on colonial sugar imports.

1848   Slavery abolished in French and Danish Antilles. French Antilles given direct representation in National Assembly.

1849–52   Narciso López expeditions against Cuba.

1853   José Martí born in Cuba.

1854   French Antillean representation in National Assembly suspended until 1871. Plans by U.S. to purchase Cuba fail.

1861–64   Santo Domingo made a province of Spain.

1863   Holland abolishes slavery.

1865   Morant Bay "revolt" in Jamaica. Crown Colony established. Santo Domingo declares its independence and becomes a republic.

1868   *Grito de Lares* in Puerto Rico. *Grito de Yara* in Cuba. "Glorious revolution" begins in Spain.

1868–78   Ten Years' War in Cuba.

1869   Puerto Rico made a province of Spain.

1873   Puerto Rico abolishes slavery. Last-known slave ship lands in Cuba. Fifty-three members of cruiser *Virginia* shot in Santiago Harbor for aiding Cuban insurgents.

1878   Pact of Zanjón ends Cuban Civil War.

1886   Cuba abolishes slavery, thereby ending legal slavery in the Caribbean.

1887   Marcus Garvey born in Jamaica.

1895–98   Second Cuban War of Independence. José Martí dies at Dos Ríos, May 19, 1895.

1897   Spain grants autonomy to Puerto Rico.

1899   Treaty of Paris. Spain cedes Cuba, Puerto Rico, and the Philippines to the United States. U.S. military occupies Cuba until 1902.

1900   Puerto Rico becomes a U.S. territory.

1902   Republic of Cuba established. Platt Amendment gives U.S. right to intervene in Cuban affairs and to establish naval base at Guantánamo

Bay. Major volcanic eruption of Soufrière in St. Vincent (kills 2,000 persons) and of Mount Pelée in Martinique (kills 40,000). Virgin Islands Legislative Council abolished. Danish legislature refuses to sanction sale of Antilles to U.S. Urban riots in Montego Bay, Jamaica, and Port of Spain, Trinidad.

1905   Riots in British Guiana. U.S. assumes control of Dominican Republic revenues.

1906   Second U.S. intervention in Cuba (until 1909).

1908   Riots in St. Lucia.

1912   Demonstrations by Afro-Cubans in Oriente, led by Estenoz and Ivonet, viciously suppressed with more than 3,000 blacks killed. Riots in Kingston, Jamaica. Revolt in the Dominican Republic.

1915   Revolt in Haiti. U.S. occupies Haiti (until 1934).

1916   U.S. occupies Dominican Republic (until 1924).

1917   Puerto Ricans become citizens of the United States. "February Revolution" in Cuba brings U.S. troops to Oriente (until 1922). Danish Antilles sold for £25,000,000 to U.S. East Indian immigration to English Antilles ends.

1919   Riots in Belize, British Honduras, and San Fernando, Trinidad.

1921   Imperial College of Tropical Agriculture opened in Trinidad.

1925   Isle of Pines issue settled in favor of Cuba. Gerardo Machado becomes president of Cuba.

1926–35   Several hurricanes sweep through the Caribbean. Earthquake tremors are felt on Montserrat for two years.

1928   British Guiana abolishes old constitution and establishes a Legislative Council.

1930   Pedro Albizu Campos elected president of Puerto Rican Nationalist Party. Trujillo assumes power in the Dominican Republic.

1933   Machado overthrown in Cuba; Fulgencio Batista emerges as strongman.

1934   U.S. abrogates the Platt Amendment.

1935   Riots in St. Vincent begin series of labor troubles throughout the British Caribbean.

1936   Constitutional change in British Honduras, British Windward, and British Leeward Islands provides for elected members to the Legislative Councils, with a majority elected in the Windwards.

1937   Riots in Barbados and Trinidad. Trujillo massacres 20,000 Haitian cane cutters in Dominican Republic.

1938   Riots in Jamaica. Political parties established in Jamaica. Moyne Commission investigates economic conditions in the British West Indies.

1940   Luis Muñoz Marín becomes Senate president in Puerto Rico. Cuba gets new constitution. Dominica separated from Leeward Islands and included in Windward Islands. Development and Welfare Organization established for all British Antilles.

1941	Anglo-American agreement grants bases to U.S. throughout the British West Indies.
1942	Anglo-American Commission established.
1943	Caribbean regiment established in the British West Indies. British Guiana gets elected majority in the Legislative Council.
1944	Universal adult suffrage granted to Jamaica, with limited self-government. Women given the vote in Barbados, British Guiana, and Bermuda.
1945	Electoral franchise extended to British Guiana and British Honduras. Aimé Césaire elected mayor of Fort de France.
1946	Puerto Rico gets first local governor, Jesus T. Piñero. Martinique, Guadeloupe, and French Guiana made overseas departments of France. First British West Indies census. Trinidad gets universal adult suffrage.
1947	Puerto Rico allowed to elect own governor. Conference held at Montego Bay, Jamaica, to discuss federation of British West Indies.
1948	Luis Muñoz Marín becomes first elected Puerto Rican governor. Colonial Development Corporation established for British West Indies. British Honduras threatened by invasion from Guatemala.
1949	Royal charter granted for the University College of the West Indies.
1950	Universal adult suffrage introduced to Barbados. Trinidad gets a new constitution. Widespread riots in Puerto Rico over constitutional issue.
1951	Riots in Antigua and Grenada. Universal adult suffrage introduced to Leeward and Windward Islands.
1952	Batista coup d'état in Cuba. Commonwealth status established for Puerto Rico. Universal adult suffrage granted to British Guiana. Dutch constitution amended to alter status of colonial possessions.
1953	Fidel Castro leads unsuccessful Moncada Barracks attack on July 26 in Santiago de Cuba. British Guiana constitution suspended.
1954	Dutch Antilles and Suriname made autonomus and equal with the Netherlands.
1956	Eric Williams forms People's National Movement in Trinidad. Fidel Castro returns from Mexico in *Granma*.
1957	François Duvalier elected president of Haiti; writes new constitution.
1958	Federation established among ten territories of the British Antilles (dissolved in 1962).
1959	Fidel Castro comes to power in Cuba.
1961	Trujillo assassinated in the Dominican Republic. U.S., Venezuela, and Colombia sever diplomatic ties with Cuba. Abortive U.S.-sponsored invasion at Playa Girón (Bay of Pigs) in Cuba. Racial violence breaks out in British Guiana.
1962	Jamaica and Trinidad and Tobago become independent. Cuba expelled from Organization of American States (OAS). Juan Bosch wins first free elections in 38 years in the Dominican Republic.

1965	U.S. invades the Dominican Republic with troops from OAS.
1966	Barbados and Guyana become independent.
1967	Trinidad and Tobago and Barbados join OAS. "Che" Guevara dies in Bolivia. Puerto Rico holds plebiscite on status issue. British Virgin Islands get new constitution.
1968	Caribbean free-trade area formed. Bermuda gets new constitution.
1969	Jamaica joins OAS. Armed clashes between Guyana and Suriname. Riots in Curaçao.
1970	Guyana becomes a republic. Riots in Trinidad. Year of the 10-million-ton sugar drive in Cuba.
1973	Fidel Castro makes two-month tour of Eastern Europe, Russia, and Africa. Bahamas gains independence.
1974	Grenada gains independence. Riots in Suriname. Poder Popular ("People's Power") implemented in Matanzas Province, Cuba. Castro visits Guyana and Trinidad en route to West Africa, Algeria, India, and North Vietnam. Jamaica, Trinidad and Tobago, Guyana, and Barbados form Caribbean Community and Common Market (CARICOM).
1975	OAS foreign ministers vote to alter 13-year boycott of Cuba and to allow individual states to reestablish normal diplomatic relations. Suriname becomes independent.
1976	Socialist constitution implemented in Cuba. Island divided into 14 jurisdictions. Trinidad and Tobago becomes a republic. Cuban troops sent to Angola.
1977	St. Lucia gains independence. Cuba and U.S. open Interests Sections in Washington and Havana.
1978	Dominica gains independence as a republic.
1979	St. Vincent and the Grenadines gain independence. Sixth summit of Nonaligned Nations in Havana. Bishop and New Jewel Movement overthrow Gairy in Grenada, replacing Parliament with People's Revolutionary Government.
1980	Tobago House of Assembly given autonomous powers over finances, economic development, and social services. Mariel boatlift brings 125,000 Cubans to the U.S. Anguilla leaves St. Kitts-Nevis-Anguilla association.
1981	Antigua and Barbuda and Belize gain independence.
1983	St. Kitts-Nevis gains independence. U.S. invades Grenada, ending People's Revolutionary Government tenure.
1986	Aruba gains separate status within Kingdom of the Netherlands. Jean-Claude Duvalier overthrown in Haiti.
1987	Cuba and U.S. agree on return of 2,500 Marielitos in exchange for 20,000 emigrants annually.
1989	Cubans agree to join talks to settle Namibian problem.
1991	Collapse of the Soviet Union. Cuba begins "Special Period in time of Peace."

1994   Association of Caribbean States formed with secretariat in Port of Spain, Trinidad.

2006   Fidel Castro hands over control to his brother, Raul.

Portia Simpson-Miller succeeds P. J. Patterson to become the first female prime minister of Jamaica.

2008   Fidel Castro resigns from the government, and the governing party elects Raul Castro president of Cuba.

2010   Massive earthquake destroys southern Haiti. Trinidad elects its first female prime minister, Kamla Persad-Bissessar.

Tables

Table 1. Africans Supplied to Barbados, 1673–1684

YEAR	NUMBER OF CARGOES	SLAVES	ESTIMATED AVERAGE DELIVERY PRICE IN POUNDS STERLING
1673	1	204	18
1674	4	1,006	20
1675	6	1,506	17
1676	7	1,833	15
1677	4	886	15
1678	8	2,053	15
1679	5	569	15
1680	6	1,340	15
1681	11	1,501	12
1682	8	1,033	14
1683	18	2,963	13
1684	6	1,380	14
Totals	84[a]	16,274[b]	

[a] Average cargo: 194 slaves

[b] Average annual importation: 1,356 slaves

NOTE: Estimated average delivery prices rounded to nearest pound sterling and based on the recalculation of Harlow's average price per cargo.

Table 2. Slave Importation Distribution by Percentages, 1600–1870

REGION	PERCENTAGE OF TOTAL TRADE			
	1600–1700	1701–1810	1811–1870	1500–1870
Br. N.A./USA	?	5.8	3.0	4.5
Brazil	41.0	31.0	60.0	40.0
British Antilles	20.0	23.0	—	18.0
Spanish America	21.8	9.6	32.0	17.0
French Antilles	12.0	22.0	5.0	16.5
Dutch Antilles	3.0	7.6	—	3.0
Danish Antilles	0.3	0.4	—	3.0
Est. total imports	1,400,000	6,000,000	2,000,000	9,500,000

SOURCE: P. D. Curtin, *The Atlantic Slave Trade.*

Table 3. Sugar Production and Slave Population Figures in Selected Colonies, 1643–1860

COLONY	YEAR	SUGAR IN TONS	SLAVE POPULATION
Barbados	1643	—	6,000
	1680	—	38,400
	1712	6,343	42,000
	1757	7,068	63,600
	1792	9,025	64,300
	1809	6,062	69,400
	1834	19,728	82,000
Jamaica	1703	4,782	45,000
	1730	15,972	74,500
	1754	23,396	130,000
	1775	47,690	190,000
	1789	59,400	250,000
	1808	77,800	324,000
	1834	62,812	311,070
Guadeloupe	1674	2,106	4,300
	1730	6,230	26,800
	1767	7,898	71,800
	1790	8,725	85,500
	1820	22,300	88,400
	1838	35,124	93,300
Saint-Domingue	1720	10,500	—
	1739	?	117,411
	1764	ca. 60,000	206,000
	1776	76,000	240,000
	1789	70,313	452,000
	1791	78,696	480,000
	1836	8	—
Cuba	1774	10,000	44,300
	1792	18,571	85,900
	1817	43,415	199,100
	1827	ca. 70,000	286,900
	1841	162,425	352,483
	1860	447,000	367,400
St. Croix	1754	ca. 730	7,566
	1770	8,230	2,364
	1786	12,100	2,850
	1803	15,700	3,030
	1821	23,000	—
	1840	7,000	—
	1860	7,600	—

Table 4. Caribbean Population by Castes, Early Nineteenth Century

COLONY	YEAR	TOTAL POPULATION	SLAVE POPULATION			FREE NONWHITE POPULATION				WHITE POPULATION		
			SLAVE POPULATION	AS % OF COLONY'S TOTAL	AS % OF NON-WHITE	NO.	AS % OF TOTAL	AS % OF ALL NON-WHITES	AS % FREE	NO.	AS % OF COLONY'S TOTAL	% FREE
BRITISH ANTILLES												
Anguilla	1819	3,080	2,388	77.5	88.0	327	10.6	10.0	47.2	365	11.0	52.8
Antigua	1832	35,412	29,537	83.4	89.3	3,531	10.0	10.7	64.0	1,980	5.6	36.0
Bahamas	1810	16,718	11,146	66.7	87.4	1,600	9.6	12.6	29.2	3,872	23.0	70.8
Barbados	1834	100,000	80,861	80.6	92.5	6,584	6.5	7.5	33.9	12,797	12.7	66.1
Barbuda		?										
Berbice	1811	25,959	25,169	97.0	99.0	240	1.0	1.0	30.3	550	2.0	69.7
Bermuda	1812	9,900	4,794	48.4	91.4	451	4.6	8.6	8.7	4,755	48.0	91.3
Demerara	1811	57,386	53,655	93.5	96.0	2,223	3.9	4.0	51.3	2,108	3.6	48.7
Dominica	1811	26,041	21,728	83.4	87.9	2,988	11.4	12.1	69.3	1,325	5.2	30.7
Essequibo	1811	19,645	18,125	92.3	96.0	757	3.9	4.0	50.0	763	3.9	50.0
Grenada & Carriacou	1811	31,362	29,381	93.6	96.0	1,120	3.9	4.0	61.0	771	2.5	39.0
Br. Honduras	1790	2,656	2,024	76.2	84.5	371	14.0	15.5	58.7	261	9.8	41.3
Jamaica	1800	340,000	300,000	88.2	89.5	35,000	10.2	10.5	70.0	15,000	4.4	25.0
Montserrat	1812	7,383	6,537	88.5	94.2	402	5.4	5.8	47.5	444	6.1	52.5
Nevis	1812	10,430	9,326	89.4	93.9	603	5.8	6.1	54.6	501	4.8	45.4
St. Christopher	1812	23,491	19,885	84.6	90.9	1,996	8.5	9.1	55.4	1,610	6.9	44.6
St. Lucia	1810	17,485	14,397	82.3	88.5	1,878	10.7	11.5	60.8	1,210	7.0	39.2
St. Vincent	1812	24,253	22,020	90.8	94.0	1,406	5.7	6.0	62.9	827	3.4	37.1

	Year											
Tobago	1811	17,830	16,897	94.8	98.0	350	2.0	2.0	37.5	583	3.2	62.5
Tortola		?										
Trinidad	1811	32,664	21,143	64.7	73.8	7,493	22.9	26.2	63.3	4,353	13.3	36.7
Virgin Islands		?										
DANISH ANTILLES												
St. Croix	1841	—	20,000			?				3,200		
St. John		?										
St. Thomas	1841	7,000	5,000	71.4	76.9	1,500	21.4	23.0	75.0	500	7.2	25.0
DUTCH ANTILLES												
Saba		?										
St. Eustatia	1850	2,500	2,000	80.0	95.2	100	4.0	4.8	20.0	400	16.0	80.0
St. Martin	1850	3,600	3,000	83.3	—	?	—	—	—	600	16.6	—
Curaçao	1833	15,027	5,894	39.2	47.4	6,531	43.5	52.6	71.4	2,602	17.3	28.6
Suriname	1830	56,325	48,784	86.6	90.6	5,041	8.9	9.4	66.8	2,500	4.4	33.2
SPANISH ANTILLES												
Cuba	1827	704,487	286,942	40.7	32.9	106,494	15.1	27.1	25.5	311,051	44.1	74.5
Puerto Rico	1860	583,181	41,738	7.1	14.8	241,037	41.3	85.2	44.5	300,406	51.5	55.5
Santo Domingo	1791	125,000	15,000	12.0	?	?						
SWEDISH ANTILLES												
St. Bartholomew	1804	7,000	?			?				?		

Continued

Table 4. Caribbean Population by Castes, Early Nineteenth Century (Continued)

COLONY	YEAR	TOTAL POPULATION	SLAVE POPULATION			FREE NONWHITE POPULATION				WHITE POPULATION		
			SLAVE POPULATION	AS % OF COLONY'S TOTAL	AS % OF NON-WHITE	NO.	AS % OF TOTAL	AS % OF ALL NON-WHITES	AS % FREE	NO.	AS % OF COLONY'S TOTAL	% FREE
FRENCH ANTILLES												
Guadaloupe	1836	107,810	81,642	75.7								
Martinique	1789	96,158	83,414	86.7	94.0	5,235	5.4	6.0	33.3	10,636	11.0	66.7
Saint-Domingue	1791	520,000	452,000	86.9	94.0	28,000	5.3	6.0	41.0	40,000	7.6	59.0
Guiana												
St. Martin	1836	3,869	2,925	75.6								
Marie Galante	1836	13,188	10,116	76.7								
Saintes	1836	1,139	569	49.9								
Desirada	1836	1,568	1,070	68.2								

Table 5a. British Antilles Sugar Production and Exports, 1815–1894

COLONY	1815	1828	1882	1894
Antigua	8,032	8,848	12,670	12,382
Barbados	8,837	16,942	48,325	50,958
British Guiana	16,520	40,115	124,102	102,502
Dominica	2,205	2,497	3,421	1,050
Grenada	11,594	13,493	1,478	3
Jamaica	79,660	72,198	32,638	19,934
Montserrat	1,225	1,254	2,314	1,801
Nevis	2,761	2,309	16,664	16,901
St. Kitts	7,066	6,060	—	—
St. Lucia	3,661	4,162	7,506	4,485
St. Vincent	11,590	14,403	8,175	2,727
Tobago	6,044	6,167	2,518	599
Tortola	1,200	663	—	—
Trinidad	7,682	13,285	55,327	46,869
Total Br. Antilles	168,077	202,396	315,138	260,211

Table 5b. Non-British Caribbean Sugar Production and Exports, 1815–1894

STATE	CA. 1815	CA. 1828	CA. 1882	CA. 1894
Martinique	15,814 (1818)	32,812	47,120	36,353
Guadeloupe	20,792 (1818)	35,244	56,592	43,041
Surinam	5,692 (1816)	11,728 (1825)	5,410 (1885)	8,023 (1895)
St. Croix	20,535 (1812)	10,576 (1830)	8,482 (1890)[a]	8,000 (est.)
Puerto Rico	1,093	31,714 (1843)	65,000 (1886)	45,500
Cuba	39,961	73,200 (1829)	595,000[b]	1,054,002[b]

[a] Average for years 1880–1890
[b] Production figures

Table 6. Haitian Export Before and After the Revolution

COMMODITY	1789	1801	1818	1820	1826	1836	1841
Sugar	141,089,831	18,535,112	5,443,765	2,517,289	32,864	16,199	1,363
Coffee	76,835,219	43,420,270	26,065,200	35,137,759	32,189,784	37,662,672	34,114,717
Cotton	7,004,274	2,480,340	474,118	346,839	620,972	1,072,555	1,591,454
Cacao	—	648,518	434,368	556,424	457,592	550,484	640,618
Indigo	758,628	804	—	—	—	—	—
Dyewoods	—	6,768,634	6,819,300	1,919,748	5,307,745	6,767,902	45,071,391
Tobacco	—	—	19,140	97,600	340,588	1,222,716	3,219,690
Castor oil	—	—	121	157	—	—	265
Cigars	—	—	—	—	179,500	33,000	728,650
Hides	—	—	—	—	—	14,891	27,126
Old rags	—	—	—	—	—	275	44,596
Wax	—	—	—	—	—	15,620	43,413
Ginger	—	—	—	—	—	15,509	15,822

NOTE: All commodities in pounds except castor oil, measured in gallons, and cigars and hides in numbers.

Table 7. Caribbean Political Configuration, 2007

	INDEPENDENT STATES	ASSOCIATED STATES	DEPENDENCIES
	Antigua and Barbuda (1981)	Aruba	Anguilla
	Bahamas (1973)	French Guiana	Bermuda
	Barbados (1966)	Guadeloupe	British Virgin Islands
	Belize (1981)	Martinique	Cayman Islands
	Cuba (1902)	Netherlands Antilles	Montserrat
	Dominica (1978)		Turks & Caicos Islands
	Dominican Republic (1865)	Puerto Rico	
	Grenada (1974)		U.S. Virgin Islands
	Guyana (1966)		
	Haiti (1804)		
	Jamaica (1962)		
	St. Kitts-Nevis (1983)		
	St. Lucia (1977)		
	St. Vincent and the Grenadines (1979)		
	Suriname (1975)		
	Trinidad and Tobago (1962)		
Total populations	35,982,948	5,306,102	317,996
Percentages of regional population	86.48	12.75	0.76

Table 8. Caribbean Populations, 2007

STATE	POPULATION	% NONWHITE
Anguilla	6,987	99
Antigua and Barbuda	100,000	99
Aruba	65,821	98
Bahamas	235,000	94
Barbados	277,000	95
Belize	160,200	92
Bermuda	57,000	61
Br. Virgin Islands	11,858	99
Cayman Islands	21,036	99
Cuba	10,200,000	63
Dominica	100,000	99
Dominican Republic	6,400,000	84
French Guiana	88,000	99
Grenada	100,000	99
Guadeloupe	300,000	95
Guyana	825,000	98
Haiti	5,498,000	99
Jamaica	2,304,000	95
Martinique	300,000	90
Montserrat	11,852	98
Netherlands Antilles	235,000	98
Puerto Rico	3,283,000	80
St. Kitts-Nevis	45,000	99
St. Lucia	100,000	99
St. Vincent/Grenadines	100,000	98
Suriname	396,000	99
Trinidad and Tobago	1,184,000	99
Turks and Caicos Islands	9,500	99
U.S. Virgin Islands	110,800	80
Total	32,451,854	

Table 9. Organized Workers and Unemployment, 1988

STATE	NUMBER UNIONIZED	UNIONIZED % OF LABOR FORCE	% UNEMPLOYED
Anguilla	—	—	26.0
Antigua and Barbuda	25,000	—	15.0
Aruba	—	—	9.5
Bahamas	15,700	26.0	20.0
Barbados	40,000	33.0	19.0
Belize	4,000	—	14.0
Bermuda	11,000	—	0.3
Cuba	2,649,000	—	3.4
Dominica	16,000	34.0	15.5
Dominican Republic	250,000	5.0	25.0
French Guiana	—	—	15.3
Grenada	6,500	39.0	21.0
Guyana	61,493	40.0	27.0
Haiti	6,000	8.0	14.0
Jamaica	222,000	43.0	25.6
Martinique	16,000	—	30.0
Montserrat	1,800	—	5.8
Netherlands Antilles	—	—	15.8
Puerto Rico	400,000	—	18.8
St. Kitts-Nevis	10,000	—	30.0
St. Lucia	10,000	27.0	24.0
St. Vincent	5,000	—	35.0
Suriname	42,000	43.0	27.0
Trinidad and Tobago	250,000	31.0	15.0
U.S. Virgin Islands	—	—	5.8

Table 10. Caribbean Profiles, 2007

STATE	AREA (SQ. MILES/SQ. KMS)	POPULATION, 2007	POPULATION GROWTH RATE (%)	PER CAPITA INCOME	UNEMPLOYMENT AS % LABOR FORCE
Anguilla	15/91	14,000	2.2	12,200	8
Antigua/Barbuda	171/442	69,481	0.52	10,900	11
Bahamas	5,380/13,934	305,655	0.6	22,700	7.6
Belize	8,866/22,963	294,385	2.6	7,800	9.4
Barbados	166/431	280,946	0.36	19,700	10.7
Cuba	44,200/114,471	11,394,043	0.27	4,500	1.9
Dominica	289/752	72,386	0.18	3,800	23
Dominican Republic	18,712/48,464	9,365,818	1.5	9,200	15.5
Grenada	133/340	89,971	0.33	3,900	12.5
Guadeloupe	628/1,628	405,500	0.88	21,780	NA
Guyana	82,990/215,000	769,095	0.23	5,300	9
Haiti	10,714/27,750	8,706,497	2.45	1,900	66
Jamaica	4,244/10,991	2,780,132	0.78	4,800	10.2
Martinique	436/1,128	399,730	NA	21,700	NA
Puerto Rico	3,515/9,164	3,967,179	0.3	19,000	12
St. Kitts/Nevis	101/261	39,349	0.62	8,200	4.5
St. Lucia	238/619	170,649	1.29	4,800	20
St. Vincent and Grenadines	131/340	118,149	0.25	3,600	15
Suriname	63,037/163,265	470,784	1.1	7,800	9.5
Trinidad and Tobago	1,980/5,128	1,056,608	0.88	21,700	6

Index

Acosta, José Julian, 194
Adams, Grantley, 212, 215, 233, 244
Adams, J. M. G. M., 240
Adams, John, 58
Adelantado, 33
Africans, 6, 132
Agramonte, Ignacio, 169
Aguilera, Francisco, 169
Albizu Campos, Pedro, 197
Alcalá de Henares, 56
Alegría, Ricardo, 5
Alfonso XII, 193
Alonso, *vecino*, 12
Altman, Ida, 49
Alvares Cabral, Pedro, 42, 46
Andean valleys, 5
Anglo-Dutch War (1665–1667), 36
Anguilla, 2, 54, 90
Antigua, 2, 5, 35, 54, 123; free villages, 131;
    Maroons in, 66; slaves in, 89
Antilles, 7, 8
Aragón, 23
Arango y Parreño, Francisco, 151
Arawaks, 8, 9
Araya, 35
Argentina, 138
Arias Dávila, Pedro, 53
Aristide, Jean Bertande, 159
Armada de la Carrera de Indias, 33
Arrowroot, 10
Artibonite Valley, 146
Aruba, 54, 139
Asiento, 41

Associated Chambers of Commerce, 222
Association of Caribbean States (ACS),
    226, 243
Atlantic Slave Trade. The (Curtin), 79
Audiencia, 40
Austin, Hudson, 223
Ávila, Alonso de, 76
Aztecs, 9
Azua, 22, 23

Baez, Buenaventura, 160
Bahamas, 1, 2, 9, 10, 26, 27, 88, 90, 135
Bahia, (Brazil), 64, 145
Bainao, 22
Balaguer, Joaquín, 162, 233, 234
Balboa, Vasco Nuñez de, 22
Baldorioty de Castro, Roman, 194
Baleares, 23
Baltimore, 145, 152
Baracoa, 27, 29, 30, 31, 65
Barbados, 2, 5, 8, 35, 36, 50, 54, 55, 56, 63,
    77, 134; Maroons in, 66; slaves in, 89, 92;
    sugar exports, 75
Barbuda, 90
Barceló, Antonio, 198
Barcelona, 42
Barclay, Alexander, 130
Barrow, Errol, 233, 244
Basques, 125
Basse-Terre, 1
Bastille, 56, 139, 140
Batista Zaldívar, Fulgencio, 161, 172,
    174, 233

Bay of Pigs, 178
Bayamo, 27, 29, 30
Beckford and Smith's College, 210
Belair, Charles, 152
Belize, 1, 89, 90. *See also* British Honduras
Bella, Ben, 183
Beltrán de Santa Cruz y Cárdenas,
    Joaquín, 168
Berbice, 89, 90
Bermuda, 86, 88, 123
Betances, Ramón Emeterio, 192
Biassou, 152
Bird, Vere, 212, 221, 233, 241
Bishop, Maurice, 223, 233, 240
Black Caribs, 231
Black Legend, 3, 22
Blue Mountains, 66
Bobadilla, Francisco de, 20
Bogle, Paul, 209
Bohío, 10, 12
Bolívar, Simón, 155
Bolivia, 9, 138
Bonao, 22, 23
Bonaparte, Napoleon, 148 150, 152, 155
Bordeaux, 144, 145
Bosch, Juan, 233, 234
Boston, 152, 154
Boulogne, 145
Bouterse, Desire, 242
Boyd-Bowman, Peter, 24, 49
Boyer, Jean-Pierre, 157, 160
Bozales, 87
Bradshaw, Robert, 212, 215, 221
Brathwaite, Edward, 91
Brazil, 9, 34, 35, 50, 53, 57, 138
Bridgetown, 56, 66
British Guiana. *See* Guiana
British Honduras, 89, 90. *See also* Belize
British North America, 139
Brulé, Etienne, 33
Buccaneers, 51, 63, 67–74
Buenaventura, 22, 23, 25
Buenos Aires, 154
Bullbrook, J. A., 16
Bunker Hill, 139
Burnham, Forbes, 215, 233, 240, 245
Bush, George H. W., 201
Bustamante, William A., 212, 214, 215,
    222, 233, 244
Butler, Uriah, 212, 215

Cabildo, 40
Cabot, Juan and Sebastian, 42
Cacique, 10, 12
Cádiz, 28
Cahiers des doléances, 146
Calabar High School, 211
Calpulli, 12
Camagüey, 29. *See also* Sancti-Spíritus
Campbell, Carl, 215
Campeche, 76
Canada, 33
Canary Islands, 23, 24, 42
Caney, 12, 29
Cánovas del Castillo, Antonio, 192
Cap Haitien, 22
Cape Verde Islands, 32
Caquetío, 9
Caracas, 9
Caribbean: defined, 1; mentioned, 2, 3, 7,
    10–12
Caribbean Community (CARICOM),
    225, 226
Caribbean Labour Congress, 222
Caribbean Union of Teachers, 222
Caribs, 5, 8, 11–14, 17, 35, 36, 42, 150
Carlisle, Thomas, 49
Carolinas, 55
Carriacou, 86, 135
Cartagena, Colombia, 31, 32, 62, 76;
    trade, 81
Carter, Martin, 224, 244
Casa de Contratación, 20, 41, 44
Cassava. *See* Manioc
Castile, 9, 21, 50
Castro, Fidel, 156, 165, 174, 175, 186, 187,
    223, 229, 233, 234, 240, 244
Catalans, 125
Cataluña, 23
Catherine d' Medici, 32
Cato, Milton, 241
*Católogo de pasajero*s, 24
Caymans, 2, 86, 90, 135
Central Aguirre Sugar Company, 196
Central America, 1, 2, 6, 7
Central Constancia, 132
Césaire, Aimé, 243, 244
Céspedes, Carlos Manuel de, 169
Champlain, Samuel de, 33
Charles II, 72, 73, 77
Charles III, 166

Charles V, 22, 33, 43, 44, 48
Charles, Eugenia, 241
Charleston, 152
Chesapeake Bay, 139
Chibcha, 9
Child, Josiah, 85
Chile, 138
Chinese, 132
Christophe, Henry, 149, 152, 156
Cibao, 25
Ciboney, 5–8, 12
Cipriani, Andrew A., 212
Clavijero, Francisco Javier, 58
Club Massiac, 147
Coard, Bernard, 223
Cockpit Country, 66
Codrington College, 210, 211
Colbert, Jean-Baptiste, 40, 72, 73
Colombia, 9, 138, 151, 152
Colonization compared, 50
Colono, 133
Columbus, Christopher: quotation from
    journal, 1; mentioned, 2, 3, 6–9, 11, 12,
    17, 19, 20–22, 24, 42, 46, 47, 76;
    crews, 3
Columbus, Diego, 25, 27, 76
Columbus, Hernando, 13
Compagnie des Iles d'Amerique, 36, 39, 75
Company of Royal Adventurers, 77
Concepción de la Vega, 22, 23
Consejo de Indias, 40
Consulado, 41
Conuco, 12, 23, 25
Cooke, S. H., 209
Cooper, James Fenimore, 59
Cordillera Central, 25
Cortés, Hernán, 19, 21, 22, 27, 28
Costa Rica, 133
Coureurs de bois, 33
Courteen, William, 39
Cox, Sandy, 212
Craton, Michael, 90
Creole, 58, 59, 90, 124, 125
Creolization, 41, 56–57, 59
Cristophe, Henri, 58
Cromwell, Oliver, 71
Cromwell, Thomas, 34
Crown Colony Govenrment, 208–9
Cuba, 1, 2, 5, 6, 8; 10, 11, 21, 22, 27, 54–56,
    63, 123–25, 127, 128, 130, 132, 139, 152,

155; maroons in, 65, 67; trade, 81;
    population, 88, 89; slaves, 92; Special
    Period, 241–42; zemis in, 9
Cuban American Sugar Company, 172
Cuban Atlantic Sugar Company, 172
Cudjoe, 65, 71
Cul-de-Sac, 146, 148
Cumaná, 35
Cundall, Frank, 231
Curaçao, 35, 54, 62, 63, 85, 123, 125; free
    port, 81; white population, 88
Curtin, Philip, 44, 79

Da Gama, Vasco, 19
Danticat, Edwidge, 244
Darien, 22
Davis, Ralph, 80
De la Cosa, Juan, 42
De Pauw, Cornelius, 55, 58
Del Castillo, Juan, 29
Demerara, 89, 90, 128; riots, 219
Deschamps, Jérémie, 72
Desirade, 135
D'Esnambuc, Pierre, 36
Dessalines, Jean-Jacques, 58, 149, 152
Díaz, Manuel, 21
Díaz del Castillo, Bernal, 19, 48
Domingo, W. A., 212, 214
Dominguez, Jorge, 175
Dominica, 1, 17, 90, 150
Dominican Republic, 2, 130, 139, 159, 161,
    162, 179, 230
Drake, Francis, 32
Ducasse, Jean-Baptiste, 73
Dujos, 13
Dunn, Richard, 50, 55
Dutch West India Company, 35, 40, 41, 53
Duvalier, François, 138, 158, 233
Duvalier, Jean-Claude, 158, 233

East Indians, 130
Ecuador, 138
Edwards, Bryan, 57, 65, 142–44, 154
Ehinger, Heinrich, 43
Elizabeth I, 32
Elliott, John, 47
Empadronamiento of 1570, 29
Encomienda, 22, 24–27, 53, 76
Engages, 36, 38, 70
English Civil War, 35

Escudero, Eusebio, 65
Esmeraldas (Ecuador), 64
Esquivel, Juan de, 21, 22, 27
Essequibo, 89, 90
Estado Libre Asociado, 198
Estenoz, Evaristo, 173
Estimé, Dumarsais, 158
Estrada Palma, Tomás, 171, 172
Exquemelin, Alexander, 69, 70
Eyre, Edward John, 209

Fabian Society, 211, 220, 221
Fajardo Sugar Company, 196
Fanmi Lavalas, 159
Faron, Louis, 10, 13
Fazenda, 49
Fedon, Jean, 150
Fedon, Julien, 150
Ferdinand, King, 20, 25
Fernández, Leonel, 162, 242
Florida, 6, 21, 22, 27
Floyd, Troy, 22
Foraker Act, 195
Francisquimé, Cristóbal, 44
François, Jean, 152
Free villages, 131
French Estates General, 124, 140, 144
French Guiana, 1
French Revolution, 139
French West India Company, 40, 73
Froude, James Anthony, 51, 54, 56, 212; quoted, 55

Gage, Thomas, 34, 37, 51
Gairy, Eric Matthew, 212, 215, 221, 233, 243
Galicia, 23
Galicians, 125
Gallego, Juan, 32
García Menocal, Mario, 172
Garrevod, Lorenzo de, Duke of Bresa, 43
Garvey, Marcus Mosiah, 212, 214, 244
Gauchos, 47
Geffrard, Fabre, 157
Gens de couleur, 58, 144, 147
Gold, 25, 28
Gomes, Albert, 212, 215
Gómez, José Miguel, 172
Gonaïves, 22
Góngora, Francisco de, 32
Gorbachev, Mikhail, 184

Gordon, George William, 209
Gorjón, Hernando, 76
Granada, 23
Grands blancs, 144–46
Grau San Martín, Ramón, 172
Grenada, 1, 36, 150, 151; East Indians in, 132; revolution, 223
Grenadines, 2, 86
Grito de Yara, 169
Guacayarima, 22
Guadeloupe, 1, 36, 54, 125, 128, 144, 150, 151; East Indians in, 132
Guagua, 12
Guajiro, 12
Guanabacoa, 29, 30
Guanahuatebey, 5, 12
Guatemala, 56
Guevara, Ernesto, 174, 179, 182, 183, 240
Guiana, 35, 54, 130, 155; free villages, 131; East Indians, 132; Maroons in, 66
Gulf of Mexico, 1, 34
Guyana, 1

Haiti, 2, 22, 128, 129, 138–40, 151, 157; coffee exports, 156
Haitian Revolution, 58, 144, 155
Hamilton, Alexander, 210
Haring, Clarence, 71
Harrington thesis, 6
Harriss, Wilson, 224
Harrison College, 211
Hatuey, 27
Havana, 12, 21, 27–33, 55; slaves in, 90
Hawkins, John, 32, 44
Hay, James, Earl of Carlisle, 35
Hearne, John, 224
Heinl, R. B. and N. G., 138
Henry, Guy V., 195
Henry the Navigator, 19
Herbert, Philip, Earl of Pembroke, 35
Heren XIX, 40
Heureaux, Ulises, 160
Heyn, Piet, 35
Higman, B.W. 64, 66
Higuey, Salvaleón de, 22
Hispaniola, 1–3, 12, 19, 21, 22, 24–27, 29, 36, 57, 63, 145; maroons in, 64; sugar in, 76; prehispanic population, 5–8; *zemis* in, 9, 10; population in 1500, 11
Holguin, 6

Hostos, Eugenio María de, 244
Huelva, 42, 76
Huguenots, 67
Hugues, Victor, 150
Humboldt, Alexander, 54
Hutson, D. M., 212

Iglesias, Santiago, 198
Imperial College of Tropical
    Agriculture, 205
Inca, 9
Irwin Estate, Jamaica, 91
Isabella, Queen, 19–21, 25, 42, 48
Isthmus of Tehuantepec, 47
Italians, 23
Ivonet, Pedro, 173

Jackson, William, 39
Jacmel, 22
Jagan, Cheddi, 215, 221, 233, 245
Jamaica, 2, 8, 10, 21, 22, 27, 37, 38, 51, 54,
    62, 63, 73, 123, 128, 152, 155; Assembly,
    83: decline of the sugar industry, 127; East
    Indians, 132; free villages, 131; prehispanic
    population, 5; slaves in, 89; trade, 81
Jamaica College, 211
James, C. L. R., 211, 214, 244
Japan, 132
Jews, 20, 51, 215
Jirajara, 9
João III, 48
Johnson, Roberta, 189, 230
Johnson, Samuel, 143
Jones Act, 196
Junta of Cádiz, 57
"Just wars," 26

Ketelholdt, Baron Maximilian von, 209
Kingston, Jamaica, 56
Kingston College, 211
Kingstown, 66
Krushchev, Nikita, 179
Kublai Khan, 48
Kumina, 218

Labat, Jean-Baptiste, 69, 70, 228, 245
La Guira, 63,
Lamming, George, 224, 244
Lares de Guahaba, 22
Las Casas, Bartolomé de, 3, 8, 22, 27, 51

Lassan, Raveneau de, 70
Las Villas, 66
La Rochelle, 144,
Lebron, Cristóbal, 76,
Le Cap Français, 145,
Leclerc, General Charles-Victor-Emanuel,
    148
Leeward Islands, 2, 8
Le Maniel (Saint-Domingue), 64, 67
Lepanto, 33
León, Ponce de, 22, 28
Les Cayes, 22
Lesser Antilles, 2, 6, 8, 38
Lewis, Arthur, 244
Lexington, 139
Liçao, Juan de, 32
Ligon, Richard: quoted, 62, 63
Lisbon, 57
Liss, Peggy , 59
Lockhart, James, 49
Lodge School, 211
L'Olonnois, Francis, 70
Long, Edward, 54, 58, 91, 125
López, Pedro, 32
López Camara, Francisco, 59
López de Velasco, Juan, 29, 30
Los Caneyes, 30
Louis XIV, 73
Louis XVI, 140
Louisiana Territory, 155
Louverture, François-Dominique Toussaint,
    58, 146, 148, 149, 155, 160, 244
Lovelace, Earl, 224
Lucayan Islands, 27
Lyttleton, Charles, 71, 73

Macaulay, Thomas Babington, 130
MacDermott, Thomas Henry, 214
MacGregor, John, 157
Machado, Gerardo, 172
MacKay, Claude, 212, 214
Madeira, 132
Magloire, Paul, 158
Magoon, Charles, 172
Mahoney, A. H., 214
Maingot, Anthony, 154
Mais, Roger, 224, 230
Maize, 10
Málaga, 42, 76
Manguana, San Juan de, 22

Manifest Destiny, 161
Manioc, 7, 10, 23
Manley, Edna, 224
Manley, Michael, 184, 233, 239, 240
Manley, Norman, 204, 212, 215, 222, 230,
   233, 244
Manning's High School, 210
Marco Polo, 48
Margarita, 22
Marie Galante, 135
Maroons, 51, 63–67, 127
Marryshow, T. Albert , 212
Martí, José, 170, 244
Martínez, Domingo, 44
Martínez Nadal, Rafael, 198
Martinique, 36, 54, 56, 123, 150
Martyr, Peter, 2
Maryland, 134, 141
Mason, George, 141
Massachusetts, 34, 134
May Decree, 147
Maya, 9, 47, 132
Mayo, 47, 132
McNeill, John, 166
McNeill, William, 51
Mendes, Alfred, 214
Menéndez de Avilés, Pedro, 33
Mesopotamia, 6
Metates, 13
Mexico, 5, 16, 20, 22, 28, 29, 57, 138
Mico Trust Training College, 210
Milton, John, 71
Mississippi River, 33
Mittelholzer, Edgar, 224
Môle, 154
Monroe Doctrine, 161
Montserrat, 1, 35, 89, 135
Moore, Richard B., 12, 212, 214
Moors, 20
Morales Carrión, Arturo, 197
Morant Bay, 133
Moreau de Saint-Méry, Medéric-Louis Elie,
   54, 56, 58, 123, 144
Morgan, Henry, 68, 70, 72, 73
Morison, Samuel Eliot, 8
Morris, Judah, 210
Morris, Mervyn, 224
Moyne Commission, 221
Muñoz Marín, Luis, 189, 197, 198, 233,
   234, 244

Muñoz Rivera, Luis, 194–96
Murcia, 23
Myal, 218

Naipaul, V. S., 205
Nanny, 65
Nantes, 142
Naparima College, 211
Narváez, Pánfilo de, 27
National Assembly, 140, 141
Navarra, 23
Navigation Acts, 41
Neiba River, 22
Nevis, 35, 54, 89, 135
New Castile, 24
New England, 55, 58
New Granada, 53, 138
New Jersey, 141
New Jewel Movement, 223
New Laws, 48
New Orleans, 152
New Spain, 21, 53, 58, 138
New World, 2, 6, 23
New York, 134, 152
New York State, 33, 35
Nkrumah, Kwame, 183, 212
North, Roger, 39
North Carolina, 141
North Province, 154
Nugent, Lady Maria, 54, 58

O'Farrill, Gonzalo, 168
Ojeda, Alonso de, 22
Old Castile, 24
Ontario, 33
"Operation Bootstrap," 199, 201, 235
O'Reilly, Alejandro, 190
Organization of American States, 162
Organization of Eastern Caribbean States
   (OECS), 225
Oriente, 32
Osgood, Cornelius, 6
Ovando, Nicolás de, 19–22, 24–27, 42, 48

Pact of Zanjón, 170
Padmore, George (Malcolm Nurse), 212
Palenque, 9
Palisadoes, 72
Palmares (Brazil), 64
Palmer, R. R., 144

Panama, 133, 138
Paraguay, 138
Paris, 56
Parry, John, 35
Pasamonte, Esteban, 76
Patriachiquismo, 58
Patronato real, 26
Peace of Utrecht (1713), 63
Peanuts, 10
Peninsula Campaign, 155
Penn, William, 37
People's Revolutionary Government, 223
Peppers, 10
Peru, 16, 20, 22, 28, 29, 57, 138
Peruvian Vale Estate, St Vincent, 91
Petión, Alexandre, 58, 146, 152, 153,
    155, 156
Petits blancs, 145, 146
Philadelphia, 143, 152
Philip II, 44
Philip IV, 37
Pinar del Río, 66
Pizarro, Francisco, 22
Plain du Nord, 147
Playa Girón, 178
Political independence, 222, 232–33
Ponce de León, Juan, 27, 28
Port Antonio, 65
Port-au-Prince, 22, 146
Port Royal, 71–73
Porto Bello, 62
Portuguese, 23, 32
Postlethwaite, Alexander, 130
Potatoes, 10
Préval, Rene, 159
Price, George, 215, 221, 245
Price, Rose, 91
Prío Socarrás, Carlos, 172
Puelche, 47
Puerto de Plata, 22, 23, 27
Puerto Príncipe, 27, 30
Puerto Real, 22, 27
Puerto Rico, 2, 8, 9, 21, 22, 27, 29, 54, 63,
    86, 90, 123, 125, 128, 155; population
    in 1500, 11; white population, 88;
    trade, 81
Punta Alegre Company, 172

Quebec, 33
Queen's College, 211

Ragatz, Lowell, 128
Raimond, Julien, 146, 153
Raleigh, Walter, 32
Ramchand, Kenneth, 154
Ramírez, Alejandro, 190
Rastafarians, 219
Reconquista, 24
Reid, Victor, 224
Reynell, Carew, 38
Richelieu, Cardinal (Armand-Jean
    du Plessis), 36, 39
Rigaud, André, 146, 152, 153
"Rights of Man," 141, 142
Rio de Janeiro, 57
Rio de la Plata, 47
Roberts, W. Adolphe, 214
Rodney, Walter, 217
Rodríguez, Carlos, 180
Roosevelt, Franklin D., 197
Rouse, Irving, 6, 7
Rousea High School, 210
Royal Africa Company, 77
Royal Commission Report, 205
Ruiz Belvis, Segundo, 192

Saba, 35, 63, 135
Sabana de Vasco Porcallo, 30
Saco, José Antonio, 128, 169
St. Augustine, Florida, 33
St. Bartholomé, 36, 86
St. Christopher, 34, 36, 39, 55. *See also*
    St. Kitts
St. Croix, 35, 54
Saint-Domingue, 38, 57, 124, 126, 127, 138,
    142, 144, 150, 151, 153–55, 165
St. Eustatius, 35, 54, 63; free port, 81, 82,
    89, 135; population, 88
St. Johns, Antigua, 90
St. Kitts, 34, 54, 89
St. Lucia, 35, 36, 54, 150
Saint Marc, 146, 147
St. Martin, 35, 36, 63, 135; as free port, 81
St. Vincent, 54, 83, 150; free villages, 131
Salamanca, 56
Salkey, Andrew, 224
Salvaleón de Higuey, 22, 23
Salvatierra de la Sabana, 22
Sanchez, Ventura, 65
San Cristóbal, 25
Sancti-Spíritus, 27, 30

San German, 27
San Juan de la Manguana, 23
San Juan de Puerto Rico, 31, 33
San Salvador, 8
Santa Clara, 29
Santa Cruz, 22, 23
Santa María, Francisco de, 32
Santana, Pedro, 160
Santiago, 22, 23, 30
Santiago de Cuba, 29, 30, 33
Santo Domingo, 23, 33, 38, 54
Sauer, Carl, 11
Schaw, Janet, 82
Scott, Sir Walter, 82
Seaga, Edward, 233, 239
Second Maroon War, 150
Seiler, Hieronymous, 43
Selvon, Samuel, 224
Senado da Camara, 49
Sepúlveda, Juan Ginés de, 22
Seven Years' War, 207
Sevilla, 28, 42
Shamans, 14
Sherlock, Philip, 35
Sierra Maestra, 66
Slaves, 76; imports, 77–79
Smith, J. A. G., 212
Smith, John, 49
Somoza García, Anastasio, 161
Soulouque, Faustin, 157
South America, 1, 2
South Atlantic System, 44, 77, 88
South Carolina, 152
South Porto Rico Sugar Company, 196
Soviet Union, 178–79
Spanish Antilles in 1570, 28
Steward, Julian, 10, 13
Stewart, John, 81–83
Sturtevant, William, 12
Sugar industry, 74–82; revolutions, 79–81
Suriname (Surinam), 1, 54, 130

Taino, 5–13, 16, 42
Tampico, 62
Ten Years War, 170
Thirty Years' War, 35, 37, 73
Thomas, John Jacob, 204, 212
Tierra Firme, 27, 81
Tobago, 35, 36, 135
Tonton Macoutes, 158

Tortuga, 72
Treaty of Alcaçovas, 43
Treaty of Basle, 160
Treaty of Breda, 77
Treaty of Cateau-Cambresis, 51
Treaty of the Hague, 73
Treaty of Madrid, 37
Treaty of Münster, 37
Treaty of Paris, 171, 195
Treaty of Ryswick, 36, 37, 73, 145
Treaty of Tordesillas, 20, 28, 32, 43
Treaty of Windsor, 73
Trinidad, 2, 16, 25, 27, 30, 130, 155;
    East Indians in, 132, 133;
    Water riots, 219
Trujillo Molina, Rafael Leonidas, 160–62,
    178, 233, 242
Tupí, 47
Turks and Caicos Islands, 135

United Fruit Company, 172
United Provinces of Central America, 138
United States of America, 57, 133, 135
University College of the West Indies,
    205, 222

Vasco Porcallo, Sabana de, 29, 30
Valencia, 23, 42
Valladolid, 22
Varela y Mortales, Félix, 169
Varona, Enrique José, 169
Vasquez, Horacio, 161
Vasquez de Mella, Pedro, 76
Vecinos, 24, 27, 29; Register of 1582, 31
Velásquez, Diego, 21, 22, 27, 28
Venables, Robert, 34, 37, 39
Venezuela, 6–9, 138
Vera Cruz, Mexico, 31, 62
Vera Paz, 22
Versailles, 140, 147
Vertientes-Camaguey Company, 172
Vespucci, Amerigo, 42
Victoria, Queen, 133
Villanueva, 22
Villanueva de Yaquimo, 22
Virgin Islands, 8, 135
Virginia, 34, 55, 134

Wagenheim, Kal, 189
Walvin, James, 90

Warao, 9
Warner, Thomas, 34, 36
Washington, George, 155, 210
Waterloo, 154, 155
West Indian Meteorological Service,
    205, 222
West Province, 154
"Western Design," 34, 37
Wilberforce, William, 128
Williams, Eric, 211, 215, 221, 222,
    233, 240
Williamson, General Adam, 143
Windward Islands, 2, 8
Windward Maroons, 65
Winthrop, John, 49, 51

Wood Report, 205
Workers trades unions, 215
Worthy Park Estate, 89–91

Yanomamö, 9
Yaque del Sur, 23
Yaqui, 132
Yibenes, Francisco de, 32
Yorktown, 139
Yucatan, 5

Zapata, Emiliano, 156, 198
Zayas, Alfredo, 172
Zemi, 9, 11, 14
Zuazo, Alonso, 76

Printed in the USA/Agawam, MA
October 19, 2018

686023.001